Anne Willan

Cooked to Perfection

An illustrated guide to achieving success with every dish

Photography by Peter Williams

Quadrille Publishing

CONTENTS

For Mark, the ultimate judge of
Cooked to Perfection

Throughout the book recipes are for four
people unless otherwise stated.
Both metric and imperial quantities are given.
Use either all metric or all imperial, as the
two are not necessarily interchangeable.

Art Director: Mary Evans
Publishing Director: Anne Furniss
Editor & Project Manager: Lewis Esson
Design: Ian Muggeridge
Photography: Peter Williams
Styling: Róisín Nield
Food for Finished Dish Photography:
    Jane Suthering
Production: Candida Lane
Indexer: Hilary Bird

First published in 1997 by
Quadrille Publishing Limited
Alhambra House
27-31 Charing Cross Road
London WC2H OLS

First published in paperback in 2000

Text © 1997 Anne Willan Inc.
Photography © 1997 Peter Williams
Design & Layout © 1997 Quadrille Publishing Ltd

The rights of Anne Willan to be identified
as the Author of this Work have been asserted
by her in accordance with the Copyright,
Design and Patents Act 1988.

Cataloguing-in-Publication Data:
a catalogue record for this book is available
from the British Library.

ISBN 1 899988 46 7 (hardback)
ISBN 1 902757 62 9 (paperback)

Colour Separations by Colourscan Singapore.
Printed in Hong Kong

The publishers would like to thank David Mellor Ltd,
4 Sloane Square, London SW1 for the use of various
kitchen equipment in photography.

List of recipes

INTRODUCTION

THIS BOOK BEGAN IN THE KITCHEN, as does much in our house. 'That looks done to me', I said one day as a student lifted a roast chicken out of the oven. And then I thought – how do I know? Cooking is a skill learned by experience, and nothing is more difficult than judging when a dish is cooked to perfection. All the senses are involved – smell, sight, touch, even hearing, with taste the last and most important of all. That roast chicken smelled heavenly; it sizzled; it looked brown and crispy, and when I wiggled a joint, it was loose. Provided the bird had been properly seasoned and basted I knew it must taste good, and it did!

From that brief beginning has developed what has proved to be an ambitious project. From the start I decided we must redefine traditional clichéd phrases such as 'until the fish flakes when tested with a fork' or 'until the cake springs back when lightly pressed with a fingertip'. We need to describe clearly and accurately in text and pictures how food looks, smells and feels when it is perfectly cooked. To illustrate this ideal state, often under- and overcooked shots are needed as well.

Then I realized that it's no good explaining what is wrong without going on to put it right. So I tell you what to do on a case-by-case basis, suggesting cheerful garnishes, appropriate seasonings for bland food, and how to remedy technical problems like curdled mayonnaise or sticky pastry dough. It is surprising how few things cannot be saved if you really try – serious scorching and oversalting are the only two I know (see opposite).

Perhaps we've had most fun developing our Quick Fixes. After 30 years in the kitchen I have a series of taste-saving devices, such as a tablespoon of Cognac, a squeeze of citrus juice or a few drops of soy sauce; together with little sauces and relishes, such as *escabeche* marinade for overcooked fish (page 15) or a yoghurt and herb dressing for vegetables (page 147). Whipped cream hides a multitude of sins in desserts, and chopped parsley will do the same for savoury dishes.

Many of the 150 Quick Fix ideas in *Cooked to Perfection* have come from the team of cooks and editors with whom I have had the pleasure of working – I would like to extend warmest thanks to Virginia Willis, who has been my right hand in bringing this book to fruition. My other leading associates in the kitchen, on the studio floor, and at the editorial desk, have been Chefs Alexandre Bird and Laurent Terrasson, together with Kevin Tyldesley, Val Cipollone and Marah Stets (among many other things, the 'hands' in our pictures). I have also had valuable help at different times from Ken Atkinson, Tim Furst, Lin Hansen, Amanda Hesser and Bongani Ngwane.

That's only half the story. There are also the teams from Quadrille Publishing in London and Reader's Digest in New York.

My mother's pea soup, page 151

I would like to acknowledge all those named on page 4, and particularly my editor Lewis Esson, who from start to finish worked with us so long and hard on this complex book. We all owe much to photographer Peter Williams – it is his vision and understanding, together with that of art director Mary Evans, which gives this book its very special visual appeal.

Which takes me back to the kitchen – to Château du Feÿ in Burgundy, where in a 17th-century panelled salon temporarily turned into a photographic studio, we all analysed the complexities of exactly when, why and how a dish is cooked to perfection. Please come and explore them with us.

THE PERILS OF OVERSALTING AND SCORCHING

The two most difficult faults in cooking to cure are oversalting and scorching. Remedies for too much salt depend on whether the food is raw or cooked. You can extract salt from small pieces of raw food, such as olives or diced bacon, by blanching them – put them in a pan of cold water, bring them slowly to the boil, then drain and rinse them. Large or very salty ingredients, such as a whole country ham or fillets of salt cod, require more lengthy treatment by soaking in several changes of cold water, for hours or even a day or two.

Too much salt in finished dishes, such as a stew or a sauce, can be counteracted by adding a bland ingredient like potato, tomato, mushroom, or a dairy product such as cream, milk or fresh cheese. In desserts, even a small amount of salt can spoil sweet fillings and frostings, so be sure to use unsalted butter unless salted butter is specified.

I find that burning is harder to disguise. When food is scorched on the surface it is relatively easy to separate the burned portion by scraping (as for toasted bread or pastry). When a sauce or stew catches on the base of the pan, spoon out the rest, leaving the burned residue behind – on no account stir, as this will mix burned and unburned food. When the burning is severe, however, a smoky taste penetrates the whole dish and little can be done.

FOOD AND HYGIENE

The best advice is to use food promptly, keeping perishable items in a well-regulated refrigerator, at around 4°C/40°F. Store cooked and uncooked foods separately, wrapping them well. Keep track of how long your purchases have been stored in the refrigerator or freezer (bacterial activity doesn't stop in the freezer, it just slows down). If there is any question of possible spoilage, throw the food out.

Clean cutting boards thoroughly between uses. Exercise special caution with raw chicken and eggs, taking them from the refrigerator only just before you are ready to prepare and cook them. Those with limited or impaired immune systems, like the very young, the elderly, pregnant women and invalids, should not risk salmonella poisoning by eating lightly cooked poultry or lightly cooked (or raw) eggs.

Certain E coli bacteria are dangerous and have been found in the food chain, notably as a result of poorly handled beef. Be sure the surface of all beef you prepare is well cooked. Ready-cooked meats can be a hazard, as can minced meat products that have not been thoroughly cooked to the centre. Pork must always be thoroughly cooked.

There is little to be said here usefully about the potential hazard of contracting CJD from cattle infected with BSE, as no preparation or cooking technique can safeguard against possible infection. However, I still happily eat good prime beef, but would certainly think twice about eating low-grade beef or products made from them.

The above cautions notwithstanding, many cooks still make use of raw eggs, (e.g. in mayonnaise) or enjoy dishes featuring lightly cooked eggs, 'pink' duck or hamburger. This book covers such techniques and recipes, but you should be aware that eating food prepared this way increases the risk of falling ill and can be life-threatening to vulnerable persons.

FISH & SHELLFISH

FISH AND SHELLFISH are surely the most difficult ingredients to cook just right. Their delicate textures and flavours can all too easily be ruined by overcooking, and a sensitive hand with the heat is important. Sometimes it's hard to tell exactly when they are done. Indeed, opinions can vary quite widely on what 'cooked to perfection' means for fish and shellfish – swordfish and tuna, for instance, can be served rare, medium or well-done, just like steak. However we all recognize – and condemn – fish that has been overcooked to a soft mush, or shellfish that has been simmered so long that it becomes inedibly tough.

Fish species and fish names vary so much from country to country, even place to place, that it's easy to be confused. When I go to the market, I keep my eye open for the best on offer that day, rather than insisting on a particular type. Most fish recipes can easily be adapted to a range of similar fish, say plaice instead of sole, or snapper instead of sea bass. We are lucky to be offered such a range of wild fish, and it may not last much longer. I've nothing against farm-raised fish – on the contrary, inexpensive and reliable supplies of species such as salmon are a boon for everyone – but farmed fish tends to lack the individuality and intensity of flavour of a catch from the wild, particularly one which has been well handled and taken to market in timely fashion.

The first criterion when choosing fish is freshness, and your nose is the best guide. Very fresh fish and shellfish have a whiff of the sea, and taste that way too. Scales should be bright, eyes plump and clear, and shellfish should be heavy in your hand. Many shellfish, notably lobster, crab and bivalves like oysters should be alive just before cooking. Since it is important to know their origins and guard against pollution, a good supplier is your best friend.

Looking at flavourings for fish, I think at once of citrus (particularly lemon and lime), saffron, ginger, the anise taste of fennel and tarragon, plus star anise and the seed itself. Don't overlook the onion family, including leek, garlic and chives. Fish without wine, oil or butter and cream is unthinkable. Tomatoes, aubergines, peppers, celery, courgettes, potatoes and mushrooms all act as agreeable background vegetables, but there are many, many more. It is not so much the type but the amount of these accompaniments that is crucial. A whisper of Cognac or chilli with fish is divine, but a blanket can easily be a disaster.

Roasted red snapper with curried
vegetables, page 17

Fish fillets

Baked, braised, grilled, pan-fried, poached, roasted, sautéed, steamed

THANK GOODNESS FOR FISH FILLETS. Free of bones, and often of skin as well, they can be cooked by almost any method and marry happily with a wide range of accompaniments. Serve them with mushrooms, tomato, or other seafood such as prawns. Try them fried with coconut as in Australia, baked with banana as in Portugal, grilled with herbs Italian-style, or poached with vinegar as in Venice. We all have our favourites. I've always had a weakness for fillets of sole Florentine, in cheese sauce on a bed of spinach.

Fish fillets should be rinsed and dried before cooking, then sprinkled with salt, white pepper (so the surface is not speckled with black) and any other seasoning called for in the recipe. When poaching and braising, be sure the cooking liquid is well flavoured. If frying or sautéing, the fat must be hot and the surface of the fish really dry so it browns rapidly. Cooking time varies with the type of fish as well as depending on the thickness of the fillet. Plaice or flounder can overcook in seconds, but monkfish and Dover sole are more resilient, a prime reason for their popularity with restaurant chefs. As accompaniment, a salad of bitter greens and chicory suits every style of cooking.

PERFECT LIGHTLY COOKED – surface firm and opaque or lightly browned depending on cooking method; when tested with knife, fish resists slightly, showing translucent inside layer. Note: for most types of fish, this layer should be about 5 mm/¼ inch thick; oily fish such as mackerel should always be well done.

PERFECT WELL-DONE – surface of fillet very firm and opaque or browned depending on cooking method; when tested with a knife, fish flakes fairly easily with no translucent layer inside; when lifted, it still holds firmly without splitting.

PROBLEMS

UNDERCOOKED
Why: cooking temperature too low; time too short.
What to do: continue until done, raising temperature if needed.

DRY AND OVERCOOKED
Why: cooked too fast; cooked too long.
What to do: moisten with melted butter, vinaigrette dressing or an oil such as olive or walnut; if very overcooked, flake to use in a soufflé or fish cakes.

TEXTURE SOFT OR STRINGY
Why: overcooked; inappropriate cooking method for type of fish.

Note: texture varies very much with variety of fish.
What to do: sprinkle with crunchy chopped spring onion or celery; serve with a velouté or butter sauce.

LACKS TASTE
Why: insufficient seasoning, particularly when grilling, poaching and steaming; poorly handled or stale fish; inappropriate cooking method for type of fish.
What to do: sprinkle with salt, pepper, lemon juice, white wine, soy sauce or other flavouring and moisten with olive or a full-flavoured oil. Season any garnish well.

John Dory with roasted garlic butter sauce

SERVES 4

John Dory is excellent pan-fried as in this recipe, but if you prefer a lighter dish, grill the fish instead. Plaice or sole fillets work equally well treated this way.

4 John Dory fillets
   (about 750 g/1½ pounds), without skin
45 g/1½ oz flour, seasoned with salt
   and pepper
1 large tomato, peeled, seeded and
   chopped
1 tablespoon chopped basil
45 g/1½ oz butter

for the roasted garlic butter sauce
1 whole head of garlic

1 tablespoon olive oil
140 g/4½ oz butter, chilled and cut into
   small pieces
3 shallots, finely chopped
75 ml/2½ fl oz white wine
75 ml/2½ fl oz dry white vermouth
1 tablespoon double cream
2 egg yolks
1 tablespoon chopped basil
salt and white pepper

First roast the garlic for the sauce. Preheat the oven to 175°C/350°F/gas4. Cut top off stem end of garlic head to expose cloves. Put in a small heatproof dish, brush with olive oil, cover with foil and roast until soft, 35-45 minutes.

When the garlic is soft, squeeze the head and, with tip of a knife, pull each clove out of its skin. Chop the cloves.

Melt 15 g/½ oz of the butter in a saucepan, add the shallots and sweat until soft but not coloured, stirring occasionally, 2-3 minutes.

Add the garlic, wine and vermouth. Boil, stirring, until reduced to 3-4 tablespoons, almost to a glaze. Stir in cream and boil for 30-60 seconds. Turn heat to low and gradually whisk in butter pieces to make a creamy sauce. Work on and off the heat, so butter softens and thickens sauce without melting to oil. Season with salt and white pepper and set aside.

Rinse fillets and pat dry with paper towels. Coat with seasoned flour, patting to remove excess. Combine tomato and basil in a small bowl and season to taste.

In a heavy frying pan, heat butter until foaming and add fillets, skinned side up. Fry over brisk heat until golden brown, 2-3 minutes. Turn over and brown other sides, until the fish is done to your taste, 3-5 minutes. Transfer fish to 4 heatproof plates.

Finish the sauce: in a medium saucepan, whisk the egg yolks with 2 tablespoons water over low heat until foamy and very thick, being careful not to 'scramble' the yolks, 1-2 minutes. Take from the heat and gradually whisk in the warm butter sauce. Stir in the basil and taste for seasoning.

Heat grill. Sprinkle chopped tomato and basil over fish, then coat with garlic sauce. Grill until the sauce is just browned, 3-5 minutes. Serve at once.

QUICK FIX

Here's a colourful topping to moisten dry fish fillets and pick up their flavour: squeeze the juice of 1 lemon or lime into a bowl; add 2 tomatoes, seeded and chopped but not peeled, then 2 stalks of very thinly sliced celery, and finally 2 tablespoons coarsely chopped dill or parsley. Moisten with 1 tablespoon vegetable oil if you like. Season with salt and pepper and sprinkle topping over fillets. Serves 4.

Fish steaks

Baked, braised, grilled, pan-fried, poached, roasted, sautéed, steamed

FISH STEAKS OFFER ALL THE VERSATILITY OF FISH FILLETS, though the bones and skin that often come with them make them less popular. Remember that it is the bones that hold steaks together and they also add considerable flavour to mild fish such as hake.

Easier to deal with are the boneless, skinless steaks cut from giant fish such as tuna, swordfish and shark. They can be thick or thin according to your taste and when carefully cooked they retain generous juices.

I think the best cooking method for steaks is to grill or pan-fry them with a minimum of fat. For garnish, look towards Mediterranean herbs, tomato, capers, olives and anchovies, or a more northern julienne of leek and carrot. In winter, why not add Vietnamese Stir-Fried Green Beans with Sesame (page 172) as accompaniment, or in summer an Indonesian Salad in Spicy Peanut Sauce (page 147). Both are an exuberant change of pace!

PERFECT LIGHTLY COOKED – when tested with a knife, centre of steak is resistant, with a translucent inside layer; surface opaque or lightly browned depending on cooking method; when pressed, edge is firm, centre fairly soft and clinging to any central bone. Note: fish such as swordfish and tuna may still have a rare centre if very lightly cooked. For most steaks, translucent layer should be about 1 cm/⅜ inch thick; oily fish like mackerel should always be well done.

PERFECT WELL-DONE – when tested with a knife, fish flakes to show no translucent layer inside; surface of steak is opaque or browned, depending on cooking method; when pressed with your fingertip, both edge and centre of steak are firm; any central bone loose when wiggled with a knife.

OVERCOOKED – texture of fish is soft or stringy, tending to fall apart when lifted; meat is dry and shrivelled; edges of steak split and flesh shrinks from any central bone; if sautéed or pan-fried, surface may be scorched.
Why: cooked too fast; cooked too long.
What to do: serve with a velouté or butter sauce (see Sauces, pages 112 and 120); if very overcooked, flake to use in a soufflé or fish cakes.

PERFECT LIGHTLY COOKED/ PERFECT WELL-DONE – when pressed, centre and edges of fish will be spongy/firm.

OTHER PROBLEMS

UNDERCOOKED
Why: cooking temperature too low; cooking time too short.
What to do: continue cooking until done, raising temperature if necessary.

DRY
Why: cooked too fast; cooked too long.
What to do: moisten with melted butter or a vinaigrette dressing.

TEXTURE SOFT OR STRINGY
Why: overcooked; inappropriate cooking method for type of fish. Note: texture varies widely with type of fish.

What to do: sprinkle with crisp garnish such as chopped celery or spring onion, or browned almonds.

LACKS TASTE
Why: insufficient seasoning, particularly when grilling, poaching and steaming; poorly handled or stale fish; inappropriate cooking method for fish.
What to do: sprinkle fish with salt, pepper, lemon juice, white wine, soy sauce or other flavouring; moisten with herb, garlic or chilli oil; be sure any garnish is highly seasoned.

Grilled swordfish with roasted corn and tomato salsa

Roasting raw kernels of corn in a heavy pan gives them a wonderful smoky flavour – the perfect foil for meaty swordfish.

4 swordfish steaks
  (about 750 g/1½ pounds),
  cut 2 cm/¾ inch thick
2 tablespoons olive oil
salt and pepper

for the roasted corn and tomato salsa
4 corn ears, husks removed
2 red peppers
2 tablespoons olive oil

1 onion, diced
2 tomatoes, peeled, seeded and
  coarsely chopped
75 g/2½ oz sun-dried tomatoes in
  oil, coarsely chopped, plus
  1 teaspoon of their oil
1 tablespoon sherry or red wine
  vinegar
3-4 tablespoons chopped coriander
juice of 1 lime

First make the salsa. Preheat the grill. While it is heating, prepare the corn. Holding each ear upright, cut off the kernels with a sharp knife. Heat a large heavy-based frying pan without any fat over a high heat until almost smoking. Add the kernels and dry-roast until tender, smoky and dark, tossing continuously as they tend to stick, 4-5 minutes. Cook the peppers under the grill, turning them until the skin chars and bursts, 7-10 minutes. Put them in a plastic bag and leave to sweat and cool so the skins loosen. Peel the peppers, discarding cores and seeds. Dice the flesh.

Heat 1 tablespoon of the olive oil in a large frying pan. Add the onion and sauté until soft but not brown, 3-4 minutes. Take the pan from the heat and stir in the roasted corn, chopped tomatoes, sun-dried tomatoes, diced peppers, vinegar and remaining oil. Heat, stirring, until hot. Take from the heat and keep warm.

Rinse the fish steaks and pat dry with paper towels. Brush with half the oil, season with salt and pepper and set on oiled grill rack about 7.5 cm/ 3 inches from heat. Grill for 3-4 minutes. Turn steaks over, brush with the remaining oil and grill until done to taste, 2-3 minutes longer.

Meanwhile, stir the coriander and lime juice into the salsa, taste and adjust the seasoning. Make a bed of salsa on 4 warmed plates and place a swordfish steak on top of each. Serve at once.

QUICK FIX

Unless already in a sauce, turn dry or overcooked fish steaks into marinated *escabeche*. In a food processor or blender, combine 1 small onion cut into pieces, 1 peeled garlic clove, pared zest of 1 orange and 1 lemon, handful of parsley sprigs, 2 teaspoons paprika, pinch of cayenne, salt and pepper. Work to a coarse purée.

Add 125 ml/4 fl oz olive oil and 3 tablespoons red wine vinegar and work again until smooth. Spread fish in a dish while still warm and spoon over the marinade. Serve at once if you like, but preferably cover tightly and refrigerate at least 8 hours. Enough for 1 kg/ 2 pounds of fish fillets, to serve 4-6.

Whole fish

Baked, braised, grilled, pan-fried, poached, roasted, sautéed, steamed

A LARGE WHOLE FISH, RESPLENDENT ON THE PLATTER, IS A JOY TO BEHOLD, especially when it is colourful like salmon and red snapper. A whole fish is ideal for grilling over charcoal, with a spicy tomato-onion relish as accompaniment; or try roasting it, Russian-style, in sour cream; or serve it with a medley of curried vegetables as opposite. A whole salmon, it seems to me, is best simply poached or steamed to develop the rich flavour, but milder fish like catfish may be baked Colombian-style with raisin sauce, or fried with lemon grass as in Vietnam.

Whatever the flavouring, a whole fish needs plenty of it to penetrate the flesh. If you like, season the fish – including the stomach cavity – thoroughly in advance and return it to the refrigerator for an hour or two before cooking so the flavours are absorbed. So the fish cooks more evenly, slash the thickest part of the fillets on the diagonal on each side and tuck in a herb sprig or a half slice of lemon. The slash will shrink attractively to display the flesh. As a guide to cooking time, measure the fish at its thickest point, using an upright ruler. Allow 10 minutes' cooking time per 2.5 cm/1 inch.

UNDERCOOKED – when tested with a knife or fork, flesh at thickest part of fish (here salmon trout) is resistant and shows a translucent layer clinging to the bone; on larger fish the eye is still translucent; if baked, barbecued, grilled or pan-fried, skin is still soft not crispy.
Why: cooking temperature too low; cooking time too short.
What to do: continue cooking until done, raising temperature if necessary.

PERFECT – when a knife or fork is inserted at thickest part of the fish, flesh nearest the bone flakes easily and is no longer translucent; eye of fish is opaque; if baked, barbecued, grilled or pan-fried, fish is attractively browned, skin slightly crisp. Note: large fish will continue to cook from residual heat, so stop cooking when slightly underdone. However, light cooking (see Fish fillets and Steaks, pages 12-15) is not recommended as it makes a whole fish on the bone hard to carve.

OVERCOOKED – eye sunken; if baked, barbecued, grilled or pan-fried, skin is dry, often scorched, and flesh is dry and stringy, falling easily from the bone; if braised, poached or steamed, skin splits, gills gape and flesh starts to shrink from the bones.
Why: cooked too long or too fast so outside overdone before heat penetrated to centre.
What to do: serve with a velouté or butter sauce, or vinaigrette dressing (see Sauces, pages 123); to add colour and draw the eye from any shortcomings in hot poached or steamed fish, serve it with a steamed green vegetable such as asparagus, broccoli or stuffed courgette boats; for cold fish, line up a row of tomato baskets; whether hot or cold, surround fish with a hedge of lettuce leaves or watercress and dress with lemon slices, a sprinkling of herbs, and add a cherry tomato eye as a humourous touch.

OTHER PROBLEMS

TEXTURE SOFT, DRY OR STRINGY
Why: overcooked; cooking method inappropriate to fish. Note: texture varies very much with variety.
What to do: sprinkle with crisp slices of celery, sweet pepper or red onion; moisten with well-flavoured olive or nut oil or vinaigrette dressing.
LACKS TASTE
Why: insufficient seasoning, particularly when poached

or steamed; poorly handled or stale fish; cooking method inappropriate to type of fish.
What to do: be sure any cooking liquid or garnish is intensely flavoured; after cooking, if necessary, sprinkle fish with salt, pepper, lemon juice, white wine, soy sauce or other flavouring, or moisten with a flavoured oil such as olive or walnut.

Roasted red snapper with curried vegetables

pictured on pages 10-11

An impressive whole red snapper is presented on a bed of roasted, spiced root vegetables. So the stomach cavity of the fish does not collapse during cooking, I suggest stuffing it with a bunch of celery tops or parsley. The garlic and shallots in the garnish retain most flavour if their skins are left on, so leave peeling to your guests.

*1 whole red snapper (about 1.8 kg/4 pounds),
  cleaned, scaled and trimmed*
1 bunch of celery tops or parsley
1 lemon, sliced
2 tablespoons vegetable oil, more if needed

for the curried vegetables
125 ml/4 fl oz vegetable oil
*500 g/1 pound carrots, peeled and quartered
  lengthwise*
500 g/1 pound turnips, peeled and quartered
*250 g/½ pound celeriac, peeled and cut into
  wedges*

500 g/1 pound potatoes, peeled and quartered
8 shallots, unpeeled
8 garlic cloves, unpeeled
1 tablespoon curry powder
2 teaspoons sugar
75 g/2½ oz whole blanched almonds
1 teaspoon salt
½ teaspoon pepper

*22.5x32.5-cm/9x13-inch flameproof
roasting pan*

Preheat the oven to 190°C/375°F/gas5. First prepare the curried vegetables: heat the oil in the roasting pan, add the carrots and sauté for 2 minutes. Stir in the turnips and celeriac and sauté for 2 minutes longer. Stir in the potatoes, shallots and garlic and sauté for 2 minutes more.

Mix the curry powder, sugar, almonds, salt and pepper in a small bowl. Sprinkle over the vegetables and toss with two spoons until well mixed. Transfer to the preheated oven and roast the vegetables, stirring occasionally, 25-30 minutes, until starting to soften and brown.

Meanwhile, rinse the snapper skin and cavity, and pat dry with paper towels. Stuff the bunch of celery tops or parsley in the cavity of the fish. Diagonally slash one side of the fish 3-4 times and insert one or two half lemon slices in each slash.

After the vegetables have roasted for 25-30 minutes, set the fish on top of them. Brush with oil and sprinkle with salt and pepper. Return the pan to oven and roast until fish is done and vegetables are tender and browned, 30-35 minutes. During cooking, baste the fish often with the cooking juices. If the fish is done before the vegetables, transfer it to a warmed platter and keep warm while the vegetables finish cooking.

Carefully lift the fish from the roasting pan and transfer to a warmed platter. Spoon vegetables and almonds around the snapper and baste it with the cooking juices. Carve it at the table.

QUICK FIX

Pretend overcooking or dryness of the fish is deliberate so flesh absorbs more of the following dressing. In a food processor or blender, combine 2 tablespoons lemon juice, 2 tablespoons white wine vinegar, 1 tablespoon chopped fresh ginger, 1 shallot, coarsely chopped, 1 tablespoon Dijon-style mustard, ¼ teaspoon freshly grated nutmeg, salt and pepper. In a slow steady stream, pour in 175 ml/6 fl oz olive oil, so the dressing emulsifies and thickens slightly. Taste for seasoning before spooning over the fish. Makes about 250 ml/8 fl oz, to serve 4. The fish may be served hot or at room temperature.

Small whole fish

In the bars of the Portuguese community in Luxembourg the special *hors d'oeuvre* is small sardines, so thoroughly cooked they are dried almost to a skeleton and are totally edible, bones and all. They are an acquired taste, but more lightly cooked small fish are easy to enjoy. Sautéed trout with almonds, brown and crispy on the plate, comes to mind at once. On the sea coast of Spain and Portugal, whole bream are baked in a salt crust, and in northern France, mackerel is poached in white wine or cider with vinegar – baby ones have their own name, *lisettes*.

Leaving small fish on the bone, with the head, adds lots of flavour. If possible, the stomach should be emptied through the gills to avoid the cut edges curling open; if the stomach has been slit, skewer the edges together with a cocktail stick. For symmetry, serve all the fish with their heads to the left – this way not only do they look good, you'll find they are easier to dismember on the plate. Tests for cooking small fish are the same as for larger ones – they should just flake easily near the bone. I find the eye a particularly good indicator as it will turn white when the fish is just done. Note that small fish overcook in just a few minutes.

PERFECT – fish (here trout) flakes easily when tested near bone with a fork and flesh is no longer translucent; eye is white; if baked, barbecued, grilled or pan-fried, skin is brown and crispy.

Whole lobster

Baked, bruised, grilled, pan-fried, poached, roasted, sautéed, steamed

NEW ENGLAND MUST BE THE WORLD'S CAPITAL FOR WHOLE LOBSTER IN ITS SHELL, enjoyed with plentiful melted butter and a bottle of chilled white wine as we did one faraway summer when lobster was $1.25 a pound. I soon learned from the natives to look for a lively lobster, heavy in its shell with plenty of meat. When boiling a lobster you should allow 5 minutes for the first 500 g/1 pound and 3 minutes more for each extra 500 g/1 pound; and when steaming, 8 minutes for the first 500 g/1 pound and 4 minutes more for each extra 500 g/1 pound. Always thoroughly season the water for boiling, allowing 1 tablespoon salt per litre/1⅔ pints of water, and add white wine, vinegar, parsley and dill stalks, bay leaf, star anise and peppercorns; dried hot red pepper is an option. The same aromatics minus the salt are good when steaming.

For steaming and boiling, a lobster is kept whole, the claws often bound so they are easy to handle. For cooking in dry heat, the lobster is most often halved lengthwise and the claws are cracked, exposing the flesh to the heat of the oven, grill or pan, a convenient way to display its spectacular shell and make the meat easy to extract. When cooked meat has been shelled, lobster salad is my first choice for enjoying its sweet flavour, perhaps with pasta and asparagus, or with potato, artichoke and pickles in the Austrian style. Classic American lobster Newburg, served hot in a cream and Cognac sauce, remains hard to beat, and I've taken with enthusiasm to contemporary French *navarin d'homard* with vegetables in a light white wine velouté sauce.

OTHER PROBLEMS

BLAND TASTE
Why: poorly handled or stale lobster; lobster frozen not fresh; lack of seasoning, especially when boiling; overcooked.
What to do: if hot, serve with a piquant sauce such as *fra diavolo* with garlic, chilli and tomato; or, if cold, serve with French *rouille*, a garlic and hot red pepper mayonnaise.

UNDERCOOKED – shell tinged blue-black (for clawed lobster), or still pink, not red (for spiny lobster); tail only starting to curl under body; meat is chewy, clings to shell and looks translucent (for whole lobster, pull off a leg); greenish meat in chest section is soft, not set when edge of shell is lifted.
Why: cooking temperature too low; cooking time too short. Note: cooking time will vary slightly with shape of lobster and thickness of its shell.
What to do: continue cooking until done, raising cooking temperature if necessary.

PERFECT – shell bright red; tail curls under but remains pliable; inside, meat is tender, moist and white, just starting to pull away from shell (for whole lobster, pull off a leg and crack open to test); lift up shell of chest section – greenish meat inside should be set, not liquid; for halved lobster, meat is lightly browned, moist and tender; when tail meat is cut, centre is opaque, not translucent; flavour full-bodied.

Whole crab

Boiled, steamed

You'll find the recipe overleaf.

QUICK FIX

When lobster is not up to standard, traditionally chefs resort to the classic Thermidor sauce. For each lobster, melt 1 tablespoon butter in a saucepan and sauté 1 chopped shallot until soft. Whisk in 1 tablespoon flour and cook until foaming. Whisk in 175 ml/6 fl oz double cream and bring to the boil, whisking constantly until the sauce thickens. Simmer 1 minute. Take from heat and stir in 2 tablespoons white wine, 2 tablespoons grated Parmesan cheese, 1 teaspoon Dijon-style mustard and 1 tablespoon chopped tarragon or 2 teaspoons dried tarragon. Season to taste. If lobster is served whole, use sauce for dipping. If lobster is split, spoon sauce over the halves. Sprinkle with a little more Parmesan and grill until brown, 1-2 minutes. Serves 1-2

LONG AGO I MASTERED HOW TO EXTRACT THE MEAT from a lobster shell, but crabs were intimidating until I took part in a Maryland crab boil, featuring huge piles of scarlet steamed crabs for each guest to dismantle with crackers and mallet. You'll find the recipe overleaf. Whole crab must be boiled with plenty of seasoning, allowing 1 tablespoon of salt per 1 litre/1¾ pints of water and adding vinegar, bay leaf, star anise, dried hot red pepper or cayenne.

The meat inside a steamed or boiled crab should be wonderfully spicy, an invitation to dipping in melted butter, or to exploring more adventurous combinations such as Spanish *centollos* with tomato sauce, sherry and brandy. *Granseola* from Italy flavoured with olive oil, parsley and lemon, is another possibility, or Scottish partan bree with anchovy, rice, cream and chicken stock.

OVERCOOKED AND TOUGH — shell white and chalky; tail curled tightly under body and stiff; often body separates from tail; meat is fibrous, dry and shrunk from shell; often claws fall off; fresh flavour is lost.
Why: lobster poorly frozen; lobster kept out of water so flesh shrank before cooking; cooked too long; lobster was slim-bodied with thin shell so heat penetrated quickly.
What to do: disguise by removing meat from shell, slicing tail meat across the grain to minimize toughness, then moistening with olive, walnut, chilli or other flavoured oil; serve hot in a white or velouté sauce (see Sauces, page 112), or stir-fried with fresh vegetables.

UNDERCOOKED — shell still partly brown, pink or blue, depending on species; inside white meat is partly translucent and clinging to shell; brown meat is not set.
Why: cooking temperature too low; time too short. Note: cooking time varies with type (large-bodied or thick-shelled take longer).
What to do: continue cooking until done, raising cooking temperature if necessary.

PERFECT — shell bright or brownish red; inside flesh is starting to pull away from shell and brown meat is set; meat is succulent and cream-coloured, with sweet slightly spicy flavour.

OTHER PROBLEMS

OVERCOOKED
Why: cooked too long; too fast; species of crab was small-bodied, long-legged (spider crab) and cooked too quickly.
What to do: serve with piquant dressing or sauce flavoured with chilli.
DRY
Why: poorly handled or stale crab; crab was frozen not fresh; overcooked.
What to do: moisten with mayonnaise, yogurt-based dressing or vinaigrette.
BLAND TASTE
Why: as Dry, or too little seasoning.
What to do: use for crab cakes or devilled crab.

QUICK FIX

Crab is good combined in a salad with orange, grapefruit, tomato or green pepper, all colourful distractions from mediocre meat. Mix 500 g/ 1 pound crab meat with this sauce: combine 125 ml/4 fl oz mayonnaise, 4 tablespoons sour cream and juice of 1 orange. Peel and slice 2 oranges, or 1 large grapefruit, and 2 large tomatoes. Core and seed 1 red or green pepper and cut it across into rings. Arrange the orange or grapefruit and tomato slices overlapping on 6 individual plates. Pile the crab meat on top and decorate with the pepper rings. Serves 6 as an appetizer or 4 as a light main course.

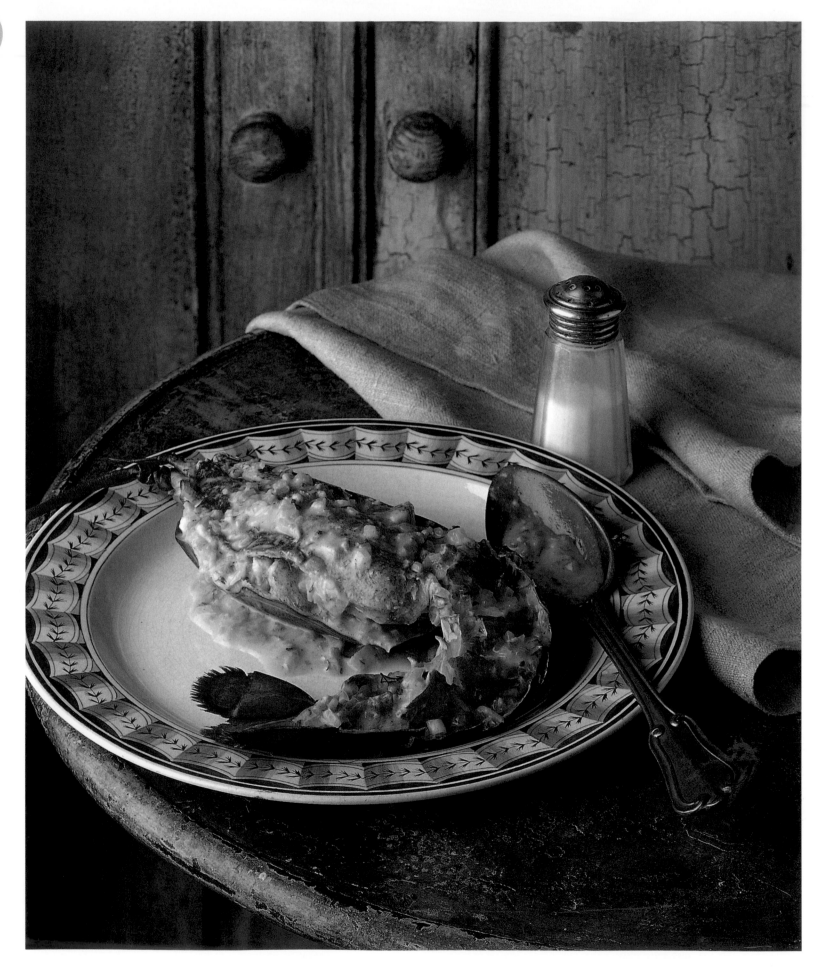

Lobster with shallots and white wine
Homard à la bordelaise

Lobster is so often served in a pungent *américaine* sauce with tomato and garlic, and I much prefer this gentle alternative. If possible, use a female lobster as the coral (eggs) will add vivid colour to the sauce.

1 whole lobster (about 750 g/1½ pounds)	4 shallots, chopped
75 g/2½ oz butter	1 tablespoon flour
salt and pepper	250 ml/8 fl oz dry white wine
2-3 tablespoons Cognac	60 ml/2 fl oz crème fraîche or double cream
1 small carrot, very finely diced (brunoise)	2 tablespoons chopped chervil or tarragon

Set the lobster on a chopping board and cover the tail with a cloth. Hold the lobster firmly by the tail. Using the point of a large knife, pierce the shell at the centre of the head all the way down to the chopping board. Continue cutting to split the tail. Turn the lobster around and, holding the head, cut it in half lengthwise. Crack the claw shells, striking them with the back of the knife. Pull out and discard the stomach sac from each half. Remove the green liver (tomalley) and any greenish black coral, chop coarsely and reserve.

Melt half the butter in a sauté pan. Lay the lobster halves, cut-side up, in the pan and season the exposed flesh with salt and pepper. Cover the pan and sauté until the meat is done, 5-7 minutes.

Add the Cognac and carefully flame either with a lighted match or by tilting the pan to catch the gas flame. Remove the lobster halves from pan.

Sauté the carrot and shallots in the pan until soft but not brown, stirring often, 3-5 minutes. Add the flour and cook for 1 minute. Add the wine and boil, stirring to dissolve the pan juices, until reduced by half, 2-3 minutes. Stir in the cream, reserved liver and coral and simmer, whisking constantly, 30-60 seconds. (The coral turns red when cooked.)

Remove from the heat and add the remaining butter in 2-3 pieces, shaking the pan until butter is fully incorporated. Stir in half of the chopped herbs, reserving the rest. Taste and adjust seasoning.

Remove the claw meat from the shell. Remove the body meat, pulling it out in pieces. Remove the tail meat and slice it on the diagonal. Trim and discard the gills (dead man's fingers) from the underside of the body shell. Set the lobster shells on individual plates. Place the body meat in the bottom of each body shell. Arrange the tail meat inside the whole shell and set the claw meat in one piece on top. Spoon over sauce and sprinkle with reserved chopped herbs. If necessary warm in a low oven, 1-2 minutes, and serve.

Lobster with shallots and white wine

Maryland steamed crabs

Spicy steamed blue crabs served in the shell – as many as you can eat – are an institution on Maryland's Chesapeake Bay. The flavouring used is equally traditional and here's my version. It is also good for steaming or boiling prawns, for flavouring fish soups and even for sprinkling on fish salads. Crabs steamed this way are delicious on their own, but you may like to give each diner a dipping bowl of melted butter.

12 blue crabs or 2-3 Dungeness or common European crabs	¼ teaspoon salt
750 ml/1¼ pints flat beer	¼ teaspoon freshly grated nutmeg
1 teaspoon ground bay leaf	¼ teaspoon ground ginger
½ teaspoon celery salt	¼ teaspoon ground cloves
½ teaspoon black pepper	¼ teaspoon paprika
½ teaspoon dry mustard	¼ teaspoon chilli powder, or to taste

Combine the beer with all the dry flavourings in a small saucepan and bring to the boil.

Put half the crabs in large pot and pour over half the flavouring liquid. Place the rest of the crabs on top and pour over the remaining liquid. Bring to the boil, cover tightly and reduce the heat. Steam the crabs until done, stirring them once, 20-25 minutes for blue crabs and 30-35 minutes for larger red crabs.

Transfer the crabs to a large warmed serving bowl and provide each person with a nutcracker or mallet for cracking the shell.

Shrimp, prawns and crayfish

Baked, braised, grilled, pan-fried, poached, roasted, sautéed, steamed

SHRIMP AND PRAWNS ARE THE MOST POPULAR SHELLFISH, and I find they are also the most mistreated by overcooking and careless seasoning. Crayfish, coming from fresh water, are even more vulnerable. It's best to buy all of them raw in the shell (live for crayfish), so you are in control of the cooking.

When boiling shrimp, prawns or crayfish, I season the water with 1 tablespoon of salt per 1 litre/1¾ pints of water, adding bay leaf, star anise, peppercorns, mustard seed, dried chilli, thick slices of fresh ginger or lemon and 1 whole onion. The same aromatics minus the salt are appropriate for steaming, or you may like to try a spicy mix of dried chilli and coriander. When stir-frying, stewing or baking in sauce, use bold flavourings such as garlic, fresh ginger, chilli and mustard. This is just a start.

For recipes like shrimp Creole with tomato, celery, wine and cayenne, or Indian prawns with crushed mustard seed, the shellfish must be peeled raw. They can be grilled, peeled or unpeeled, with an olive oil or vodka marinade, or boiled in dill court-bouillon or just sea water. In Brazil, prawns are cooked Bahia-style in coconut milk with okra, celery and peppercorns; in Mexico, they are dressed with lime, tomato, coriander, onion and radish, and an American low-country boil features shrimp, crab, corn, potato, sausage, onion and herbs.

Whatever the recipe, rinse and drain the shellfish before you start. If peeled, dry on paper towels, season them well with salt, pepper, soy sauce or cayenne, and leave them to absorb the flavours, 10-15 minutes.

UNDERCOOKED – shells may have some trace of blue or grey, depending on species; shells soft when pinched; meat is still slightly translucent and clings to shell.
Why: cooked too slowly, cooking time too short.
What to do: continue cooking, raising cooking temperature if necessary.

PERFECT – shells a deep pink with no trace of blue or grey, depending on species; shells firm when pinched; shells are slightly loose and can be peeled easily from meat; inside meat is white tinged with pink, plump and succulent; for peeled shellfish, meat is juicy, a pearly white, lightly or deeply tinged with pink depending on species; flavour is sweet and slightly spicy.

OVERCOOKED – shells dry, starting to lose colour and crack easily when pinched; tail very tightly curled; meat is shrunken, fibrous for large prawns, pasty for small ones; worst of all, fresh sea flavour is lost.
Why: cooked too long or too fast.
Note: peeled shrimp and prawns are delicate and easily dried out by high heat.
What to do: serve with a savoury cheese sauce, tomato salsa or white butter sauce (see Sauces, page 120).

OTHER PROBLEMS

BLAND TASTE
Why: poorly handled or stale seafood; lack of seasoning, especially when boiling; overcooked. Note: any chlorine taste comes from overuse of commercial sulphite preservative.
What to do: moisten with dressing –

shallot, garlic, thyme and lime or lemon juice are good flavours.
TEXTURE FIBROUS OR SOFT
Why: poorly handled or stale shellfish; shellfish frozen not fresh; overcooked.
What to do: sprinkle with nuts, particularly cashews or browned flaked almonds.

PEELED SHELLFISH WATERY
Why: seafood poorly frozen or stored; too much seafood in pan so juices ran.
What to do: drain excess liquid, then finish cooking in small batches over high heat to ensure browning.

Thai hot-and-sour prawn soup

There are two schools of thought on this classic Thai soup. Traditional Thai cooks leave all the flavourings in the soup so the diner has to extract the edible parts. Westerners often strain out the flavourings before adding the prawns and mushrooms.

Feel free to adjust the amounts of chilli and lime juice to your taste, remembering that balance between the hot and sour flavours is the key.

500 g/1 pound medium raw prawns, in shells
small bunch of coriander
3 stalks of lemon grass
400 ml/13 fl oz coconut milk
125 g/4 oz straw mushrooms
    or thinly sliced button mushrooms
2 tablespoons fish sauce (nam pla)
juice of ½ lime, or to taste
salt

for the flavoured bouillon
1 tablespoon oil
2 garlic cloves, finely chopped
750 ml/1¼ pints water
4 kaffir lime leaves,
    or pared zest of 2 limes
white pepper
2-4 fresh chilli peppers, cored, seeded
    and cut into thin strips

Peel and devein the prawns, reserving the shells. Strip and chop the leaves from the coriander, reserving the stems. Cut the dry leafy tops from the lemon grass and peel away the outer layers to reach the moist tender cores. Reserve the outer layers. Crush the core of the lemon grass with the flat side of a knife and thinly slice it

Make the flavoured bouillon: heat the oil in a medium saucepan, add the prawn shells and sauté until they turn pink, 2-3 minutes. Add the garlic and reserved outer layers of lemon grass and sauté, stirring, until fragrant, 1-2 minutes. Stir in the water, reserved coriander stems, lime leaves or zest, white pepper and half the chillies. Bring to the boil, cover and simmer until well-flavoured, 20-25 minutes.

Strain the bouillon into another saucepan, stir in the coconut milk and bring to the boil. Season the prawns with salt and add to the bouillon with the mushrooms and sliced lemon grass. Simmer until the prawns and mushrooms are just done, 2-3 minutes. Stir in the fish sauce, remaining chillies, lime juice, and chopped coriander leaves. Taste and adjust hot and sour flavourings. Serve at once, while still very fragrant.

QUICK FIX

If I suspect shrimp, prawns or crayfish are bland, I often make a quick seafood salad. For every 375 g/¾ pound peeled, cooked, chopped shellfish, combine 150 g/5 oz chopped celery, 125 ml/4 fl oz mayonnaise, 1 medium onion, finely chopped, 4 coarsely chopped hard-cooked eggs, the juice of ½ lemon, ½ teaspoon paprika, salt and pepper. Add the shellfish and stir to mix. Season to taste and pile on a bed of salad greens. Serves 3-4.

Shucked clams, mussels and oysters

Baked, grilled, pan-fried, sautéed, simmered, stewed

COOKING SHUCKED CLAMS, MUSSELS AND OYSTERS in their own natural container, the half shell, is an international habit. In America you'll find baked clams Casino, topped with green pepper and bacon (overleaf) and oysters baked à la Rockefeller with spinach and cheese sauce. In Colombia, oyster cocktail comes with garlic, vinegar, chopped onion and tomato. Belgians load their outsized mussels with toppings of onion, tomato and cheese. As for the French, as far as I can discover the only half-shell cooking they countenance is aristocratic oysters in Champagne sauce. On the American seaboards you'll find shucked clams and oysters sold in jars by size, which are perfect for soups, stews and fritters. Otherwise shuck them yourself for dishes such as devilled oysters or angels on horseback, with the oysters wrapped in bacon. I once tried a peacemaker, a Southern sandwich of stewed oysters in cream sauce in a baguette. A memorable treat!

Before shucking and cooking, clams, mussels and oysters must be well scrubbed, discarding any open shells that do not close when tapped – they may be dead. If shells are very dirty before shucking, it is wise also to clean the meat inside with a soak in sea or salt water for an hour or so to wash off sand and grit.

PERFECT — meat plump, juicy and just warmed through, with edges curled; flavour is sea-fresh and piquant; any coating or sauce lightly browned.

OTHER PROBLEMS

SANDY
Why: shells gathered near sand or after a storm.
What to do: remove shellfish from shell, rinse meat and shell and replace meat (some flavour will be lost).

SALTY
Why: too much salt or salty flavourings, such as bacon, used; overcooked.
What to do: best solution is to under-season any toppings or accompaniments.

OVERCOOKED — meat dry and shrivelled, aromatic flavour lost; a coating or sauce is often dried or separated.
Why: cooked too long or too fast. Note: When on half shell, meat continues to cook in heat of shell; if shells tip, juice is lost.
What to do: dress shellfish on half shell with a drizzle of melted butter, oil or vinaigrette dressing, and sprinkle with chopped tomato, herbs, crisp bacon or, as contrast to a white sauce, a spoonful of caviar; for shucked shellfish, add a flavoured oil such as chilli or dark sesame, or vinaigrette dressing laced with shallot. If very overcooked, chop to serve in a lively salsa or in tomato sauce for topping pasta (see Sauces, pages 126-7).

QUICK FIX

Chop overcooked shellfish and make pancakes. For every 175 g/6 oz chopped cooked shellfish, sift together in a bowl 125 g/4 oz flour, 1¾ teaspoons baking powder, ½ teaspoon salt, ½ teaspoon sugar and ¼ teaspoon ground black pepper. Strain clam or mussel liquid through muslin or a fine sieve and measure 60 ml/2 fl oz. Make a well in the centre of the flour and add the measured liquid with 175 ml/6 fl oz milk, 2 teaspoons melted butter and 1 egg. Stir with a whisk until mixed, then gradually draw in flour to form a smooth batter. Stir in the chopped clams or mussels with 1 tablespoon chopped thyme. In a 10-cm/ 4-inch frying pan, heat 1-2 tablespoons butter until foaming. Using a ladle, add 2-3 tablespoons batter to form a pancake. Fry briskly until firm and browned, 2-3 minutes, flip and brown other side. Fry remaining pancakes, adding more butter as needed. Serve with sour cream. Makes 10-12 pancakes, to serve 4-6.

Whole clams and mussels

Roasted, steamed

IF NEW ENGLAND IS THE PLANET'S LOBSTER CAPITAL, Dieppe in Normandy is home to the world's best mussels, deeply appreciated by our whole family when we had a summer villa just along the coast. Most often we cooked them *à la marinière*, with onion, white wine and parsley, until their shells just opened. Other good ways to enjoy mussels or clams in their shell include steaming them with samphire, simmering them Portuguese-style with sausages and garlic, and baking them with corn, lobster and chicken in a clambake. Whatever you do, keep it simple!

Before cooking, both clams and mussels must be well scrubbed, discarding any open shells which do not close when tapped – these bivalves may be dead and should not be eaten. If the clam or mussel shells are dirty, it's a good idea to clean them by soaking in sea or salt water for an hour or two so the meat is purged of sand and grit. Mussels and clams are often salty, so do not add salt until cooking is finished, then taste them first.

UNDERCOOKED – few shells open but most still shut. *Why:* heat too low; cooking time too short; pan not covered and heat uneven.
What to do: stir to distribute heat evenly and cover pan; continue cooking, if necessary increasing heat.

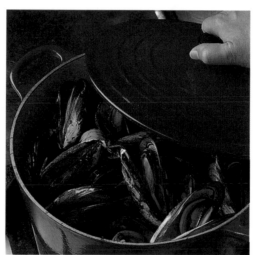

PERFECT – shells open, with meat inside juicy and plump; smell is sea-fresh, flavour piquant. Note: if a few shells remain closed, discard them.

OTHER PROBLEMS

SANDY
Why: shells gathered near sand, or after a storm.
What to do: strain cooking juices through muslin. If meat is gritty, nothing can be done.

SALTY
Why: salt or salty ingredients added; overcooked.
What to do: counteract salt with bland ingredients such as cream, tomato and potato.

OVERCOOKED AND TOUGH – shells gaping wide with meat inside shrivelled; salty flavour intensified and juices fallen to bottom of pan.
Why: cooked too long; not tossed during cooking.
What to do: see Quick Fix.

QUICK FIX

Overcooked clams and mussels are inedibly tough. The only answer is to shell and chop them, discarding the neck of clams or rubbery ring around mussels, then add them to pasta. For 175 g/6 oz chopped cooked shellfish, cook 250 g/½ pound of pasta. Strain clam or mussel liquid and add water to make 250 ml/8 fl oz. In a frying pan, heat 2 tablespoons olive oil, add 2 chopped garlic cloves and sauté 30 seconds. Add cooking liquid, 125 ml/4 fl oz double cream, pinch of nutmeg and pepper. Simmer over high heat until slightly thickened and sauce coats a spoon. Stir in shellfish, 30 g/1 oz chopped parsley and 30 g/1 oz chopped stoned black olives. Toss with pasta. Serves 2.

Squid and octopus

Squid and octopus used to be culinary jokes in non-Mediterranean countries. I well remember my Yorkshire-born father scoffing at a stew of squid in its ink, which I insisted on trying one year in Portugal.

No longer … We're all familiar with deep-fried squid, and may even have encountered char-grilled octopus or dishes such as pasta salad of squid with red onion, or Greek stuffed squid with rice, currants and lots of garlic.

They are not difficult to prepare, just remember that careful cooking is vital as both squid and octopus can turn so rubbery that you can't eat them.

They should either be very lightly cooked for a few moments, as when sautéed, deep-fried or poached, or simmered long and slowly in a Mediterranean-style stew with garlic, wine, olive oil, tomato and lots of herbs. At first they will toughen, then they gradually soften to be tender but still slightly chewy. A connoisseur's delight!

PERFECT – squid tender enough to cut with a thumbnail; juicy with no trace of toughness; flavour delicate, with a touch of salt.

Clams on the half shell with garlic, green pepper and bacon

SERVES 4

This recipe, commonly called clams Casino, is equally good made with oysters or large mussels. Here I call for lemon slices to steady the shells on the baking sheet instead of the more usual coarse sea salt, which all too easily strays into the clam shells.

24 littleneck or cherrystone clams
4 lemons
1 tablespoon vegetable oil
1 green pepper, cored, seeded and
   finely diced

2 garlic cloves, finely chopped
6 thin slices of bacon
   (about 250 g/½ pound)

Preheat the oven to 220°C/425°F/gas7. Scrub the clams under cold running water. Shuck the clams: hold each clam in a cloth in the palm of your hand and insert the tip of a small knife between the shells near the hinge. Twist the knife, prying the shells apart. Cut the clam meat from the bottom and top shells. Rinse the bottom shells and set the clam meat back on this half shell. Squeeze the juice from 1 lemon and slice the remaining lemons – you need 24 slices. Set the shells on a baking sheet on lemon slices to keep them steady.

Heat the oil in a small frying pan, add the green pepper and sauté until soft, 3-5 minutes. Add the garlic and continue cooking until fragrant, 1-2 minutes. Cut the bacon into pieces the same size as the clams.

Sprinkle a little lemon juice over each clam, spoon over the green pepper and garlic and top with a piece of bacon. Bake in the oven until the bacon is crisp and brown and clams are just done, 8-10 minutes. Transfer the clams on the lemon slices to individual plates and serve at once.

Clams on the half shell with garlic, green pepper and bacon

Spaghetti with red mussel sauce

SERVES 4

The fewer the ingredients, the better they must be – the freshest of mussels and the ripest of tomatoes are important here.

500 g/1 pound spaghetti
60 ml/2 fl oz olive oil
salt and pepper
2 tablespoons chopped parsley

for the red mussel sauce
1.8 kg/4 pounds small mussels
2 tablespoons olive oil
2 onions, finely chopped
6 garlic cloves, finely chopped
1.4 kg/3 pounds tomatoes, peeled,
   seeded and chopped
1 bay leaf

Bring a large pan of salted water to the boil for the spaghetti. Scrub the mussels for the sauce under cold running water, pulling off beards with a small knife. Discard any mussels which do not close when tapped on the counter.

Steam the mussels open: put them in large pan, cover tightly and cook over medium heat until done, stirring once, 4-5 minutes. Take the mussels from the pan, reserving their liquid. Cover the mussels to keep them warm, discarding any which are still closed.

Make the sauce: heat the olive oil in a sauté pan, add the onions and sauté until lightly browned, 4-5 minutes. Add the garlic and continue cooking until fragrant, 1-2 minutes. Add the reserved mussel juice to the pan, taking care to leave any sandy deposit behind. Then add the tomatoes and bay leaf and simmer until sauce is concentrated and just falls easily from a spoon, 5-8 minutes.

Add the spaghetti to the boiling water and simmer, stirring occasionally until *al dente*, tender but still firm to the bite, 5-7 minutes. Drain, return spaghetti to the pan and toss with olive oil. Transfer to a large serving bowl and keep warm.

Discard the bay leaf from the sauce and add the sauce to the mussels. Stir to mix and reheat for 1 or 2 minutes. Taste and adjust the seasoning – salt may not be necessary as the mussels are already salty. Spoon mussels and sauce over the spaghetti, sprinkle with parsley and serve.

Spaghetti with red mussel sauce

Scallops

Baked, grilled, pan-fried, poached, roasted, sautéed, simmered

LOBSTER IS REGARDED AS THE KING OF SHELLFISH, but I reckon a freshly roasted scallop, caramelized in butter and bursting with juices, runs a close second. Personally I prefer large sea scallops, but smaller bay, calico and queen scallops have their partisans. Before cooking, season scallops with salt and pepper having first drained them and dried them thoroughly on paper towels. Then give them a simple treatment, perhaps pan-frying them with fennel, or poaching them in cider and cream as in Normandy, or spearing them to grill on kebabs with cherry tomatoes, or baking them as a breadcrumb-topped gratin with onion, garlic and ham, as in Spain. Scallops take kindly to sweet spices such as cumin, coriander and saffron. Never, never allow them to overcook.

PERFECT LIGHTLY COOKED – meat is plump and white or delicately browned, depending on cooking method; when pressed, meat offers no resistance (Thumb Test, first finger stage, see right); flavour is sweet and aromatic.

PERFECT WELL-DONE – meat is plump and white or lightly browned depending on cooking method; when pressed, meat resists (Thumb Test, third finger stage, see right); flavour is sweet and aromatic.

THE THUMB TEST FOR FIRMNESS

A simple way to judge the cooking of a piece of fish, meat or poultry is to compare its resilience to that of your thumb muscle. As shown, the further the thumb has to reach, the more resilient the muscle becomes.

FIRST-FINGER STAGE
for lightly cooked fish and underdone/blue meat – touch your thumb to its opposing first finger and press the ball of your thumb with the tip of a finger of the other hand – the ball will offer no resistance.

SECOND-FINGER STAGE
for rare meat – touch your second finger to your thumb and press the ball of the thumb – the ball will feel spongy.

THIRD-FINGER STAGE
for well-done fish and medium-cooked meat, game or duck – touch your third finger to your thumb and press the ball of your thumb – the ball will feel resistant.

FOURTH-FINGER STAGE
for well-done meat or poultry – touch your fourth finger to your thumb and press the ball of your thumb – the ball will feel firm.

PROBLEMS

OVERCOOKED AND TOUGH
Why: cooked too long or too fast.
What to do: moisten with a flavoured oil such as olive or walnut, melted butter or vinaigrette dressing, or serve with a rich white butter or hollandaise sauce (see Sauces, pages 120 and 118).

TASTELESS
Why: scallops stale or poorly stored; too much phosphate in preserving liquid; under seasoned; overcooked.
What to do: serve with white butter or velouté sauce (see Sauces, pages 120 and 112) well flavoured with saffron, fresh ginger, tomato or herbs, like basil or dill.

WATERY, HARD TO BROWN
Why: not well drained; scallops poorly preserved in phosphate liquid; too many cooked at once; pan not hot enough.
What to do: after cooking, drain excess liquid then finish in small batches over high heat to ensure browning.

Grilled scallops with prosciutto cream sauce

SERVES 6-8 as an appetizer, or 4 as a main course

Deceptively simple, this velvety sauce made with prosciutto and mushrooms is the perfect foil for fresh, sweet scallops. By all means replace the button mushrooms with wild varieties when you can find them.

750 g/1½ pounds scallops
30 g/1 oz butter
vegetable oil for the grill rack

for the prosciutto cream sauce
75 g/2½ oz thinly sliced prosciutto
30 g/1 oz butter
1 tablespoon olive oil
1 garlic clove, finely chopped
1 shallot, finely chopped

1 small carrot, very finely diced (brunoise)
3 tablespoons white wine
165 g/5½ oz button mushrooms, diced
60 ml/2 fl oz double cream or crème fraîche
30 g/1 oz butter, chilled and cut into pieces
salt and pepper
2 tablespoons chopped parsley

Make the prosciutto cream sauce: cut the prosciutto in thin strips about 2 cm/¾ inch long. Heat the butter and olive oil in a saucepan, add the garlic and shallot and sauté until fragrant, 1-2 minutes. Add the carrot and sauté until beginning to soften, 1-2 minutes. Pour over the white wine and boil, stirring, until reduced by half. Stir in the mushrooms and cook until slightly softened, 1-2 minutes. Stir in the cream or crème fraîche with the prosciutto strips and boil until slightly thickened, 1-2 minutes.

Turn the heat to low and gradually whisk in the butter pieces to make a smooth creamy sauce. Work on and off the heat, so that the butter softens and thickens the sauce without melting to oil. Season to taste with salt and pepper. Keep the sauce warm on a rack over a pan of hot but not boiling water.

Preheat the grill. Discard the small crescent-shaped muscles at the sides of the scallops. Rinse the scallops and pat dry with paper towels. Place them on an oiled grill rack, dot with butter and season with salt and pepper. Set the rack about 7.5 cm/3 inches from the heat and grill the scallops until done, 2-3 minutes on each side.

Meanwhile, stir all but 1 teaspoon of the parsley into the sauce. Spoon the sauce on 4 warmed plates, arrange the grilled scallops on top and sprinkle with reserved parsley. Serve at once.

QUICK FIX

Dress scallops which are overcooked, tough or tasteless as a pasta salad. For 750 g/1½ pounds scallops, cook 500 g/1 pound coloured or tri-coloured pasta such as shells or fusilli. In a small bowl, combine the juice of 3 lemons, 2 limes and 1 orange. Whisk in 75 ml/2½ fl oz vegetable oil

and 30 g/1 oz coarsely chopped parsley. Drain any sauce from the scallops and cut them across in thin rounds to minimize toughness. Add to the pasta, pour over the dressing and toss to mix. Season to taste. Serves 4.

Marinated raw fish and shellfish

Recipes for marinated raw fish and shellfish fall into two main categories: very thin slices of fish that are sprinkled with flavourings, often called carpaccio after the Italian beef preparation, and Latin American seviche, with its spicy strips or chunks of fish or shellfish. In each case, the acid present in the marinade lightly cooks the fish. For carpaccio, the fish must be sliced wafer-thin so that the acid and other flavourings sprinkled on top penetrate quickly, for serving within a few minutes. A typical seviche is marinated with lime juice or vinegar and hot with chilli, but mild versions can be made with a simple vinaigrette. Marinating time can be lengthy, even a day or two, producing almost a pickle.

Fish for marinating must be super-fresh, and only a few firm, sweet-fleshed types are suitable. Salmon and scallops are prime favourites, though sea bass, plaice, white tuna, red snapper, sole and squid are very good as well.

PERFECT right – clear white or pink colour of fish (here salmon) slightly blanched by action of acid and highlighted by vivid garnish; flavourings a good balance of acid and piquant, lively without overwhelming delicate flavour of very fresh raw fish or seafood.

OVERDONE left – colour faded and patchy; fresh flavour of seafood lost.

Why: too much acid, particularly citrus; too many piquant ingredients such as green peppercorns, chopped onion, chilli pepper; seafood marinated too long – 5 minutes is enough for very thinly sliced fish, or up to 12 hours for thicker slices or strips of seafood.

What to do: very little can be done; a sprinkling of oil helps balance acidic flavour.

Deep-fried fish and shellfish

BRITISH FISH AND CHIPS, Japanese tempura, American deep-fried oysters, Italian *fritto misto*, French *petite friture* – it is no accident that deep-fried fish is everyone's national dish. Sealed by a coating of flour, batter or crumbs, the delicate juices and flavour of fish are effectively trapped, to arrive piping hot on your plate. Little else is needed, except a squeeze of lemon juice, a drizzle of vinegar, or possibly a light Oriental dip. Richer sauces such as piquant French tartare or Greek *skordalia*, laden with garlic, are tempting but by no means mandatory.

When deep-frying, all the action comes at the last minute, so efficient preparation is vital. Rinse the fish and pat dry. If using egg and breadcrumbs, coat the fish ahead of time, then spread the pieces on a baking sheet and chill – this will dry the coating and make it all the crisper. However, coating with flour or batter should be done at the last minute just before cooking. While the fat is heating to the correct temperature, assemble the equipment you'll need – frying basket, draining spoon or 'spider', and a tray lined with paper towel for draining. Even when using a thermostat, test the temperature of the fat with a drop of batter or a small piece of fish. Then finally launch into cooking. It will only take a few minutes.

Deep-frying doesn't take long, but it really does have to be done at the last minute. Drain the fried fish or shellfish on paper towels and, if you need to keep it warm briefly while frying more, put it in a low oven with the door open.

QUICK FIX

Try a cover-up of deep-fried herbs. While the hot oil cools slightly, rinse a large bunch of parsley, detach sprigs and dry them thoroughly on paper towels. Wash a bunch of basil and/or sage, detach and dry leaves. Toss a handful of parsley into the fat, fry about 30 seconds until sputtering stops and at once scoop out with a wire scoop or basket. Repeat for the remaining herbs. Sprinkle over fish and serve.

UNDERCOOKED – batter or breadcrumb coating is pale, often soggy and falling from the fish or shellfish; inside, the seafood is firm, shellfish soft and partly translucent.
Why: fat not hot enough (depending on size of seafood pieces, correct temperature is 175-190°C/350-375°F); too much seafood added at once to fat, thereby lowering temperature; frying time too short.
What to do: remove seafood and drain, reheat fat to correct temperature and re-fry until done.

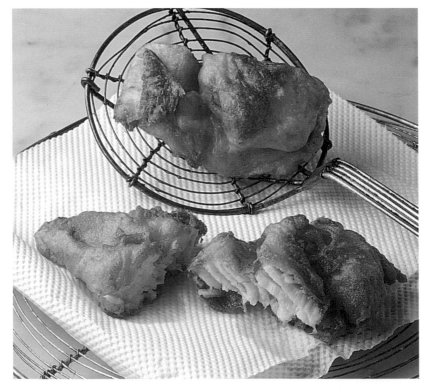

PERFECT – fish or shellfish is moist and opaque with no translucent centre; coating of batter or breadcrumbs is even and cooked to a crisp golden brown; flavour is juicy and full-bodied.

OTHER PROBLEMS

OVERCOOKED
Why: fat too hot so coating scorched before seafood was cooked; fried too long.
What to do: not much can be done. Try adding accompaniments such as skinny French fries and a fresh salsa such as the Salsa of Tomato and Coriander on page 129.

TASTELESS
Why: seafood or coating not sufficiently seasoned; bland type of fish or shellfish; oil overpowers flavour of fish.
What to do: serve with lemon or vinegar for sprinkling, plus a piquant sauce such as tartare or wasabi vinaigrette.

COATING SOGGY
Why: batter too thin or crumbs not dry; temperature too low.
What to do: drain seafood thoroughly; heat fat to 190°C/375°F and re-fry briefly.

COATING FALLS OFF
Why: seafood not dried before coating; batter too thin or crumbs not dry; frying temperature too low.
What to do: nothing possible.

Seafood trio in beer batter

SERVES 4-6

Here I suggest three favourite fish for deep-frying but many others will do equally well. Buy what is freshest, if possible with a contrast of texture. Beer is a popular addition to batters as it cuts the richness of deep-fried food as well as making the batter light. I often serve deep-fried fish with the Oriental dressing in the Quick Fix on page 35 as a dipping sauce.

250 g/½ pound salmon fillets, without skin
250 g/½ pound cod fillets, without skin
250 g/½ pound catfish or whiting fillets, without skin
45 g/1½ oz flour, seasoned with salt and pepper
oil for deep-frying

for the beer batter
150 g/5 oz flour
½ teaspoon salt
1 egg, separated
300 ml/½ pint beer
1 tablespoon vegetable oil

Make batter: sift flour and salt into a large bowl and make a well in the centre. Add egg yolk and half the beer and whisk, gradually drawing in flour to form a smooth paste. Stir in remaining beer with the oil. Note: don't overmix or batter will become elastic. Cover and leave to stand so starch in flour expands and lightens the batter, 15-30 minutes.

Heat oil for deep-frying to 190°C/375°F. Rinse fish fillets and pat dry with paper towels. Cut each type of fish fillet into 4 equal pieces.

Beat the egg white for the batter until stiff peaks form when the whisk is lifted. Fold the beaten white into the batter.

Coat the fish pieces with flour, patting to remove the excess. Dip a piece into the batter and lower it into the hot oil. Repeat with 3-4 more pieces and fry until done, 3-4 minutes depending on the thickness of the fish. Drain on paper towels and keep warm. Repeat with remaining pieces of fish, frying them in 1 or 2 batches.

Arrange a piece of each fish on 4 warmed plates. Set a ramekin of dipping sauce beside the fish and serve at once.

Fish and shellfish stews

STEWS WERE ONCE REPOSITORIES FOR TRASH FISH — coarse-textured fish with large bones, fish with too many bones to make filleting easy, or simply damaged fish with no other use. Given the high price of fish today, this is no longer the case and any recipe that extracts the maximum flavour from heads and bones as well as the edible flesh is bound to be a hit. Almost all types of fish and shellfish can be pressed into service, the more the merrier, resulting in a wonderfully exotic range of flavours and recipes. Among my favourites are peppery shrimp and okra gumbo from Louisiana, Breton *cotriade* with cod, potato, mussels and cream, and of course Provençal *bouillabaisse* flavoured with saffron. Then there's Flemish *waterzöi* of eel flavoured with leek and celery, or Italian-American *cioppino* of sea bass, clams and crab with tomato and garlic.

Irrespective of its origins, the guidelines for a fish stew are the same. Quick-cooking fish should be in large pieces, with slower-cooking types cut smaller. Add the different seafood according to cooking time, with those taking longest on the bottom. Be sure the cooking liquid is highly seasoned, and don't drown the fish — it should be barely covered, no longer swimming in a sea.

PERFECT — fish pieces firm and lightly cooked, with translucent line in centre, or well-done according to taste; shellfish plump, tender but still firm when pinched between finger and thumb; sauce may be a concentrated broth or thick enough lightly to coat the back of a spoon; must have lively flavour and vivid colour.

QUICK FIX

Transform overcooked fish into a soup: remove pieces of fish and shellfish from the liquid, discard skin and bones and set shellfish aside. Purée fish in 2-3 batches with a little liquid. Pour into a soup pan, add remaining liquid, bring to the boil and season with cayenne, salt and pepper. If very thick, thin with a little cream, milk or water. Replace shellfish, heat gently and taste, adding white wine, lemon juice, tomato purée or cayenne as you like. Serve with croutons.

OTHER PROBLEMS

TASTELESS
Why: poorly handled or stale seafood; under-seasoned; lacking pungent flavourings.
What to do: add vegetables such as onion, leek, fennel and celery to stew, and lively flavourings such as fresh ginger, garlic and saffron; be sure cooking liquid is well seasoned, if you like with white wine, soy sauce, herbs such as bay leaf, dill, coriander, parsley or tarragon; pick up flavour before serving with salt, pepper, chilli oil, hot sauce, vinegar, Southeast Asian fish sauce, soy sauce, cayenne, lime or lemon juice.
BROTH OR SAUCE THIN AND TASTELESS
Why: poorly handled or stale seafood; too much liquid.
What to do: remove seafood, boil until well-flavoured and replace seafood; see also Tasteless
SEAFOOD COOKED UNEVENLY
Why: seafood cut in uneven pieces or added in wrong sequence; layers of seafood too deep so those on bottom are done before top.
What to do: transfer cooked fish to bowls and keep warm while continuing to cook the rest.
OVERCOOKED — fish pieces disintegrating and shellfish tough; sauce lacks sparkle.
Why: stew boiled rather than simmered; cooked too long.
What to do: avoid stirring as it can break up fish pieces; for minimum handling, serve stew in warm individual bowls rather than a tureen; serve with a pungent sauce.

Stir-fried fish and shellfish

ONCE AN ORIENTAL EXCLUSIVITY, QUICK LIGHT STIR-FRYING IN A WOK has gone international. It's no longer a surprise to hear of cross-cultural dishes like stir-fried mako shark with peppery greens, or prawns with carrot, daikon radish and leek. Yet it's hard to beat such classics as Chinese clams in black bean sauce or Vietnamese *ca sao mang tuoi* (grouper with bamboo shoots and dried mushrooms).

Asian cooks are expert at marinating seafood before stir-frying in piquant ingredients such as soy sauce, rice wine, lemon or lime juice, mirin, rice vinegar, fish sauce, or chopped garlic and ginger. They pay particular attention to chopping or slicing each ingredient to exactly the right size, not to mention adding them in the right order at the right moment. Like deep-frying, stir-frying calls for quick reactions and careful timing.

UNDERCOOKED – fish or shellfish translucent on outside; other ingredients still almost raw so textures conflict and flavours have not started to blend and mellow.
Why: overcrowded wok; temperature not high enough; cooking time too short.
What to do: turn up heat and continue cooking; if seafood and other main ingredients are already browned, cover wok and leave over low heat until they are done.

PERFECT – fish or shellfish is opaque outside and just firm; centre may be lightly cooked and translucent, or well-done as preferred; other ingredients are lightly cooked also, adding colour as well as crisp or smooth contrast of texture; flavours are lively.

OTHER PROBLEMS

OVERCOOKED – fish soft, shellfish tough
Why: cooking too slow, often because too many ingredients added too quickly; cooking time too long.
What to do: drain excess liquid and disguise by stirring in crisp and colourful fresh ingredients such as chopped celery, spring onion, radish, water chestnut or jícama.

FLAT TASTE
Why: lack of seasoning; overcooked.
What to do: season with soy sauce, rice wine, lemon or lime juice, Tabasco, chopped lemon grass or spring onion.

DULL COLOURS
Why: poor choice of ingredients; overcooked.
What to do: sprinkle with chopped sweet pepper, tomato or herb such as coriander.

COOKING UNEVEN – some ingredients almost raw, others overcooked
Why: ingredients added in wrong sequence so some are ready before others.
What to do: if possible, separate out those ingredients that are cooked and keep cooking those that aren't.

Black-and-white stir-fried bream

SERVES 4

The black of dried mushrooms contrasts with white strips of bream in this lively stir-fry. For best flavour, use Chinese black mushrooms or black chanterelles; tree ears will add colour and chewy texture but little taste.

30 g/1 oz dried black mushrooms
500 g/1 pound bream fillets, free
*   of skin and bones*
3 tablespoons vegetable oil
1.25-cm/½-inch piece of ginger,
*   finely chopped*
2 garlic cloves, finely chopped
2 dried red chilli peppers
2 spring onions, sliced
500 g/1 pound bok choy or chard,
*   stems and green leaves*
*   shredded*
125 ml/4 fl oz fish or chicken stock

2 tablespoons soy sauce
1 tablespoon rice wine
1 tablespoon cornflour, mixed to a
*   paste with 2 tablespoons water*

for the marinade
1 tablespoon rice wine or dry sherry
½ teaspoon salt
¼ teaspoon shrimp paste
¼ teaspoon pepper
1 egg white, whisked until frothy
1½ tablespoons cornflour
1 tablespoon oil

First soak the mushrooms: put the dried mushrooms in a bowl and pour over boiling water to cover generously. Leave them to soak 20-30 minutes, then drain and dry them on paper towels. Trim any tough stems and cut the mushrooms into 5-cm/2-inch pieces.

Meanwhile, marinate the fish: wash the fillets, dry on paper towels and cut them in 5-cm/2-inch strips. Put the strips in a bowl with the rice wine, salt, shrimp paste and pepper. Mix well, then add egg white, cornflour and oil and stir until smoothly coated. Cover and chill, 15-30 minutes.

When ready to cook, heat the wok over high heat until very hot. Pour in oil to coat the base and sides, reserving 1 tablespoon. Heat over high heat for 30 seconds. Add the ginger, garlic and red chilli peppers and stir-fry until fragrant, about 30 seconds. Add the fish and spring onions and stir-fry rapidly 2-3 minutes until the fish turns white. Discard the chilli peppers, transfer the fish mixture to a bowl and set aside.

Wipe the wok with paper towels and heat again until very hot. Add the remaining oil and heat for 15 seconds. Add the shredded bok choy and mushrooms and stir-fry over high heat until the stems of the bok choy are crisp-tender and the mushrooms are hot, 2-3 minutes. Stir in the stock, soy sauce and rice wine, mixing thoroughly.

Return the fish mixture to the wok and stir well. Add the cornflour paste and continue stirring over high heat until the sauce thickens, 1-2 minutes. Remove wok from the heat, taste and adjust the seasoning with soy sauce.

Serve the stir-fry immediately.

Smoked fish and shellfish

Smoking has long been used as a method of preserving fish and shellfish – salmon, herring, oysters, mussels and clams are good examples – as the process prevents the fats in fish from turning rancid. These days the emphasis is mainly on flavour and chefs seem to be smoking anything from trout to eel to bay scallops. Smoke from a fire of tea leaves, corn cobs, maple, hickory, birch or mesquite flavours fish beautifully, while fruit woods such as apple, cherry and vine cuttings provide added fragrance. When done, the texture of smoked fish and shellfish should be firm, but certainly not tough. The flavour and aroma of the smoke should be evident and, depending on the process, it should colour the fish from light to dark amber.

In most cases, fish is salted or dipped in brine before being smoked in one of two ways. In cold-smoking, a true preserving technique, fish is exposed to cold (32°C/90°F) smoke, so it dries and pickles rather than cooks. Fish that has been cold-smoked for 24 hours can be stored up to two weeks. This process is safest done commercially under strict controls. In hot-smoking, the fish is cooked by smoke at 38-88°C/100-190°F, which only partially preserves it. Hot-smoked fish should be eaten within a few days. Some hot-smokers have a chamber for liquids such as water, beer, wine or fruit juice, which impart even more flavour to the fish as it smokes. Fish that has been hot-smoked too long looks shrivelled, with uneven colour and a sour smell.

PERFECT – fish (clockwise from top: salmon, scallops and mackerel) moist; colour glossy and golden, not too dark; firm to the touch; just flakes easily when tested with a fork; flavour full-bodied but not overpowering. Note: a stringy appearance denotes that the fish has been overcooked.

Fish and shellfish pâtés and mousselines

FISH PÂTÉS AND MORE DELICATE MOUSSELINES MADE FROM PURÉED RAW FISH OR SHELLFISH, bound with egg white and enriched with cream, are a part of the classic culinary repertoire. They are inseparable from France in recipes like salmon stuffed with a scallop mousseline, and turban of sole fillets baked in a circular mould with a mousseline of pink prawns. Contemporary cuisine chimes in with simpler ideas such as a warm mousse of sea bass with fennel and saffron, or halibut mousse with dill sauce, while from Asia come ideas like Vietnamese *cha tom*, a type of prawn pâté.

All of these recipes need well-flavoured shellfish or fish with a fine texture such as pike, whiting or scallops. Salmon is valued for its colour. You should avoid fish like mackerel and sardine as their high oil content can break down the texture of the pâté. The raw seafood is finely puréed – a food processor is convenient, though the traditional drum sieve gives a finer texture. Use only a stainless steel or nylon sieve to avoid discolouring the fish. Seasoning with salt helps stiffen and bind the mixture, and be sure to chill the seafood over ice before beating in the cream.

Key before any cooking is to test a ball of the mixture in gently simmering water to see if it falls apart; if it does, work in more egg white. At the same time, taste the cooked mixture and add more seasoning if needed. A water bath must be used to control the heat during cooking, as these delicate mixtures can easily separate. Don't worry, even when overcooked or separated they remain appetizing.

UNDERCOOKED – mixture moist and disintegrating; when unmoulded and cut, sides sag and centre is soft; mixture offers no resistance when pressed (first-finger stage, see page 28); a skewer inserted in the centre for 30 seconds is scarcely warm to the touch when withdrawn; meat thermometer inserted in centre registers less than 70°C/160°F; flavour not yet developed.
Why: cooking temperature too low; cooking time too short.
What to do: continue cooking, if necessary, first bringing water bath to the boil.

PERFECT – texture of the pâté or mousseline is light and smooth, just holding firm; mixture is firm when pressed (fourth-finger stage, see page 28); a skewer inserted in the centre is hot to the touch when withdrawn after 30 seconds; meat thermometer inserted in centre registers 70°C/160°F; taste is subtle and fresh, with colour pale and clear.

OVERCOOKED AND SEPARATED – texture dry, rough and almost curdled; mixture discoloured and shrinks from sides, with juices expelled around edges; skewer inserted in centre for 30 seconds is very hot when withdrawn; thermometer inserted in centre registers 70°C/160°F or more; fresh flavour lost.
Why: heat too high or cooking too long; if separated, type of seafood unsuitable or frozen; poorly puréed; proportions incorrect, especially too much cream; mixture not chilled during mixing.
What to do: add a herb butter sauce or parsley mayonnaise to counteract dryness, or a Japanese silver sauce of dashi, soy sauce, ginger and lemon. Garnish with colourful chopped tomato, alfalfa sprouts, wilted greens, or sprigs of watercress.

Fish quenelles

Quenelles, or dumplings, are closely related to mousseline, being basically the same mixture reinforced with a flour-based *panade* (often simply choux pastry). Most quenelles are of French origin, but a few ethnic recipes such as Jewish gefilte fish of pike bound with matzo meal also meet the definition. The dumpling mixture is firm enough to hold together if shaped with spoons and poached in stock or water. As it cooks, the quenelle puffs and lightens, floating to the top when done. When making quenelles it is important to poach a sample as for the mousseline in the terrine recipe overleaf, both for consistency and taste. If the quenelle is heavy or tastes of flour, it is most likely underdone. If thoroughly cooked but still disappointing, I usually beat a whole egg or two into the mixture to lighten it. The mixture will probably also need more seasoning.

UNDERCOOKED *left* – mixture flabby, scarcely holds shape.
PERFECT *centre* – slice is firm, smooth and moist.

OVERCOOKED AND SEPARATED *right* – mixture stringy and falling apart.

PERFECT – quenelles are lightly puffed, firm to the touch, and holding a clear shape. When cut, the texture is soft and smooth with fresh colour and definite flavour.

OTHER PROBLEMS

LACKS TASTE
Why: not enough seasoning; poorly handled or unsuitable fish or shellfish.
What to do: disguise bland taste with a lively sauce or dressing (see Overcooked and separated, and Quick Fix).

GREYISH COLOUR
Why: poor colour of fish or shellfish; metal sieve discoloured mixture; overcooked.
What to do: distract attention with colourful additions such as diced blanched sweet peppers, truffles or pistachio nuts.

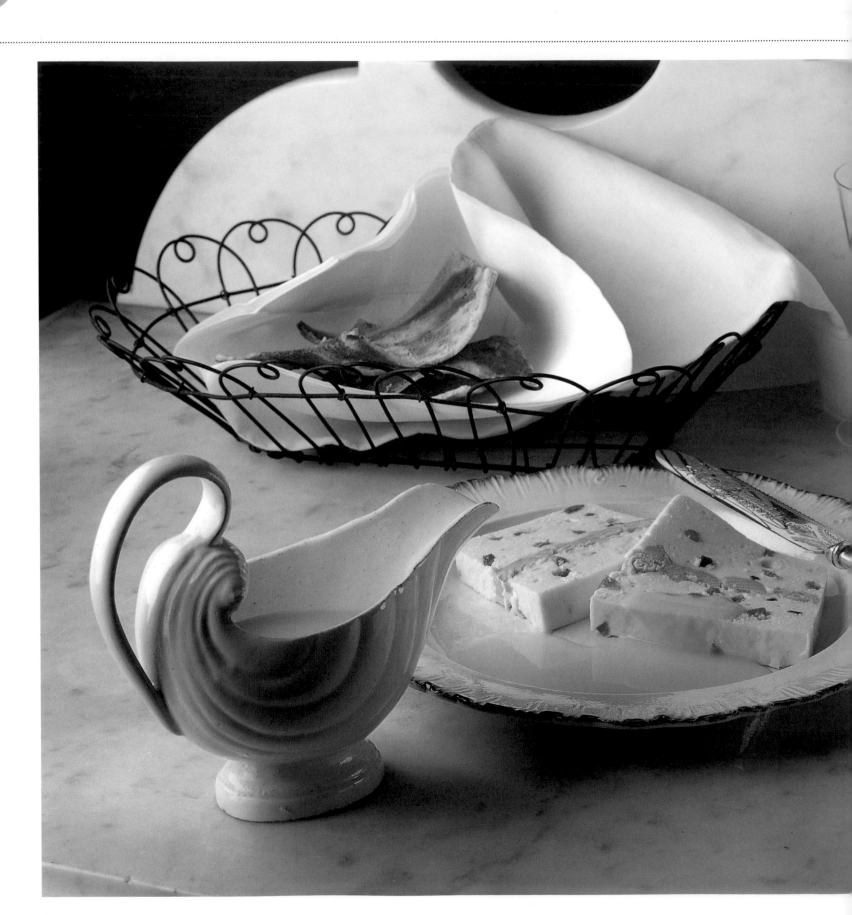

Salmon and scallop terrine with ginger sauce

Delicate scallop mousseline, striped with pink-fleshed salmon fillets, is equally good served hot with this tangy fresh ginger sauce or chilled with either a piquant mayonnaise or a walnut oil vinaigrette. Accompany with melba or whole-wheat toast.

250 g/½ pound salmon fillet, without skin, cut into strips
½ green pepper, cored, seeded and chopped
½ red pepper, cored, seeded and chopped
2 canned truffles, with liquid (optional)
bunch of watercress (optional)

for the scallop mousseline
750 g/1½ pounds sea scallops
3 egg whites
pinch of grated nutmeg
salt and white pepper
250 ml/8 fl oz double cream

for the ginger sauce
375 g/12 oz butter, cold and cut into pieces
2 garlic cloves, crushed
1 small onion, sliced
1 shallot, sliced
bouquet garni
5-cm/2-inch piece of fresh ginger, chopped
125 ml/4 fl oz white wine

1.25-litre/2-pint terrine mould or loaf pan

Preheat the oven to 175°C/350°F/gas4 and butter the mould or loaf pan. Bring a small pan of salted water to the boil, add red and green peppers and boil for 1 minute to blanch them. Drain, rinse in cold running water and drain again thoroughly. Drain the truffles, if using, and reserve their liquid; chop one of them and slice the other.

Make the scallop mousseline: whisk the egg whites until foamy. In a food processor, work the scallops to a fine purée. With the blades still turning, gradually work in the egg whites. Season with nutmeg, salt and white pepper. Transfer to a metal bowl and chill in the refrigerator until very cold, 10-15 minutes.

Set the chilled bowl in a larger bowl of ice and water. Using a wooden spoon, beat the mixture 1-2 minutes. It will thicken slightly. Beat in the cream by spoonfuls, beating well between additions – the mixture should be very thick. Beat in the peppers with the chopped truffles and truffle liquid if using.

Bring a small pan of water to the boil and poach a teaspoon of mixture for 1-2 minutes. Taste and adjust seasoning of the remaining mixture if necessary – it should be highly seasoned. The mixture should hold shape after poaching; but, if soft, beat in another egg white and chill again very thoroughly.

Pack half of the mixture in the buttered mould or loaf pan. Arrange strips of fish lengthwise on the mixture. Add the remaining mixture, smooth the top and cover with the lid or several layers of foil.

Half fill a roasting pan with water for a water bath. Set the terrine in the pan and bring the water to the boil on top of the stove. Transfer to the preheated oven and cook until done, 40-50 minutes.

Meanwhile, make the ginger sauce: in a medium saucepan, melt 2 tablespoons of the butter, add the garlic, onion, shallot, bouquet garni and ginger and sauté until soft but not browned, 3-5 minutes. Stir in the white wine and simmer until reduced by half, 1-2 minutes. Whisk the remaining butter into sauce a few pieces at a time, working on and off the heat so the butter softens and thickens the sauce without melting to oil. Strain the sauce into another saucepan, pressing the vegetables well to extract all their juices. Taste, adjust the seasoning and keep warm on a rack over a pan of warm water.

When the terrine is cooked, let it stand 10-15 minutes to reabsorb its juices. Run a knife around the edge and turn it out on a chopping board. Note: The peppers will have given off water so dry the edges of the terrine with paper towels. Cut it into 1.25-cm/½-inch slices and arrange them on a warmed platter or individual plates. Spoon over a little of the sauce and serve the rest separately. Decorate the slices of terrine with sliced truffles and watercress if you like.

POULTRY & GAME

How lucky we are! Can you imagine having to cook without a constant supply of inexpensive poultry that comes so conveniently in various forms – whole, in pieces, even boneless. Yet it was only in the 1950s that battery henhouses brought poultry within common reach. In my childhood, chicken was a treat, totally absent from school or weekday meals.

Now chicken has taken centre stage, its accommodating taste a strength as well as a weakness. Mild enough to blend with almost any other ingredient, chicken can be spiced up or left plain, mixed with vegetables, with meats like bacon and sausage, or even with shellfish such as prawns. For a lively approach, don't hesitate to adopt some of the flavouring ideas in my Quick Fixes.

There's much debate on the merits of free-range chickens and I've yet to be convinced that any but the very best are worth the extra cost. What matters more is how the chicken was fed – some foodstuffs taint the meat. When it comes to duck, however, you'll find that the lean birds available through speciality outlets and Chinese markets are far superior to the average fatty supermarket variety. The same goes for whole turkey or goose, my personal choice. Here's where money is well spent on a cosseted free-range bird. The difference in flavour can be dramatic. Appropriate seasonings and accompaniments range widely for all four types of domestic bird.

I haven't even mentioned the most interesting poultry category of all, that of game birds. They are rapidly becoming domesticated in the sense that more and more farm-raised varieties are available, including ostrich, emu, pheasant, guinea fowl, wild duck, pigeon and quail, in descending order of size. Tenderness is almost guaranteed when they are cooked right, and flavour offers a mild adventure which I urge you to try.

Poultry, particularly chicken, adapts well to virtually every cooking method. The high heat of roasting and grilling assures crisp skin and uncomplicated flavour – the danger is dryness, for which you'll find all sorts of remedies in this chapter. With the lower, moist heat of sautéing, braising and poaching, flavours become more elusive; it's here that the French insistence on simmering sauces to reduce and concentrate them is so important.

BIRDS

Lemon roast duck with olives and capers, page 53

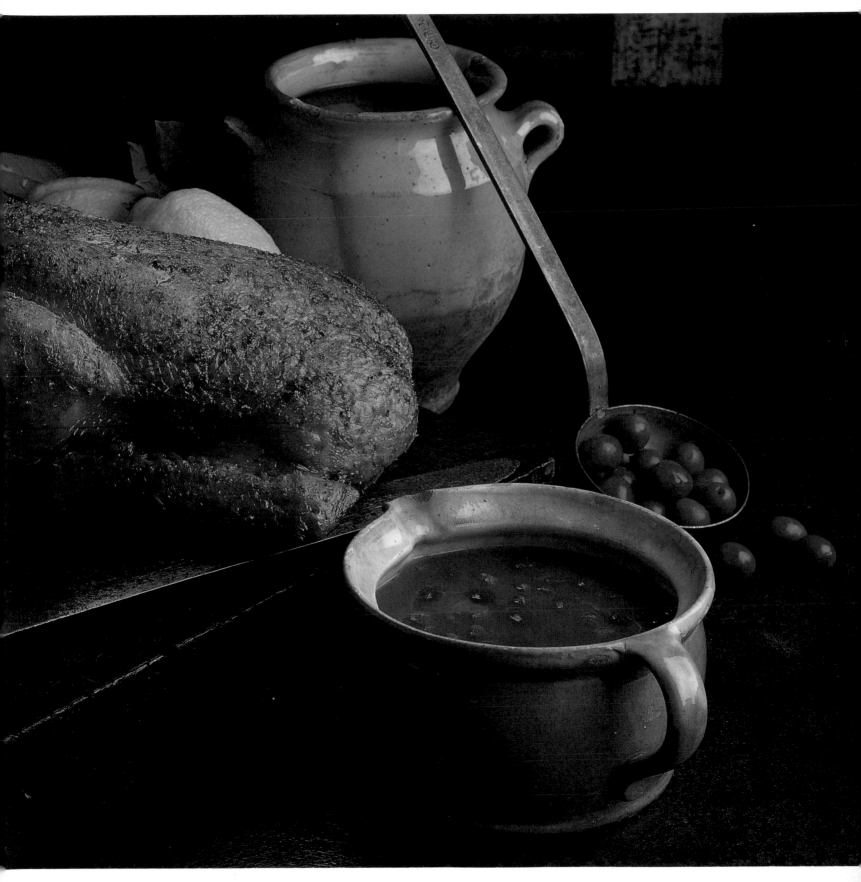

Whole chicken

Baked, braised, pot-roasted, roasted, spit-roasted

A WHOLE ROASTED OR BRAISED CHICKEN IS COMFORT FOOD, and happily within reach of a modest budget. We eat it at least once a week, so I feel I'm an expert in dressing up the average bird. Dry the surface of the chicken inside and out with paper towel. Then try seasoning the skin and cavity, not just with salt and pepper but with a brushing of soy sauce or white wine and olive oil, or rub the skin with a dry marinade of mustard, ground ginger, nutmeg, paprika or ground coriander. If you can, return the bird to the refrigerator for 1-2 hours before cooking so the flavours permeate the meat. You may also want to stuff it with a bundle of herbs, a whole onion or the pared zest of a lemon. Always truss or tie it with string to keep its shape. So heat penetrates more evenly, start the bird roasting on its back and then, once it starts to brown, turn it from one leg to the other, then finally on its back. Constant basting is the key to prime roast chicken – my mother stations herself by the oven with a good book so she can baste every 10 minutes. Let the bird stand in a warm place at least 10 minutes before serving, so the juices are redistributed uniformly throughout the meat. Butter is the favourite basting medium for poultry, though Italians favour a mix of olive oil, garlic and rosemary.

UNDERCOOKED – cavity juices pink; skin pale and not crisp; when drumstick pulled, joint rigid; flesh resistant when pierced with a fork; thermometer between thigh and breast reads less than 83°C/180°F; carved breast meat tinged with pink and thigh joints very pink.
Why: cooking temperature too low; cooking time too short.
What to do: cook until done, raising temperature if needed.

PERFECT WHOLE CHICKEN – when lifted with fork, juices from cavity run clear; skin evenly golden and crisp; when drumstick pulled, joint feels slightly flexible; flesh plump and tender when pierced with fork, and just starting to shrink from end of leg; thermometer inserted between thigh and breast reads 83°C/180°F; when carved, meat moist with no trace of pink. Note: thermometer unreliable for chickens under 1.4 kg/3 pounds.

DRY AND OVERCOOKED – flesh stringy and shrinking from bones; skin may be scorched; leg collapses when end is pulled; if not trussed, cooking may be uneven.
Why: cooked too long; too fast; if roasted, not basted enough.
What to do: moisten with brown sauce, gravy or salsa (see Sauces, pages 114-5 and 127); decorate with watercress, and add colourful accompaniment such as a sweet pepper or baked tomato.

OTHER PROBLEMS

BIRD IS TOUGH
Why: chicken too mature (boiling fowl); undercooked.
What to do: if pot-roasting or braising, ensure plenty of liquid and continue; if roasting, add liquid, cover and cook until tender.

LACKS TASTE
Why: meat of bird bland; insufficient seasoning.
What to do: serve with piquant gravy, brown sauce or

salsa (see Sauces) and contrasting accompaniments.
WET AND FATTY
Why: bird poorly frozen and defrosted; undercooked; temperature too low; if braised or pot-roasted, used too much liquid; if roasted, not basted often enough.
What to do: continue cooking 5-10 minutes uncovered at high heat, basting often if roasting.

QUICK FIX

For simply roasted chicken that is dry and overcooked or bland: brush the hot cooked bird with an Oriental mix of 2 tablespoons soy sauce, 2 teaspoons dark sesame oil, 1 garlic clove, finely chopped, 1 tablespoon chopped fresh ginger, juice of ½ lime and 1 tablespoon chopped fresh coriander. Add an Oriental accompaniment of Vietnamese Stir-Fried Green Beans with Sesame (page 172).

Whole chicken

Poached, steamed

MUCH OF MY ADVICE ON WHOLE BRAISED AND ROASTED CHICKEN also holds good for poached and steamed birds. Trussing is particularly important, as the limbs will shrink from the carcass during cooking if left undone. For poaching, look for a large chicken, if possible an older bird (boiling fowl). It will take longer to cook, but has so much more flavour. For maximum flavour when poaching or steaming, be sure the cooking liquid is laced with aromatics such as onion, garlic and herbs. To make a sauce, boil the liquid to reduce it well and don't hesitate to pick up the taste with lemon juice or Cognac.

Poached or steamed chicken is far from plain, even if it implies cooking with water. From my birthplace in northern England comes 'hindle wakes', simmered chicken stuffed with prunes in a lemon cream sauce; Italians sometimes stuff the bird with beet greens, ricotta and Parmesan. Perhaps my favourite dish of this sort is the archetypal French *poule au pot*, stuffed with herbs, smoked ham, chicken liver and breadcrumbs, and simmered in stock with vegetables.

TOUGH AND UNDERCOOKED – when thickest part of thigh is pierced with fork, meat is resistant and juices run pink; meat wet and fatty, still tinged with pink, especially in gap between breast and leg; joint is rigid when leg is pulled; meat thermometer inserted between thigh and breast reads less than 83°C/180°F.
Why: cooking temperature too low; cooking time too short.
What to do: continue cooking until tender, if necessary raising temperature.

PERFECT – meat is tender and juices run clear when thickest part of thigh is pierced with two-pronged fork; chicken is plump and meat is just starting to shrink from end of leg; when leg is pulled, joint feels slightly flexible; a meat thermometer inserted between thigh and breast reads 83°C/180°F; when carved, the meat is full-flavoured and moist but not flabby.
Note: Whole birds will continue to cook from residual heat, so stop cooking when slightly underdone. Thermometer is not reliable for birds under 1.4 kg/3 pounds.

OTHER PROBLEMS

OVERCOOKED
Why: cooked too long; cooked too fast; if not trussed, cooked unevenly.
What to do: cut chicken in pieces, trimming bones well, and coat with a velouté or vegetable-thickened sauce (see Sauces). If very overdone, discard bones and skin, pull meat into shreds and serve in sauce or moistened with an herb and shallot vinaigrette.

LACKS TASTE
Why: meat of bird bland; insufficient seasoning.
What to do: if serving hot, sprinkle meat lightly with salt and pepper and serve with a lively vegetable-thickened sauce or salsa (see Sauces); if cold, marinate 1-2 hours in vinaigrette, or simply oil and lemon juice.

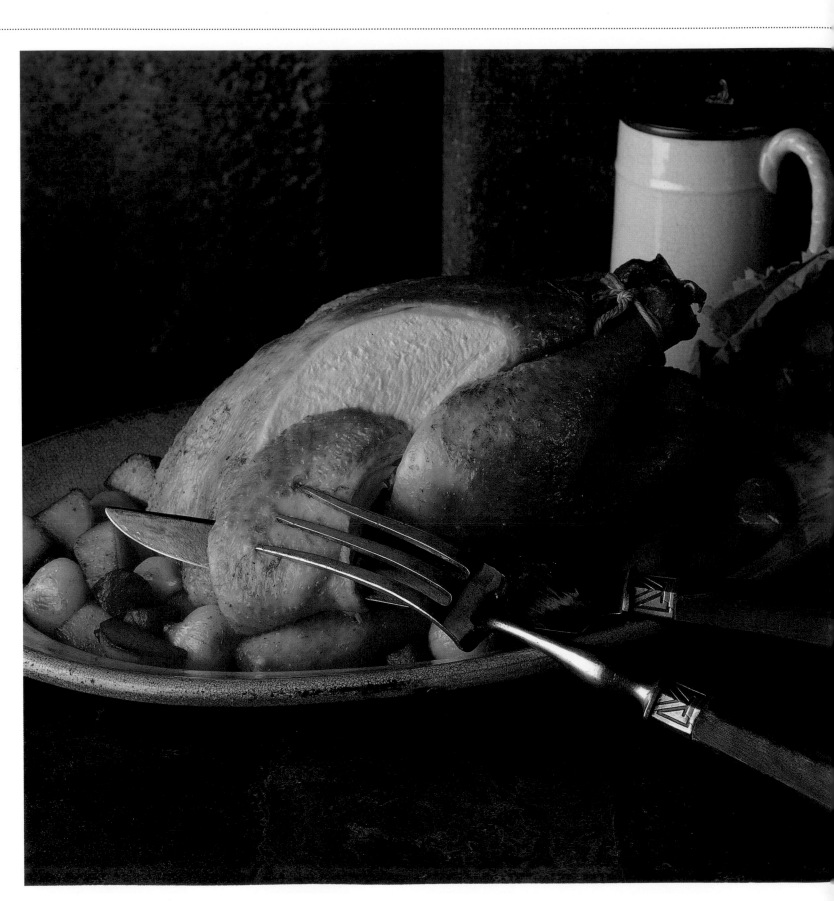

Pot-roasted chicken with potatoes, bacon and onion

SERVES 4

The classic *bonne femme* garnish of potatoes, bacon and onion makes this dish a meal in itself.

1 chicken (about 1.75 kg/3½ pounds)	625 g/1¼ pounds potatoes, peeled and cut into 2-cm/¾-inch chunks
45 g/1½ oz butter	salt and pepper
125 g/4 oz lean bacon, diced	
20-24 baby onions, blanched and peeled	trussing needle and string

Preheat the oven to 175°C/350°F/gas4. Season the skin and cavity of the chicken with salt and pepper and truss it.

In a flameproof casserole, melt the butter, add the bacon and onions and cook until brown, stirring often, 8-10 minutes. Remove them, add the potato chunks, season with salt and pepper and brown these, 8-10 minutes. Take them out, add the chicken and brown well on all sides, 8-10 minutes.

Set the chicken in the casserole on its back, cover tightly and roast in the preheated oven, turning the bird from time to time, until it is almost tender, 35-45 minutes.

Lift out the chicken and discard excess fat from the casserole if necessary, leaving about 2 tablespoons. Add the browned onions, bacon and potatoes to the bottom of pan and set the chicken on top. Cover and continue cooking until the chicken is done and vegetables are very tender, 15-20 minutes longer.

Discard the trussing strings and set the chicken on a serving platter. Taste the bacon and vegetables, adjust the seasoning if necessary and spoon them around the chicken, together with the cooking juices.

Pot roasted chicken with potatoes, bacon and onion

Poached chicken with salsify and cream

SERVES 4

All the ingredients are white in this traditional Norman wedding dish. You may substitute baby turnip or celeriac for the salsify, a slender root which resembles white asparagus in shape and taste.

1 chicken or boiling fowl (about 1.8 kg/4 pounds)	2 litres/3¼ pints chicken stock or water, more if needed
salt and white pepper	1 kg/2 pounds salsify
1 onion, studded with 2 cloves	
2 carrots, quartered	for the cream sauce
2 garlic cloves	75 g/2½ oz butter
bouquet garni, including tarragon	45 g/1½ oz flour
300 ml/½ pint white wine	375 ml/12 fl oz crème fraîche or double cream
	trussing needle and string

Season the skin and cavity of the bird and truss it. Put it in a pot into which it fits quite tightly, together with the onion, carrots, garlic and bouquet garni. Pour in the wine and enough chicken stock or water just to cover, add a little salt and pepper and bring to the boil. Cover and simmer over low heat, skimming occasionally, until the bird is done, 1-1¼ hours for chicken and 1½-2 hours for boiling fowl.

About one-half hour before the end of cooking, peel the salsify and cut it in 5-cm/2-inch lengths. Put it in a pan and add enough stock from the bird to cover it generously. Cover and simmer until tender, 25-35 minutes. Drain and return the stock to the pot.

When the bird is done, transfer to a cutting board. Discard the strings and cover the bird with foil to keep it warm. Skim any fat from surface of stock and measure 1 litre/1⅔ pints. Boil this until reduced to 750 ml/1¼ pints.

Make the cream sauce: melt the butter in a pan, whisk in the flour and cook until foaming. Strain in the reduced stock, stir and bring to the boil, whisking constantly until the sauce thickens, 1-2 minutes. Simmer for 2 minutes, then add the crème fraîche or cream. Taste and adjust the seasoning. Continue simmering the sauce until it lightly coats the back of a spoon, 3-5 minutes.

Add the salsify to the sauce and heat gently for 1-2 minutes. Carve the chicken in 6-8 pieces and arrange it on a platter. Spoon the salsify and some sauce around the chicken and serve the rest separately.

Whole turkey

Baked, braised, pot-roasted, roasted, spit-roasted

A FEW REMINDERS ARE BOUND TO BE HELPFUL when facing the annual challenge of cooking the Christmas turkey. First of all, the bird does not have to be roasted – it can be braised or pot-roasted with flavourings and wine or stock to keep it moist, a less risky procedure which needs little attention. I often take a middle road: a few hours before cooking I rub the bird with a dry marinade. Later I roast it until it starts to brown, then I add stock or wine and cover the bird with foil so it continues cooking in moist heat.

The bigger the turkey, the lower the oven temperature should be, so that heat penetrates slowly and thoroughly without drying the surface. However a temperature below 160°C/325°F is risky for large birds, as the heat can take too long to reach the centre and harmful bacteria may flourish. Stuffing also slows the cooking, so I prefer to leave the bird empty, and bake the stuffing separately in a large dish or individual dishes so it develops a crusty brown top. When the bird is done, let it stand in a warm place at least 10 minutes before carving so the juices are redistributed uniformly throughout the meat.

A whole turkey is best kept simple. For festive effect, I often load the plate with accompaniments – roasted potatoes, braised chestnuts, glazed onions, Brussels sprouts or broccoli or Glazed Root Vegetables (page 175). Stuffings such as sausage meat with chestnuts, celery with dried fruits and walnuts, or the spiced onion, raisin, almond and rice combination favoured in Greece, are all good choices.

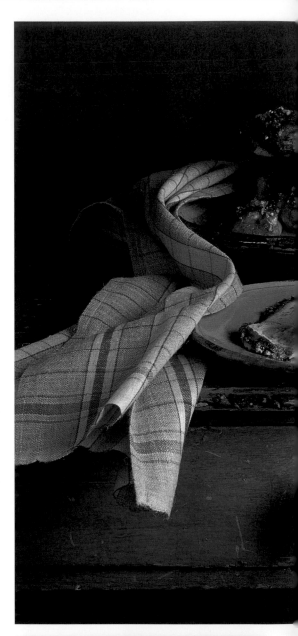

UNDERCOOKED – when drumstick is pulled, leg joint is rigid; skin is not yet crisp and meat looks flabby; juices run pink when thickest part of thigh is pierced with a fork; meat thermometer inserted between thigh and breast reads below 83°C/180°F.
Why: cooking time too short; cooking temperature too low.
What to do: continue cooking until done, if necessary raising temperature.

PERFECT – when drumstick is rotated towards breast, it feels slightly loose; skin is evenly golden brown and crisp; meat is plump and starting to shrink from end of leg; juices run clear when thickest part of thigh is pierced with a two-pronged fork; meat thermometer inserted between thigh and breast reads 83°C/180°F; when turkey is carved, meat is moist and full of flavour.

QUICK FIX

Draw attention from less-than-perfect birds: decorate the platter with tomato baskets filled with diced celery or cucumber for a crisp contrast. For a lavish approach, pile on some grilled cocktail sausages and little rolls of crispy bacon. Disguise problems with the bird itself – skin not browned, split or scorched – with sprigs of watercress, branches of herbs, even a strategically placed flower or two. Purists may frown, but turkey is a celebration and the situation calls for a touch of fantasy.

Moroccan roast turkey with honey and almond glaze

SERVES 8

Basting with a honey-and-almond glaze keeps this turkey moist and makes the skin deliciously crisp and dark golden-brown. Couscous is a good accompaniment, flavoured with saffron and raisins if you like.

1 turkey (about 4.5 kg/
  10 pounds), with giblets
2 tablespoons sesame seeds
175 g/6 oz blanched almonds, very
  finely chopped
2 tablespoons ground cinnamon
1 tablespoon ground cumin
1 tablespoon ground coriander
2 teaspoons ground ginger
1 teaspoon ground cloves
1 teaspoon salt

1 teaspoon pepper
1 onion, studded with 6 whole
  cloves
30 g/1 oz butter, softened
2 cinnamon sticks
125 ml/4 fl oz honey
500 ml/16 fl oz chicken stock,
  more if needed

trussing needle and string

Preheat the oven to 175°C/350°F/gas4. Spread the sesame seeds and chopped almonds in a single layer in a shallow pan and roast them, shaking the pan occasionally, until golden, 8-10 minutes. Set aside to cool.

In a small bowl, mix the ground cinnamon, cumin, coriander, ginger and cloves with the salt and pepper. Rub both the skin and cavity of the turkey with this spice mixture. Put the onion studded with the cloves in the cavity and truss the bird. Place the bird on its back in a roasting pan and spread the skin with softened butter. Cut the giblets in pieces and add them to the pan with the cinnamon sticks. Combine the honey and half the stock and pour this over the bird.

Roast the bird in the preheated oven, turning it on one side, then the other, and then returning it to its back, until done, 2½-3 hours. Baste often and, when stock and honey begin to brown, add the remaining stock.

About 15 minutes before the turkey is due to be done, remove it from the roasting pan and strain the pan juices into a small saucepan. Skim off the fat and boil the juices to reduce them if necessary – there should be about 250 ml/8 fl oz of this glaze. Stir in the toasted sesame seeds and almonds. Return the turkey to the roasting pan, spread the glaze over the top and continue roasting, basting very often, until the skin is dark golden brown and crisp, 10-15 minutes.

Discard the trussing strings. Transfer the turkey to a warmed platter, spoon over any remaining glaze, cover with foil and leave to stand for 10-15 minutes before carving.

OTHER PROBLEMS

DRY AND OVERCOOKED

Why: cooked too long; too fast; if roasted, not basted enough; bird very large, so outside dried before centre was cooked.
What to do: serve with brown sauce or gravy (see Sauces); add moist and colourful accompaniments, such as red-skinned potatoes, chestnut or pumpkin purée, mashed potatoes, cranberry sauce or tomato confit.

TOUGH

Why: undercooked; if roasted, not basted often enough.
What to do: if pot-roasting or braising, ensure enough liquid used, and cook until tender; if roasting, add stock or wine, cover and continue.

LACKS TASTE

Why: meat bland; underseasoned.
What to do: before serving, brush with mix of soy sauce and pepper flakes, or vinaigrette; serve with a piquant sauce.

Split small birds and small game birds

Baked, grilled, roasted

LITTLE BIRDS ARE EVERYONE'S FAVOURITES, whether devilled and barbecued, grilled to serve with figs and olives as in Italy, or lacquered with black sesame seeds as in Hong Kong. One of my happiest memories is of mesquite-grilled quail in a basket, eaten with bucket-sized margueritas at the Cadillac Bar in Houston, Texas. The cook had them just right, toasted and juicy, and we must have demolished at least half a dozen per person. I suspect they were also marinated, a great help with little birds – try brushing them an hour or two before cooking with a light barbecue sauce, or perhaps with mustard, Worcestershire sauce or lemon juice and crushed bay leaf.

To grill small birds, I often first 'spatchcock' them, splitting and skewering them flat so they cook evenly (see the recipe opposite). Plump birds do well if the meaty parts are also slashed so heat penetrates more evenly. No matter what the flavouring, a side order of matchstick potatoes or ultra-thin French fries are a must with any spatchcocked bird.

UNDERCOOKED – meat is pinkish and pink juice runs when thigh is cut with a knife; meat is flabby and skin may not be brown.
Why: cooking temperature too low; bird too far from heat source; cooking time too short.
What to do: continue cooking until done; if necessary raise temperature or adjust rack so it is closer to heat.

PERFECT – meat of baby chicken is evenly cooked throughout and white; juices run clear when thickest part of thigh is cut with a knife; skin is crisp and well browned with no scorched patches; meat is moist and full-flavoured.

DRY AND OVERCOOKED – meat stringy, skin scorched; little or no juice runs when thigh is cut.
Why: cooked too long; cooked too fast; bird too close to heat; not basted often enough.
What to do: before serving, brush bird with melted butter, oil, or basting sauce; serve with a brown sauce or salsa (see Sauces); Oriental sauces such as hoisin or plum are also good, with relishes like mango chutney, or spicy pickled vegetable condiments such as chow-chow or piccalilli.

OTHER PROBLEMS

LACKS TASTE
Why: meat of bird bland; not enough seasoning.
What to do: serve with a tangy devil sauce, barbecue sauce, or salsa (see Sauces).

SURFACE SCORCHED AND COOKING UNEVEN
Why: too close to heat; bird not correctly flattened.
What to do: part way through cooking move rack further from heat, or wrap bird loosely in foil and transfer to 175°C/350°F/gas4 oven; see Dry and overcooked for serving suggestions.

QUICK FIX

Small birds are often deliberately cooked until dry to act as foil for a dipping sauce like this one. In a small saucepan, combine 4 tablespoons tomato ketchup, 3 tablespoons red wine vinegar, 30 g/1 oz butter, 1 tablespoon brown sugar, and a dash of Tabasco. Bring mixture to the boil, stirring, and taste, adding more Tabasco if you like. Brush sauce over birds and serve the rest on the side as a dipping sauce. Enough for 4 small birds, to serve 4.

Spatchcock of baby chicken with confit of shallot

SERVES 4

To spatchcock means to split and flatten a bird for cooking, leaving it joined at the breast. Here I'm suggesting little birds, but you can also spatchcock larger chickens to serve 2 people. Leftover confit keeps well in the refrigerator for up to two weeks.

4 baby chickens	for the shallot confit
(about 500 g/1 pound each)	500 g/1 pound shallots
60 g/2 oz butter	60 ml/2 fl oz white wine
salt and pepper	60 ml/2 fl oz white wine vinegar
2 tablespoons Dijon-style mustard	150 g/5 oz sugar
	½ teaspoon salt
8 wooden or metal skewers	

Split and flatten the birds: cut the backbones and wing-tips from the birds with shears or scissors. Snip the wishbones to sever them. (If you like, simmer trimmings to make stock.) Flatten the birds with the palm of your hand, breaking the breastbone. Make a small incision between each leg and bottom end of the breastbone and pass through ends of legs to hold them in place. Thread a skewer through the wings of the birds to hold them flat. Thread a second skewer through the legs.

Make the shallot confit: peel the shallots and slice them very thinly. Put the white wine, vinegar, sugar, salt and a little pepper in a large pan and heat gently, stirring occasionally, until the sugar is dissolved. Bring just to the boil and stir in the shallots. Cover and cook over a very low heat, stirring often, until shallots are translucent and very tender, 20-25 minutes. Taste the confit and adjust the seasoning.

Meanwhile, preheat the grill and brush the rack with oil. Melt the butter and brush the chickens with half melted butter. Season with salt and pepper. Put the chickens on the grill rack, skin-side up, about 7.5 cm/ 3 inches from the heat. Grill for about 10 minutes, basting occasionally with butter. Turn the chickens over, baste with the remaining butter and continue grilling for about 10 minutes. Turn the chickens over again and brush with the mustard. Continue grilling, skin-side up, until the birds are done, about 10 minutes more.

To serve: remove the skewers from the birds and arrange them on individual plates. Spoon some confit beside the birds and serve the rest separately.

Boneless rolled whole chicken and turkey

Boneless whole chicken and turkey, tied in a neat cylinder for roasting, is almost as common as boneless poultry breast. It could hardly be easier to cook, behaving in the oven like a boneless pork or veal roast. Don't use too much liquid as the meat can be watery. Flavour is mild, so add plenty of seasonings and baste often during cooking. To dress up the roast further, before cooking remove the net or strings, open up the meat and spread it with a savoury stuffing or sprinkle it with flavourings such as chopped onion, garlic, shallot, fresh ginger or herbs, then re-roll and tie it.

Serve with lively garnishes such as a fruit conserve of baked figs, caramelized peaches or cherries, plus colourful accompaniments – braised red or green cabbage, green peas, orange lentils or pumpkin purée are just a start.

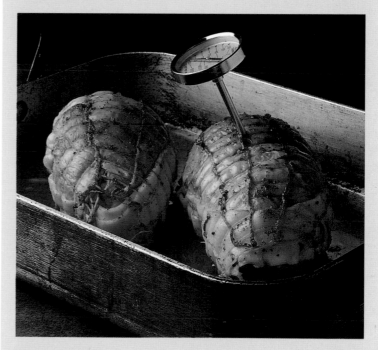

PERFECT BONELESS ROLLED CHICKEN – meat thermometer in centre of meat reads 83°C/180°F; outside is golden and juices run clear when meat is pierced with two-pronged fork or skewer; a skewer inserted in centre of meat is hot to touch when withdrawn after 30 seconds.
Note: large pieces of rolled poultry will continue to cook inside from residual heat, so stop cooking when slightly underdone.

Chicken, duck, turkey and game bird pieces

Baked, braised, grilled, pan-fried, poached, roasted, sautéed, stewed

CHICKEN PIECES OFFER A PLEASANT DILEMMA – do you choose a whole cut-up bird, thus giving diners a choice of colour and piece of meat, or opt for using only thighs, legs or breasts, so they cook at the same pace and are easier to handle on the stove? I'm never sure which way to go. In any case I try to season pieces before cooking, rubbing the skin with dried herbs such as herbes de Provence, or marinating them in wine or soy sauce. A full-scale wine marinade can also serve as a cooking medium. Take the classic *coq au vin*, for example, or duck marinated in balsamic vinegar, red wine and garlic, a dish which dates back to Renaissance Italy. Pieces of poultry offer a wonderful range of recipes, from simple southern fried chicken or grilled buffalo wings to turkey in a Mexican *mole* sauce flavoured with chocolate and chillies. In Spain, you'll find the Christmas turkey is cut into pieces to simmer with onion, herbs and saffron.

TOUGH AND UNDERCOOKED – juices run pink when pieces are pierced with fork, meat clings to fork; skin is pale; meat is flabby not firm.
Why: bird mature or poorly handled; cooking temperature too low; cooking time too short.
What to do: continue cooking until done, if necessary raising temperature. If still tough, slice breast meat thinly for serving; reserve dark meat for another use such as salad.

PERFECT – juices run clear when pieces are pierced with a two-pronged fork, pieces fall easily from fork; skin is evenly coloured; meat is firm, tender and moist; flavour is full-bodied.

DRY AND OVERCOOKED – meat and skin shrink from bones; meat is stringy.
Why: cooked too long; cooked too fast; bird poorly handled; if baked, grilled or barbecued, pieces not basted often enough.
What to do: if very overcooked, take meat that's been cooked in a sauce from bones and pull into pieces. Serve it in the sauce over pasta or rice, adding colourful garnish such as chopped tomatoes or herbs. If dry-cooked, take meat from bones to use in a salad.

OTHER PROBLEMS

LACKS TASTE
Why: meat of bird bland; insufficient seasoning.
What to do: serve with a piquant brown or white sauce (see Sauces) flavoured with mushroom and tomato, or a roasted red pepper sauce, caramelized onion purée or fresh coriander pesto; add hearty accompaniments such as pasta with pesto or a grain such as kasha or cracked wheat.

SURFACE DRY, COOKING UNEVEN
Why: heat too high, especially when barbecuing and grilling; heat is uneven, especially on hob.
What to do: lower the heat, shift pieces and continue cooking.

WET AND FATTY
Why: undercooked; bird poorly frozen and defrosted; if braised, poached or stewed, cooked with too much liquid.
What to do: continue cooking, uncovered, at high heat to dry out meat. Be sure any accompanying sauce or dressing is highly flavoured.

SAUCE SEPARATED
Why: overcooked; too much liquid evaporated.
What to do: add more stock, or water if flavour is already concentrated, and whisk to emulsify sauce.

Sauté of chicken with paprika

Try this spicy coating for bland or overcooked poultry pieces, no matter the bird or how cooked. First drain any sauce and reserve. Brush poultry with oil. For 6-8 pieces, combine 60 g/2 oz dry brown or white breadcrumbs, 2 teaspoons dry mustard, 1 teaspoon ground ginger, 1 teaspoon ground allspice, 1 teaspoon ground black pepper, a large pinch of grated nutmeg and ¼ teaspoon ground hot red pepper, or more to taste, and pour into a large plastic bag. Add poultry pieces, close bag and shake vigorously to coat with spiced breadcrumbs. Lay pieces on an oiled baking sheet and grill 3-5 minutes each side until browned, turning once. Reheat any sauce and serve separately.

A few spoonfuls of sour cream set off the brilliant red of the paprika sauce. Fresh noodles are a classic accompaniment.

1 chicken (about 1.4 kg/3 pounds), cut into 6 pieces
salt and pepper
2 tablespoons sweet red paprika
2 tablespoons vegetable oil
1 onion, chopped
175 ml/6 fl oz chicken stock, more if needed
3 red sweet peppers
2 tablespoons tomato purée
75 ml/2½ fl oz sour cream, double cream or crème fraîche

Season the pieces of chicken with salt and pepper. Sprinkle them with paprika, patting with your hands until thoroughly coated. Heat the oil in a sauté or frying pan. Beginning with the legs, add the chicken pieces, skin side down. When they begin to brown, add the wing pieces and finally the breasts. (Note: do not use too high a heat or the paprika may scorch.) When all the pieces are well browned, turn them over and brown them on the other sides, 8-10 minutes total.

Remove the chicken from the pan and add the onion. Sauté until soft but not browned, 3-4 minutes. Return the chicken to pan and add half of the stock. Cover tightly and cook over low heat until the chicken is done, 30-35 minutes. Add more stock during cooking if the pan gets too dry.

Meanwhile, roast the peppers either over an open flame or under a preheated grill, turning them until the skin chars and bursts, 7-10 minutes. Put them in a plastic bag to allow them to steam and the skin to loosen, and leave to cool. Peel the cooled peppers, discard their cores and seeds, and cut the flesh into strips.

When the chicken is cooked, remove the pieces from the pan. By now, the pan juices should be reduced to a glaze; if not, boil them well to reduce them. Discard any fat from pan, stir in the tomato purée and remaining stock and bring just back to the boil. Return the chicken pieces to the pan with the pepper strips and heat gently, 1-2 minutes. Taste sauce for seasoning.

Arrange the chicken on a warmed platter or on individual plates and spoon the sauce on top. Spoon over the cream or crème fraîche as a contrast to the sauce and serve at once.

Boneless chicken and turkey breasts

Baked, braised, deep-fried, grilled, pan-fried, poached, roasted, sautéed, stewed, stir-fried

CHICKEN AND TURKEY BREASTS HAVE CLEAR ADVANTAGES. They are universally available, of reliable quality, simple to cook and with a mild flavour which adapts to almost any seasoning. On the down side, they dry out easily and can become tough and stringy. This is why it is a good idea to marinate them, however briefly, before cooking and to score them so moisture penetrates. I always cook them with a basting sauce, liquid or small amount of fat.

Boneless chicken and turkey breasts usually come stripped of skin and trimmed of fat. However the underside contains a sinew which toughens and shrivels during cooking. To remove it, loosen the white, visible end with a knife. Grasp tightly with a cloth and strip it out with the finger and thumb of your other hand. The breast underside also includes a loose piece called the fillet; if it becomes detached, cook it separately, allowing just a few minutes.

Think of chicken and turkey breasts as a blank page for your artistic designs. Cheerful ideas include baked lemon chicken breast with artichokes and wild mushrooms, and sautéed turkey breast with balsamic tomato vinaigrette. More traditional renderings include a *feuilletée* of chicken with sweetbreads, chicken *cordon bleu* stuffed with ham and cheese and chicken Kiev filled with herb butter and then deep-fried. Chicken breasts can also be butterflied and spread with a colourful stuffing such as vegetable julienne and goats' cheese or prosciutto with ricotta. When rolled and baked, they are then sliced to show a pretty spiral pattern. Chicken or turkey breasts are also ideal for stir-frying as in *tung an*, the Chinese chicken dish with spring onion, dried black mushrooms and rice wine, or the evocative 'explosion chicken' with cashews, sweet pepper and bamboo shoots ignited with chilli and hoisin. For an easy stir-fry, see Quick Fix.

PERFECT – when pressed with your fingertip, meat feels spongy (Thumb test, second-finger stage, see page 28); breast falls easily from a two-pronged fork and juices run clear; meat is moist, full-flavoured and tender.

PROBLEMS

TOUGH AND UNDERCOOKED
Why: breasts poorly frozen; cooking temperature too low; cooking time too short.
What to do: continue cooking until done, if necessary raising temperature.

DRY AND OVERCOOKED
Why: inferior bird; cooked too fast; temperature too high; if baked, barbecued, grilled, smoked or pan-fried, not basted enough during cooking. Note: boneless breast of chicken or turkey dries out very easily.

What to do: baste often; serve with cooking juices or a white, brown or butter sauce (see Sauces) and lively accompaniments such as roasted garlic, onions or shallots, or sliced yellow squash, tomato and aubergine baked with a topping of olive oil and chopped fresh herbs.

LACKS TASTE
Why: meat bland; insufficient seasoning.
What to do: serve with a fruity or piquant sauce (see Sauces), confit of onions, mango chutney, a cucumber and yogurt raita, or Salsa of Tomato and Coriander (page 129).

Italian stuffed chicken breasts with tomato concassée

SERVES 4

This is the perfect simple dish for a summer evening when fresh tomatoes are at their peak. Tomato *concassée* is a seasoned mixture of tomatoes that have been peeled, seeded and chopped.

4 boneless chicken breasts, without skin
2 thin slices of cooked ham (about 45 g/1½ oz)
8 thin slices of Mozzarella cheese (about 125 g/4 oz)
1 bunch of basil
salt and pepper

for the tomato concassée
75 ml/2½ fl oz olive oil
3 tomatoes, peeled, seeded and chopped
juice of 1 lemon

Preheat the oven to 190°C/375°F/gas5. Prepare the ham and Mozzarella stuffing: cut each ham slice in half, to about the same size as a Mozzarella slice. Strip the basil leaves from their stems and reserve 4 sprigs for decoration; chop half of the remaining basil leaves and set aside for the sauce. Set a piece of ham on top of a Mozzarella slice. Lay 2-3 of the basil leaves on top and cover with another slice of Mozzarella. There should be 4 packages.

Butter a medium baking dish. Turn breasts skin down and strip the tendon from the centre of each, stroking with the tip of a sharp knife to remove it cleanly. Reserve the loose strip of fillet that comes off with it. Turn breasts skin side up. Cut a horizontal pocket, working the whole length of each breast and taking care not to cut all the way through.

Stuff each pocket with a ham, Mozzarella and basil package and then the reserved strip of meat, tucking it in to seal the gap. Set the chicken breasts skin side up in the baking dish. Season them with salt and pepper, cover tightly with foil and bake in the preheated oven until done, 30-35 minutes.

When the chicken is almost done, make the tomato *concassée*: heat the oil in a small pan and stir in the tomatoes and lemon juice. Season to taste.

When the chicken breasts are done, slice them diagonally and arrange each in a fan on individual warmed plates to show the stuffing. Stir the reserved basil into the *concassée* and heat until very hot. Spoon it over the breasts and top with a reserved basil sprig. Serve at once.

QUICK FIX

I often rely on the crisp vegetables and energetic flavourings of a good stir-fry to revive cooked chicken breast. Cut breasts in thin strips. For every 375 g/12 oz cooked meat, mix 2 tablespoons dark soy sauce, 2 tablespoons rice wine, a pinch of sugar and 2 teaspoons cornflour. Mix with chicken and leave to marinate. Heat 2 tablespoons oil in a wok. Add 6 chopped spring onions, 2 small dried chillies, a 2.5-cm/1-inch piece of fresh ginger, finely chopped, and 1 garlic clove, finely chopped. Stir-fry until fragrant, about 30 seconds. Add 250 g/½ pound shredded bok choy or white cabbage and stir-fry until beginning to soften, about 1 minute. Drain chicken, reserving marinade, and add to wok. Stir-fry until very hot, about 2 minutes. Add marinade to wok, stirring constantly until marinade thickens and coats chicken and peas. Discard chilli peppers, taste for seasoning and serve at once. Serves 4.

Whole duck and goose

Baked, braised, pot-roasted, roasted, spit-roasted

ROAST DUCK WITH CORNBREAD STUFFING, duck with plum sauce, duck braised with sauerkraut or olives, Russian goose with walnut stuffing, Austrian stuffed Christmas goose with apple and prunes – don't the very ideas make you hungry? They do me. I love all those succulent dark-fleshed birds which go so well with tart and fruit flavours. Roasting is the cooking method of choice if you like crisp skin, though braising or pot-roasting will ensure that an elderly bird becomes moist and tender.

Despite their richness, duck and goose can be dry if not carefully treated. My advice on seasoning and trussing of whole chickens (pages 40-41) also applies to duck and goose. Start cooking at high heat, turning it down once the duck or goose skin starts to brown. To allow the fat to be released, I prick the skin before cooking begins and then I baste often. You should set aside the excess fat to fry the world's crispest potatoes. Both birds make tasty gravy, but do be sure to drain off all fat before you deglaze the pan. If roasting, remember to let the bird stand in a warm place for at least 10 minutes before serving so the juices are redistributed uniformly throughout the meat.

PERFECT LIGHTLY COOKED – when carved, breast meat of duck is rosy pink and juicy; skin crisp and an even golden-brown; when duck or goose is lifted, juices from centre cavity run pink; when leg is pulled, joint is rigid, and meat is firm when thigh is pierced with a two-pronged fork; a meat thermometer inserted between thigh and breast reads less than 83°C/180°F; full meaty flavour. Note: legs will be tough and undercooked and must be cooked further, usually by grilling.

PERFECT WELL-DONE – when carved, breast meat is well-done but still juicy and tender; skin crisp and a deep golden brown; when duck or goose is lifted, juices from centre cavity run clear, not pink; meat shrinks from end of leg, which feels slightly flexible when pulled; a meat thermometer inserted between thigh and breast reads 83°C/180°F; generous meaty flavour. Note: legs will be well-done and tougher than breast.

OTHER PROBLEMS

UNDERCOOKED
Why: cooking time too short; cooking temperature too low.
What to do: continue cooking until done, if necessary raising temperature.

BIRD IS TOUGH
Why: bird too mature or poorly handled; bird was undercooked.
What to do: if pot-roasting or braising, be sure plenty of liquid is used, then continue cooking until tender; if roasting, transform into a pot-roast by adding liquid, covering pan tightly with a lid or foil and cooking until tender.

MEAT IS FATTY
Why: fatty breed of bird; stuffing kept meat too moist; bird undercooked; if braised or pot-roasted, cooked with too much liquid.
What to do: continue cooking for 10-15 minutes uncovered at high heat, basting often if roasting; serve with a piquant orange, peppercorn or other brown sauce or gravy (see Sauces) and accompaniments such as pickled red cabbage, turnips or wild rice pilaf.

Lemon roast duck with olives and capers

pictured on pages 38-9

QUICK FIX

Distract attention from disappointing duck or goose with this colourful salad in a sweet-sour dressing. Core 4 large tomatoes and thinly slice them. Cut the peel and skin from 4 large oranges and thinly slice them across. Interleave tomato and orange slices on 4 salad plates. In a small bowl, whisk together 4 tablespoons port, 2 tablespoons raspberry vinegar, 2 tablespoons lemon juice, 1 tablespoon honey and salt and pepper to taste. Spoon dressing over fruits and top each plate with a mint sprig. Serves 4.

OVERCOOKED AND DRY — when carved, breast meat is dry and stringy, shrinking from breastbone as well as legs; skin is dry, lacking brilliance, and may be scorched; leg falls from carcass when end is pulled.

Why: cooked too long; cooked too fast; if roasted, not basted often enough.

What to do: moisten bird with orange or brown sauce or gravy (see Sauces); add aromatic accompaniments such as celeriac purée, saffron rice, roasted garlic and shallots or Wild Mushroom Fricassee with Hazelnuts (page 170).

This recipe borrows flavours from the Mediterranean to update classic *canard à l'orange*. A *gastrique*, made by dissolving caramelized sugar in vinegar, enlivens many fruit sauces such as this one.

1 duck (about 2 kg/4½ pounds), with giblets	75 ml/2½ fl oz wine vinegar
salt and pepper	750 ml/1¼ pints chicken or veal stock
2 lemons	1 onion, diced
3-4 bay leaves	1 carrot, diced
½ teaspoon whole cloves	2 tablespoons flour
60 ml/2 fl oz olive oil	60 g/2 oz mild brine- or oil-cured black olives
for the sauce	1 tablespoon capers, rinsed and drained
60 g/2 oz sugar	trussing needle and string
4 tablespoons water	

Preheat the oven to 230°C/450°F/gas8. Season the skin and cavity of the duck with salt and pepper and prick the skin so that the fat escapes during roasting. Pare the zest from the lemons and put this inside the duck together with the bay leaves and cloves. Truss the duck, place it on its back in a roasting pan and rub the skin with olive oil and the juice of 1 of the lemons. Cut the giblets into pieces and add them to the pan.

Roast the duck in the preheated oven until it starts to sizzle, about 15 minutes. Reduce the heat to 200°C/400°F/gas6, turn the duck on one side, baste it and roast for 15 minutes. Turn the bird on the other side, baste and roast 15 minutes more. Finally return the duck to its back and continue roasting, basting often, until done to taste, 1-1¾ hours.

For the sauce, prepare a caramel-vinegar *gastrique*: in a small pan, heat the sugar in the water until it has dissolved, then boil steadily to a light-brown caramel. Remove the pan from the heat and at once add vinegar. (Note: stand well back, because vapour from the vinegar will sting your eyes.) Heat the *gastrique* gently until the caramel is dissolved. Add the stock and the juice of the remaining lemon. Bring to the boil and simmer until reduced, 3-5 minutes.

When the duck is cooked, transfer it to a warmed platter. Cover with foil and leave it to stand before carving, 10-15 minutes. Pour off all but 1 tablespoon of fat from the roasting pan. Add the onion and carrot to the giblets in the pan and cook until well browned, 5-7 minutes. Stir in the flour and cook, stirring, until well browned, 1-2 minutes. Pour in the *gastrique* and bring to the boil, stirring to dissolve the pan juices. Simmer until slightly thickened, 4-5 minutes. Strain the sauce into a saucepan, pressing down on the vegetables and giblets to extract all the liquid. Simmer until the sauce is well reduced, glossy and lightly coats the back of a spoon, 4-5 minutes.

Add the olives and capers to the sauce. Heat gently without boiling, taste and adjust seasoning. Spoon a little sauce over the duck and serve the rest separately.

Whole game birds

Baked, braised, pan-fried, pot-roasted, roasted, sautéed, spit-roasted

MY FATHER WAS A HUNTER and each autumn our diet was the same: over-roasted pheasant, dry as a bone and often tough to boot, at least three times a week. What was my mother thinking? I still cannot convince her that roast game birds should be juicy, possibly even pink. Nor can she countenance marinating and braising a wild bird to tenderize and to add flavour with red wine, vinegar, herbs and vegetables.

She was, however, adamant about hanging game birds to age and develop flavour – an admirable practice which helps distinguish wild from relatively bland farm-raised birds. Game birds are also helped by barding – wrapping in thinly sliced pork fat or, as my mother does, with bacon. Truss or tie the bird in shape and during cooking turn it from one leg to another, finishing on its back. Most importantly when roasting, baste often; if braised or pot-roasted in a closed pot in moist heat, the bird needs less attention.

Even the mildest farm-raised game birds have distinct woodsy flavours, an invitation to pairing with wild mushrooms, grains like buckwheat and root vegetable purées. Larger birds are usually roasted or braised, perhaps with a flavouring of salt pork or grapes. Quail and other little birds are more versatile – in Australia I've had them pickled and then deep-fried, and in Italy pan-fried with pancetta and herbs.

PERFECT LIGHTLY COOKED – juices from centre cavity run pink when bird is lifted; skin is lightly browned; when drumstick is pulled, leg joint is rigid; meat is firm when thigh is pierced with a two-pronged fork; when carved, breast meat is pink and juicy with meaty-to-gamy flavour depending on type of bird and how long it has been aged. Note: legs will be tough and undercooked and are often cooked further in a ragout or stew.

PERFECT WELL-DONE – juices from centre cavity run clear, not pink when bird is lifted; skin is golden brown; meat shrinks from end of leg, which feels slightly flexible when drumstick is pulled; when carved, breast meat is well-done but still juicy and tender with generous meaty flavour; legs are likely to be tough. Note: whole birds will continue to cook from residual heat, so stop cooking when slightly underdone.

PROBLEMS

DRY AND OVERCOOKED
Why: cooked too long; cooked too fast; if roasted, not basted often enough.
What to do: serve with gravy or a piquant brown sauce (see Sauces) to counteract dryness, and moist accompaniments such as celeriac, pumpkin or sweet potato purée. If very overcooked, take meat from bones and serve in sauce over pasta or polenta.

UNDERCOOKED
Why: cooking time too short; cooking temperature too low.

What to do: continue cooking until done, if necessary raising temperature.

BIRD IS TOUGH
Why: poor-quality or old bird; bird was undercooked. Note: old wild game birds are very tough and should be pot-roasted or braised.
What to do: if pot-roasting or braising, be sure plenty of liquid is used, then continue cooking until tender; if roasting, transform into a pot-roast by adding liquid, covering pan tightly with a lid or foil and cooking until tender.

Braised pheasant with lentils

Bacon mashed potatoes act as foil for a dry or overcooked bird (and be sure to make plenty of gravy or sauce). Allow a medium potato per person and to speed cooking, bring a pan of water to the boil. Meanwhile thickly slice the potatoes without peeling them. Add to the water and simmer until very tender, 10-15 minutes. Dice 1 thick slice of bacon per person and fry until browned. Drain on paper towel, reserving the fat. Drain the potatoes, return them to the pan and dry over low heat, 1-2 minutes. Mash with a potato masher in the pan. For each potato, add 1 tablespoon reserved bacon fat with 2 tablespoons milk and beat over low heat with wooden spoon until potatoes are fluffy, 3-5 minutes. Beat in bacon bits and season with pepper and salt if needed.

The green lentils from Le Puy, in the volcanic mountains of central France, are renowned. This recipe is also excellent with guinea fowl or rabbit.

2 pheasants, each about
   750 g/1½ pounds
1 tablespoon oil
15 g/½ oz butter
250 g/½ pound bacon, diced
1 onion, chopped
1 carrot, diced
bouquet garni
250 ml/8 fl oz white wine

250 ml/8 fl oz chicken stock,
   more if needed
salt and pepper

for the lentils
250 g/8 oz Le Puy or other
   dark green lentils
1 onion, studded with a clove
1 garlic clove
bouquet garni

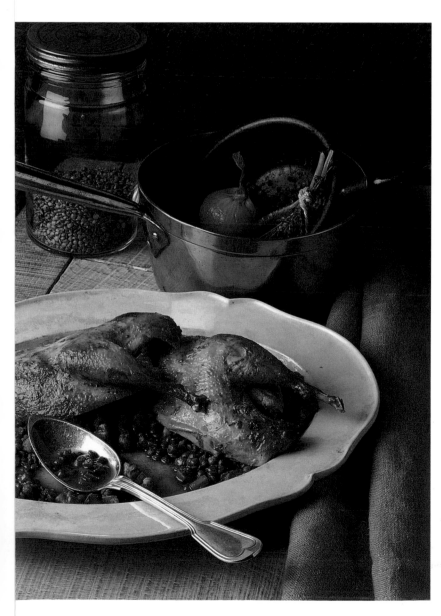

Preheat the oven to 190°C/375°F/gas5. Truss the pheasant. Heat the oil and butter in a heavy flameproof casserole, add the bacon and fry until lightly browned. Remove the bacon, add the pheasants and brown well. Add the onion and carrot and cook over medium heat until soft, 5-7 minutes.

Return the bacon to the casserole with the bouquet garni, wine, stock, salt and pepper. Bring just to the boil, cover and braise in the oven until the birds are done to your taste, 1-1½ hours. Baste occasionally during cooking and add more stock if the pan is dry.

Pick over the lentils, discarding any stones, and wash them well. Put them in a pan with the clove-studded onion, the garlic and bouquet garni and enough water to cover generously. Bring to the boil and skim any scum. Partially cover and simmer until the lentils are tender and most of the water is absorbed, 30-45 minutes. Stir occasionally, and if the lentils get dry add more water. At the end of cooking they should be moist but not soupy. If too wet, drain off excess liquid. Discard the onion, garlic and bouquet garni.

When the pheasants are cooked, remove them from the casserole. Discard the strings and bouquet garni and strain the cooking juices into a pan, reserving the bacon and vegetables. Transfer the lentils to the casserole and stir in the bacon and vegetables. Taste, adjust seasoning and cook over a low heat to blend flavours for about 10 minutes.

Meanwhile, cut the pheasants in half, discarding their backbones, and trim the wing-tips and ends of the legs. Place pheasant halves on top of the lentils. Discard excess fat from reserved cooking juices and, if necessary, boil them to concentrate the flavour. Taste and adjust the seasoning.

Serve the pheasants and lentils from the casserole or transfer them to a platter. Spoon some cooking juices on top of the pheasants and serve the rest separately.

Magret of duck with green peppercorn sauce

SERVES 2

Magret is the French name for boneless duck breast, traditionally the plump meat on a bird which has been flattened for foie gras. The legs of the bird are used for *confit*.

1 large or 2 small boneless duck breasts
  (about 375 g/12 oz)
1 tablespoon oil
salt and pepper

for the green peppercorn sauce
3 shallots, finely chopped
375 ml/12 fl oz red wine
60 ml/2 fl oz brown beef or veal stock
2 tablespoons crème fraîche or double cream
1 teaspoon green peppercorns, drained and crushed
1 tablespoon butter

Heat the oil in a heavy frying pan. Season the duck breast(s) on both sides with salt and pepper and score the skin so fat will escape during cooking. Fry skin-side down over high heat until the skin is well browned, 3-5 minutes. Turn the breast(s) over, lower the heat to medium and continue frying until cooked to your taste, 3-7 minutes. Transfer to a carving board and keep warm.

Make the green peppercorn sauce: discard all but a tablespoon of fat from the pan. Add the chopped shallots and sauté 1 minute. Add the red wine, whisk to dissolve the pan juices and boil until reduced by half. Whisk in the stock and boil to concentrate the flavour if necessary. Add the cream and peppercorns and simmer 2-3 minutes.

Carve the duck breast(s) in diagonal slices and arrange on 2 individual warmed plates. (The skin can be discarded if you prefer.) Drain any juice from the duck into the sauce. Take the sauce from the heat and add the butter in 2-3 pieces, shaking the pan until the butter is fully incorporated. Taste the sauce and adjust the seasoning. Spoon over the duck and serve at once.

Magret of duck with green peppercorn sauce

Stir-fried spicy velvet chicken with mange-touts and cashews

SERVES 4

Here, a technique called 'velveting' is used to seal the chicken, keeping it from drying out in the searing heat of the wok. First the chicken is coated in a flavoured cornflour mixture, then it is simmered briefly, so it takes on a silky texture when stir-fried.

500 g/1 pound boneless
  chicken breasts,
  without skin
2 tablespoons vegetable oil
4 dried red chilli peppers
2.5-cm/1-inch piece of
  fresh ginger, chopped
250 g/½ pound mange-tout
  peas, cut into thirds on
  the diagonal
75 g/2½ oz salted cashews

for the velvet coating
½ teaspoon salt
1 tablespoon dry rice wine
  or dry sherry
1 large egg white, whisked
  just until broken up

1 tablespoon cornflour
1 tablespoon oil
1 litre/1⅔ pints water

for the sauce
1½ teaspoons cornflour
1½ tablespoons dry rice
  wine or dry sherry
2 tablespoons dark soy
  sauce
1½ tablespoons rice vinegar
1 teaspoon sugar
½ teaspoon salt
1½ teaspoons dark sesame
  oil, or to taste

First coat the chicken: cut the breasts in 1.25-cm/½-inch cubes, slicing first lengthwise with the grain, then across into cubes. Put the cubes in a bowl with the salt and rice wine. Mix well, then add the egg white, cornflour and oil and stir until coated. Cover and chill for 30-60 minutes.

Simmer the chicken: bring the water to the boil in a medium pan. Add the chicken, stirring to separate the pieces. Bring back to the boil and simmer for 1 minute, stirring constantly. Drain and let cool to room temperature. Meanwhile, whisk together the sauce ingredients.

Heat the wok over a high heat for 30 seconds. Drizzle in oil to coat the bottom and sides and heat for 30 seconds. Lower the heat, add the chillies and toss until they begin to brown, about 1 minute. Add the ginger and stir-fry a few seconds. Discard the chillies. Increase heat to high, add the mange-tout peas and stir-fry for 30-60 seconds until just starting to wilt. Add the chicken and stir-fry until very hot, about 30-60 seconds. Give the sauce a quick stir and add to the wok, tossing to coat chicken and mange-tout peas. Stir in the cashews and heat briefly. Taste and adjust seasoning. Transfer to a serving dish and serve at once.

MEAT & GAME

Of all main-dish ingredients, I find meat is the most forgiving. A hint of dryness, a few minutes' overcooking, a drab appearance – all can be taken care of with little trouble, as I hope to show you in this chapter.

For a start, let's look at the general characteristics of the different meats. Beef is juicy and full-flavoured but is apt to be tough. Bold flavourings come to mind, such as mustard, paprika, chilli powder, horseradish, red wine and garlic. To complement lamb, the other domestic red meat, I tend to turn to the Mediterranean and capers, olives, rosemary, thyme and garlic, not forgetting the mint from my mother's English garden. Given how differently veal cooks from beef, you might never think it comes from the same animal. As a young meat, veal is rarely tough but it can easily be dry; plenty of liquid and no more than medium heat are advisable. Veal's flavour is best developed with lemon, nutmeg, mace, rosemary, parsley and white wine … and don't stint on the cream, butter or olive oil. Pork, the other white meat, is wonderfully rich and varied – think of all those chops, hams and sausages which are so good with honey, apples, brown sugar, sage and spices. Despite its richness, however, pork dries easily, just like veal.

As for game, toughness is the great danger, especially with wild meat. When making sauce, wine and beer will serve you well, as will dark earthy seasonings such as juniper, bay leaf, garlic and molasses. I'm a partisan of juniper and a splash of gin. In fact the odds are that you can guess a cook's national origin from their choice of meat accompaniments!

Remember that good cooking cannot change the quality of the meat itself. Carefully raised and butchered meat is pricey, especially beef and lamb which have been aged for greater tenderness and flavour, then properly trimmed. Provided you cook it correctly, it's much better to get the top grade of a cheaper cut than a cheap grade of a premium cut. Flank can rival fillet any day, but it must be treated right.

*Roast pork loin with figs
and port, page 69*

Large cuts of beef, lamb and game

Grilled, roasted, spit-roasted

I AM HAPPY TO SAY I AM OF THE GENERATION that remembers Sunday lunch with roast beef and Yorkshire pudding – real roast beef on the bone with plenty of crispy trimmings. My mother sought out English sirloin, with well-marbled loin and fillet meat so we could have one firm slice full of flavour, the other butter-soft. She cooked it the way she liked it, very well done, with juices which darkened in the pan for a memorably rich gravy. You cannot do better than follow her lead. Pick the cut of meat you like best – lean beef fillet perhaps, or a leg of lamb. (Only thin tender cuts, such as butterflied leg of lamb or boned saddle of venison, are suitable for roasting on an open grill.) Cook the meat the way you want – there are four different stages for a beef roast, each of them perfectly acceptable (see Stages in roasting and grilling meat, overleaf). With other meats, you have less choice.

Beef, lamb and most game are robust and juicy, so should tolerate dry heat, but I often judge by appearance. If the surface of a roast starts to look dry before it tests as done, I add wine, stock or even water to the pan, cover the meat loosely with foil and turn down the temperature before I continue cooking.

To add flavour before cooking, you may want to rub the meat surface with pepper, dry mustard and spices such as paprika or allspice, or aromatic herbs such as thyme and rosemary. Then refrigerate it for an hour or two to allow it to mellow. Add salt only at the last minute as this draws out juices which will dampen the uncooked surface. For added crispness, sprinkle the surface of the roast with flour. Score any surface fat and moisten the meat with a tablespoon or two of oil so the meat browns well. To help smaller cuts to start cooking rapidly, it's a good idea to brown the meat on the hob first.

Once in the hot oven, the roast will soon sizzle and need to be basted – with the pan drippings if roasting, or with basting liquid if you are grilling. Instead of basting only with fat, you may like to add stock, red or white wine, soy sauce or a barbecue sauce. Constant basting is vital – the finest roast can be spoiled by lack of attention. Lastly, when the meat is done let it stand in a warm place at least 10 minutes, or longer for a large cut, so the juices are redistributed uniformly.

These are the ground rules. For more ambitious roasting and grilling ideas, you may be inspired by the cut itself, shaping a loin of ribs into a crown, or boning a shoulder so you can add a well-flavoured stuffing – mushroom duxelles, herbs and onion, spinach and pancetta are just a beginning. Tougher cuts such as beef round, lamb shoulder and leg of venison will benefit from a preliminary soak in a wine or other marinade which can be used as the basis of a sauce for serving.

Accompaniments are just as traditional as the roast itself. Depending on the country, beef may come flanked with oven-roasted potatoes, puréed swede, Yorkshire pudding and horseradish sauce. In France, lamb demands fresh haricots verts, dried flageolet beans and a creamy potato gratin, while in England baby boiled potatoes and mint sauce are more likely. Roast venison evokes dark wine sauces warm with cracked pepper and cinnamon, offset by purées of chestnut, pumpkin, celeriac and perhaps a poached pear.

Long before it reaches the plate, a grand roast of meat tantalizes the eye and the nose. Among my favourites are pecan-smoked rack of lamb from the American South, Breton roast leg of lamb with white beans and tomato, Swedish roast saddle of venison with sour cream, juniper and redcurrant jelly, and maple venison ham from Canada, not forgetting the international beef Wellington with liver pâté baked in pastry and served with truffle sauce.

TYPICAL CUTS

for grilling, roasting and spit-roasting
Beef: bottom round, rib, rib eye, rump, sirloin, fillet, top round
Lamb: breast, leg, loin, rack, saddle, shoulder
Game: leg, rack, saddle

COOKING METHODS FOR MEAT

When cooking meat, much depends on temperature. The high heat of roasting and grilling is simple and quick, but it also dries meat, making no concessions to toughness, so you need to choose your cuts with care. By contrast, long slow cooking when you braise or stew meat with plenty of liquid has a moistening effect and greatly contributes to flavour – a much more accommodating approach.

With cuts that are suited to roasting, grilling or pan-frying, the outside of the meat is often seared so that the juices caramelize and add flavour. Then the heat is allowed to penetrate to the centre to a greater or lesser degree depending on preference (see Stages in roasting and grilling meat, page 64). You must take care not to go too far – if the cooking process continues too long, juices start to dry and fibres toughen, eventually making the meat almost inedible.

However, tougher cuts that should be braised, pot-roasted or boiled (more correctly, poached) tolerate – indeed require – much longer cooking, so that slow moist heat breaks down the tissues and tenderizes the meat. This takes time, varying from 15-20 minutes for thinly sliced delicate meats like veal escalopes to several hours for large cuts of beef and game. A famous French dish is *gigot de sept heures*, seven-hour leg of lamb.

Roast fillet of beef with coffee pan gravy, see overleaf

STAGES IN ROASTING AND GRILLING MEAT

Four stages can be defined when roasting and grilling meat:
• When underdone/blue, surface of meat is hot but centre remains blue; texture is soft to the touch. Only beef steak and game such as ostrich are ever served this way.
• When rare, centre of meat starts to lose blue colour. Juices are pink and spurt out when pierced with a two-pronged fork. Tenderness is at a maximum, ideal for steak, lamb chops and most game, though old game animals may remain tough.

• As cooking continues, heat reaches centre and meat becomes medium-cooked, still very tender, though juices are less pink. All meat can be served medium-cooked.
• When well-done, meat stiffens and toughens. Centre is hot with no trace of pink juices. To avoid a dry chewy texture, it is important not to roast or grill meat beyond this stage.

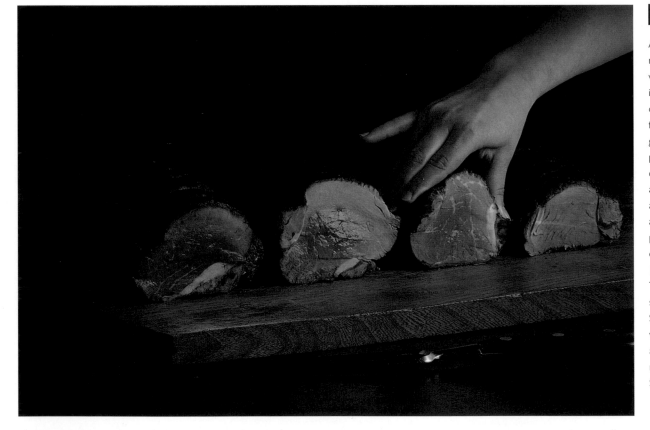

from left to right

PERFECT BLUE *for beef and very lean game such as ostrich* – surface browned but meat (here, beef fillet) still clinging to any bone; when carved, surface of meat is well done, the rest rare to almost blue; a skewer inserted in the meat is cold to the touch and juices are not warm enough to run; meat thermometer registers less than 52°C/125°F. Note: only a few people prefer beef cooked this way.

PERFECT RARE *for beef, lamb, buffalo, venison and ostrich* – surface well browned, meat starting to pull from any bone; when carved, surface meat is well done with centre red, very juicy and full-flavoured; a skewer inserted in the meat is cool to the touch and juices run red; thermometer registers 52°C/125°F. Note: after being removed from oven, large cuts will continue cooking for 5-10 minutes from their own residual heat.

PERFECT MEDIUM *for beef, lamb, buffalo, venison, wild boar* – surface dark brown and meat shrinking from any bones; when carved, meat is juicy and aromatic, shading from crusty well-done surface to rose-pink in centre; a skewer inserted in the meat is warm to the touch and juices run deep pink; meat thermometer registers 60°C/140°F.

PERFECT WELL-DONE *for beef, lamb, all game* – surface crusty brown and whole roast visibly shrunken; when carved, meat has no trace of pink and surface is dry and fibrous; skewer is hot to the touch and juices run clear; meat thermometer registers 70°C/160°F. Note: beef and game can be very dry if well done.

Roast fillet of beef with coffee pan gravy

It was the cooks of the American South who first thought of using coffee to flavour their ham gravy. Now some modern French chefs have taken up the practice with delicious results. Unusual flavourings for gravy include a tablespoon of whole-grain mustard, whisked in after straining the gravy. A tablespoon of toasted sesame seeds plus a few drops of dark sesame oil will add Oriental depth, as will a teaspoon of soy sauce, but the effect should be subtle so don't overdo it.

1.15-kg/2½-pounds piece of beef fillet
salt and pepper
2 tablespoons vegetable oil
250 ml/8 fl oz brown beef or veal stock
2 tablespoons coffee beans

250 ml/8 fl oz black coffee
30 ml/1 fl oz bourbon whiskey (optional)
2 tablespoons cold butter, cut into pieces

trussing string

Preheat the oven to 260°C/500°F/gas10 or to its highest possible setting. Trim any sinew, membrane or excess fat from the beef fillet. Fold under the tapered end to give the roast an even cylindrical shape and tie the roast neatly at regular intervals. Measure the diameter of the roast with a ruler. Note: the cooking time is much better gauged by measuring the thickness of the fillet than by using its weight.

Season the beef with salt and pepper. Heat the oil in a roasting pan and brown the roast on all sides over high heat, 5-7 minutes. Transfer to the oven and roast until done to your taste, allowing 8-9 minutes per 2.5 cm/1 inch for rare meat, 9-10 minutes for medium-cooked and 10-12 minutes for well-done. About 5 minutes before the roast is going to be done pour half the stock over the meat. Note: stand back as the stock will sputter.

Coarsely chop the coffee beans, pulsing them 2-3 times in a coffee grinder. Alternatively, put the coffee beans in a plastic bag and crush them lightly with a rolling pin.

When the beef is done, transfer the pan to the top of the stove. Set the meat on a platter and cover with foil to keep warm. Add the coffee, bourbon if using and the remaining stock to the roasting pan and bring to the boil, stirring to dissolve pan juices. Add the coffee beans to the pan and boil to reduce and concentrate flavour, 8-10 minutes. Strain this gravy, bring it back to the boil, taste and adjust the seasoning with salt and pepper. Take the pan from the heat, add the pieces of cold butter and shake the pan to swirl the gravy until the butter is melted and incorporated. Discard the trussing strings from the meat, moisten the meat with a little gravy and serve the rest separately.

PROBLEMS

UNDERCOOKED AND OUTSIDE PALE
Why: cooking temperature too low; roasting time too short.
What to do: continue roasting, increasing temperature if necessary.

OVERCOOKED AND DRY
Why: meat (especially beef) has little marbling of fat; meat cooked too long; temperature too high; cut of meat long and narrow, so cooks quicker; not basted often enough; meat carved when very hot so juices leaked.
What to do: carve across grain of meat to minimize toughness; serve with lots of brown sauce or gravy (pages 114-5); hold attention with colourful accompaniments such as carrots, Brussels sprouts or green cabbage for beef, green beans, courgette or baby onions for lamb, and red cabbage or pumpkin for game.

TOUGH
Why: meat (especially beef) has little marbling of fat; wrong cut for cooking method; old animal (especially game); meat fresh not aged; poorly handled when frozen; not basted often enough; overcooked.
What to do: if inedibly tough, slice meat and simmer in sauce as a stew until tender.

LACKS TASTE
Why: bland meat; meat not aged; insufficient seasoning.
What to do: serve with a lively sauce such as horseradish (for beef), mint or redcurrant jelly (for lamb), red wine and pepper sauce or sour cream sauce for game.

OUTSIDE NOT BROWN AND CRISP
Why: undercooked; not basted often enough; meat poorly handled when stored or frozen so surface wet; meat salted ahead of time so surface wet; temperature too low.
What to do: increase heat to very high towards end of cooking to encourage browning.

ROASTING TIMES AND TEMPERATURES

Roasting temperature is a matter of debate and I favour the French habit of starting with a very high heat of 230°C/450°F/gas8 for 15 minutes until the meat is browned. After that, much depends on the size and type of meat. For a big cut I then turn down the heat to 175°C/350°F/gas4 to ensure the heat penetrates evenly to the centre of the meat. Approximate timings are: 12 minutes per 500 g/1 pound for underdone (blue) meat, 14-16 minutes per 500 g/1 pound for rare, 16-18 minutes per 500 g/1 pound for medium and 18-20 minutes per 500 g/1 pound for well-done meat. However, a plump cut takes longer and the long skinny shape of a beef fillet needs the highest possible heat for a short time (see the recipe above).

Large cuts of veal

Roasted, spit-roasted

A VEAL ROAST CALLS FOR MORE DELICATE TREATMENT THAN THE RED MEATS (beef, lamb and venison) though much of the advice on preparation, seasoning and basting holds true. You can choose between lightly roasted veal so it remains slightly pink, as I prefer it, or veal roasted until well done. Either way it's important not to let roast veal overcook and become dry, so a longer time in the oven at a lower temperature is the wiser approach. I generally set the oven at 175°C/350°F/gas4, allowing about 20 minutes per 500 g/1 pound for medium-cooked meat and 2 minutes longer per 500 g/1 pound for well-done.

Butter is the preferred basting fat for roast veal, both for flavour and because it helps brown the surface, which is often moist. Many veal roasts are taken off the bone, an invitation to stuffing with herbed breadcrumbs and onions or a colourful mixture of spinach and ricotta cheese. Be sure the veal is tied compactly as it tends to shrink in the oven, and let the meat stand at least 10 minutes before carving so the juices are redistributed uniformly throughout the meat.

TYPICAL CUTS

for roasting and spit-roasting are breast, centre rib, crown roast, loin, round, rump, saddle, sirloin

UNDERCOOKED – outside scarcely browned; skewer cool to touch when withdrawn after 30 seconds and juices run deep pink; thermometer registers less than 66°C/150°F; when carved, meat in centre is pink and translucent.
Why: cooking temperature too low; roasting time too short; cut of meat plump or includes bone so cooks more slowly.
What to do: continue roasting, raising temperature if necessary.

PERFECT MEDIUM – outside of meat (here, rolled breast of veal) is lightly browned; skewer is warm to the touch when withdrawn after 30 seconds and juices run lightly pink; meat thermometer registers 66°C/150°F; when carved, meat is juicy, slightly pink in centre and aromatic. Note: after being removed from oven, large cuts will continue cooking for 5-10 minutes from their own residual heat.

PERFECT WELL-DONE – outside golden brown; when pressed, meat feels firm (Thumb test, fourth-finger stage, see page 78); skewer is hot to touch when withdrawn after 30 seconds and juices run clear; meat thermometer registers 70°C/160°F; when carved, meat has no trace of pink but remains juicy and full-flavoured.

OTHER PROBLEMS

OVERCOOKED AND DRY
Why: roasted too long; temperature too high; cut of meat long and narrow, so cooks quickly.
What to do: serve with generous amounts of brown or velouté sauce or gravy (see pages 112 and 114-5) and colourful mounds (bouquets) of carrots, turnips, baby onions and creamed spinach.

TOUGH OR LACKS TASTE
Why: veal not milk-fed; wrong cut for cooking method; poorly handled when stored or frozen; not basted often; insufficient seasoning, overcooked.
What to do: carve across the grain to minimize toughness; add bold accompaniments such as spinach sautéed with garlic and onion, spaetzle noodles or Carrot Purée with Cardamom (page 177).

QUICK FIX

I make this raw tomato, garlic and basil salsa often as a punchy condiment to mask blandness in everything from meat and poultry to fish. In a small bowl, whisk together 75 ml/2½ fl oz balsamic vinegar, 3 chopped garlic cloves, salt and pepper. Gradually whisk in 150 ml/5 fl oz olive oil so the dressing emulsifies and thickens slightly. Core and halve 3 tomatoes and squeeze out the seeds. Chop the halves and stir into dressing with shredded leaves from small bunch of basil. Taste for seasoning. Makes 250 ml/8 fl oz, to serve 4.

Roast veal with sorrel and spinach purée
Rôti de veau à la purée d'oseille et d'épinards

SERVES 6-8

TESTS FOR ROASTING

There are three tests for the cooking of roasted meat, one using a thermometer, another a skewer and the third with your fingers. Using a good-quality meat thermometer is the most accurate.

THERMOMETER – insert a meat thermometer into the thickest part of the meat, without touching any bone, and allow at least 1 minute for temperature to register. Juices which emerge also indicate stage of cooking. Note: after being removed from oven, large cuts will continue cooking for 5-10 minutes from their own residual heat. Internal temperatures rise during this period, so compensate by taking the roast from the oven when it's just shy of the right temperature.

SKEWER – insert a metal skewer into the thickest part of the meat, without touching any bone, and wait 30 seconds; if the skewer is cold to your touch when withdrawn, the meat is underdone; if cool, the meat is rare; if warm, the meat is medium-cooked; if hot, it is well done. Juices which emerge when skewer is removed are red for rare meat, pink for medium-cooked and clear when meat is well done. You'll also notice that, when rare, meat clings to any bone, gradually pulling away during further cooking.

FINGERS – press or pinch the roast with your fingers. With experience you will learn to judge the difference between the firm resilience of meat which is well done and the spongier feel of a roast that is still rare in the centre.

I like to use boneless loin or round of veal for roasting – breast is less expensive and good too. Larding the meat with strips of pork fat or barding with bacon helps keep it moist and tender. If sorrel is not available, you can substitute watercress, boiling the leaves with the spinach.

1 veal roast as above
   (about 1.25 kg/2½ pounds)
125-g/4-oz piece of pork or bacon fat,
   cut into short strips
salt and pepper
2 tablespoons vegetable oil
1 carrot, thinly sliced
1 onion, sliced
175 ml/6 fl oz white wine
175 ml/6 fl oz brown beef or veal stock,
   more if needed

for the sorrel and spinach purée
750 g/1½ pounds sorrel
750 g/1½ pounds spinach
30 g/1 oz butter
175 ml/6 fl oz double cream

trussing string

Preheat the oven to 175°C/350°F/gas4. Lard the veal roast: pierce the meat with the point of a sharp knife and insert a strip of pork or bacon fat in each incision. Roll the veal into a neat cylinder and tie it at regular intervals. Season the roast with salt and pepper.

Heat the oil in a roasting pan and brown the veal on all sides. Add the carrot and onion and fry, stirring, until lightly browned, 3-5 minutes. Add the wine and boil until reduced by half, then stir in the stock. Roast the veal in the preheated oven until done to your taste, 1-1¼ hours. Baste often and add more stock, if necessary, to keep the meat moist.

Meanwhile, make the sorrel and spinach purée: wash the sorrel and spinach thoroughly in several changes of water. Pick over the leaves, discarding the stems. Put the sorrel in a large pan with a little salt, cover and cook over high heat until wilted, stirring once or twice, 3-5 minutes. Add the butter and cream to the pan and cook, stirring, until the sorrel thickens to a purée which falls easily from the spoon, about 5 minutes. Set it aside. Pack the spinach into another pan with 2 cm/¾ inch water. Cover and cook the spinach over high heat until the leaves start to wilt. Stir, cover and continue cooking until completely wilted, 1-2 minutes. Drain, let cool, then press to remove excess water. Chop the spinach and stir into the sorrel purée. Taste the purée and adjust the seasoning.

Transfer the veal to a carving board and cover with foil to keep warm. Strain the cooking juices and, if necessary, boil them until reduced and well-flavoured. Discard the trussing strings and carve the veal into 1.25-cm/½-inch slices. Reheat the purée if necessary and pile it down the centre of a warmed serving dish. Arrange the veal slices overlapping on top. Moisten them with a little gravy and serve the rest separately.

Large cuts of pork

Grilled, roasted, spit-roasted

TYPICAL CUTS

for grilling, roasting and spit-roasting are blade, crown, fresh ham, leg, loin

BEEF MAY BE THE ARISTOCRAT OF GRAND ROASTS and veal the choice for fine cuisine, but when it comes to a family feast I hope you'll agree that pork wins hands down. When stuffed with garlic, onion and herbs, then basted constantly as it cooks with wine and meat juices, pork is fit for a king. Pigs are now bred to be lean, so the meat dries all the more easily. I prefer a cut which includes the bone to keep it moist such as fresh leg, or loin including the ribs. Whether you are roasting or grilling, you'll find moderate rather than intense heat is best.

Pork must always be cooked until well done (a few pink juices are acceptable), leading to plenty of crispy trimmings. I like to use a moderately hot oven at 190°C/375°F/gas5, allowing 18 minutes per 500 g/1 pound for medium, or 20 minutes for well-done meat. Best of all is the skin, left on the roast in some countries and a prime part of suckling pig. To help the skin dry and crisp, score it deeply, rub it with salt and spices, and shortly after cooking begins, pour over a cup or two of boiling water. Remember to let the meat stand at least 10 minutes before carving, so the juices are redistributed uniformly throughout the meat.

By itself, barbecued or roasted pork can be a bit plain. I like to sweeten it with dried figs or prunes, or flavour it with orange or cranberry. Roast pork goes well with hot pepper jelly, apple sauce, roast garlic and accompaniments such as cornbread, polenta, sauerkraut and mashed potatoes. In Austria it is served with a raisin pudding, and in Mexico suckling pig is roasted with cumin, paprika and orange juice, wrapped in banana leaves. What a surprise package!

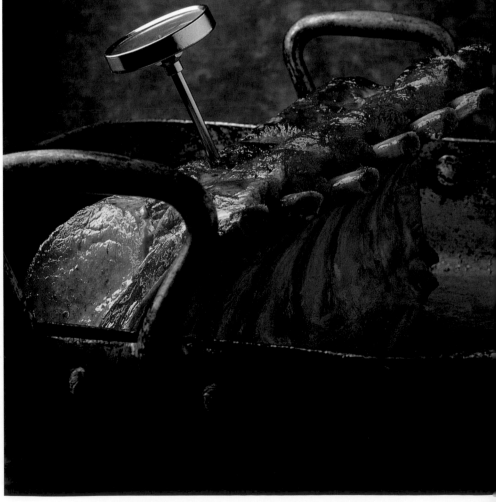

UNDERCOOKED *above* – outside lightly browned and meat clings to bones; skewer cool or warm to the touch when withdrawn after 30 seconds and juices run pink; meat thermometer registers less than 70°C/160°F; when carved, meat is pink in centre.
Note: cooking pork to an internal temperature of 70-75°C/160-170°F destroys any possible parasites that cause trichinosis, though the risk of contamination is very low.
Why: cooking temperature too low; roasting time too short; cut of meat plump or includes bone so cooks more slowly.
What to do: continue roasting, raising temperature if necessary.

Roast pork loin with figs and port

pictured on pages 60-61

QUICK FIX

For dry, tired pork, make this honey mustard sauce. In a small bowl, combine 3 tablespoons finely chopped dill, 2 tablespoons whole grain mustard, 2 tablespoons honey, 1 tablespoon Dijon-style mustard and 1 tablespoon sugar. Stir until mixed. Makes 75 ml/2½ fl oz sauce, to serve 4.

Look for figs that are still a bit firm so they bake well, giving up generous juices for the rich sauce. A pilaf of wild rice or cracked wheat is an excellent accompaniment.

1 rolled pork loin roast
*   (about 1 kg/2 pounds)*
salt and pepper
2 teaspoons ground cinnamon
8 large figs (about 375 g/¾ pound)
15 g/½ oz butter
1 tablespoon vegetable oil
250 ml/8 fl oz brown beef or veal stock,
*   plus more if needed*

250 ml/8 fl oz port
1 tablespoon brown sugar
2 tablespoons red currant jelly
juice of ½ lemon
1½ teaspoons cornflour, mixed to a paste
*   with 2 tablespoons cold water*

trussing string

PERFECT *left* – outside of meat (here, centre rib roast) well browned and crusty, pulling away from bones; meat thermometer registers 70°C/160°F for medium-cooked, and 75°C/170°F for well-done; skewer very warm or hot to the touch when withdrawn after 30 seconds and juices run very light pink (medium) or clear (well-done); meat is tender when pierced with two-pronged fork; when carved, meat is juicy and full-flavoured with slight or no trace of pink. Note: after being removed from oven, large cuts will continue cooking for 5-10 minutes from their own residual heat.

Preheat the oven to 190°C/375°F/gas5. Unroll the flap of meat attached to the loin. Slice halfway through the loin to make a pocket, leaving the ends of the loin uncut so the stuffing does not fall out during roasting. Season the pocket and cut side of the roast with salt, pepper and half the cinnamon. Trim 2 figs and cut them into quarters. Tuck these fig quarters into the pocket. Re-roll the roast and tie at regular intervals. Season with salt, pepper and the rest of the cinnamon.

Heat the butter and oil together in a roasting pan until foaming. Add the pork and brown it on all sides. Pour over the stock and transfer the pan to the preheated oven. Roast, turning and basting the meat occasionally, until done, 1-1¼ hours. If the pan gets dry, add more stock to keep the meat moist.

Meanwhile, glaze the figs: slice a cross-hatch in the top of each remaining fig and open it slightly like a flower. Pack the figs in a small baking dish, pour over half the port and sprinkle with the sugar. Bake in the oven with the pork until the figs are tender and glazed, 15-20 minutes. Remove them and keep warm.

When the roast is done, transfer it to a carving board and cover with foil to keep warm. Add the remaining port, jelly and lemon juice to the roasting pan and bring to the boil, stirring to dissolve the pan juices. Strain the sauce into a small saucepan and skim excess fat. Add the juices from the cooked figs to make about 375 ml/12 fl oz in total; if necessary, add more stock. Bring to the boil and whisk in the cornflour paste so the sauce thickens slightly. Taste and adjust seasoning.

Discard the trussing strings and carve the roast into 1-cm/⅜-inch slices. Arrange the slices overlapping on a warmed platter and spoon over a little sauce. Set the figs around the sides of the platter and serve the remaining sauce separately.

OTHER PROBLEMS

OVERCOOKED AND DRY

Why: cooked too long; temperature too high; cut of meat long and narrow so cooks quickly.
What to do: serve with generous amounts of cream sauce, gravy or fruit sauce (see Sauces) and dominating accompaniments such as poached dried fruits or sauerkraut.

TOUGH OR LACKS TASTE

Why: wrong cut for cooking method; meat poorly handled; not basted often enough; overcooked.
What to do: carve across grain of meat to minimize toughness and serve with crisp vegetables, such as stir-fried celery and carrot or mange-tout peas; if very tough, slice and simmer in gravy or a spicy sauce until tender.

Large cuts of beef, veal, lamb, pork and game

Boiled, braised, poached, pot-roasted

COMPARE MY LIST BELOW OF TYPICAL CUTS WHICH BRAISE WELL with the few that are good for roasting and you'll see why I often tell friends 'when in doubt, play safe and braise'. The plain truth is that most parts of an animal tend to be tough and benefit from slow moist heat to break down the tissue. Even expensive roasts can be chewy if the meat is of indifferent quality or lacks a marbling of fat (increasingly common with the current trend towards lean meat). There are no halfway measures for such meats – they must be cooked slowly and thoroughly until meltingly tender, allowing the juices to drain into the sauce or broth. Incidentally, the term 'boiled beef' is a misnomer; the key for such dishes is to poach the meat at a gentle simmer so the heat penetrates evenly to the centre. The more gently meat is simmered, the better it will be.

Most countries boast a traditional, slowly cooked braise, from German sweet-and-sour *Sauerbraten* to American pot roast and French *boeuf en estouffade*. Australians are even known to braise kangaroo meat in red wine. One-pot meals in which the meat is simmered with vegetables and aromatics to make a rich broth are equally universal: Brazil has its *cozido* with beef, ham, garlic sausage and vegetables, Austria its beef flank with beer, juniper, bacon and vegetables, Britain its hot-pot and France its *pot au feu*.

Some recipes go even further, calling for meat to be cooked until almost falling apart and soft enough to cut with a spoon. Beef tends to be the meat of choice in this case, but lamb gives rise to classics like Greek lamb shanks in lemon sauce and British boiled leg of lamb with capers. No matter what the recipe, meat should always be brought slowly to the boil in cold liquid (usually water), then poached just short of a simmer. If immersed in boiling liquid or simmered too fast, the surface of the meat will turn disagreeably hard. Salted meats such as brisket must be blanched before simmering and some cooks like to blanch other meats, particularly veal, to draw out impurities.

Before cooking, the meat for braising or pot-roasting is often soaked in a wine or other marinade, which is then used to make a sauce. The cooking liquid itself may include beef or veal stock, red or white wine, beer or vinegar. Be sure it is highly flavoured with vegetables, such as onion, carrot, leek and celery, herbs such as bay leaf, thyme, parsley and oregano, and spices such as allspice, pepper, nutmeg, juniper, clove and dried chilli. Given such a choice it's no wonder no two recipes are alike!

Boiled meats are delicious with condiments like mustard, pickles, coarse salt, redcurrant jelly (for lamb and game), plum or apricot preserves (for pork). For all, a starch such as pasta, boiled or mashed potatoes, boiled rice or a grain pilaf is mandatory to soak up the juices.

TYPICAL CUTS

for boiling, braising, poaching and pot-roasting
Beef: arm, back ribs, blade, brisket, chuck, eye and bottom round, flank, rump, shank
Veal: rump, shank, shoulder, sirloin
Lamb: breast, leg, saddle, shank, shoulder
Pork: chops, fresh ham, leg, shoulder, spare ribs
Game: leg, saddle, shoulder.

PERFECT – surface of meat (here, braised leg of lamb) moist, and brown if braised or pot-roasted; skewer is hot to the touch when withdrawn after 30 seconds and juices run clear; meat is very tender when pierced with two-pronged fork, starting to pull from bones; meat thermometer registers 70°C/160°F; when sliced, meat is evenly cooked, moist and succulent. Note: after being removed from oven, large cuts will continue cooking for 5-10 minutes from their own residual heat.

PERFECT WELL-DONE – surface of meat drier and very brown if braised or pot-roasted; skewer is very hot to the touch when withdrawn after 30 seconds; meat is soft enough to cut with a spoon and shrinks from bones; meat thermometer registers more than 70°C/160°F; when sliced, meat is very tender, almost falling into shreds

Braised leg of lamb with garlic and wild mushrooms

SERVES 6-8

PROBLEMS

UNDERCOOKED

Why: cooking temperature too low; cooking time too short; cut of meat plump or includes bone so cooks more slowly.

What to do: continue cooking, raising temperature if necessary and basting often.

OVERCOOKED AND DRY

Why: cooked too long; temperature too high; cut of meat long and narrow so cooks quickly; wrong cut for cooking method; if braised or pot-roasted, not enough liquid.

What to do: slice meat and coat with cooking gravy or sauce, then warm 5 minutes in a low oven to moisten meat.

TOUGH AND STRINGY

Why: wrong cut for cooking method; meat had little marbling of fat (especially beef); old animal (especially game); not milk-fed (veal); meat fresh not aged; poorly handled when stored or frozen; if boiled or poached, cooking started in hot not cold liquid; cooked too fast (especially veal); overcooked.

What to do: carve across grain of meat to minimize toughness.

LACKS TASTE

Why: meat was bland or not aged; poorly handled when stored or frozen; insufficient seasoning; overcooked.

What to do: revive sauce or gravy for dark meats with Cognac, mustard, soy sauce or Tabasco, or for white meats with sherry, balsamic vinegar or lemon juice.

GREY COLOUR, MAINLY WHEN BOILING OR POACHING

Why: meat poorly handled when stored or frozen so lost juices; white meats not blanched before cooking.

What to do: serve with colourful vegetables, such as carrot, leek, green cabbage and red potatoes.

QUICK FIX

When cooking has been a bit haphazard, I often shred meats for a salad. For every 375 g/¾ pound shredded or thinly sliced meat, mix 1 tablespoon Dijon-style mustard, 1 tablespoon coarse-grain mustard, 2 finely chopped shallots, salt and pepper in a medium bowl. Gradually whisk in 125 ml/4 fl oz olive oil so the dressing emulsifies. Add meat, stir until coated and season to taste. Serves 4.

Here I call for my favourite wild mushroom – the cep – but feel free to substitute whichever type happens to be available and fresh. You can economize by substituting common mushrooms for part or all of the wild ones.

1 leg of lamb (about 2.25 kg/5 pounds)	bunch of thyme
4 garlic cloves, peeled and cut into slivers	bunch of rosemary
salt and pepper	375 ml/12 fl oz white wine
3 tablespoons oil	500 ml/16 fl oz brown beef or veal stock,
15 g/½ oz butter	more if needed
2 onions, sliced	175 ml/6 fl oz double cream or crème
2 carrots, sliced	fraîche
1 stalk of celery, sliced	2 tablespoons chopped parsley
500 g/1 pound ceps, sliced	

Preheat the oven to 175°C/350°F/gas4. With the point of a small knife, make several incisions in the lamb and insert slivers of garlic in them. Season the lamb with some salt and pepper.

Heat 2 tablespoons of the oil and the butter in a large flameproof casserole. Brown the lamb on all sides and remove to a tray. Add the onion, carrot and celery to casserole and sauté until browned, 5-7 minutes. With a slotted spoon, transfer these to the tray.

Heat the remaining oil until very hot, add the ceps and sauté, stirring, until they give up their liquid. When this liquid begins to reduce, remove the mushrooms with the slotted spoon and set aside.

Return the onion, carrot and celery to the casserole with the thyme and rosemary. Set the lamb on top, pour over the white wine and simmer for 1 or 2 minutes. Add the stock, bring to the boil, cover and transfer to the preheated oven. Braise the lamb until done to your taste, 2-2½ hours. Baste the lamb occasionally and add more stock if the casserole gets dry.

When the lamb is done, transfer it to a cutting board and cover with foil to keep warm. Strain the braising liquid, skim off any fat and return it to the casserole. Bring to the boil and, if necessary, boil to reduce to about 250 ml/8 fl oz. Stir cream into sauce, add the mushrooms and simmer until they are tender, 2-3 minutes. Taste, adjust seasoning and stir in the chopped parsley.

Carve the lamb and replace the slices on the bone or arrange them on a warmed serving platter. Spoon the mushrooms and some sauce around the sides of the meat and serve the rest separately.

Whole and half ham

Boiled, baked, braised, pot-roasted, roasted, simmered

DIFFERENT TYPES OF HAM CALL FOR QUITE DIFFERENT PREPARATION, as hams vary far more than any other cut of meat. They may come raw or cooked, mild or salty, smoked or cured with a zesty pepper or spice mix. Strictly speaking, all hams are cut from the leg of pork, but today the term is often extended to include other cuts, such as pork shoulder. Don't be distracted by the term 'fresh ham' sometimes applied to fresh leg of pork.

Mildly cured and precooked hams are good cooked with very little liquid, baked or roasted in dry heat. Large cuts of bacon and gammon can be treated in the same way, or they can be sliced into steaks to pan-fry (see Pork chops, spare ribs and ham steaks, page 82). On the other hand, well-aged or strongly cured hams, particularly those with a dry-salt cure, must first be soaked in water for 24 hours or longer, changing the water several times. Trim the skin, and to reduce fat, cut away all but a thin layer and then score it so it cooks evenly. Rather than being baked, braised, pot-roasted or roasted, such hams should be simmered in water with flavourings such as apple, onion, bay leaf and thyme (no salt).

Sugar and spice are nice as a glaze for basting ham, balancing the salt. A typical glaze calls for brown sugar or maple syrup, cloves and a fruit such as pineapple or orange. I've come across a Maryland recipe where the ham is boned and stuffed with a mixture of grits and peppery greens, while in Burgundy around Chablis, sliced ham is baked in a white wine cream sauce with vinegar, onion, shallot, juniper and peppercorns. Note: if a ham is pallid or greyish, it is either not properly cured or stale. Don't use it.

PERFECT – meat is starting to shrink from bone and bone feels loose; skewer is hot to the touch when withdrawn after 30 seconds; meat thermometer registers 75°C/170°F; if baked, braised, pot-roasted or roasted, surface is scored and well browned with a caramelized glaze; when carved, meat is juicy and clear or deep pink, depending on cure; flavour vigorous but not salty. Note: after being removed from oven, large cuts will continue cooking for 5-10 minutes from their own residual heat.

PROBLEMS

UNDERCOOKED, WET AND FLABBY
Why: ham was of poor quality, with water injected to increase weight; cooking time too short.
What to do: if boiling, drain ham and bake or roast to finish cooking; if braising or pot-roasting, remove cover, raise oven temperature and continue cooking.

OVERCOOKED, DRY AND STRINGY
Why: ham aged or dried too long; cooked too long; oven heat too high.
What to do: moisten with gravy or fruit sauce (see Sauces), serve with forthright accompaniments such as fresh or dried fruits, sauerkraut, leaf spinach with raisins or sweet potato purée.

SALTY
Why: salty cure; ham not soaked before cooking; too little liquid used in cooking; overcooked.
What to do: serve with a fruit or sweet sauce such as plum, apple or apricot. If very salty, cut up ham to mix with pasta, rice or potatoes.

BLAND
Why: ham too lightly cured; overcooked.
What to do: slice ham and bake in white wine vinegar sauce, mustard cream sauce or port wine gravy.

QUICK FIX

To help ham that is wet, stringy, salty or bland, add a sweet-hot topping. If not already done, score the ham fat deeply in a lattice pattern. For a ham for 6-8 people, mix 4 tablespoons Dijon-style mustard and 100 g/3¼ oz dark brown sugar to a paste and spread over fat. Spear the centre of each diamond in the lattice with a whole clove. Roast ham in a 200°C/400°F/gas6 oven, basting every few minutes, until the sugar is melted and surface a rich dark brown, 15-20 minutes.

Braised ham in apple juice with ginger stuffed apples

To cook ham with apple is a tradition in Normandy, where pigs are often raised beneath the apple trees. Use mildly cured ham and apples on the tart side for this braise.

1 uncooked ham (1.4 kg/3 pounds)	for the ginger stuffed apples
1 tablespoon vegetable oil	6-8 small tart apples
15 g/½ oz butter	(about 1.15 kg/2½ pounds),
2 carrots, peeled and sliced	preferably Granny Smith
2 onions, chopped	60 g/2 oz butter
1 stalk of celery, sliced	60 g/2 oz dark brown sugar
1 teaspoon whole cloves	30 g/1 oz raisins
750 ml/1¼ pints apple juice, more	2 tablespoons chopped preserved
if needed	ginger
1 tablespoon cornflour mixed to a	½ teaspoon ground nutmeg
paste with 3 tablespoons of the	75 ml/2½ fl oz apple juice
apple juice	
pepper	

Preheat the oven to 160°C/325°F/gas3. Heat the oil and butter in a large flameproof casserole. Add the carrots, onions, celery and cloves and sauté until soft, stirring occasionally, 5-7 minutes.

Trim away any skin and all but a thin layer of fat from ham. Score the fat in a lattice pattern. Set the ham on top of vegetables, pour over the apple juice and bring to the boil. Cover, transfer to the preheated oven and braise until the ham is done, 1-1¼ hours. Baste the ham often and if the casserole gets dry during braising, add more juice.

Meanwhile, prepare the apples: cut them in halves at their equators and scoop out the cores. Trim the stem and flower ends, but do not peel. Put the apples cut-side up in a shallow baking dish. Cream the butter and beat the sugar into it until soft and light. Stir in the raisins, ginger and nutmeg. Spoon the mixture into the apple cavities. Pour the apple juice into the baking dish and bake the apples in the oven with the ham, basting occasionally, until the apples are very tender, 40-50 minutes. Transfer to a dish and cover with foil to keep warm. Reserve the juices in baking dish.

When the ham is done, transfer to a cutting board. Cover to keep warm. Strain the cooking juices into a pan and skim off the fat. Stir in the juices from the baked apples – there should be about 375 ml/12 fl oz in total. If necessary, boil them until reduced. Whisk enough cornflour paste into the boiling juices to thicken the sauce until it lightly coats the back of a spoon. Taste and adjust the seasoning.

Carve the ham and arrange the slices on a warmed platter, or carve it at the table. Arrange the baked apples around the ham. Moisten both with a little sauce and serve the rest separately.

Beef steaks, lamb chops and game medallions

Grilled, pan-fried, sautéed

STEAKS AND LAMB CHOPS ARE BY FAR THE MOST POPULAR MEATS in any cook's repertoire. Medallions and noisettes, small tender pieces which are easy to cook, are equally sought after when it comes to game. My instinct is to cook such luxury cuts very simply as in the Mixed Grill opposite, adding at most a pat of herb butter. If you are pan-frying, a reduction sauce of shallot, herbs and red wine takes only a few moments and it's hard to beat.

Looking at the more complex traditional sauces for grilled and pan-fried meats, we find truffle and Madeira sauces with beef, their expense a reflection of steak's prestige. Béarnaise, perhaps made with mint instead of tarragon, is right for lamb as well as beef, as are vegetable-thickened sauces of garlic, sweet pepper or shallot, or Middle Eastern confections based on yogurt. For game, I would go spicy with a black pepper *poivrade* sauce, or sweet with the redcurrant jelly, orange and port of a Cumberland sauce.

Top-quality meat, marbled with plenty of fat for beef and lamb, is essential for successful grilling and pan-frying. Unfortunately, there are few cuts which are tender enough to withstand such dry heat. Only in kebabs can a plainer cut of meat (such as lamb shoulder) pass muster, with distractions such as crunchy onion, mushroom, bursting cherry tomatoes and aromatic herbs.

Marinating red meats in red wine or other acids before cooking adds flavour and helps tenderize them, but only on the surface. Other methods of tenderizing, by pounding or sprinkling with a commercial mix, tend to break down fibres so juices are lost. A better bet is to rub the surface of the meat with dry seasonings such as mustard, pepper and paprika up to half an hour before cooking, then add salt at the last minute. There's much debate about this: I am a firm believer in salting before cooking as heat helps the salt penetrate the surface of the meat. However many cooks salt steaks and chops only after cooking, for fear that the meat juices will be drawn out and prevent browning.

Different nations tend to add their own favourite ingredients to steaks and chops. Hearty German cooks top steak with a fried egg in Holstein style; Italians coat lamb chops with Parmesan and breadcrumbs before frying; Australians stuff beef with oysters to make carpetbag steak. Wild boar medallions turn up in Italy with prunes, chocolate and cinnamon, and in France with juniper.

OTHER CUTS
for grilling, pan-frying and sautéing
Lamb: escalopes, noisettes
Game: noisettes

Mixed grill, see overleaf

OVERC
Why: co
cut too
What t
béarnai
such as
sautéed
fried po
Hazeln
TOUGH
Why: w
little m
(especi
handle
What t
minimi
lean st
and sir
LACKS
Why: n
season
What t
ground
and nu
sauce
accom

QU

As ev
au po
overc
2 tabl
bag a
1½ tal
175 m
2 tabl
and 1
salt. S

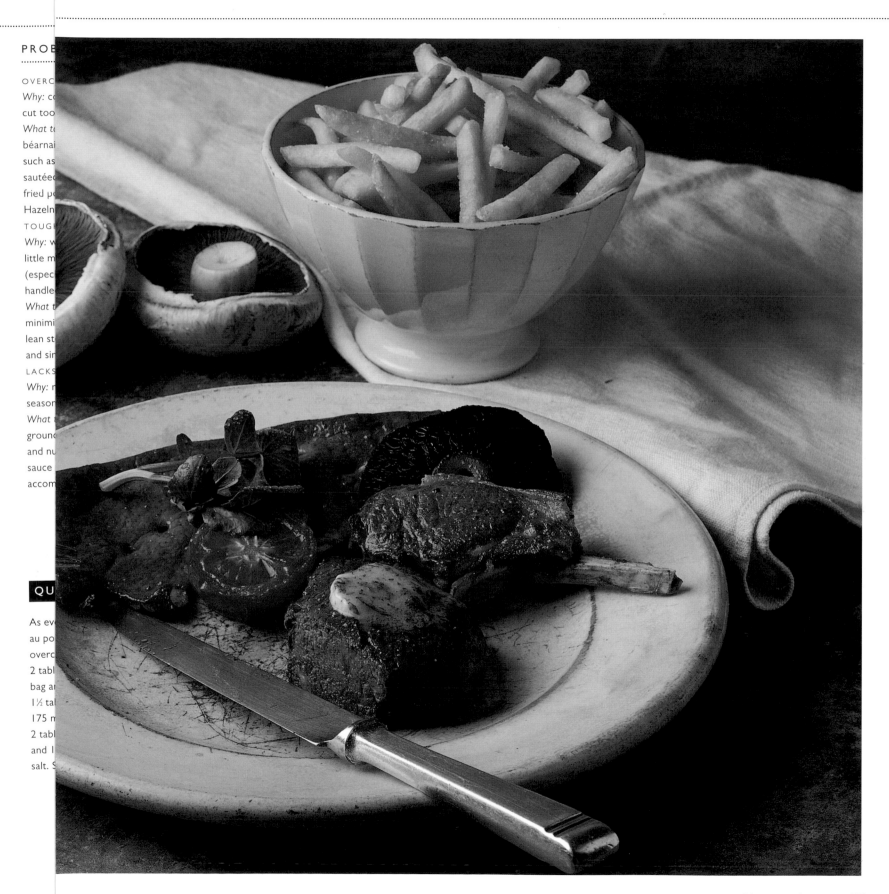

Veal chops, medallions and small cuts
Grilled, pan-fried, sautéed

WE ARE SPOILED IN FRANCE, where top-quality veal is taken almost for granted. I find that its tenderness and delicate flavour show best in small cuts like chops and medallions, provided they are simply cooked. The main danger is dryness, so before pan-frying or grilling, I often brush veal generously with oil, or even better, marinate it in olive or walnut oil flavoured with lemon juice or balsamic vinegar and herbs. For another approach, coat veal with flour to help retain juices and keep the surface of the meat crisp.

Older veal is easily spotted by its dark pink colour. You can whiten these pieces somewhat by soaking them in milk before cooking, but little can be done about the texture, which is liable to be tough. The best solution is to braise or stew older veal (see Steaks, chops and game pieces, opposite), an option made all the more tempting by recipes such as veal Marengo with tomato, mushrooms and white wine, or veal shank with onion, leek, carrot and cider vinegar, which is popular in Germany.

Mediterranean ingredients seem to do well with veal – vegetables such as aubergine and courgette and herbs like sage, rosemary and basil. Veal and mushrooms, especially morels, is a classic pairing, particularly when simmered in cream.

PERFECT MEDIUM – surface (here, medallions) lightly browned and meat spongy when pressed in centre, firm at sides (Thumb test, second-finger stage, right); beads of juice on surface are pink; when cut, meat is juicy, faintly pink and aromatic.

PERFECT WELL-DONE – surface golden brown, crusty if grilled; meat firm when pressed in centre (Thumb test, fourth-finger stage, right); beads of juice on surface clear; when cut, no pink juices visible but meat still moist and well-flavoured.

PROBLEMS

UNDERCOOKED
Why: time too short; temperature too low.
What to do: continue cooking, raising heat if necessary.
OVERCOOKED AND DRY
Why: meat poorly handled when stored or frozen; cooked too long; temperature too high; no liquid or basting sauce used during cooking.
What to do: moisten with a Madeira or herb butter sauce and serve with colourful accompaniments – saffron risotto, creamed spinach and glazed baby onions and carrots are classic.

TOUGH
Why: wrong cut for method; veal not milk-fed; poorly handled when stored or frozen; cooked too fast; overcooked.
What to do: continue in low heat until tender; if necessary, add stock or wine to keep meat moist.
TASTELESS
Why: meat was bland; poorly handled when stored or frozen; underseasoned; overcooked.
What to do: sprinkle with salt, pepper and lemon juice and chopped sage or thyme; add a lively sauce like Fresh Tomato with Roasted Red Peppers (page 129).

THE THUMB TEST FOR FIRMNESS

A simple way to judge the cooking of a piece of meat, poultry or fish is to compare its resilience to that of your thumb muscle. As shown below, the further the thumb has to reach across the hand, the more resilient the muscle becomes.

FIRST-FINGER STAGE
for underdone/blue meat and lightly cooked fish – touch your thumb to its opposing first finger and press the ball of your thumb with the tip of a finger of the other hand – the ball will offer no resistance.

SECOND-FINGER STAGE
for rare meat – touch your second finger to your thumb and press the ball of your thumb – the ball will feel spongy.

THIRD-FINGER STAGE
for medium-cooked meat, game or duck or well-done fish – touch your third finger to your thumb and press the ball of your thumb – the ball will feel resistant.

FOURTH-FINGER STAGE
for well-done meat or poultry – touch your fourth finger to your thumb and press the ball of your thumb – the ball will feel firm.

Steaks, chops and game pieces

Baked, braised, stewed

Escalopes

Escalopes are versatile as well as popular. They can be floured and sautéed as *saltimbocca*; the classic *Wiener Schnitzel* is breaded and deep-fried in butter, while for veal cordon bleu, they are stuffed with ham and cheese. Rolled veal escalopes, called 'birds' or *paupiettes*, may be stuffed with herbs, lemon and breadcrumbs, sausage or chopped mushrooms. The best veal escalopes are cut from the round; for tenderness, they should be sliced across the grain with little or no seam of connective tissue. Watch out for cheaper imitations from less desirable veal cuts as they are liable to be stringy.

When escalopes are mentioned, veal is generally understood, but slices from turkey and chicken breasts are gaining ground as an inexpensive alternatives. Many recipes advise flattening escalopes between sheets of paper, but be gentle; if you pound them to pieces they will lose all their juices. They need equally delicate cooking as they overcook in minutes.

PERFECT VEAL ESCALOPES – lightly browned on both sides; when cut, meat is white and juicy with no trace of pink.

BRAISING, BAKING OR STEWING IN MOIST HEAT IS THE WAY TO GO with beef brisket and back ribs, with less expensive steaks from the round, chuck or blade, together with lamb shoulder chops, neck slices, riblets and shanks, and game leg or shoulder slices and shanks. They may be boneless or on the bone. It's also safest for almost any small piece of wild game as only the best cuts of farmed venison can be relied upon to be tender in the dry heat of grilling. The advantages of cooking in moist heat are many, but it must be handled correctly. Cooking is long and must be sufficiently slow to allow the meat fibres to soften and relax instead of toughening under high heat.

A multitude of flavourings can be added: the classic French braise combines onion, carrot and celery with garlic, wine and a bouquet garni of herbs. A simple Indian curry mix of cumin, cinnamon, black pepper and cloves is an alternative. In Spain, lamb shanks are simmered with onion, garlic, paprika, vinegar and red wine, while Americans add beer and onions to brisket of beef. You can win twice over if you marinate the meat for 2-3 days in the refrigerator with vegetables and wine, vinegar or other acidic ingredients, then let the marinade cook down with the meat to make the ideal companion sauce.

PERFECT – meat (here, braised rump steak) very tender, pulling from bone and falling easily from a two-pronged fork; meat is moist and very well flavoured, with tender gelatinous tissue.

QUICK FIX

Tunisian tabbouleh salad makes a really refreshing accompaniment to any dish of meat in sauce. Pour 250 ml/8 fl oz boiling water over 175 g/6 oz instant couscous with 1 teaspoon salt, stir and leave to soak. Pare zest of 2 lemons, halve zest strips and purée in food processor with juice from lemons. Cut 1 onion into pieces and combine in processor with leaves from large bunches of mint and parsley. Using pulse button, purée until chunky. Pour over couscous. Core and halve 3 tomatoes. Squeeze out seeds, dice halves small and add to couscous. Pour over 175 ml/6 fl oz olive oil and toss. Season to taste. Serves 4-6.

PROBLEMS

UNDERCOOKED
Why: cooking temperature too low; cooking time too short.
What to do: continue cooking, raising temperature if necessary.

OVERCOOKED AND DRY
Why: wrong cut for cooking method; cooked too long; cooking temperature too high; not enough cooking liquid.
What to do: add hearty accompaniments such as potato and cheese gratin, saffron rice or kasha; beef is helped by horseradish sauce and a baked tomato, while lentils or roasted fennel are good with lamb, and a fruit chutney with venison.

TOUGH AND STRINGY
Why: meat lacks marbling of fat; old animal (especially game); meat fresh not aged; poorly handled when stored or frozen; cooked too fast; undercooked.
What to do: continue simmering even if meat starts to break up; for serving suggestions, see Overcooked and dry.

LACKS TASTE
Why: meat was bland; meat not aged; poorly handled when stored or frozen; insufficient seasoning; sauce too thin; overcooked.
What to do: if sauce is thin, lift out meat, simmer sauce until well flavoured and replace meat; serve with pungent accompaniments such as mustard and pickles for beef, aubergine caviar or Moroccan preserved lemons for lamb, pickled mushrooms and cranberry or lingonberry sauce for game.

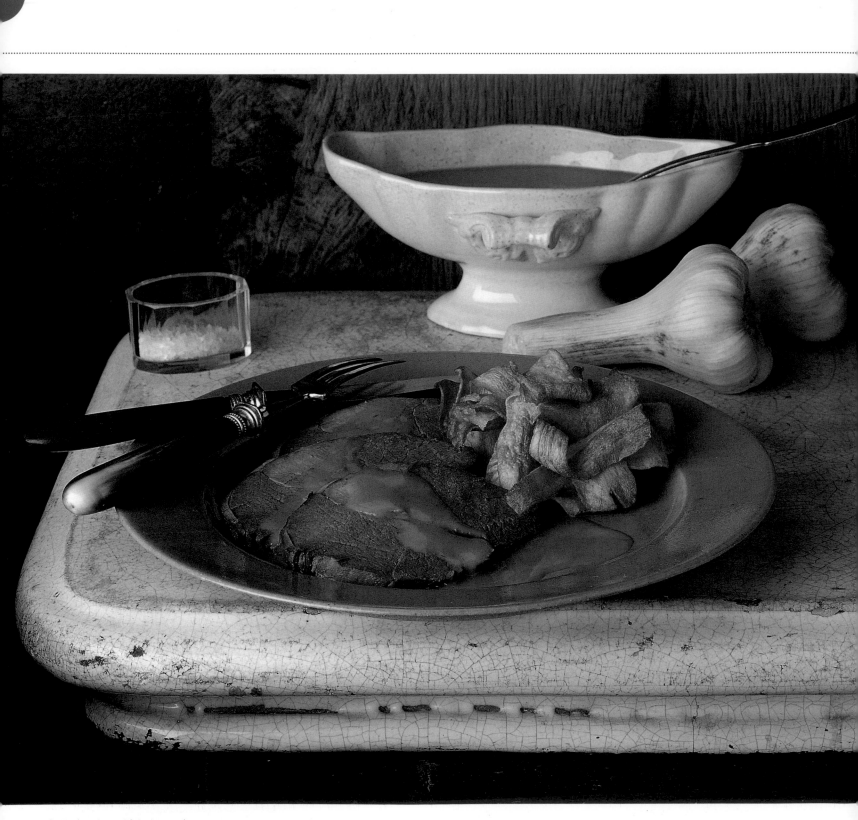

Braised venison with juniper and cream

Braised venison with juniper and cream

SERVES 4

This braise can be made with other game, including wild boar. Choose tougher cuts such as those from the leg, which benefit from slow cooking in moist heat. Cooking time varies with the age of the animal.

1-kg/2-pound piece of boneless leg of venison	for the marinade
15 g/½ oz butter	1 bottle (750 ml/1¼ pints) red wine
3 tablespoons vegetable oil	2 onions, quartered
2 tablespoons flour	4 shallots, halved
salt and pepper	3 garlic cloves, finely chopped
250 ml/8 fl oz crème fraîche or double cream	1 leek, trimmed, split and thinly sliced
	2 carrots, sliced
	1 tablespoon juniper berries, crushed
	2 tablespoons vegetable oil

Make the marinade: combine the wine, onions, shallots, garlic, leek, carrots and juniper berries in a saucepan. Bring to the boil and simmer 10 minutes. Leave the marinade to cool.

Tie the meat at regular intervals. Put meat and marinade in a deep non-metallic bowl and spoon over the oil. Cover and leave to marinate in the refrigerator, stirring occasionally, 1-2 days.

Preheat the oven to 170°C/325°F/gas3. Drain the meat and vegetables, reserving the marinade. Pat the meat dry with paper towels. Heat the butter and 2 tablespoons of the oil in a sauté pan or large flameproof casserole. Brown the venison over high heat on all sides, 5-7 minutes. Remove the meat to a plate.

Add the remaining oil with the drained vegetables and flavourings from the marinade to the casserole and sauté until lightly browned, 4-6 minutes. Sprinkle over flour and cook, stirring, until browned, 1-2 minutes. Return the venison to the casserole and stir in the marinade, salt and pepper – the meat should be completely covered. Cover with a lid and bring to the boil. Transfer to the preheated oven and cook, stirring occasionally, until meat is done, 2-3 hours. If the casserole gets dry during cooking, add a little water.

Transfer the venison to a platter and cover with foil to keep it warm. Strain the cooking juices into a saucepan, pressing down on the vegetables to extract all the liquid. Skim off any fat and boil, stirring often, to reduce and concentrate the flavour, 5-10 minutes – the sauce should be thick enough to coat the back of a spoon. Stir in the cream and bring just back to the boil. Taste and adjust the seasoning. Discard the trussing strings from the venison, cut it into slices, moisten them with some sauce and serve the remaining sauce separately.

Veal chops with lemon and roasted red pepper relish

SERVES 4

The simpler the recipe, the more important are the quality and freshness of the ingredients, so prime veal chops will be highlighted here. The red pepper relish smooths and mellows if it is made ahead and reheated when pan-frying the chops.

4 veal chops, cut 2 cm/¾ inch thick (about 250 g/½ pound each)	for the red pepper relish
1 lemon	3 red sweet peppers
75 ml/2½ fl oz olive oil	2 tablespoons olive oil
4 tablespoons water	2 onions, thinly sliced
2 tablespoons chopped parsley	2 garlic cloves, finely chopped
salt and pepper	15 g/½ oz chopped mixed herbs (basil, oregano, marjoram, parsley, thyme)
	sugar to taste

Grate the zest from the lemon and squeeze the juice. Combine all but 2 tablespoons of the olive oil, the lemon juice, salt and pepper in a non-metallic bowl. Lay the chops in a deep tray and pour over the olive oil mixture. Cover and leave to marinate in the refrigerator for 2 hours, turning occasionally.

Meanwhile, make the red pepper relish: preheat the grill. Roast the peppers under the grill, turning them for 7-10 minutes or until the skin chars and bursts. Put them in a plastic bag or cover them with wet paper towels to loosen the skin, and leave to cool. Peel the peppers, discard the cores and seeds, and cut the flesh into 1-cm/⅜-inch strips. Heat the oil in a frying pan. Stir in the onion and garlic and sauté until soft but not browned, 3-4 minutes. Add the pepper strips, herbs, salt, pepper and a pinch of sugar. Sauté until heated through and the flavours are blended, 2-3 minutes. Taste and adjust the seasoning. Set aside and keep warm.

Drain the chops, reserving the marinade. Heat the remaining olive oil in a large frying pan, add the chops and fry over fairly high heat until browned, then turn and brown the other sides – allow 4 minutes per side for lightly cooked meat, or 5 minutes per side for well-done meat. Transfer the chops to a warmed platter and keep warm.

To make a *jus*: skim the fat from the pan, then add the water and remaining marinade. Stir for 1-2 minutes over a low heat to dissolve the pan juices. Take the pan from the heat and stir in the lemon zest and chopped parsley. Taste the sauce and adjust the seasoning, if necessary. Spoon it over the chops and serve with the red pepper relish.

Pork chops, spare ribs and ham steaks

Baked, braised, grilled, pan-fried, roasted, sautéed

I WAS BROUGHT UP IN YORKSHIRE, PORK COUNTRY. On the main street of our local town, for every two butchers specializing in pork there was only one for beef and lamb. So I am a firm believer in a plump juicy pork chop, moistened with a splash of wine and a generous serving of fried onions on the side.

The pork we eat today is considerably leaner than even 10 years ago. Less fat means less protection in cooking, so it's no surprise that chops and other lean cuts like medallions or fillet slices are often best braised or stewed, perhaps with raisins and marsala as in Italy, or Scandinavian-style with red berries pickled in vinegar. I like my pork thoroughly cooked, while recognizing that the meat should remain tender and full of its natural juices. However, lighter cooking is quite acceptable.

In any case, pork does well on the bone, one reason why spare ribs are so popular, and so delicious. Spare ribs call for creative basting sauces such as spicy Classic Barbecue Sauce (opposite), or an Oriental mix of soy sauce, brown sugar and rice wine, or the green chilli braising sauce with courgette and chayote to be found in Mexico. Many of the same combinations are also good with a thick ham steak, as fruity and spicy flavours complement the salty cure. Much depends on the ham and if it is strongly cured, you may want to soak it in cold water to leach out some salt before cooking.

UNDERCOOKED – surface lightly browned and meat clings to bone; when cut with a knife, meat is very pink; beads of juice on surface are pink; meat is firm at sides, spongy in centre when pressed with a fingertip (Thumb test, second-finger stage, see page 78). Note: cooking pork to an internal temperature of 70-75°C/160-170°F destroys any possible parasites that cause trichinosis, though the risk of contamination is very low.
Why: cooking time too short; temperature too low.
What to do: continue cooking, raising heat if necessary.

PERFECT – surface browned (especially pork) and meat (here, pork chops) starting to pull from bone; when cut with a knife, meat is juicy; beads of juice on surface are very light pink when medium-cooked or clear for well-done; for medium-cooked, meat is firm at sides and centre resists when pressed with a fingertip (Thumb test, third-finger stage, see page 78); when well-done, meat is firm at sides and centre when pressed with a fingertip (fourth-finger stage).

OTHER CUTS

for baking, braising, grilling, pan-frying, roasting, sautéing are medallions, back ribs, fillet slices

Grilled pork chops with classic barbecue sauce

SERVES 4

Constant basting with this lively sauce ensures moist chops and plenty of flavour. Warm Potato Salad with Tarragon and White Wine (page 167) is the natural accompaniment.

4 pork loin chops
    (about 250 g/½ pound
    each), cut 2.5 cm/1 inch
    thick
salt and pepper

for the classic barbecue
sauce
2 tablespoons vegetable oil
1 onion, finely chopped
1 garlic clove, finely
    chopped

1 lemon
100 g/3¼ oz brown sugar
60 ml/2 fl oz vinegar
125 ml/4 fl oz tomato
    ketchup
1 tablespoon
    Worcestershire sauce
½ teaspoon Tabasco sauce,
    or to taste
¼ teaspoon chilli powder,
    or to taste

Make the barbecue sauce: heat the oil in a frying pan and sauté the onion and garlic until soft and lightly browned, 4-5 minutes. Grate the zest from the lemon and squeeze the juice. Add the lemon zest, half the lemon juice, the sugar, vinegar, ketchup, Worcestershire sauce, Tabasco sauce and chilli powder to the onion and simmer gently, 5 minutes. Taste, adjust the seasoning and let cool.

Preheat the grill or light the barbecue. Season the pork chops with salt and pepper and brush with the cooled barbecue sauce. Grill them, basting often, 5-7 minutes. Turn over and continue grilling and basting until the chops are done, 5-7 minutes longer.

OTHER PROBLEMS

DRY AND OVERCOOKED
Why: cooked too long; temperature too high; meat cut too thinly.
What to do: moisten with plenty of pan gravy, apple chutney or a ginger beetroot sauce.

TOUGH
Why: wrong cut for cooking method; inferior meat; meat poorly handled when stored or frozen; temperature too high; overcooked.
What to do: add accompaniments such as sauerkraut, plus potato purée flavoured with bacon and dripping or olive oil and sage.

TASTELESS
Why: meat was bland; meat poorly handled when stored or frozen; lack of seasoning; overcooked.
What to do: serve in a piquant or devil sauce; or take the sweet-and-sour route of pickles and a fruit chutney such as cranberry, apricot or mango.

HAM TOO SALTY
Why: salty cure; overcooked.
What to do: to balance salt, serve with a fruit sauce such as plum or apple; if very salty, use ham in soup, or to flavour pasta, rice or potatoes.

QUICK FIX

For dry or salty cooked ham make this paprika sauce: melt 15 g/½ oz butter in a large frying pan and sauté 1 sliced onion until soft. Add 1 tablespoon paprika and cook gently, stirring constantly, 1 minute. Add 2-3 tablespoons vodka and flame. Stir in 250 ml/8 fl oz double cream and bring to the boil. Add ham and heat gently until hot, basting well. Taste for seasoning. Serves 4.

Meat stews

A GOOD STEW DISPLAYS ITS CHARACTERISTICS WITH EXUBERANCE. Flavours are intense, the result not just of good seasoning but also of long simmering and reduction of the cooking liquid to a vivid sauce. If the meat is first to be browned as in *boeuf bourguignonne*, do so thoroughly, then add the toughest vegetables first so that everything finishes cooking at the same time; be sure to use herbs and spices generously. Let's face it, what makes a stew special is not the meat itself, but the way all the other ingredients have been blended into a perfect sauce. A stew provides a chance to use all of those odd pieces – ribs, breast, flank, shank – which old-fashioned cooks managed so well. More orthodox cuts which are also good for stewing are listed on the right. If meat is on the bone, as with ribs, veal shank or neck, flavour is all the more intense.

When choosing meat for a stew don't be put off by sinew, nor by a bit of fat. Well-marbled beef or lamb will be all the more tasty and tender, and exterior fat can be trimmed off to your taste. Sinew dissolves after lengthy cooking, turning meltingly tender and adding rich gelatine to the sauce. Whenever you can, I would advise marinating meat for stew, whether by way of a lengthy soak in a wine marinade, or simply a quick seasoning of the meat with dry spices such as allspice, nutmeg, coriander or paprika.

TYPICAL CUTS

for stewing
Beef: chuck, short ribs, skirt, top round
Veal: neck, rump, short ribs, shoulder, top round
Lamb: breast, neck, riblets, shoulder
Pork: hocks, neck, ribs

QUICK FIX

When sauce for a meat stew lacks body or colour, stir in 2-3 teaspoons tomato purée.

TOUGH AND UNDERCOOKED – meat pieces resist when pinched between finger and thumb and cling to a two-pronged fork; sauce is thin, lacking flavour.
Why: cooking time too short; meat fresh not aged (especially beef); old animal (especially game); not milk-fed (veal); poorly handled when stored or frozen; cooked too fast.
What to do: continue simmering until tender; for serving suggestions, see Overcooked.

PERFECT – when pinched between finger and thumb, meat crushes with little resistance; meat pieces are tender and fall easily when pierced with a two-pronged fork; meat is well-browned (for beef, lamb and game), or lightly browned or white (for pork and veal); sauce is rich, glossy and aromatic.

OVERCOOKED – pieces are soft, starting to fall apart; sauce is muddy, with fat separated on surface.
Why: cooked too long; cooked too fast; pieces cut too small.
What to do: serve with lively accompaniments such as herbed rice pilaf, cornbread or freshly baked focaccia topped with thyme or sage; if very overcooked, shred meat and stir back into sauce to serve tossed with pasta or over rice.

OTHER PROBLEMS

LACKS TASTE
Why: meat was bland; poorly handled when stored or frozen; insufficient seasoning; sauce too thin; overcooked.
What to do: if sauce is thin, lift out meat when cooked and simmer sauce until well-flavoured and thickened; season sauce well, adding lemon juice, vinegar, chopped anchovy or an alcohol such as Cognac or whisky to sharpen flavour, with chopped herbs, grated citrus zest, dark sesame oil for perfume, and nutmeg, dried hot red pepper, soy sauce or a fortified wine such as Madeira or port for depth of flavour.

SAUCE SEPARATED
Why: overcooked; too much liquid evaporated.
What to do: add more stock, or water if flavour is already concentrated, then whisk to re-emulsify sauce.

Spicy lamb stew with almond and coconut
Badami roghan josh
SERVES 3-4

This dark sauce from northern India goes equally well with lamb or beef. Serve the stew with rice pilaf or Indian Wholewheat Flat Bread (page 269).

1 kg/2 pounds boned shoulder of lamb,
    cut into 2.5-cm/1-inch pieces
salt and pepper
75 ml/2½ fl oz vegetable oil
1 teaspoon whole cloves
2 small dried red chilli peppers
1 teaspoon whole peppercorns
2 onions, finely chopped

for the almond and coconut sauce
60 g/2 oz blanched flaked almonds

2 teaspoons ground cumin
1 tablespoon ground coriander
2 tablespoons unsweetened grated coconut
4 garlic cloves, cut into pieces
2.5-cm/1-inch piece of fresh ginger, chopped
1 teaspoon ground allspice
125 ml/4 fl oz brown beef or veal stock, plus
    more if needed
1 tablespoon tomato paste
75 ml/2½ fl oz plain yogurt

Trim the lamb of most of the fat. Season the pieces with salt and pepper. Heat the oil in a flameproof casserole, add the cloves, chilli peppers and peppercorns, and heat gently, stirring until the spices are fragrant and infuse the oil, 3-5 minutes. Using a slotted spoon, transfer the spices to a food processor. Increase the heat to high, add the lamb to the casserole in 2-3 batches and brown well on all sides. Remove the lamb to a plate, add the onions to the casserole and sauté until well browned, stirring occasionally, 5-7 minutes.

Meanwhile, make the almond and coconut sauce: chop half the almonds, reserving the rest. Heat a heavy frying pan over a low heat for 3-5 minutes. Add the cumin, coriander, coconut and chopped almonds and roast, stirring, until the spices are fragrant and the nuts are golden, 5-7 minutes. Add the roasted spices and nuts to those in food processor together with the garlic, ginger, allspice and stock. Process until smooth.

Stir the sauce and tomato paste into the browned onions in the casserole and simmer, stirring to dissolve pan juices, 5 minutes. Stir in the yogurt. Return the meat to the casserole, bring to the boil, cover and simmer, stirring occasionally, until done, 1-1¼ hours. If the casserole gets dry, add more stock.
Note: the yogurt will separate but this is intentional here.

When the lamb is done, taste the sauce and adjust the seasoning. Transfer the stew to a warmed serving bowl or serve directly from the casserole, sprinkled with the reserved almonds.

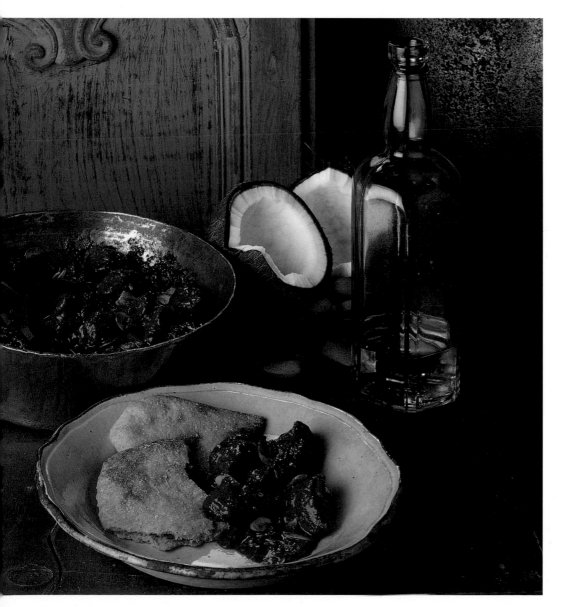

Minced meats

Baked, grilled, pan-fried, roasted, sautéed, simmered, stewed

MINCED MEAT DISHES FROM OTHER COUNTRIES somehow seem so much more tempting than one's own. I would always pick Lebanese *kibbeh* of minced lamb with bulghur, nuts, yogurt and parsley, or Scandinavian *frikadeller* (right) in preference to British shepherd's pie of minced lamb topped with mashed potato. Yet gourmet versions of shepherd's pie are now popular the world over. Perhaps the minced meat recipe with the most universal appeal is hamburger. Let's look at what constitutes a good one.

First of all, the meat must be freshly prepared: minced meat starts to deteriorate within 12 hours even when tightly wrapped in the refrigerator. The justification for mincing meat is to render tough pieces palatable, so a relatively inexpensive cut is fine provided it has no sinew and little fat. If possible, mince the meat yourself in a traditional mincer – note that a food processor pounds rather than cuts fibres and will make the meat heavy. For lightness when mixing in seasonings, work the meat using a wooden spoon, and if you like add some breadcrumbs soaked in milk or water.

Hamburger and meatball mixtures should always be seasoned with salt, pepper and herbs or spices. For a taste test, fry a small ball of mixture and adjust the seasoning before cooking the rest. Even after seasoning, the ultimate flavour of minced beef, lamb or veal depends very much on how it has been cooked. Burgers and patties rely on high heat to produce a crisp brown surface, whereas meat sauces such as bolognese must be cooked slowly from the start if the consistency is to be smooth and the flavour rich.

Don't forget sausages. Around the world, more minced meat, particularly pork, must be consumed in sausage casings than any other way. American country sausage of pork, veal and herbs, Spanish smoked pork *chorizo* flavoured with red pepper, German veal *weisswurst* with parsley and cream, Canadian venison sausage and the British pork and sage 'banger' are just a few. Like hamburger, a good sausage calls for top-quality meat, gentle handling and intense seasoning.

TYPICAL CUTS
for minced meat
Beef: chuck, flank, neck, round
Veal: breast, round, shoulder
Pork: shank, shoulder, sirloin
Lamb: breast, shank, shoulder

QUICK FIX

For overcooked or bland minced meat, make up a quick tomato salsa. Cut 500 g/ 1 pound fresh plum tomatoes in halves, squeeze to remove seeds and chop the halves. Then mix with 2-3 tablespoons red wine vinegar, 2 chopped garlic cloves, salt, pepper and lots and lots of chopped mint. Serves 4.

PERFECT LIGHTLY COOKED *for beef, lamb, game and veal (please see the note on E. coli 0157 on page 9)* – if dry-cooked, surface is crusty brown and beads of juices on surface are pink; if simmered or stewed, surface is brown and moist; when pressed, centre of patty or ball is spongy, edges are firm (Thumb test, second-finger stage, see page 78), centre slightly resistant; inside meat is juicy and full-flavoured, deep red to pale pink depending on type of meat.

PERFECT WELL-DONE *for beef, lamb, game, pork and veal –* if dry-cooked, surface is crusty, slightly charred, and beads of juice on surface are clear; if simmered or stewed, surface is well browned and moist; when pressed, both centre and edges of patty or ball are firm (Thumb test, fourth-finger stage, see page 78); inside meat is still well-flavoured and juicy with no trace of pink. Note: when well-done, beef and game can be very dry. However, pork should always be cooked thoroughly to destroy any possible parasites that cause trichinosis, though the risk of contamination is very low.

Scandinavian meat dumplings with mushroom sauce *Frikadeller*

SERVES 4-6

Frikadeller are often served as a main course with boiled potatoes and pickled beetroots, or you can add them to soup, cooking the dumplings in the broth.

375 g/¾ pound veal, minced	for the mushroom sauce
375 g/¾ pork, minced	75 g/2½ oz butter
2 slices of white bread	30 g/1 oz flour
250 ml/8 fl oz milk	375 g/¾ pound mushrooms, thinly sliced
1 small onion, grated	2 shallots, finely chopped
2 egg yolks	1 garlic clove, finely chopped
¼ teaspoon grated nutmeg	2 tablespoons chopped parsley
¼ teaspoon allspice	
salt and pepper	
1 litre/1⅔ pints veal or chicken stock	
125 ml/4 fl oz white wine	
125 ml/4 fl oz white wine or cider vinegar	

Pull the bread into pieces and soak it in the milk. In a bowl, combine the veal, pork, onion, egg yolks, nutmeg, allspice, salt and pepper, and beat with a wooden spoon to mix. Squeeze excess liquid from the soaked bread, pull it apart into crumbs and add to the meat mixture. Beat until smooth, adding a little milk if the mixture is dry.

Bring a small pan of water to the boil and poach 1 teaspoon of the seasoned mixture. Taste and adjust the seasoning of the remaining mixture, if necessary – it should be quite highly seasoned. Shape the mixture into walnut-sized meatballs.

Bring the stock, white wine and vinegar to the boil. Add half the meatballs and simmer until done, 8-10 minutes. With a draining spoon, transfer them to a baking dish, cover with foil and keep warm in a low oven. Simmer the remaining meatballs and drain. Boil the stock until reduced by half and set this aside for the sauce.

Make the mushroom sauce: in a small bowl, work half the butter with the flour to a paste with a fork to make kneaded butter; set it aside. Melt the remaining butter in a frying pan, add the mushrooms and sauté, stirring occasionally, until tender, 2-3 minutes. Add the shallots, garlic, salt and pepper and sauté until the mushrooms are browned and the shallots are tender, 1-2 minutes. Stir in the reserved reduced stock and simmer 5 minutes. Whisk the kneaded butter into the simmering sauce, a few pieces at a time, whisking constantly so the sauce thickens evenly. It should lightly coat the back of a spoon; if it is thin, continue simmering to reduce it.

Stir in the chopped parsley, taste the sauce and adjust the seasoning if necessary. Add the simmered meatballs to the hot sauce and heat gently so the flavours blend, 3-5 minutes. Taste the sauce again and adjust the seasoning again if necessary. Serve at once.

PROBLEMS

UNDERCOOKED

Why: patties or balls too large; cooking time too short; temperature too low.
What to do: continue cooking, raising heat if necessary.

OVERCOOKED AND DRY

Why: patties or balls too small; cooked too long; temperature too high.
What to do: serve beef with a piquant barbecue sauce or salsa (see Sauces), and the classic accompaniment of roasted corn and baked potato, or branch out with a spicy lentil dhal, a raita of cucumber and yogurt and warm pitta bread, especially for lamb.

CHEWY

Why: meat contained sinew and fat; wrong cut for cooking method; old animal (especially game); poorly handled when stored or frozen.
What to do: little can be done but add creative accompaniments, see Overcooked and dry.

FATTY

Why: meat had too much fat; wrong cut for cooking method.
What to do: serve with mustard, pickles, or a julienne of celeriac tossed in lemon juice; rice or pasta helps balance an excess of fat.

HEAVY

Why: fatty meat; meat puréed in food processor; meat mixture overworked.
What to do: serve with a crisp relish of corn kernels and celery, or with roasted baby onions in fruit vinegar, a tart berry chutney or sweet pickles.

LACKS TASTE

Why: bland meat; meat not freshly ground; insufficient seasoning; overcooked.
What to do: highly season any cooking liquid or sauce; for serving suggestions, see Overcooked and dry.

DISINTEGRATES

Why: mixture too dry; cooked too fast; stuck to rack or pan; overcooked.
What to do: break up meat as finely as possible and stir into sauce for pasta or rice.

Meat terrines

DON'T THINK OF TERRINES AS MERELY A FANCY FRENCH AFFAIR; plain meat loaves and homely meat puddings belong to the same family. All are a wonderful way to dress up various minced meats. Pork, including pork liver, is the top choice for richness, with beef and game runners-up for flavour; veal or chicken add delicacy, but can be dry. Only lamb is off limits as in a terrine it tends to taste unpleasantly strong.

You cannot go far wrong if you take your flavouring ideas for meat terrines from sausages, using aromatic herbs like thyme, sage and bay leaf, even a bit of chilli in moderation. You may want to add colourful blanched pistachios, cooked black wild mushrooms, chopped dried fruits, diced ham or tongue, all of which add colour and texture to the cooked mixture. Strips of meat such as liver, veal or poultry breast, with pork fat for richness, are other options, adding a pleasing mosaic when sliced. Uncooked strips of meat should first be sautéed so they do not shrink and break up the terrine as it cooks.

The basic seasoning formula for a good terrine is 1 tablespoon of salt and ¾ teaspoon of ground black pepper per 1 kg/2 pounds of meat. Chefs often add ground allspice and perhaps cloves, coriander or nutmeg, as well as a few spoonfuls of Cognac to improve flavour and extend storage time. To check that seasoning is adequate, fry a small ball of mixture and taste it – it should be quite spicy as flavours mellow after the terrine or loaf is cooked.

Careful cooking of a terrine or meat loaf is as important as the quality of the mixture itself. To help the heat spread evenly, use a heavy mould and oil it or line it with barding fat or bacon to keep the contents moist. Delicate terrines are sealed with a flour-and-water paste and then baked in the oven in a water bath (the water must be brought to the boil on the hob first so cooking time can be estimated accurately). To make a terrine easier to slice, press it with a weight as it cools – a brick is ideal. More robust puddings and loaves can be baked uncovered so they form a crisp brown crust; they do not need pressing.

OTHER PROBLEMS

CHEWY TEXTURE
Why: tough meat; meat poorly handled when stored or frozen; meat puréed in processor; meat too coarsely minced; terrine under- or overcooked; cooked too fast.
What to do: serve with country bread and crunchy ingredients such as pickled onions, dill pickles, walnuts or browned hazelnuts.

LACKS TASTE
Why: lack of seasoning; inferior or bland meats; not enough fat in mixture.
What to do: add garnishes such as cucumber pickle fans, black and green olives.

DULL COLOUR
Why: pallid meats; overcooked and juices lost.
What to do: serve colourful garnishes, such as radish and tomato roses, and watercress or alfalfa sprouts.

CRUMBLING TEXTURE
Why: mixture too coarse; lacks binder such as egg; mixture stuck to mould; overcooked; not well pressed while cooling.
What to do: cut with serrated knife using sawing motion; for distracting garnishes, see Dry and overcooked.

UNDERCOOKED – mixture is soft in centre when pressed; a skewer inserted in centre is cool or warm to the touch when withdrawn after 30 seconds; meat thermometer inserted in centre registers less than 75°C/170°F; juices pink; when cut, texture wet and flabby.
Why: cooking temperature too low; cooking time too short.
What to do: continue cooking, if necessary first bringing water bath to the boil.

PERFECT – mixture shrinks from sides of mould and is firm when pressed; a skewer inserted in centre is hot to the touch when withdrawn after 30 seconds; meat thermometer inserted in centre registers 75°C/170°F; juices run clear not pink; when cut, texture of terrine is firm and moist with rich full flavour. Note: after being removed from oven, terrines will continue cooking for 5-10 minutes from their own residual heat.

DRY AND OVERCOOKED – shrunken, surrounded by melted fat and juices; skewer inserted in centre is very hot when removed after 30 seconds; thermometer registers more than 75°C/170°F; when cut, terrine is dry, crumbling on outside.
Why: mould too thin; cooked too long or too fast so outside overdone before centre cooked; dryness can result from overweighting, so juices expelled.
What to do: serve with moist sauce, such as herbed mayonnaise.

Country terrine with hazelnuts
Pâté de campagne aux noisettes

Make this classic French terrine at least 3 days and up to a week ahead so the flavours have time to mellow and blend. Fat bacon can be substituted for barding fat.

250 g/½ pound lean pork, minced	pinch of ground cloves
250 g/½ pound fat pork, minced	pinch of grated nutmeg
250 g/½ pound veal, minced	2 eggs, beaten to mix
250 g/½ pound chicken livers, minced	2 tablespoons brandy
250 g/½ pound barding fat	1 teaspoon salt, more if needed
15 g/½ oz butter	¾ teaspoon pepper
1 onion, chopped	45 g/1½ oz hazelnuts, toasted and skinned
2 garlic cloves, finely chopped	1 bay leaf
¾ teaspoon ground allspice	sprig of thyme
	1.5-litre/2⅓ pint terrine mould

Line the bottom and sides of the mould with barding fat, reserving some of it for the top. Preheat the oven to 175°C/350°F/gas4. Half fill a roasting pan with water for a water bath.

Melt the butter in a pan and sauté the onion until soft but not brown. In a bowl, combine the onion, lean and fat pork, veal, chicken livers, garlic, spices, eggs, brandy, salt and pepper. Beat with a wooden spoon to mix flavourings thoroughly. Stir in the hazelnuts. Melt some butter in a pan and sauté a small piece of the mixture. Taste and adjust the seasoning of remaining mixture if necessary – it should be highly seasoned. Continue beating mixture until it holds together, pulling away from sides of bowl, 2-3 minutes.

Pack mixture into lined mould, smooth top and cover with remaining barding fat. Set the bay leaf and thyme on top. Cover terrine with lid, set in the water bath and bring water to the boil on the hob. Transfer to the preheated oven and bake until done, 1¼-1½ hours. If the water in the bath evaporates, add more.

When terrine is cooked, remove from bath and leave until tepid. Remove cover and set a 1-kg/2-pound weight on top so that the terrine is compressed and firm for slicing. Store weighted terrine in refrigerator.

Discard the bay leaf and thyme. Serve from the mould or turn it out and cut it in 1-cm/⅜-inch slices.

Meat terrine (here Country Terrine) *from left to right*
UNDERCOOKED – terrine is still pink in the centre, texture is wet and flabby.
PERFECT – texture is firm and moist with full rich flavour.
DRY AND OVERCOOKED – terrine is dry, crumbling on the outside with dense texture.

QUICK FIX

Garnish individual plates of a terrine that is dry or overcooked with a cornucopia of raw vegetables, such as radishes and carrot, celery and courgette, cut into sticks. If serving the terrine on a platter, arrange slices overlapping to mask damage and surround them with piles or bouquets of raw vegetables. Add a variety of olives, marinated peppers, artichoke hearts or okra, if you like, and don't forget your favourite mustard.

EGGS

REMEMBER ONE SIMPLE FACT ABOUT COOKING EGGS – they coagulate rapidly at relatively low temperatures, 63°C/145°F for whites and 66°C/150°F for yolks. This is why it is so important to cook them at moderate, rather than high, temperatures. If you look at the various cooking methods, eggs are invariably shielded from direct heat, either by the shell, by a heavy dish or pan, or by cooking in water or a water bath. The high heat needed for a folded omelette is an exception, but even then a thick pan is mandatory.

The egg itself provides a variety of shapes and textures, not to mention eye-catching colour. Its flavour is an ideal background for other more robust ingredients, like bacon, spinach, truffles or cheese – in small quantities of course. Whatever the flavouring, a careful hand is needed, for it's all too easy to overwhelm the delicate aroma of a freshly laid egg with chilli or soy sauce, even with too much salt and pepper. It is hard to beat simple dishes like scrambled eggs with fresh herbs, or a baked egg seasoned with salt and pepper and topped with a spoonful of cream.

We are all warned not to eat too many eggs and, as it happens, a proper serving is difficult to gauge. While a single soft-boiled egg is surprisingly satisfying, a two-egg omelette or portion of scrambled eggs can seem sadly deficient. On the other hand, a more modest serving of one poached or baked egg does well as a first course, providing a generous garnish is included.

Remember that cooked eggs cannot sit for long. A soufflé is the classic example of a dish we must wait for, rather than it wait for us. Omelettes, baked and fried eggs, even a lightly boiled egg, are all the better for serving promptly. Then their simple freshness can be appreciated to the full.

As many of the preparations and recipes in this chapter contain raw or lightly cooked eggs, please read the note about salmonella on page 9.

Hard-boiled eggs with garlic and
herb topping, page 95

Boiled eggs

SURELY WE ARE ALL FAMILIAR FROM CHILDHOOD WITH BOILED EGGS, preferably served with 'soldiers' of buttered toast cut into sticks for dipping. It's reassuring that there are so many recipes for grown-ups, too – standbys like stuffed devilled eggs, French *oeufs mayonnaise* and Scotch eggs wrapped in sausagemeat and deep-fried. In Italy, boiled eggs are served on *crostini* in a tempting tarragon sauce.

You'd think boiling an egg would be a walk-over, but there are snares even to this simple process. Very fresh eggs take a minute or two longer to cook, as do extra-large ones. Shells crack all too easily during cooking, particularly those from battery hens, so start cooking in cold water so the egg heats slowly, and time from the moment the water comes to the boil. Allow 3-4 minutes for a soft-boiled egg, 5-7 minutes for *mollet* (resembling a poached egg, with a firm white and moist yolk) and 10-12 minutes for a classic hard-boiled egg.

Boiling is, in fact, a misnomer as eggs should be simmered, both to keep the shells intact and so as not to toughen the whites. To seal any egg white which does start to leak from the shell, it helps to add a spoonful of vinegar or salt to the water. As an egg ages, an air pocket forms at the end of the shell. It is the expansion of this air when the egg is heated that often causes the shell to crack, so some cooks like to prick the flat end of the egg to let air escape. There's even a small gadget for the purpose. Note: it is not a good idea to store hard-boiled eggs in the refrigerator, whether peeled or unpeeled, as the cold will make the whites tough.

PERFECT SOFT – yolk is soft and runny, white lightly set or firm depending on your taste.

PERFECT MOLLET *top* – yolk is soft but not runny and vivid in colour, white is set; shell can be peeled with care. Often served in a sauce or aspic, like a poached egg.
PERFECT HARD-BOILED *centre* – both yolk and white are firmly set; yolk is slightly pale in colour; shell is easy to peel. Used for slicing, stuffing and serving hot in sauce or cold with mayonnaise.
OVERCOOKED *bottom* – yolk is decidedly pale in colour and a greenish-grey line encircles it; white is tough and egg smells and tastes slightly of sulphur.
Why: boiling time too long; eggs very small, so timing off.
What to do: for *mollet* and hard-boiled eggs, stop cooking at once by plunging in cold water; if very overcooked, shred whites so toughness is less obvious and sieve yolks to make fluffy yellow mimosa.

OTHER PROBLEMS

UNDERCOOKED
Why: boiling time too short; eggs extra-large; eggs very fresh.
What to do: if first egg peeled is undercooked, continue simmering the rest.

TASTES OF SULPHUR
Why: eggs overcooked; eggs very stale.
What to do: disguise with strong flavour, like anchovy or olive.

SHELL CRACKS DURING BOILING
Why: eggs transferred to hot water from very cold refrigerator; thin or faulty eggshells.
What to do: after peeling, shred eggs, discarding moist parts.

COOKED EGGS HARD TO PEEL
Why: eggs very fresh and skin clings to cooked white.
What to do: peel eggs under cold running water.

Poached eggs

POACHED EGGS CAN BE TRICKY, BUT THERE'S NO DENYING THEIR VERSATILITY. They bolster a bowl of soup or add body to a salad such as *salade lyonnaise* (overleaf). Plain poached egg on toast is a breakfast dish; in Greece, poached eggs come in yogurt sauce; while when combined with diced bacon, mushrooms and a light red wine sauce, poached eggs are transformed into *oeufs pochés en meurette*, one of the great classics of Burgundian cuisine.

Success in poaching depends almost entirely on the freshness of the eggs. Really fresh eggs work best, as the white is less likely to break away from the yolk once the egg is added to the boiling water. Adding 3 tablespoons of vinegar or 1 tablespoon of salt to each 1 litre/1⅔ pints of water helps prevent this from happening. Always drop each egg (four is the usual maximum) into a briskly bubbling patch of boiling water so the egg white is swirled around the yolk. Then lower the heat until the water scarcely bubbles, so the eggs cook gently without breaking. This is what poaching means.

Of course, you can also poach an egg in one of those special moulds, but that's cheating. The egg loses its natural freeform shape, and is baked rather than poached directly in contact with the water.

PERFECT – yolk is still soft when gently prodded with fingertip; white is lightly set and clings to yolk; skin around yolk is opaque, with soft yolk inside.

WHITE FORMS STRINGS – white no longer clings to yolk and may almost separate from it.
Why: egg not fresh; egg not dropped into briskly bubbling patch of water.
What to do: trim strings and, if possible, wrap white around yolk. Conceal egg with a white, velouté or hollandaise sauce to serve hot, or top with mayonnaise or salsa to serve cold (see Sauces).

QUICK FIX

For poached eggs which are overcooked or with untidy whites: for each egg, blanch a large lettuce leaf in boiling salted water for 20-30 seconds. Remove, refresh under cold running water and pat dry with paper towels. Wrap a leaf around each egg. Serve plain or with whatever sauce was intended.

OTHER PROBLEMS

TOO SOFT – when gently prodded, white is very soft and still partly transparent; skin on yolk has not yet whitened to be opaque.
Why: eggs very fresh; cooking time too short.
What to do: return egg to water and continue poaching.

WHITE IS TOUGH, YOLK IS FIRM
Why: overcooked (common when poached egg is reheated in sauce).
What to do: serve with plenty of sauce. Note: though overcooked, the egg still tastes good.

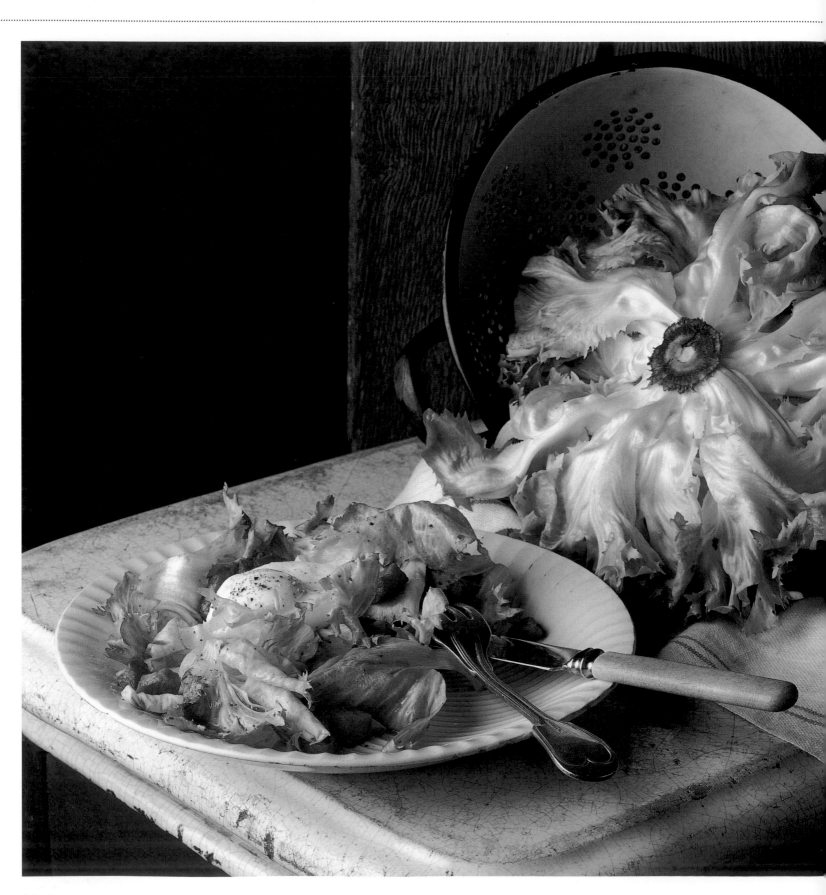

Salad with hot bacon dressing
Salade lyonnaise

SERVES 4 as an appetizer or 2 as a main course

This salad of chewy winter greens wilted with hot bacon and topped with a poached egg is a favourite in the bistros of Lyons.

750 g/1½ pounds curly endive or escarole	for the hot bacon dressing
4 eggs	1 tablespoon oil
2 tablespoons vinegar	175 g/6 oz thickly sliced lean smoked bacon, diced
	2 garlic cloves, thinly sliced
	75 ml/2½ fl oz red wine vinegar
	freshly ground black pepper

Discard any tough outer green leaves from the curly endive or escarole and pull apart the central white leaves. Wash them, dry well and put in a salad bowl.

Poach the eggs: fill a large shallow pan two-thirds full of water, add the vinegar and bring to the boil. Break the eggs one at a time into a patch of bubbling water. Regulate the heat so the water barely simmers and poach the eggs until done, 3-4 minutes. Note: it's important the yolks remain soft so they act as a dressing on the salad leaves. With a slotted spoon, transfer the eggs to a bowl of hot water to keep warm.

Heat the oil in a frying pan, add the bacon and fry, stirring often. When the bacon is well browned and the fat is rendered, lower the heat and add the garlic slices. Cook until the garlic is soft and fragrant but not browned, about 30 seconds. Discard some fat if you have more than 3-4 tablespoons. Pour the hot fat, bacon and garlic over the greens and toss thoroughly so they wilt slightly.

Return the pan to the heat, add the vinegar and boil for a few seconds until reduced by half, stirring to dissolve pan juices. Pour over the salad and toss again. Add pepper to taste and spoon the salad on to 4 warmed individual plates or into bowls.

Drain the eggs on paper towels, set them on top of the salad and serve at once.

Salad with hot bacon dressing

Hard-boiled eggs with garlic and herb topping

SERVES 6   *pictured on pages 90-91*

Serve a tomato and fresh basil salad with this simple little recipe from the Italian island of Sardinia.

6 eggs	3 tablespoons dry breadcrumbs
salt	2 teaspoons finely chopped parsley
60 ml/2 fl oz olive oil	
4 teaspoons red wine vinegar	
1 garlic clove, finely chopped	

Put the eggs in a medium pan, generously cover with cold water and add 2 teaspoons salt to help seal any egg white which may start to leak from the eggshells. Bring to the boil and simmer until hard-boiled, 10-12 minutes. Cool the eggs in cold water. Peel, rinse them under cold running water and dry them. Slice each egg in half lengthwise.

Heat the oil, vinegar and a large pinch of salt in a frying pan. Add the egg halves, cut side down, and cook over low heat until the vinegar has evaporated, 3-5 minutes. Turn the eggs once or twice during cooking. With a slotted spoon, transfer the eggs to a warmed platter, arranging them cut-sides up, and keep warm.

Add the garlic to the frying pan and sauté over low heat until soft, about 1 minute. Stir in the breadcrumbs and cook until golden, 1-2 minutes. Spoon the mixture over the eggs. Sprinkle with the parsley and serve warm.

Fried eggs

THE FLAVOUR OF FAT, BE IT BUTTER, OLIVE OIL OR LARD, comes through loud and clear when frying an egg. Allow about 1 tablespoon per egg, so you can baste and cook the upper surface with hot fat, and use a heavy pan to discourage scorching. Most eggs are fried on one side only, or 'sunny side up', but they can also be flipped 'over easy' to brown the other side. For a low-fat alternative, eggs can be cooked with a minimum of fat in a non-stick pan, but the result is more like a baked than a fried egg.

A fried egg somehow demands a meaty partner, a slice of bacon, or a juicy sausage perhaps. A fried egg is equally tempting 'on horseback', set on a hamburger, steak or veal escalope. When added to *croque monsieur*, a toasted ham and cheese sandwich, the dish changes gender to become *croque madame*. Personally I go for fried eggs with a forceful vegetable such as spinach or escarole sautéed with garlic. Others prefer Mexican spicy *huevos rancheros* (right), which has become a classic.

PERFECT — skin on yolk is slightly opaque with yolk inside soft; white is set, lightly browned underneath, and clings to form a ring around the yolk.

PROBLEMS

SOGGY, WHITE NOT SET
Why: undercooked; fried too slowly; too much fat (allow about 1 tablespoon per egg); too many eggs in pan.
What to do: if necessary, remove some fat; turn up heat and fry briskly so white sets and browns slightly.
OVERCOOKED WITH SCORCHED EDGES
Why: base of pan thin, so heat spreads unevenly; fat too hot when egg was added; fried too long.
What to do: see Quick Fix.
WHITE DETACHES FROM YOLK, RUNS ALL OVER PAN
Why: egg dropped carelessly into pan; stale egg.
What to do: break egg into a cup or saucer before sliding into pan.

QUICK FIX

For untidy or overcooked eggs, trim egg with a pastry cutter to neaten the white and remove scorched edges.

Fried eggs with tomato-chilli sauce *Huevos rancheros*

SERVES 4

The seeds and internal white ribs hold much of a chilli's heat. To control the spice of this tomato-chilli sauce, I generally discard both seeds and ribs, but if you have macho taste buds, you can include them.

4 corn or flour tortillas, 15 cm/6 inches across
75 ml/2½ fl oz vegetable oil
4 eggs
30 g/1 oz grated sharp Cheddar or Monterey Jack cheese
1 tablespoon chopped coriander

for the tomato-chilli sauce
½ small onion, cut into pieces
3-4 small fresh hot green chilli peppers, seeded and cut into pieces
2 garlic cloves, cut into pieces
750 g/1½ pounds tomatoes, peeled, seeded and cut into pieces
1 tablespoon vegetable oil
salt

Make the tomato-chilli sauce: put the onion, chillies and garlic in a food processor and work until quite finely chopped. Add the tomatoes and work to a coarse purée. Heat the oil in a medium frying pan. Add the tomato purée to the pan and simmer, stirring constantly until the sauce thickens enough to coat the back of a spoon, 8-10 minutes. Remove from the heat, taste and adjust seasoning with salt. Keep warm.

Meanwhile, heat a large heavy-based frying pan over high heat until very hot. Roast the tortillas in the dry pan one at a time until hot and starting to brown, 2-3 seconds on each side. Set them on 4 warmed plates.

Reduce the heat under the pan to medium. Add the oil and heat until a drop of water sizzles. Break 1 egg into a cup and slide it into the pan. Repeat with the remaining eggs and fry over medium heat, basting constantly until done, 2-3 minutes. Using a slotted spoon, set the eggs on the tortillas.

Reheat the sauce if necessary and spoon it over the eggs to cover the whites and tortillas. Sprinkle with cheese and coriander and serve at once.

Rolled omelette

THE KEY TO THE PERFECT OMELETTE IS THE PERFECT PAN. Every cook has their favourite. Personally I go for the classic French cast-steel omelette pan, with gently sloping sides and a handle at just the right angle to make turning out easy. Before use, the pan must be 'seasoned' – baked with a layer of salt and oil so it does not stick. To clean the pan after use, simply wipe it out with a damp paper towel; never wash it. A non-stick pan is another option, though I find it doesn't brown the eggs so well.

A few more omelette tips: for good flavour, be sure to brown the surface by cooking the omelette over high heat so the outside browns while the inside remains soft; with fillings that stick, such as grated cheese, fish or vegetable mixtures, begin cooking the eggs in the pan before adding the filling; use the right size pan – too few eggs in a large pan will thicken fast and toughen, while too many in a small pan will cook slowly rather like scrambled eggs.

A rolled omelette is a great home for a few spoonfuls of lively flavourings such as mixed herbs, ham, tomato or sautéed mushrooms. German *Königinomelett* is filled with creamed chicken and mushrooms, and Mexican *tortilla de huevo* includes tomato, avocado, onion and chilli. Remember, a filling is meant to highlight, not overwhelm the flavour of the eggs.

PALE AND UNDERCOOKED – surface of omelette not browned, so toasted flavour lacking.
Why: too many eggs for pan; not hot enough when eggs added; cooked too slowly; time too short.
What to do: if eggs still soft, turn up heat and quickly brown surface; if already set, nothing can be done.

PERFECT SOFT CENTRE – surface of omelette is lightly browned with tender texture, and centre of omelette is still slightly runny when folded over with a fork.

PERFECT FIRM – surface of omelette is evenly browned with no trace of scorching at any point; eggs are completely set throughout, with a firm but fluffy texture.

OTHER PROBLEMS

SCORCHED, TEXTURE TOUGH
Why: butter too hot when eggs added; omelette cooked too fast; pan too thin; pan too large for eggs; cooking time too long.
What to do: see Quick Fix.
LACKS TASTE
Why: eggs underseasoned; eggs stale.
What to do: sprinkle omelette with salt and pepper before folding; add a lively filling such as grated

cheese, crisp bacon dice, fried onions, ratatouille.
STUCK TO PAN
Why: seasoned pan scrubbed with water instead of simply wiping out to clean; butter not hot when eggs added.
What to do: loosen omelette from pan with a metal spatula and turn on to plate, adding leftover bits on top; sprinkle generously with chopped parsley or grated cheese.

QUICK FIX

For an omelette which is overcooked or sticks to the pan: leave omelette flat in the pan, moisten it with 2-3 tablespoons double cream and sprinkle with grated cheese. Grill until browned, 1-2 minutes. To serve, cut omelette in wedges like a cake.

Flat omelette

A FLAT OMELETTE IS ONE OF MY SUNDAY NIGHT SPECIALS, a hearty dish which adapts to all sorts of fresh and cooked ingredients. Unlike a rolled omelette, where eggs are the leading ingredient, in a flat omelette the eggs are there to bind the filling. Classic combinations include: Spanish *tortilla a la gallega* flavoured with pimento, potato and chorizo; Swedish *bondomelett* has onion, ham and potato, and in Italian *frittata alla romana* you'll find beans, onion and herbs. I use whatever happens to be on hand, be it smoked fish, cooked chicken or vegetables, backed up by sautéed onion, garlic and chilli, with ham, bacon, anchovy or olives for piquancy and celery, cooked greens or croutons for texture. Try to use colourful ingredients that add robust texture as well as flavour.

Most flat omelettes are browned on both sides to a firm cake, which can be cut into wedges for serving. Exceptions include English omelette Arnold Bennett, filled with smoked haddock then topped with Parmesan and browned under the grill. All these omelettes are cooked quite quickly, but Italian frittata is different, cooked over the lowest possible heat so the eggs puff in the pan rather like a soufflé. No matter what the nationality or style, however, what you're looking for in the perfect flat omelette remains the same.

PERFECT – firmly set, often glossy on top and brown on underside before being flipped over; when done, evenly browned on both sides; filling is generous, so egg acts as binder; flavour is robust, often with some crunchy or chewy texture. Note: if omelette is not holding firmly enough to flip, brown under the grill.

PROBLEMS

PALE AND FALLING APART
Why: cooking time too short; flavouring ingredients, particularly vegetables, too watery.
What to do: continue cooking omelette over high heat until firmly set and browned.

TEXTURE SOFT, LOOKS UNAPPETIZING
Why: lacking full-bodied, colourful ingredients.
What to do: be sure omelette is well browned on both sides; sprinkle with colourful crisp ingredients such as chopped spring onion, celery or sweet pepper.

SCORCHED, TEXTURE TOUGH
Why: butter too hot when eggs added; omelette cooked too fast; cooking time too long.
What to do: moisten warm omelette with vinaigrette dressing made with olive oil.

LACKS TASTE
Why: eggs or flavourings underseasoned.
What to do: sprinkle cooked omelette with salt, pepper and condiments such as Tabasco, soy sauce, lemon juice or dark sesame oil.

QUICK FIX

If a flat omelette is overcooked, falls apart or looks unattractive, use it as filling for a sandwich on baguette or pitta bread.

SOUFFLÉ OMELETTES

Soufflé omelettes are light, and light-hearted. Savoury ones are made by beating the eggs for 5 minutes or more until mousse-like and thick enough to hold a light ribbon trail. The omelette may be flat or folded, and fillings are usually simple, some herbs or a little grated cheese so the eggs keep their lightness. The legendary prototype was created by Mère Poulard (a pseudonym meaning 'Mrs Plump Chicken') at Mont St. Michel in Normandy. Her fluffy omelettes were whisked in the traditional copper bowl, then cooked in a long-handled pan over an open fire.

For sweet omelettes, the eggs are separated, the whites are beaten with a little sugar to make a light meringue and then folded back into the yolks. A sweet omelette may be cooked completely on the hob, using low heat – it will take up to 10 minutes – or first browned on the underside and then quickly baked in the oven. Either way, a filling of warm fruit jam is customary, then the omelette is folded, dusted with icing sugar and hurried to the table like a true soufflé (see page 104).

Both savoury and sweet soufflé omelettes are quickly made and quickly spoiled. They should remain slightly soft in the centre and if overcooked are rubbery and dry. They quickly deflate, too. A spoonful or two of cream counteracts dryness but texture cannot be revived.

Blue cheese and walnut omelette

SERVES 2-3

Any moist blue cheese works well in this omelette – choose strong or mild according to your taste.

5-6 eggs
45 g/1½ oz butter
1 small onion, chopped
salt and pepper
125 g/4 oz blue cheese, crumbled

30 g/1 oz walnuts, chopped
1 tablespoon double cream

23-cm/9-inch omelette pan

Melt one-third of the butter in a frying pan, add the onion, salt and pepper and sauté over moderate heat until soft but not brown, 3-4 minutes. Take the pan from the heat and stir in the cheese, walnuts and cream.

Whisk the eggs in a bowl with a little salt and pepper until slightly foamy. In the omelette pan, heat the remaining butter over fairly high heat until it stops sputtering and just starts to brown. Add the eggs and stir briskly with a fork, pulling the cooked egg from the sides of pan to the centre until the eggs start to thicken, 20-25 seconds. Stir in the blue cheese mixture and continue cooking, stirring constantly, until the egg is lightly set. Stop stirring and leave the omelette to brown underneath and cook until soft or firm according to your taste, 1-1½ minutes.

Tip the pan towards you and fold over one side of omelette. Roll and slide the omelette towards you on to a warmed platter. Serve at once.

Summer prawn omelette

SERVES 4

This colourful and tasty flat omelette makes a perfect summertime dinner. Enjoy it with a rocket salad and a glass of crisp dry white wine.

8 eggs
2 corn ears, husks removed
45 g/1½ oz butter, more if needed
1 large potato, diced
1 red pepper, cored, seeded and sliced
4 spring onions, sliced

salt and pepper
125 g/4 oz cooked peeled medium prawns
75 g/2½ oz cooked green peas

23-cm/9-inch omelette pan or frying pan

Bring a large pan of water to the boil, add the corn ears and cook until tender, 5-7 minutes. Drain and cut the kernels from the cob.

Melt half the butter in a frying pan, add the potato and sauté, stirring often, until browned, 10-15 minutes. Add the pepper, spring onions, salt and pepper and cook until the pepper is wilted, 2-3 minutes. Stir in the prawns, corn kernels and peas. Taste the mixture and adjust seasoning.

Whisk the eggs in a bowl with salt and pepper until slightly foamy. In the omelette pan or frying pan, heat the remaining butter over fairly high heat until it stops sputtering and just starts to brown. Add the eggs and stir briskly with a fork, pulling the cooked egg from the sides to the centre of pan, until the eggs start to thicken, 8-10 seconds. Stir in the prawn mixture. Continue cooking the omelette, stirring constantly, until the egg is lightly set, 1-1½ minutes. Stop stirring and leave until brown underneath and almost firm on top, 2-3 minutes.

Take the pan from the heat, set a heatproof plate on top of it and invert both together to turn out the omelette. Add more butter if the pan is dry. Slide the omelette back into the pan and brown the other side, 1-2 minutes. Slide the omelette on a warmed platter and serve at once.

Summer prawn omelette

Scrambled eggs

THE BEST SCRAMBLED EGGS ARE SMOOTH, creamy and lightly thickened or firm, depending on your taste. They really need very little flavouring – salt, pepper, a few chopped herbs or sautéed mushrooms are enough, though sometimes scrambled eggs are used to bind more complex mixtures such as the Basque dish *pipérade* of red and green sweet peppers, onion and tomato. Scrambled eggs are also the ideal foil for expensive ingredients like fresh truffle, caviar or smoked salmon. Serving them in a crisp container of puff pastry, or simply on a slice of toasted bread, offers a nice contrast of texture.

Some cooks like to control temperature by using a double boiler or water bath when scrambling eggs, but this really isn't necessary. I simply use a heavy pan over very low heat, stirring constantly with a wooden spoon and allowing at least 3 minutes to thicken 4 or more eggs. Don't be tempted to hurry the process, though there's no need to go to the lengths of purists who heat the eggs so slowly they take half an hour or more to thicken. No wonder chefs competing for the highest honour in French cuisine – that of *meilleur ouvrier de France* – are often put to the test with scrambled eggs!

PERFECT SOFT – eggs are creamy in texture and leave a trail when stirred; soft enough to pour, smooth and with light curds; colour varies with the egg yolks, so use deep orange yolks when you can.

PERFECT FIRM – eggs just hold a shape when stirred, with soft smooth curds; for best flavour, use very fresh eggs. Note: keep stirring scrambled eggs after taking them from the heat so they do not coagulate around the sides of the pan.

STIFF AND SEPARATED – curds are lumpy not smooth, often watery around edges.
Why: eggs insufficiently mixed before cooking so whites not fully blended; cooked too fast so eggs did not thicken smoothly; cooked too long; left in hot pan so cooking continued off the heat. Note: if cream, milk or water have been added, scrambled eggs separate more easily.
What to do: off the heat, stir in a raw egg which has been whisked until very smooth.

OTHER PROBLEMS

BLAND TASTE
Why: lack of seasoning; stale eggs.
What to do: add seasoning, particularly salt, pepper and a very little cayenne; enliven eggs with flavourings such as grated Parmesan cheese, chopped olives, anchovy, herbs, bacon or smoked salmon.

WATERY
Why: salt added to eggs more than 5 minutes before cooking; too much water, milk or cream mixed with eggs; too many moist flavourings added, such as fresh tomato.
What to do: serve in a pastry case, fried croûte, biscuit or other crisp container for contrast of texture.

QUICK FIX

For stiff, separated or watery scrambled eggs: for each serving portion, toast a slice of white bread or round of French bread. Cut 6-cm/2½-inch rounds from the warm toast and brush with melted butter or oil. With an ice cream scoop or two tablespoons, shape balls of scrambled egg and set on the toast rounds. Top with crossed slivers of pimento, smoked salmon or a slice of truffle.

Scrambled eggs with fresh herbs on tomato toasts

SERVES 4

No matter what kind of herbs you have available – chives, tarragon, chervil, even parsley – as long as they're fresh, they'll make all the difference in this simple dish.

8 eggs
2 tablespoons chopped mixed herbs, plus sprigs for garnish
30 g/1 oz butter

for the tomato toasts
2 large tomatoes
8 slices of French baguette or 4 slices of a larger French loaf, cut 1 cm/⅜ inch thick
2 tablespoons olive oil
salt and pepper

Make the tomato toasts: cut each tomato across into 4 slices, discarding the ends. For the French loaf, cut the slices in half. Preheat the oven to 175°C/350°F/gas4. Brush both sides of each slice of bread with olive oil, and lay the slices on a baking sheet. If using baguette, place them touching one another. Set a tomato slice on top of each bread slice, season lightly with salt and pepper and bake in the preheated oven until the bread is crisp and the tomato begins to soften, 12-15 minutes. Remove to a plate and keep warm. Crush the tomato slices with a fork to release the juices into the toast.

Whisk the eggs with salt and pepper until slightly frothy. Stir in the chopped herbs. Melt the butter in a heavy saucepan, copper if possible. Add the eggs and stir constantly with a wooden spoon over very low heat until cooked to your taste, at least 8-10 minutes. The more slowly the eggs cook, the better they will be. Note: they will continue to cook in the pan after it has been removed from heat.

Taste the eggs and adjust the seasoning. Spoon them over the tomato toasts, garnish with herb sprigs and serve at once.

Baked eggs

BAKED EGGS COME IN ONE OF TWO WAYS: *en cocotte* in deep ramekins for one or two eggs, or *au plat* in a shallow baking dish, looking more like fried eggs. Often the eggs are seasoned simply with salt and pepper – always sprinkled on the bottom of the dish to avoid spotting the surface of the egg – and topped with a spoonful of cream. You can add interest with a garnish spread in the dish, or spooned on top or around the eggs after baking. There are many possibilities: American baked eggs may come with oysters, Portuguese baked eggs are flavoured with salt cod and tomato, the French use wild mushrooms, tomato and parsley, the Spanish are fond of baking the yolk covered with beaten white, and you'll find baked eggs with cheese absolutely everywhere.

For a handy supper dish, I sometimes take leftover rice pilaf or risotto, or chopped cooked vegetables, and spread them in an oiled baking dish. I scoop hollows, drop in eggs and bake in a 175°C/350°F/gas4 oven until the eggs are set.

PERFECT – egg has a shiny 'mirror' surface, with yolk lightly thickened, white just set; surface opaque, not transparent.

HARD AND OVERCOOKED – yolk is firm, white is dry and starting to crack on the surface – more common when egg is baked in a flat dish rather than ramekins.
Why: cooked too fast; cooked too long.
What to do: to disguise dry surface, sprinkle eggs with paprika, chopped chives or grated cheese.

OTHER PROBLEMS

SPOTTED OR PITTED SURFACE
Why: egg sprinkled with dark seasoning such as pepper; egg white was sprinkled with salt, which pock-marked surface.
What to do: top each egg with a very thin slice of tomato and a herb sprig.
LACKING FLAVOUR
Why: underseasoned; eggs stale.
What to do: add seasoning and top with a garnish such as fried onions, sweet peppers, bacon, mushrooms or croutons.

QUICK FIX

To disguise overcooked eggs: moisten them with a spoonful of double cream or drizzle of melted butter or walnut oil and top with a sprig of basil, two crossed chive stems or a halved black olive.

Soufflé

A HOT SOUFFLÉ INVOLVES A VIRTUOSO PERFORMANCE, a bravura display of skill and I love it – both in the kitchen and on my plate. Assuming you're familiar with the underlying principle that a soufflé consists of a flavoured base puffed in the oven by whipped egg whites, here are a few signposts to success.

The taller the dish, the higher the soufflé will rise, but the more likely it is to spill over – hedge your bets with a shallower dish. When preparing the dish, brush it generously with melted butter, especially at the rim, then freeze and coat again. Much depends on correctly beating the egg whites (see page 223) and on the consistency of the basic mixture. If this mixture is too heavy or sticky, the egg whites cannot lighten it; if it is too thin, it will be difficult to fold in the egg whites. Vivid flavouring is important so that the basic mixture balances the inherent blandness of egg whites – think in terms of herbs, garlic, anchovy, mustard, and Tabasco, Worcestershire and soy sauces, with lemon juice, rum, kirsch and liqueurs for a sweet soufflé.

It is essential to fold egg whites into the basic soufflé mixture as gently as possible. It helps if you warm the mixture and stir about a quarter of the whites into it so they cook and lighten it. Then fold this mixture carefully into the remaining bulk of the egg whites – a metal spoon is my preferred tool for folding, though many chefs use a wooden spoon or rubber spatula. If the mixture seems to soften and lose air towards the end of folding, stop at once. A few bits of unmixed egg white are better than a flat soufflé.

Set the soufflé in the bottom third of the oven on a preheated baking sheet so the mixture gets a boost of bottom heat. Shield it from any convection fan and turn the dish during cooking so the mixture rises evenly. Note: a well-made soufflé will rise in almost any heat – the hotter the oven, the more quickly it bakes.

You may prefer a soufflé to be soft, so it forms a sauce for the firm sides. This is ideal for cheese and sweet soufflés and calls for baking at a relatively high heat, while heavier fish and vegetable soufflés are best done at a slightly lower temperature until firm in the centre. In any case, guests must wait for the soufflé, never the contrary; you can keep it warm in the oven with the door open for 2-3 minutes, but no more.

QUICK FIX

There is no quick fix for a fallen soufflé, the cook just has to brazen it out. Serve collapsed savoury soufflé with a green salad, if possible cutting the mixture into wedges like quiche Lorraine. Serve a fallen sweet soufflé like a pudding, topping it with whipped cream or ice cream.

PERFECT SOFT – soufflé (here, with cheese) browned and risen high, but top still slightly concave; mixture wobbles when dish lightly shaken; centre is runny; texture smooth and light, flavour delicate and aromatic.

PERFECT WELL-COOKED – soufflé browned and risen high with flat top; mixture is firm when dish is lightly shaken; inside, mixture is cooked through and just firm in the centre; texture is light and flavour definite.

Fish soufflé with curry sauce

SERVES 4

OTHER PROBLEMS

UNDER-RISEN AND WOBBLES WHEN SHAKEN

Why: not baked long enough.

What to do: continue baking – even if an underbaked soufflé has been taken from the oven for a few moments, it will often rise again if rebaked.

COARSE, RATHER DAMP TEXTURE

Why: egg whites overbeaten and coarse-textured before folding; basic mixture has chunks of moist ingredients such as onion; soufflé mixture not baked at once, so egg whites separated slightly.

What to do: serve savoury soufflés with a vegetable sauce or coulis, or sweet soufflés with a caramel or chocolate sauce or fruit coulis.

SOUFFLÉ HEAVY, ROSE POORLY

Why: too few egg whites (allow 3-4 egg whites per 250 ml/8 fl oz of basic mixture); basic mixture too heavy or sticky for egg whites to lighten; basic

mixture too thin, so egg whites were difficult to fold; egg whites overfolded so lost air; overbaked.

What to do: transform soufflé into a mousse, see Overbaked.

BLAND TASTE

Why: flavour of basic mixture was not sufficiently robust to balance bland egg whites.

What to do: serve savoury soufflés with a brisk sauce such as mustard or curry; baste sweet soufflés with a tablespoon or so of liqueur, opening hole in centre of soufflé with spoon.

SOUFFLÉ DEFLATES AFTER COOKING

Why: soufflé caught in a draught or was held too long before serving, so air in egg whites contracted.

What to do: if soufflé just starting to fall, reheat it 1-2 minutes in oven so it puffs again; if shrunk and cool, nothing can be done.

OVERBAKED – soufflé loses height and shrivels; inside texture is uneven and tough.

Why: baked too long.

What to do: pretend soufflé is a mousse: unmould it into a serving dish, spoon over a sauce and reheat in the oven. For savoury soufflés, use white or velouté sauce, or simply cream warmed with flavourings such as curry powder or grated cheese. For sweet soufflés, use cream flavoured with powdered instant coffee or chocolate.

ROSE UNEVENLY – one side of soufflé flat, often sticking to rim, other side rises and may spill over.

Why: dish unevenly buttered so soufflé mixture stuck to rim; heat of oven uneven, especially if door ill-fitting; egg whites poorly beaten.

What to do: if soufflé is not done and heat is uneven, turn dish and continue cooking; try to loosen crust with point of knife, wrap collar of buttered foil around dish and continue cooking, turning dish if heat uneven.

This soufflé is cooked for longer than usual, so it is fairly firm in the centre. You'll need a full-flavoured fish, such as cod, snapper or salmon, and the spicy curry sauce provides a delicious contrast.

300 g/10 oz cooked flaked fish
60 ml/2 fl oz double cream
pinch of dry mustard
4 egg yolks
6 egg whites

for the béchamel sauce
500 ml/16 fl oz milk
1 large slice onion
1 bay leaf
½ teaspoon black peppercorns
45 g/1½ oz butter

30 g/1 oz flour
salt and white pepper
generous pinch of nutmeg

for the curry sauce
30 g/1 oz butter
2 shallots, finely chopped
2-3 teaspoons curry powder
60 ml/2 fl oz double cream
125 ml/4 fl oz milk

1.25-litre/2-pint soufflé dish

Preheat the oven to 190°C/375°F/gas5. Butter the soufflé dish.

Make the béchamel sauce: scald the milk with the onion, bay leaf and peppercorns. Cover and leave to infuse off the heat, 10-15 minutes. In a heavy-based saucepan, melt the butter, whisk in the flour and cook, stirring, until the flour is foaming but not browned, about 1 minute. Off the heat, strain in the hot milk, whisk well, then bring to the boil, whisking constantly until the sauce thickens. Season to taste with salt, pepper and nutmeg and leave to simmer 1-2 minutes.

Pour half the béchamel sauce into a bowl and reserve. Beat the fish, cream and mustard into the remaining sauce, taste and adjust seasoning – the mixture should be highly seasoned. Heat the fish mixture until very hot, then take from the heat and beat in the egg yolks so they cook and thicken the mixture slightly.

In a copper bowl if possible (see page 223), beat the egg whites until stiff. Reheat the fish mixture until it is hot to the touch, add about one-quarter of the egg whites and stir until well mixed. Add this to remaining egg whites and fold together as gently as possible. Pour the mixture into prepared soufflé dish and smooth the top. Bake in the preheated oven until the soufflé is puffed and brown, 25-30 minutes.

Meanwhile, make the curry sauce: melt the butter in a saucepan, add the shallots and curry powder and cook gently, stirring occasionally, 3-4 minutes. Whisk in the reserved béchamel sauce, cream and milk, and bring to the boil. Taste and adjust the seasoning. Serve the soufflé as soon as it is ready, passing the curry sauce separately.

SAUCES

IT'S NO ACCIDENT THAT IN A PROFESSIONAL KITCHEN the sauce chef is at the top of the hierarchy. A sauce demands a skilled hand to balance taste and consistency just right – a mastery needed as much for contemporary butter sauces and salsas as for the grand classics like hollandaise and espagnole. This is also true at home – remember how grandmother was judged by her gravy? So important are basic sauces, such as white, velouté, brown, hollandaise, white butter and mayonnaise, that they are called 'mother sauces' with whole families of sauces descended from them.

Today we're fortunate to enjoy a much broader range of sauces than even a generation ago. Steak, for instance, may appear with a traditional Madeira or truffled brown sauce, with béarnaise, with a reduction sauce mounted with butter in the pan, with a gravy thickened with roasted garlic, or with a crispy salsa heightened with chilli and coriander. Duck may be paired with green peppercorns in place of orange, turkey with a spiced chocolate *mole* instead of cranberries, and sea bass with a *tapenade* of green olives instead of a white wine velouté.

When making a sauce, remember that it cannot exert its magic in limbo. By definition, its purpose is to complement and highlight the food which it accompanies. When tasting, don't judge a sauce on its own, like soup, but if possible pair it with the food it accompanies. This is particularly important for salad greens, which often lack intrinsic flavour. Consistency is also important. Do you want a sauce to be as thin as unthickened gravy, or lightly coat food, or mask it, or be thick enough to bind ingredients together? Judging the consistency of a sauce just right can make all the difference to a dish.

Lastly, consider the impact of a sauce. Whether delicate like egg custard, tart with a red fruit, or dark and pungent with a reduction of red wine, a sauce should have the same intensity as its companion ingredient.

As many of the preparations and recipes in this chapter contain raw or lightly cooked eggs, please read the note about salmonella on page 9.

White sauce

Where would we be without white sauce? If we followed the exhortations of some contemporary chefs to leave it behind, so many familiar dishes simply would not exist. We'd have no macaroni cheese, no moussaka or creamed spinach, we'd lose half our cannelloni and lasagne, and soufflés would scarcely rate a mention. White sauce is the basis of half a dozen key creations, such as cream, mushroom, onion and oyster sauces, not to mention the French herb-and-nutmeg-scented béchamel, and mornay or cheese sauce (page 110), most important of them all. Vigorous whisking is the key to smooth consistency and a glossy finish.

PERFECT THIN – shiny, very pale cream colour; lightly coats back of spoon but runs off quickly; flavour is light but not bland. At this consistency, white sauce is thin enough to be the base of a soup.

PERFECT MEDIUM – generously coats back of spoon but still flows easily; smooth and glossy; flavour is creamy and fragrant. Used for lightly coating eggs, fish, poultry, white meats and vegetables, particularly for gratins.

PERFECT THICK – glossy, unctuous and a rich cream colour; thick enough to bind a mixture, but still falls easily from the spoon; flavour is rich and full-bodied. Acts as a base for soufflés, stuffings and croquettes.

PERFECT BINDING (panade) – smooth and stiff enough to hold mark of spoon; flavour robust, with no trace of uncooked flour. Use to bind ingredients together, as in choux pastry, fritters and quenelles.

PROBLEMS

CONSISTENCY TOO THIN
Why: too little flour; sauce not fully cooked.
What to do: simmer, stirring often, until reduced to right consistency.

CONSISTENCY TOO THICK
Why: too much flour; simmered too long so milk evaporated.
What to do: thin by whisking in more milk.

LUMPS IN SAUCE
Why: cooked too fast; not whisked enough while thickening; not stirred while simmering, so caught on the pan; skin formed on surface when sauce cooled.
What to do: take at once from heat and whisk vigorously or use immersion blender to smooth lumps; if unsuccessful, work through a strainer; keep sauce covered while it cools.

TASTES OF FLOUR
Why: not fully cooked; too much flour.
What to do: continue simmering 3-5 minutes.

BROWN SPOTS IN SAUCE
Why: scorching due to overheating or lack of whisking. Note: black dots can be caused by seasoning with black (not white) pepper.
What to do: work through strainer into another pan, taking care not to scrape bottom of scorched pan. Note: if badly burned, sauce is unusable.

Gratin of leeks and ham

SERVES 6-8 as an appetizer, or 4 as a main course

When we lived in Paris, this gratin was a favourite supper dish, the complex flavours of the béchamel marrying plain leeks and ham to unexpected harmony. Braised chicory is an alternative to the leeks.

4 medium leeks
   (about 1.25 kg/2½ pounds)
8-10 thin slices of cooked ham
   (about 375 g/¾ pound)

for the béchamel sauce
500 ml/16 fl oz milk
1 large slice of onion

1 bay leaf
½ teaspoon peppercorns
45 g/1½ oz butter
3 tablespoons flour
salt and white pepper
generous pinch of nutmeg

Preheat the oven to 175°C/350°F/gas4 and butter a medium gratin dish. Bring a large pan of salted water to the boil. Trim the leeks, discarding the roots and tough tops. Slit the trimmed leeks lengthwise, leaving them attached at root end, and wash thoroughly under cold running water. Tie the leeks together with string so they hold their shape in cooking. Add the leeks to the boiling water and simmer, uncovered, until tender, 10-15 minutes depending on their size.

Meanwhile, make the béchamel sauce: scald the milk with the onion, bay leaf and peppercorns. Cover and leave to infuse off the heat for 10-15 minutes. In a heavy-based saucepan, melt the butter, whisk in the flour and cook, stirring, until the flour is foaming but not browned, about 1 minute. Off the heat, strain in the hot milk. Whisk well, then bring to the boil, whisking constantly until the sauce thickens. Season to taste with salt, pepper and nutmeg and leave to simmer 1-2 minutes. Take off the heat, cover and set aside.

Drain the leeks, rinse with cold water and drain again thoroughly, squeezing them in your fists to extract any water. Cut the leeks into 8-10 pieces about 10 cm/4 inches long. Strip off 2-3 outer green leaves from one of the leeks. Lay these flat, slice them lengthwise into julienne strips and set aside for garnish.

Roll each leek section in a slice of ham and pack tightly in the buttered gratin dish. Spoon béchamel sauce on top and bake in the preheated oven until bubbling, 20-25 minutes. If not browned on top, grill 2-3 minutes until golden. Sprinkle the leek julienne on top and serve at once.

WHITE SAUCE PROPORTIONS

Knowing standard proportions is very useful when making white sauce.
For 250 ml/8 fl oz sauce, you need:

Thin: 15 g/½ oz butter and 7 g/1 tablespoon flour
Medium: 20 g/¾ oz butter and 10 g/1½ tablespoons flour
Thick: 30 g/1 oz butter and 15 g/2 tablespoons flour
Binding: 45 g/1½ oz butter and 20 g/3 tablespoons flour

CRÈME FRAÎCHE

Crème fraîche, the thick, nutty-flavoured cream found in France, is quite easily recreated using double cream and cultured buttermilk. The cream should be high in butterfat and the buttermilk must be labelled 'active'. To ensure the high acidity needed for the culture, I also add lemon juice.

To make 1 litre/1⅔ pints: in a saucepan, stir together 750 ml/1¼ pints double cream, 250 ml/8 fl oz active buttermilk and the juice of 1 lemon until mixed. Warm, stirring, over low heat to about 30°C/85°F – just below body temperature. Use a thermometer, or test the temperature with the tip of your finger.

Half cover the cream and leave in a warm place at 21-27°C/70-80°F until it thickens and develops a slightly tart flavour, at least 12 and up to 24 hours. Timing depends on the buttermilk culture and temperature of the cream.

When it is thick enough to hold the mark of a spoon, cover the cream and store it in the refrigerator. Crème fraîche keeps well for a week or more in the refrigerator.

THICKENING AGENTS FOR SAUCES

Thickeners for sauces can be divided into two groups: those which are part of the sauce from the beginning, and those added at the end of cooking.
- A roux of flour and butter provides a stable robust base for white velouté and brown sauces. For brown sauces the roux should be well browned to add flavour before any liquid is added.
- Beurre manié or kneaded butter is a version of a roux made by working butter and flour together, designed for addition in small pieces at the end of cooking.
- Fruit and vegetable purées also add a full-bodied flavour, and those of colourful vegetables like carrots and fruits like berries can improve the colour of a sauce.
- Egg yolks, sometimes whole eggs, are used to emulsify and lightly thicken sauces (see Emulsions and Emulsifiers, page 123).
- Egg yolks and cream, or simply egg yolks may be added at the end of cooking to white sauces and soups to enrich and thicken them slightly. To avoid curdling it is advisable to add some of the hot sauce to the egg and cream mixture off the heat and then stir this back into the sauce and reheat until it thickens, without boiling.

- Cornflour, potato starch and arrowroot are invaluable for last-minute thickening of liquids or thin sauces. The starch should first be mixed to a thin paste with cold liquid before being added to the hot sauce, stirring constantly. On average, 1 teaspoon of starch will thicken 250 ml/8 fl oz of liquid. Starch thickening does not hold up well, so if you leave the sauce standing over heat, or reheat it, it may slacken and you will have to add more thickener.
- Breadcrumbs, fresh or dried, may be added at any point. Used in moderation, the effect is surprisingly light, though never very smooth. A breadcrumb-thickened sauce will thicken perceptibly on standing or being reheated.
- Blood, usually pigs' blood, is a traditional thickener for dark wine sauces, particularly of game. It is whisked into the hot sauce just before serving and must never be boiled, or it will coagulate and curdle the sauce.

Cheese sauce

CHEESE SAUCE SHARES THE CLAIM OF WHITE SAUCE to being the most useful of all sauces, and personally I think it has the edge. White sauce can be bland, but cheese sauce can never be, provided it is properly seasoned. Just think of a cheese sauce – delicately golden, rich but not sticky – with fillets of sole, with sea scallops, with cauliflower, as a filling and topping for crêpes, moistening pasta or browned on top of a vegetable gratin.

Cheese sauce is as easy to make as white sauce, but remember this – always whisk in the cheese off the heat and do not reheat the sauce, as it may separate and the cheese cook into strings.

PERFECT – sauce has a deep cream colour, surface is glossy, and sauce generously coats the back of spoon; flavour is lively. Note: use when a cheese sauce of thick and binding consistency is required, as in seafood and vegetable gratins, and macaroni cheese.

STRINGS IN SAUCE – sauce is thick and long strings form when whisk is lifted.
Why: sauce was boiled, reheated or kept warm too long, so protein in cheese coagulated. Note: this is less likely to happen with hard aged cheese such as Parmesan.
What to do: nothing can be done.

OTHER PROBLEMS

CONSISTENCY TOO THIN
Why: too little flour; sauce not fully cooked.
What to do: before cheese added, simmer, stirring often, until reduced to right consistency; after cheese added, whisk in 1-2 egg yolks and heat very gently, whisking until sauce thickens.

CONSISTENCY TOO THICK
Why: too much flour; simmered too long so milk evaporated.
What to do: thin by whisking in more milk.

LUMPY
Why: cheese not fully melted; cooked too fast; not whisked enough while thickening; not stirred while simmering, so caught on the pan; skin formed on surface when cooled.
What to do: if cheese not melted, heat very gently, whisking constantly; if flour in sauce has formed lumps, take at once from heat and whisk vigorously; if unsuccessful, work sauce through a sieve.

LACKS FLAVOUR
Why: lack of seasoning; not enough cheese; cheese bland (Parmesan, Gruyère or dry sharp Cheddar are best).
What to do: adjust seasoning, particularly with dry or Dijon-style mustard and salt; add more cheese.

Twice-baked cheese and herb soufflés

SERVES 6

This recipe is an exception to the rule that soufflés must be served at once. The mixture is baked, left to cool, then unmoulded and coated with a cream sauce. It can be held up to a day in the refrigerator before being baked a second time. A mixture of Parmesan and Gruyère cheeses is recommended for this soufflé, but you can also use a sharp Cheddar. As for the herb, chives and cheese are natural partners, but thyme or parsley are good too.

60 g/2 oz butter
30 g/1 oz flour
375 ml/12 fl oz milk
pinch of nutmeg
salt and pepper
375 ml/12 fl oz single cream
5 egg yolks

100 g/3¼ oz grated cheese
bunch of chives, chopped
whites of 6 eggs

six 250-ml/8-fl oz ramekins and
six 15-cm/6-inch gratin dishes

Generously butter the ramekins and chill them. In a heavy-based saucepan, melt the butter, whisk in the flour and cook until foaming but not browned, about 1 minute. Whisk in the milk, nutmeg, salt and pepper and bring to the boil, stirring constantly until the sauce thickens. Simmer for 2 minutes. Take from the heat and transfer about one-third to a small saucepan. Pour over the cream and set aside.

Whisk the egg yolks one at a time into the remaining sauce so they cook in the heat of sauce and thicken it slightly. Take the sauce from the heat and whisk in the grated cheese and the chives, reserving 3-4 tablespoons of cheese and 1 tablespoon of the chives for sprinkling. Taste the sauce and adjust the seasoning – the mixture should be highly seasoned. Cover with cling film or rub the surface of the sauce with butter to prevent a skin forming.

Preheat the oven to 175°C/350°F/gas4. Bring a roasting pan of water to the boil on the stove for a water bath. Preferably in a copper bowl (see page 223), beat egg whites until stiff. Warm the cheese sauce gently until the pan is hot to the touch. (Note: do not overheat or cheese will become stringy.) Add about a quarter of egg whites to the sauce and stir until well mixed. Fold this mixture into the remaining egg whites as gently as possible. Fill the ramekins with the mixture, smoothing the tops with a palette knife. Run a thumb around the edge of each dish to detach the mixture so the soufflé will rise straight.

Set the ramekins in the water bath. Bring back to the boil on the hob and transfer to the oven. Bake until the soufflés are puffed, browned and just set in the centre, 15-20 minutes. They should rise well above the rim of the dish. Remove from the water bath and leave to cool – the soufflés will shrink back into the ramekins, pulling away slightly from the sides.

Turn each soufflé out into a gratin dish. Whisk the cream with the reserved sauce until smooth and bring just to the boil. Season to taste and pour on top of the soufflés, allowing it to pool around sides. Sprinkle with the reserved cheese. The soufflés can be prepared to this point up to 24 hours ahead and kept covered in the refrigerator.

To finish: preheat the oven to 220°C/425°F/gas7. Bake the soufflés until browned, slightly puffed and sauce is bubbling, 5-7 minutes. Sprinkle with the reserved chives and serve at once.

Velouté sauce

VELOUTÉ SAUCE IS MADE WITH STOCK or the liquid from poaching veal, poultry or fish and is usually served with its parent ingredient. This mundane definition gives little clue to the aromatic richness of a good velouté, so poetic French chefs herald it with titles like *suprême* (chicken velouté with lemon and mushrooms) or *à la reine* (chicken breast in velouté sauce). Add a puff pastry case and the dish is indeed fit for a queen.

Velouté is outstanding with fish, often enhanced with white wine in classics such as *sauce normande* with mussels, mushrooms and prawns, or *sauce cardinale* with lobster butter. Velouté can also stand alone, flavoured with capers or tomato (*aurore*), or with lemon juice and parsley (*poulette*). It's far too versatile to be exclusively French. Greek *avgolemono* sauce is none other than lemon velouté; the German herbed meatballs called *Königsberger Klopse* involve a velouté, and in my native northern England we serve a velouté caper sauce with lamb.

PERFECT – sauce lightly coats back of spoon but runs off quickly; colour a rich cream, glossy, with no tinge of grey; sauce has full-bodied flavour of stock – veal, chicken or fish – used to make it.

PROBLEMS

CONSISTENCY TOO THIN
Why: too much liquid.
What to do: simmer until reduced to right consistency.
CONSISTENCY TOO THICK, GUMMY
Why: not enough liquid, or over-reduced.
What to do: thin with stock or, if flavour is strong, with water.

LACKS GLOSS
Why: not whisked enough when thickening; not simmered long enough.
What to do: whisk vigorously 1 minute, then leave to simmer 3-5 minutes and skim any scum.

LACKS TASTE
Why: poor stock or lack of seasoning.
What to do: adjust seasoning; add meat, chicken or fish glaze if available; continue reducing even if sauce gets slightly thick; bolster taste with teaspoon or two of brandy, Madeira or sherry.

Chicken breast on horseback with tarragon velouté

SERVES 4   *pictured on page 106*

Pungent tarragon is a pick-me-up for this chicken breast served on a crisp potato cake.

4 boneless chicken breasts, without skin	for the tarragon velouté large bunch of tarragon
500 g/1 lb baking potatoes	1 litre/1⅔ pints chicken stock
60 ml/2 fl oz double cream	60 g/2 oz butter
salt and white pepper	30 g/1 oz flour
	juice of ½ lemon, or to taste

Preheat the oven to 175°C/350°F/gas4. Start the sauce: strip half the tarragon leaves from the stems, reserving the stems and 4 small sprigs for decoration. Chop the leaves and set aside. In a saucepan, bring the stock to the boil with the remaining tarragon and reserved stems.

Arrange the chicken breasts in a medium baking dish, then pour over the stock and its tarragon. Cover with buttered foil and bake until tender when pierced with a two-pronged fork, 15-20 minutes. Remove them to a plate and cover with foil to keep warm. Reserve the cooking liquid. Raise the oven temperature to 200°C/400°F/gas6.

Meanwhile, make the potato cakes: peel the potatoes and coarsely grate them using a food processor or grater. Squeeze in a cloth to remove water and put them in a large bowl. Stir in the cream, salt and pepper. Note: work quickly or the potatoes will discolour. Brush a baking sheet with vegetable oil and add the potatoes in 4 mounds. With a spatula, flatten them into 6-mm/¼-inch thick cakes. Bake in the preheated oven until brown, 12-15 minutes, then turn and continue baking until crisp, 12-15 minutes more.

Finish the tarragon velouté sauce: melt the butter in a heavy-based saucepan, whisk in the flour and cook until foaming but not browned, 30-60 seconds. Whisk in the reserved cooking liquid, with the tarragon stems, and bring to the boil, whisking the sauce constantly until it thickens. Season lightly with salt and pepper – the flavour will concentrate as the sauce reduces. Simmer until done, skimming occasionally, 15-30 minutes.

Strain the sauce into another pan, bring just to the boil and stir in the chopped tarragon and lemon juice. Taste and adjust the seasoning. Place the potato cakes on 4 individual plates. Slice the chicken breasts on the diagonal and arrange in a fan shape over the cakes. Partially coat the chicken with sauce and top with a tarragon sprig. Serve at once, passing the remaining sauce separately.

Making stocks

STOCKS MADE FROM FISH, chicken, veal or beef bones and vegetables, simmered with seasonings to extract maximum flavour, form the basis of many sauces and soups. Good stock is full-flavoured, fresh for fish stock, and more mellow for chicken and meat. All should be rich with gelatine, extracted from the bones. Colour varies from almost clear for fish, to light golden for chicken and white veal stock to a warm golden for brown veal and beef stock, given by thorough browning of the bones and vegetables. White veal stock is made like brown stock, but the bones and vegetables are not browned. The bones must first be blanched by bringing them to the boil and draining before they are simmered to make the stock. To intensify flavour, simmer stock until it is reduced and concentrated – if boiled further, stock eventually becomes a glaze (see page 114). For this reason, you'll see that I do not add salt to stock as it can so easily become salty when reduced. Stock can be kept for up to 3 days in the refrigerator, or it can be frozen. I often boil it down, freeze it in ice cube trays and store the cubes to use in small quantities. For vegetable stock, see page 165.

PERFECT – stock clear and transparent; colour bright, pale for fish and vegetable, light golden for chicken and veal, darker for beef; flavour lively and concentrated, fresh for fish and vegetable, mellow for poultry and meat.

CLOUDY – appearance muddy, colour often dark; flavour cloying.
Why: bones not washed; stock boiled.
What to do: whisk 2 egg whites into warm stock and bring slowly to the boil, simmer 5 minutes, strain through cheesecloth.

OTHER PROBLEMS

FATTY
Why: bones were fatty, not drained after browning; stock was boiled.
What to do: chill and lift off solid fat.

FLAVOUR THIN
Why: too much water; cooking too short.
What to do: continue cooking; after straining, boil rapidly to concentrate.

QUICK FIX

Strips of paper towel are very useful for quick skimming, as well as removing any lingering fat globules from the hot stock by floating them on the surface.

Brown veal and beef stock

MAKES ABOUT 2.5 LITRES / 4½ PINTS

Veal stock is made with veal bones only, whereas beef stock has half veal bones (for gelatine) and half beef (for flavour). Vegetables suggested here are just a start and you can add many others including leeks, carrot tops, tomatoes for colour and herbs for taste; never add roots as they disintegrate. Bones and vegetables for brown stock must be well browned and this easiest in the oven – the onion skins also add colour. At least 4 hours' simmering (and preferably 5-6) is needed to extract full flavour from the bones.

2.5 kg/5 pounds veal (or half beef, half veal) bones, cracked in large pieces
2 unpeeled onions, quartered
2 carrots, quartered
1 stalk of celery, cut into pieces
bouquet garni
1 teaspoon peppercorns
1 tablespoon tomato purée
3-4 garlic cloves, unpeeled (optional)
5 litres/9 pints water, more if needed

Preheat oven to 260°C/500°F/gas10 or its highest setting. Put bones in a roasting pan and roast until well browned, 30-40 minutes. Stir, add onions, carrots and celery and continue roasting until bones and vegetables are very brown, almost charred around the edges, 30 minutes more.

Transfer to a stockpot and add the bouquet garni, peppercorns, tomato purée, garlic if using and enough water to cover. Bring slowly to the boil, skimming often. Simmer very gently, skimming occasionally, 5-6 hours, adding more water if needed to cover. Strain and, if flavour is not concentrated, boil it until well reduced. Chill and skim off fat before using.

Chicken stock

Chicken stock is made by the same general method as above, but substitute 1.4 kg/3 pounds raw chicken backs, necks and bones for the veal bones and do not brown them. Simmer with 1 quartered onion, 1 quartered carrot, a stalk of celery, cut into pieces, a bouquet garni, 1 teaspoon peppercorns and 4 litres/7 pints of water, allowing 2-3 hours to extract full flavour. Skim often and add more water if necessary to keep the bones covered. You can also substitute a whole chicken for the bones (use the cooked meat for another dish such as a salad) or cooked chicken carcasses, for a milder flavour. This makes about 1.5 litres/2¾ pints stock.

Fish stock

Fish stock is the only type of stock which is boiled rapidly for a short time to extract maximum flavour from the bones while still retaining a fresh taste. If the bones are not carefully washed or boiled too long, fish stock can be bitter. To make about 1 litre/1⅔ pints, boil 750 g/1½ pounds thoroughly washed fish bones and heads, cut into pieces, with 1 onion, sliced, and a bouquet garni, 1 teaspoon peppercorns, 250 ml/8 fl oz dry white wine or 4 tablespoons white wine vinegar and water just to cover. Bring to the boil, skimming often, and simmer rapidly for 20 minutes, skimming occasionally.

Brown sauce, thickened gravies

BROWN SAUCE IS BASIC TO A PROFESSIONAL KITCHEN but it also turns up at home as thickened gravy, the much-loved accompaniment to mashed potato, roast meats and poultry. Brown sauce, whether the traditional slowly simmered *espagnole* based on a roux of flour and oil, or the more modern veal stock thickened with starch dissolved in water, is a test of culinary skill involving multiple ingredients and long simmering. Whisking should be done with discretion, just enough to prevent sticking. Too much can froth and cloud brown sauces. Flavourings are always added to the basic sauce, leading for example to Madeira sauce, *sauce périgueux* (with truffles), *charcutière* (with reduced white wine, shallot and gherkin pickles) and *bordelaise* (with reduced red wine, shallot and bone marrow). Other versions of brown sauce or gravy include Italian *salsa piemontese* with anchovy, shallot and white truffles, and the white pepper gravy so popular with fried chicken in the southern states of the USA.

GLAZES

Meat, poultry and fish glaze is made by boiling down stock until it is reduced to the syrupy consistency characteristic of a glaze. 2 litres/3½ pints of stock will produce a scant 250 ml/8 fl oz of glaze. Be sure the original veal, beef, poultry or fish stock has plenty of gelatine, extracted by simmering bones. When cold, glaze sets and will keep in the refrigerator for several months. Just a teaspoonful packs powerful flavour – add it before adjusting the seasoning of a sauce as glaze can be salty. Glaze can also be diluted to make a nutty-tasting stock.

CONSISTENCY TOO THIN – looks pale; scarcely thickened and runs quickly off surface of spoon or plate; lacks taste.
Why: too much stock; poor-quality stock; not enough caramelized meat juices (for gravy).
What to do: simmer until thoroughly reduced; add meat glaze if available; thicken with arrowroot or cornflour dissolved in cold water, then whisk enough into boiling sauce to give right consistency.

PERFECT – glossy, light to deep mahogany colour (darker for red meats and game); very lightly coats a spoon or plate; flavour intense and well balanced.

CONSISTENCY TOO THICK – muddy colour; texture sticky, generously coating a spoon or plate.
Why: too much flour or starch thickener; reduced too far.
What to do: thin with stock or, if flavour is strong, with water.

OTHER PROBLEMS

LUMPY
Why: thickener poorly mixed with liquid; sauce not whisked while coming to the boil and thickening.
What to do: work through fine or tamis sieve.

LACKS TASTE
Why: poor stock; underseasoned; not reduced enough.
What to do: adjust seasoning; add meat glaze if available; continue simmering to concentrate flavour.

BITTER
Why: over-reduced; flour scorched.
What to do: thin with water; mask with Worcestershire sauce, Tabasco or mustard; if badly scorched, nothing can be done.

MUDDY COLOUR, LACKS GLOSS
Why: stock cloudy; sauce insufficiently whisked before it thickened; boiled rather than simmered to reduce; not skimmed during reduction.
What to do: add cold stock or water and simmer, skimming often.

QUICK FIX

Madeira adds richness and colour as well as flavour to a pallid sauce. For best results, add several tablespoonfuls and simmer the sauce for 5-10 minutes. Then whisk in a last tablespoon of Madeira to sharpen the flavour just before serving. Marsala can be used in the same way to give Italian richness, or you can use a mixture of port and Cognac.

Unthickened gravies

GOOD UNTHICKENED GRAVY, OFTEN CALLED BY ITS FRENCH NAME *JUS*, is normally made from the caramelized juices which coagulate on the bottom of the pan after roasting or pan-frying meat or poultry. These juices are deglazed (dissolved) with stock, wine or water; the more copious they are, the better the gravy will be. If the juices are not well browned, cook them down in the pan before adding any liquid. Meat or poultry juices will always include some drippings or fat which emulsify (page 123) and help thicken the finished gravy. Only a small amount of fat is needed – 1 or 2 tablespoons, not more – so you should discard excess before deglazing the pan. Finally, when liquid is added, brisk boiling of gravy is essential so it reduces to be full-flavoured and rich. The choice of liquid for making gravy is an amusing insight into national character. As you might expect, the French favour wine, red or white depending on the meat. Italians incline towards Marsala, and the Portuguese to Madeira or port. British cooks will tell you to economize and use the water from boiling vegetables, while Americans use coffee to make an excellent gravy for ham called red eye. Try my version for beef tenderloin (page 65), it's delicious!

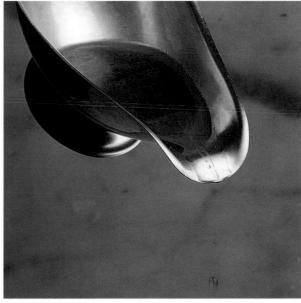

PERFECT – golden brown colour (darker for red meats and game), full-bodied flavour, slightly thickened as juices emulsify when reduced.

FAT SEPARATED – heavy layer of fat separates from darker juices beneath.
Why: excess fat; gravy not emulsified by boiling.
What to do: skim off almost all fat, preferably before adding liquid; boil hard to emulsify liquid and fat.

OTHER PROBLEMS

CONSISTENCY TOO THIN
Why: not enough caramelized juices in pan; gravy not sufficiently reduced; water used, not stock or wine.
What to do: continue boiling until emulsified and slightly thickened.

LACKS TASTE
Why: poor stock; lack of meat juices in pan; too little seasoning.
What to do: add a few tablespoons red wine, Madeira or port (for pork or duck) and simmer 1-2 minutes; add meat glaze if available.

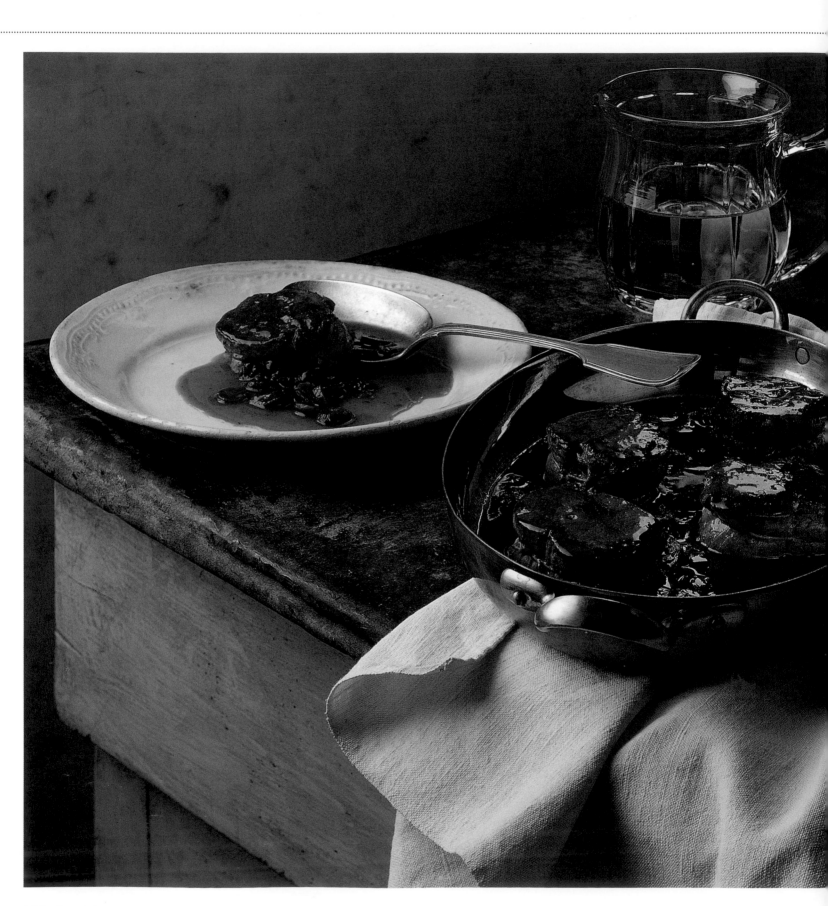

Pork fillet with muscat wine and dried cranberries

SERVES 4

Pork fillet can be tied with string to form medallions of meat, ideal for pan-frying to serve with this sweet-and-sour gravy and an accompaniment of celeriac, turnip or potato. Other dried fruits, such as cherries or apricots, can be substituted if dried cranberries are hard to find.

2 pork fillets (about 750 g/1½ pounds)
1 teaspoon ground cinnamon
salt and pepper
15 g/½ oz butter
1 tablespoon oil
60 g/2 oz dried cranberries
250 ml/8 fl oz sweet white muscat wine
250 ml/8 fl oz brown beef or veal stock
1 tablespoon redcurrant jelly
squeeze of lemon juice

Trim any skin and fat from the fillets. Lay them head to tail and tie them together with 8 pieces of string at even intervals to make a cylinder. Cut between each piece of string to make 8 medallions about 4 cm/1½ inches thick. Season the medallions with cinnamon, salt and pepper.

Heat the butter and oil in a frying pan until foaming. Add the medallions and sauté them until brown, 3-5 minutes. Turn them over, lower the heat and leave until browned on the outside and just cooked to your taste, 5-7 minutes. Transfer them to a plate and keep warm.

Discard all but a teaspoon of fat from the pan. Add the dried cranberries, wine and stock and boil until reduced by half, stirring to dissolve pan juices, 10-12 minutes Add the redcurrant jelly and lemon juice and stir until dissolved. Taste and adjust the seasoning.

Add the medallions to the sauce in the pan and reheat for 1 minute. Discard the strings, arrange the medallions on 4 warmed individual plates and spoon over the sauce. Serve at once.

Pork fillet with muscat wine and dried cranberries

Steak with red wine sauce

SERVES 4

Chefs have abandoned the traditional *espagnole* sauce, which took days to make, but reduction by simmering remains the key to a glossy, mellow brown sauce. Even the 20 minutes called for here makes a difference.

2 sirloin steaks (about 750 g/1½ pounds), cut 2.5 cm/1 inch thick
2 tablespoons oil
salt and pepper
bunch of watercress for decoration

for the red wine sauce
30 g/1 oz butter
3 shallots, finely chopped
500 ml/16 fl oz red wine
½ teaspoon coarsely ground black pepper
¼ teaspoon grated nutmeg
375 ml/12 fl oz brown veal or beef stock
1 teaspoon arrowroot or potato starch mixed to a paste with 1 tablespoon cold water

Brush the steaks with oil, season both sides with pepper and leave to marinate.

Start the red wine sauce: melt half the butter in a heavy-based saucepan, add the shallots and sauté gently until soft, 2-3 minutes. Add the wine, black pepper and nutmeg. Boil until reduced by half. In another saucepan, bring the stock just to the boil and strain the red wine reduction into it. Simmer to reduce the sauce again by about half, 15-20 minutes.

Meanwhile, preheat the grill. Season the steaks on both sides with salt and set them on the grill rack. Grill about 5 cm/2 inches away from the heat, cooking the steaks to your taste (page 76), 6-10 minutes, turning them once halfway through cooking.

Finish the sauce: bring the sauce back to the boil and whisk in just enough arrowroot or potato starch paste to thicken it slightly. Remove the pan from the heat, taste the sauce and adjust the seasoning. Add the remaining butter, cut into pieces, swirling the pan so that butter is incorporated smoothly into sauce.

To serve: cut the steaks in diagonal slices, discarding any fat, and arrange on a warmed platter or individual plates. Spoon a little sauce over the steaks. Decorate with watercress and serve at once, with the remaining sauce passed separately.

Hollandaise sauce

HOLLANDAISE NEEDS NO INTRODUCTION. Apart from its starring role in classics such as eggs Benedict with poached egg, ham and English muffin, or *sole bonne femme* with mushrooms in a white wine sauce, hollandaise must be the most popular of all accompaniments to boiled vegetables and poached or steamed fish. Hollandaise browns well on the top of gratins and a spoonful or two is useful for enriching cream soups and sauces. It can also be lightened with whipped cream or enhanced with a discreet flavouring of mustard, herbs, tomato or blood orange, as in *sauce maltaise*.

To ensure that hollandaise is thick and rich enough to act as a coating, be sure the foundation mousse of egg yolk and water is well thickened before adding butter – the mousse should hold the trail of the whisk for at least 3 seconds. Since the sauce relies on butter for flavour, use only the best unsalted butter and clarify it to get rid of the whey impurities. I learned my lesson in Moscow, when I whipped up a hollandaise with the local butter – it tasted disconcertingly, though not unpleasantly, of cheese.

Everyone warns of the dangers of curdling hollandaise – it is indeed based on a fragile emulsion (page 123) and must be cooked and kept warm over very gentle heat. Never let it get more than hand-hot. Some cooks like to use a water bath, though I find a heavy pan sufficient protection during cooking (here's where the expense of a lined copper saucepan really pays off). Even if the worst happens, you'll see there are several ways to restore hollandaise.

CONSISTENCY TOO THIN – frothy consistency; lacks body and falls very easily from spoon; flavour faint.
Why: mousse of egg yolk and water not sufficiently thickened before adding butter.
What to do: continue cooking sauce to right consistency over very low heat or in water bath, whisking constantly 1-2 minutes.

PERFECT – rich consistency, sauce holds trail of whisk for 10-15 seconds; flavour is delicate, rich with light touch of lemon.

CURDLED – butter separates, depositing curds of cooked egg.
Why: mousse of egg yolk and water cooked too quickly; butter added too quickly; sauce cooked over too high a heat, or for too long; eggs stale.

What to do: cool pan at once by dipping base in cold water. Add an ice cube to sauce and whisk beside the cube, gradually working curdled sauce into melting cube to re-establish emulsion. If not successful, see Quick Fix.

OTHER PROBLEMS

TASTES EGGY OR BLAND
Why: lacks seasoning; too little butter; butter poor-quality or not clarified.
What to do: adjust seasoning especially with lemon juice; add more clarified butter.

DULL, GREYISH COLOUR, METALLIC TASTE
Why: egg and acid reacted with aluminium or other pan or whisk.
What to do: nothing can be done. Next time use pan lined with metal such as stainless steel.

QUICK FIX

When hollandaise curdles, the best remedy is to start again, using the curdled sauce in place of more melted butter. Whisk 1 egg yolk with a tablespoon of water over low heat to make a light mousse which just holds the trail of a whisk. Take from heat and gradually whisk in curdled sauce, starting with a teaspoonful of sauce, then adding it more quickly once emulsion begins. Note: if original sauce is severely overcooked so that egg yolk curds are cooked until firm, it cannot be saved.

Eggs with spinach, brown butter hollandaise
Oeufs pochés à la florentine
SERVES 4

Classic poached eggs *à la florentine* are coated with cheese sauce, but I much enjoy this version with brown butter hollandaise. Serve the eggs with sliced baguette to mop up the sauce.

4 eggs
3-4 tablespoons white vinegar
1 kg/2 lb spinach
30 g/1 oz butter
1 shallot, finely chopped
salt and white pepper

for the brown butter hollandaise sauce
175 g/6 oz butter
3 tablespoons water
3 egg yolks
juice of ½ lemon, more to taste

Poach the eggs: fill a large shallow pan two-thirds full of water, add the vinegar and bring to the boil. Break the eggs, one at a time, into a patch of bubbling water. Lower the heat so the water barely simmers and poach the eggs until the white is set but the yolk is still soft, 3-4 minutes. With a slotted spoon, transfer the eggs to a bowl of hot water to keep them warm.

Tear the stems from the spinach leaves. Wash the leaves well in plenty of cold water and drain most of the water from the leaves. Pack the spinach in a large heavy-based saucepan, cover and cook just until wilted, stirring occasionally, 3-4 minutes. Let the spinach cool, then squeeze it in your fists to extract water.

Melt the butter in a large frying pan over medium heat. Add the shallot and cook until soft, 1-2 minutes. Add the drained spinach and sauté, stirring until hot and all liquid has evaporated, 1-2 minutes. Taste, adjust seasoning and keep warm.

To make the brown butter hollandaise sauce, first brown the butter. In a small heavy-based pan, heat the butter gently, skimming the froth from its surface. Continue simmering, stirring occasionally, until the butter stops sputtering and the sediment in the pan is golden with a nutty aroma, 5-7 minutes. Pour into a bowl and let cool to tepid.

Wipe out the pan with some paper towel, add the water and egg yolks with a little salt and pepper, and whisk until thoroughly combined and the eggs lighten slightly in colour. Set the pan over a low heat or in a water bath and whisk vigorously to form a mousse that is creamy and thick enough to hold a ribbon trail for 3 seconds, 3-5 minutes. Note: the base of the pan should never be more than hand-hot or the yolks will cook too quickly.

Take the pan from the heat. Whisk in the brown butter, a little at a time, until the sauce starts to thicken slightly . Continue whisking in the butter in a slow steady stream, leaving the brown sediment at the bottom of the bowl. Stir in the lemon juice, taste and adjust the seasoning of the sauce.

Spoon a layer of spinach on 4 warmed individual plates. Drain the eggs and pat them dry on paper towels. Set the eggs on the beds of spinach. Spoon the brown butter hollandaise sauce over the eggs and serve at once.

Béarnaise sauce

Béarnaise sauce, named after the feisty French province of Béarn, is a pungent version of delicate hollandaise. Flavour is piquant rather than mild, with a reduction of tarragon vinegar, tarragon stems and shallot replacing the water used in hollandaise. Boil this reduction down well so the flavour is concentrated. The texture should be thick and rich, stiffer than hollandaise. To achieve this, before adding melted butter, the basic egg yolk mousse must be cooked until it holds the trail of the whisk for at least 15 seconds. Once the sauce is strained, to give it a final boost chopped tarragon and ground black pepper are added – be sure both are fresh. If the flavour is flat, try a squeeze of lemon juice and a pinch of cayenne. Béarnaise can curdle, just like hollandaise, and is saved in the same way.

Béarnaise is a favourite of mine. Don't limit it to classic fillet steak and lamb chops, but try it with poached or grilled fish, such as turbot and salmon, and even with *magret* of duck.

PERFECT – whisk leaves clear trail through sauce on base of pan for 10-15 seconds; texture creamy and just drops easily from spoon; flavour is assertive, fragrant with tarragon.

White butter sauce and other butter sauces

LIKE HOLLANDAISE AND BÉARNAISE, white butter sauce relies on an emulsion (see page 123) for its consistency – but it is even more delicate because the milk solids and whey in the butter act as the emulsifier. (This is why butter sauce cannot be made with clarified butter, from which the whey has been removed.) As always, the key to white butter sauce is to establish the emulsion right from the start by vigorously whisking in a small amount of cold butter. Then you'll do fine. Here let me whisper the professional trick of adding a spoonful of double cream as an additional emulsifier – purists protest a loss of flavour, but it works.

Flavourings for butter sauces may range from the classic combination of white wine, white wine vinegar and shallot (*sauce beurre blanc*) to red wine and shallot (*sauce beurre rouge*); you can also add herbs, lemon, saffron, or sharp tastes like soy sauce or anise liqueur for additional flavour. Be sure all these elements are thoroughly reduced, usually to a glaze, before cold butter is added. Most delicate of all is a plain mounted butter sauce made by whisking butter into a spoonful of water, with no added flavourings except perhaps a squeeze of lemon juice or a spoonful of chopped herbs. Butter sauces began as an accompaniment to steamed and grilled fish, but now you find them with poultry and meat, particularly when flavoured with a reduction (glaze) of the liquid from cooking. Perhaps best of all is a butter sauce with vegetables.

Keep a butter sauce warm on a rack over gently steaming water, and please don't leave it for long. If it separates, try the Quick Fix; or simply serve the sauce as a deliciously seasoned melted butter.

CONSISTENCY TOO THIN – almost transparent and scarcely coats spoon. *Why:* flavourings not reduced to a concentrated, syrupy glaze before adding butter; butter not chilled when added; butter added too fast and sauce not whisked vigorously. *What to do:* take from heat and whisk very vigorously by hand or stick blender.

PERFECT – lightly coats a spoon and clear trail is left when finger is drawn across back of spoon; flavouring ingredients evenly blended (sometimes strained out); flavour delicate, well balanced, with lingering hint of shallot, wine and vinegar.

SEPARATED – butter separates to top of sauce, leaving flavourings at bottom. *Why:* butter not whisked in vigorously at start to form emulsion; sauce cooked over too high a heat or kept warm for too long. *What to do:* if sauce starts to thin, stop stirring and cool pan at once by dipping base into cold water. Then follow instructions in Quick Fix.

OTHER PROBLEMS

TASTES TOO BUTTERY
Why: too few or poor-quality flavourings; lacks seasoning.
What to do: adjust seasoning, especially with vinegar; add flavourings such as chopped herbs or grated citrus zest.

TOO SALTY
Why: salted butter used; too much seasoning.
What to do: add flavourings such as anise liqueur, chopped herbs, saffron or a spoonful of double cream.

QUICK FIX

For 250 ml/8 fl oz separated butter sauce: in a separate saucepan, reduce 2 tablespoons double cream, whisking constantly, until thick, 1-2 minutes. Over a low heat, whisk 1 teaspoon of the broken butter sauce into reduced cream so it emulsifies. Whisk in 2-3 more spoonfuls, then whisk in remaining sauce in a slow steady stream. Taste sauce and adjust the seasoning. This fix does not have the staying power of a perfect sauce, but will hold up to 5 minutes without breaking.

Steamed sea bass with fennel butter sauce

SERVES 4

In Provence, pastis, the local anise liqueur, is accorded a respect that most French reserve for their Cognac. Here it is used to bolster the flavour of fennel when steaming another Mediterranean favourite, sea bass, known locally as *loup de mer* or 'sea wolf'. This recipe is also good with hake or sea trout.

4 sea bass fillets (about
    750 g/1½ pounds), with skin
salt and pepper

for the court bouillon
1 onion, spiked with 1 clove
1 carrot, sliced
1 tablespoon fennel seeds
bouquet garni
250 ml/8 fl oz white wine
500 ml/16 fl oz water

for the fennel butter sauce
250 g/8 oz cold butter, cut into
    pieces
2 shallots, finely chopped
1 teaspoon fennel seed
125 ml/4 fl oz white wine
2 tablespoons pastis or other anise
    liqueur

Put all the ingredients for the court bouillon in the base of a steamer, cover and simmer until fragrant, 15-20 minutes. Meanwhile, rinse the fish fillets and pat dry with paper towels. Season with salt and pepper.

Set the fillets skin-side up on the steamer rack, put the rack over the court bouillon and cover. Steam until the fish is done to your taste (page 12), 10-12 minutes. Remove the fish and keep warm. Strain the steaming liquid into a medium saucepan and boil over high heat until reduced to 2-3 tablespoons of syrupy glaze, 7-10 minutes.

Meanwhile, make the fennel butter sauce: in a medium saucepan, melt 30 g/1 oz of the butter, add the shallots and fennel seeds and sauté until the shallot is soft but not browned, 1-2 minutes. Stir in the white wine and half the pastis or other liqueur and simmer until it is reduced to about 2 tablespoons. Whisk the remaining butter into the sauce a few pieces at a time, working on and off the heat so the butter softens and thickens the sauce without melting to oil. Strain the sauce into the saucepan of fish glaze, crushing the shallots to extract all their juices. Whisk the sauce and glaze together until mixed, then stir in the remaining liqueur. Taste and adjust the seasoning.

Spoon pools of the sauce on 4 warmed serving plates. Set a piece of fish on top, skin-side up, and serve at once, passing the remaining sauce separately.

Fennel butter sauce

Mayonnaise

MAYONNAISE IS SAID TO BE TRICKY AND IT HELPS TO KNOW WHY. For its satiny, rich consistency, mayonnaise depends on an emulsion (opposite page) of vinegar, oil and raw egg yolk – 175 ml/6 fl oz of oil per egg yolk are standard proportions. Several conditions are needed for this emulsion to form. First, all the ingredients must be at room temperature; if the eggs come from the refrigerator, you may need to warm both them and the bowl. Whisk the egg yolks and seasonings with a teaspoon of vinegar or lemon juice for at least a minute before you add the oil, first drop by drop and then in a trickle. (You can follow my example and use an immersion blender or hand-held electric mixer to do the work.) Without this small amount of liquid, the egg yolks and oil will not emulsify. Once the emulsion is formed and the mayonnaise starts to thicken, you should have no trouble and you'll be rewarded by a mayonnaise so thick it will hold a spoon upright. Given the hazards of raw egg yolks, take care to refrigerate mayonnaise and use it within 24 hours.

When measured against what you can achieve at home, bottled mayonnaise is a limited substitute for the real thing. For a start, your vinegar can be based on white wine, red wine, or cider, or flavoured with garlic and herbs, or replaced by lemon juice. Walnut or hazelnut oils are a delectable alternative to olive oil, or you may opt for a neutral mayonnaise of vegetable oil, the better to display a flavouring of herbs, tomato, garlic or pickles. Let your choice be guided by the dish you are preparing – fish, eggs, meat or cooked root vegetables.

Mayonnaise has many country cousins, such as the Provençal *aïoli*, which is heady with fresh garlic, and rusty-red *rouille* with hot red pepper. In the US, mayonnaise is lightened with sour cream, chives and tarragon as green goddess dressing, and everyone recognizes tartare sauce which is simply a mayonnaise with capers, shallot, pickles and chopped hard-boiled egg.

PERFECT MEDIUM – holds mark of whisk; glossy, cream colour; vinegar and other flavourings nicely balance richness of oil.

PERFECT THICK – holds a whisk upright; colour a clear golden; flavour pungent.

SEPARATED – pours easily from a spoon; coarse-textured, with eggs clearly separated from oil.
Why: egg yolks and oil too cold; sauce not whisked vigorously at start; oil added too rapidly.
What to do: see Quick Fix.

OTHER PROBLEMS

CONSISTENCY TOO THIN AND POURS EASILY
Note: will probably separate on standing.
Why: egg yolks and oil too cold; sauce not whisked vigorously at start to form emulsion; oil added too rapidly; too much vinegar, not enough oil.
What to do: stop adding oil, set bowl in a warm water and whisk very vigorously until it thickens; if too much vinegar, whisk in more oil.
TASTES OILY
Why: too strong an oil used; too little vinegar, lemon juice or seasoning.
What to do: adjust seasoning, especially with salt and vinegar or lemon juice.
TASTES ACID
Why: too much vinegar or lemon juice; poorly seasoned.
What to do: add more salt; beat in more oil, particularly flavoured oil such as olive.

Vinaigrette dressing

EMULSIONS & EMULSIFIERS

An emulsion is formed when two substances which would normally separate, for example oil and vinegar, are combined to a smooth, lightly thickened mixture. Sauces which rely on an emulsion include hollandaise, béarnaise, white butter sauce, mayonnaise and vinaigrette dressing.

Several factors help to create an emulsion. One is to add an emulsifier – an ingredient that helps other ingredients to combine in this way. Common examples are egg yolks (in hollandaise, béarnaise and mayonnaise), Dijon-style mustard (in mayonnaise and vinaigrette), the milk solids in butter and cream (in butter sauces), spices and herbs.

Next is vigorous whisking, typically adding one liquid to the emulsifier, starting drop by drop. It is crucial to establish the emulsion right at the beginning. Once off to a good start – you can tell by the slight but perceptible thickening of the mixture – the liquid may be added more quickly.

Other factors which help an emulsion to form include following proportions carefully, and having the ingredients and utensils at the right (usually room) temperature. It is difficult, for example, to make mayonnaise with eggs which have come straight from the refrigerator.

'BE A PRODIGAL WITH THE OIL, a miser with the vinegar and whisk like the devil himself' runs an adage on vinaigrette dressing, and I couldn't agree more. Standard proportions for vinaigrette are three parts oil to one vinegar, but I vary them all the time depending on the inherent strength of the oil or vinegar. Natural marriages of flavour include olive oil with red wine vinegar or lemon juice (allow five parts oil to one part lemon juice), walnut oil with sherry vinegar, and hazelnut oil with raspberry or balsamic vinegar.

A good vinaigrette dressing should be lightly emulsified by vigorous whisking so it coats salad leaves or whatever food it accompanies – a spoonful of Dijon-style mustard or cream will help the oil and vinegar combine, but is not essential. On standing, the dressing separates, but can easily be recombined by whisking – see Quick Fix. Don't refrigerate vinaigrette as the oil will congeal.

Careful seasoning is key to good vinaigrette and I like to season with salt and freshly ground pepper three times, first adding it to the vinegar, then to the finished dressing, and finally to the salad itself. (The theory that salt will not dissolve in a dressing once the oil is added is nonsense.) Add other flavourings to the vinegar, such as very finely chopped shallot, garlic or liquids like soy sauce. However, chopped herbs must be a last-minute addition as they quickly lose colour and fragrance.

Vinaigrette dressing need not be limited to cold or warm salads. It acts as a handy marinade and basting sauce for grilling. It appears with poached fish and steamed vegetables. I've come across lamb chops with tamarind vinaigrette and warm chicken breast with walnuts and blue cheese, a tribute to the versatility of this universal sauce.

PERFECT *right* – lightly thickened and ingredients smooth and emulsified; flavour balanced and seasoning vivid.
THIN, NOT EMULSIFIED *left* – oil and vinegar lose emulsion and form separate layers.
Why: dressing not whisked vigorously when oil added; dressing left to stand.
What to do: thin vinaigrette is quite usable, it simply does not coat ingredients smoothly; if not already mixed with other ingredients, re-emulsify it, see Quick Fix.

OTHER PROBLEMS

BLAND TASTE
Why: lacks seasoning; bland ingredients
What to do: whisk in flavourings such as very finely chopped onion, shallot, garlic, fresh ginger, chilli or chopped herbs; add a few drops of soy sauce, Worcestershire sauce, Cognac, Tabasco or, for fruit salads, liqueur.

TASTES ACID
Why: underseasoned; too little oil; harsh vinegar; too much onion, shallot or other acid ingredient.
What to do: season again with salt and (for sweetened dressings only) a small amount of sugar; add more oil, particularly flavoured oil such as olive.

TASTES OILY
Why: underseasoned; too little acid.
What to do: season again with salt; add more vinegar, lemon juice or mustard.

QUICK FIX

When vinaigrette dressing is thin or separated, try whisking vigorously by hand or with an immersion blender so the dressing emulsifies and thickens slightly. If unsuccessful, start again in a small bowl with an emulsifier such as 1 teaspoon of Dijon-style mustard, 1 tablespoon of yogurt or double cream, or 1 very finely chopped shallot. Gradually whisk in the separated dressing, adding it slowly at first until an emulsion is established, then in a thin stream. Taste dressing and adjust seasoning.

Rocket with grapefruit and prosciutto in balsamic vinaigrette

SERVES 4

Balsamic vinegar suits fruit, its mellowed flavour pairing particularly well with fresh citrus. Feel free to use olive or vegetable oil, as you prefer.

3 pink grapefruits
125 g/4 oz thinly sliced prosciutto
large bunch of rocket
   (about 175 g/6 oz)

for the balsamic vinaigrette
3 tablespoons balsamic vinegar
2 teaspoons Dijon-style mustard
salt and freshly ground black
   pepper
125 ml/4 fl oz olive or vegetable oil

Pare the zest from 1 of the grapefruits and cut this zest into julienne strips. Bring a small saucepan of water to the boil, add the strips of zest, simmer 2 minutes and drain.

Slice off top and bottom of each grapefruit, then cut away the zest, pith and skin, following the curve of the fruit. Cut the grapefruit segments from the membranes.

Make the vinaigrette: combine the vinegar, mustard, salt and pepper in a mixing bowl and whisk until smooth. Gradually whisk in the oil so the vinaigrette emulsifies and thickens slightly. Taste and adjust the seasoning.

Toss the rocket with about a third of the vinaigrette. Taste and adjust the seasoning again. Make a bed of greens on 4 individual plates. Arrange the grapefruit sections and slices of prosciutto, curled into roses, on top of the rocket. Spoon over the remaining dressing and sprinkle the salad with grapefruit julienne. Serve at once.

Celeriac with piquant mayonnaise
Céleri rémoulade

SERVES 4-6

A *rémoulade* mayonnaise usually calls for the addition of capers, gherkin, anchovy and chopped herbs, but *céleri rémoulade* needs only mustard to highlight the distinctive bite of the celeriac.

1 celeriac root (about 750 g/1½ lb)
1 lemon, halved

for the piquant mayonnaise
1 large or 2 small egg yolks

2 teaspoons Dijon-style mustard,
   or to taste
2 tablespoons white wine vinegar
salt and white pepper
175 ml/6 fl oz vegetable oil

Make the mayonnaise: in a small bowl, whisk the egg yolks with the mustard, half the vinegar and a little salt and pepper until slightly thickened, 1-2 minutes. Add the vegetable oil, drop by drop, whisking constantly. When 2 tablespoons of oil have been added, the mixture should be very thick. The remaining oil can be added a little more quickly, either 1 tablespoon at a time, beating thoroughly between each addition, or in a thin steady stream. When all the oil has been added, stir in the remaining vinegar. Taste the mayonnaise and adjust the seasoning – it should taste clearly of mustard.

Peel the celeriac and rub it with the cut lemon to prevent discoloration. Cut the root in julienne strips on a mandoline slicer or with a knife. Put the celeriac in a pan of cold salted water, bring to the boil and simmer for 1 minute. Drain, refresh and drain again. If the celeriac is fibrous, several minutes' blanching may be needed – it should be crisp but not tough.

Mix the mayonnaise thoroughly with the celeriac and season to taste with lemon juice, salt, pepper and more mustard if needed. Cover and refrigerate to allow flavours to mellow, at least 1 hour and up to 12 hours.

Rocket with grapefruit and prosciutto in balsamic vinaigrette

Tomato sauces and cooked salsas

ITALIAN COOKS ARE MASTERS OF TOMATO SAUCE, so it's surprising that they developed a passion for the tomato barely 150 years ago. Only in Italy do you find such an array of tomato sauces, whether for pasta and pizza, or to accompany fish, poultry, meat and vegetables. Simplest is a *coulis* of fresh tomatoes seasoned with salt, pepper and fresh herbs, so lightly cooked it is only just hot. Marinara-style sauces are more full-bodied, backed with onion and garlic (page 129). At the far end of the spectrum come terracotta-gold essences of tomato so concentrated that a teaspoonful conveys a whole fruit.

The French, like the Italians, will often cook a simply flavoured tomato sauce down until nearly all the moisture has evaporated. This preparation is called *tomates concassées* because the tomatoes are first peeled, seeded and chopped. Elsewhere, cooks may approach tomatoes differently, for example adding hot chilli and roasting the tomatoes with garlic and onion for a cooked Mexican salsa. Whatever their name or origin, the same criteria of quality apply to all cooked tomato sauces: they should be full-flavoured without being too sweet or acid, richly coloured and as thin or thick as you require.

Vegetable-thickened sauces

Vegetable-thickened sauces are both ancient and modern. They date back to medieval times and beyond, when pulses and grains were included in stews much like Indian curries and other ethnic dishes we know today. Then for centuries vegetable thickeners fell into disuse, only to be revived some years ago in recipes like Roasted Red Pepper Sauce and Salsa of Tomato and Coriander (pages 179 and 129).

Roots such as onion, garlic and sweet potato, together with tomato, pumpkin and other pulpy vegetables, are top choices for thickening as they add flavour as well. Dried pulses – lentils, kidney beans and the like – bind even more effectively but must be used sparingly as they can be sticky. A pulpy effect is perfectly acceptable for most vegetable sauces, particularly when they form part of a meat or poultry stew. For a smoother consistency, purée the sauce, and possibly strain it to remove fibres.

PERFECT MEDIUM – slightly chunky, drops easily from spoon but too thick to pour; rich, vivid colour; flavour mellow and concentrated.

PERFECT THICK – liquid evaporated so sauce clearly holds mark of spoon without being sticky; flavour intense but not salty or acid; colour earthy.

PERFECT *left* – sauce (here red pepper cream sauce) coats back of spoon, consistency rich; flavour may be pungent or aromatic and mellow.
GRAINY *right* – texture coarse; liquid may seep at edges of sauce; flavour is undeveloped.
Why: vegetables too firm, undercooked or fibrous with little starch; not puréed enough.
What to do: purée more thoroughly; work through sieve or food mill to remove fibres.

Vegetable-thickened sauces often also suffer from coarse texture or muddy colour. Pep them up with chopped mint, oregano or parsley, or with olive, chilli or garlic oil. If necessary, colour with tomato purée.

PROBLEMS

CONSISTENCY TOO THIN
Why: undercooked; too many liquid ingredients.
What to do: simmer rapidly until thickened.
STICKY TEXTURE
Why: overcooked.
What to do: hard to remedy, but add crisp ingredients such as chopped cucumber, onion or more fresh tomato, thin with stock or water and cook 3-5 minutes.
ACID OR BITTER
Why: unripe tomatoes; sauce too reduced.
What to do: add 1-2 teaspoons sugar or a pinch of bicarbonate of soda (which neutralizes acid).

QUICK FIX

When tomato sauce or salsa is heavy or overcooked, or tastes flat, here are some simple additions. Choose whatever is appropriate to the dish:

- 125 ml/4 fl oz double cream.
- 2-3 seeded and chopped tomatoes.
- Enough red wine to restore the consistency you want.
- 2-3 tablespoons finely chopped celery and/or sweet onion.
- Adjust seasoning, particularly with lemon juice, vinegar, mustard, fresh herbs.

Fresh salsas

A GOOD FRESH SALSA IS CRISP, CRUNCHY AND BURSTING WITH TASTE. The colourful ingredients – green, red and gold – should say 'New World'. Salsa is not just the indispensable accompaniment to tacos, empanadas, burritos and other dishes from its native Mexico. Consider it a versatile condiment on the lines of a relish to accompany all manner of grilled and sautéed fish, poultry and meats, rather than the traditional smooth sauce designed to act as a coating.

The flavour of a fresh salsa must be forceful, even crude, so typically it is based on chopped sweet onion, diced cucumber, celery, radish, jícama, sweet pepper and chilli. Typical herbs include coriander, basil, thyme and dill. To bind all of this, chopped tomato is customary, but other juicy fruits such as avocado, mango, peach or plum may take its place. The mixture may be chopped coarsely or finely, to your taste, but do be careful not to bruise delicate herbs such as basil or coriander.

I like to leave flavours to mellow for an hour or two, even overnight, but don't overdo it, as some fruits – notably stone fruits such as peach – will discolour and lose their aroma.

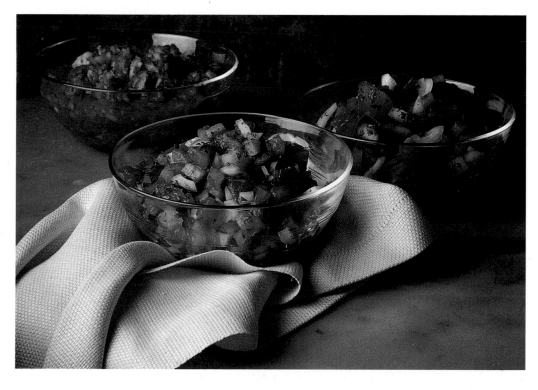

from left to right
WATERY – ingredients flabby, liquid separates at bottom of salsa; colour faded and flavour flat.
PERFECT FINE – ingredients finely chopped; flavour is lively and fragrant.
PERFECT CHUNKY – ingredients coarsely chopped, though small enough to blend; flavour of individual ingredients more pronounced.

PROBLEMS

WATERY
Why: juicy ingredients, particularly fruits, not drained or chopped too finely; salsa left too long so salt and sugar draw out juices.
What to do: drain through a sieve and stir in more coarsely chopped vegetables.

LACKS FLAVOUR
Why: lack of seasoning; poor ingredients particularly tomatoes and herbs; stored for too long (often best within 1-2 hours).

What to do: pick up flavour with lemon juice, vinegar, soy sauce, Tabasco and herbs; for tomato and other fruit, add a little sugar.

TASTES BITTER
Why: original ingredient bitter, particularly cucumber; ingredients, especially onion or herbs, bruised during chopping.
What to do: disguise with strong flavourings such as chilli, Tabasco, lemon or lime juice.

QUICK FIX

When salsa seems dreary, try this. First drain excess liquid. Next sharpen taste with citrus juice, particularly lime, then stir in an aromatic chopped herb such as basil, dill or coriander. Finally add zip with a splash of Tabasco.

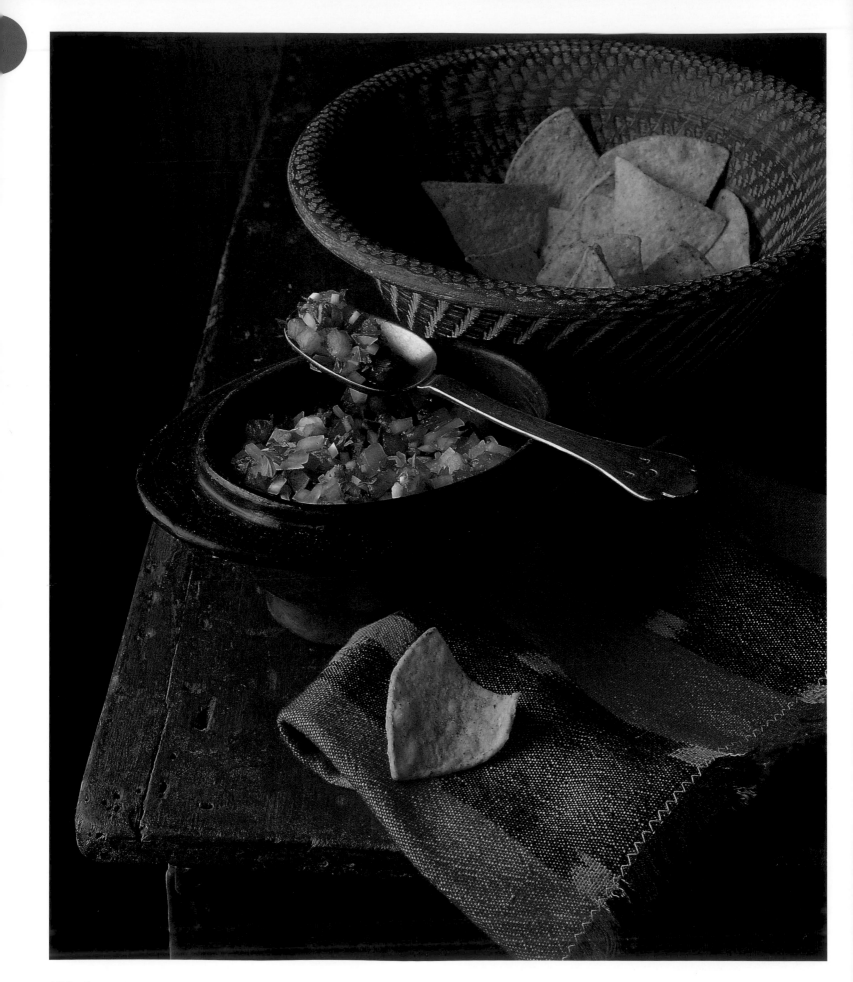

Salsa of tomato and coriander

MAKES 750 ML/1¼ PINTS

The salsas of Mexico are a national tradition, varying remarkably from region to region. In the northern region of Sonora they are mild, rarely calling for any of the country's wide selection of chillies, but in southern Mexico's Yucatán peninsula, cooks often spice things up with fiery habaneros? This mild fruity tomato salsa can be made hotter with more chillies, if you like.

500 g/1 pound tomatoes, peeled, seeded and chopped
2 garlic cloves, finely chopped
1 large onion, chopped
1 green or red sweet pepper, cored, seeded and chopped
small bunch of coriander leaves, chopped
1-2 jalapeño chilli pepper(s), cored, seeded and chopped
juice of 1 lemon
salt and pepper

Mix together the tomatoes, garlic, onion, sweet pepper, coriander and jalapeño(s) in a non-metallic bowl. Stir in the lemon juice and season to taste with salt and pepper. Let stand at room temperature at least 30 minutes.

Before serving, stir the salsa well to blend the juices, then taste and adjust the seasoning. Serve the salsa at room temperature or chilled. It can be kept 2-3 days, but it is best on the day of making.

Fresh tomato sauce with oregano
Salsa marinara

MAKES 1 LITRE/1⅔ PINTS

Tomato-based salsa marinara varies widely with the season and what the cook happens to have on hand. By varying its cooking time and thickness, it can be used for both pasta and pizza.

1.4 kg/3 lb tomatoes, peeled, seeded and chopped
75 ml/2½ fl oz olive oil
3 onions, chopped
5 garlic cloves, finely chopped
90 ml/3 fl oz tomato purée
3-4 tablespoons chopped oregano
pinch of sugar
salt and pepper

Heat the oil in a large deep heavy-based saucepan. Add the onions and fry over medium heat until soft and lightly browned, 4-5 minutes. Add the garlic and cook until fragrant, 1 minute. Stir in the tomatoes, tomato purée, oregano, sugar, salt and pepper. Cover and cook over low heat until the tomatoes are very soft, 10-15 minutes.

Uncover the pan and continue cooking the tomato sauce, stirring occasionally, until lightly thickened for pasta, 5-10 minutes, or until very thick and concentrated, 20-25 minutes, for pizza sauce. Taste the sauce and adjust the seasoning.

Fresh tomato sauce with roasted red peppers

On the island of Majorca I came across an interesting version of tomato sauce which includes roasted red pepper. It is often used for topping the island version of pizza, called coca am pebres. Make Fresh Tomato Sauce with Garlic and Oregano as described above and leave to simmer for 10-15 minutes until thick enough just to fall from the spoon.

While it is cooking, roast 3 red peppers under the grill, turning them until the skins char and burst, 7-10 minutes. Put them in a plastic bag to retain steam and loosen the skins. Let them cool, then peel them. Cut them in half, discard the cores and seeds and cut them in strips. Stir them into the tomato sauce, taste and adjust the seasoning. Makes 1.25 litres/2 pints.

Salsa of tomato and coriander

Custard sauce

LOOK AT ANY DESSERT MENU AND YOU'RE SURE TO FIND CUSTARD SAUCE in one form or another, often disguised under its French name *crème anglaise*. It marries with almost any flavouring from anise to coffee to zest of citrus, and accompanies many hot and cold puddings, soufflés, mousses, cakes and fruit compote. Custard is also the base of cold soufflés, bavarians, charlottes and such eternal favourites as floating islands and trifle. The finest ice cream is often made from a custard base, taking on a new spin with tastes like cinnamon apple and lavender honey.

The best custard is home-made from whole milk, thickened with egg yolks and sweetened with sugar – standard proportions are 500 ml/16 fl oz milk, 5 egg yolks and 50 g/1¾ oz sugar. Flavour is easily tainted, so use fresh, previously unopened milk and be sure utensils are clean. Sometimes a light thickener is added – for more about that see Pastry cream and Thickened custard sauces (opposite).

The main danger when making custard is curdling – it thickens at 82°C/180°F, and overcooks at only 6°C/10°F more, so must never be allowed to boil. It will only thicken slightly, with less body than flour-based custard. To spread the heat evenly, I use a heavy pan, preferably made of copper, and stir steadily with a wooden spoon over low to medium heat. Use a water bath if you like, but it will take you much longer. Egg yolks and sugar can be lightly beaten before adding the heated milk, but during cooking do not be tempted to whisk the custard itself. The aim is a smooth rich finish, not a foamy one.

CONSISTENCY TOO THIN – same consistency as milk; custard runs together when finger is drawn across back of spoon.
Why: custard not sufficiently cooked; too few egg yolks used.
What to do: continue cooking over low to medium heat, stirring constantly; if too few egg yolks, whisk in 1-2 teaspoons cornflour mixed to a paste with 1-2 tablespoons water and continue cooking until custard thickens.

PERFECT – creamy, smooth and clear trail is left when finger is drawn across back of spoon; flavour is delicate, perfumed with vanilla.

OTHER PROBLEMS

'OFF' FLAVOUR
Why: egg custard is delicate and can easily be tainted by other flavours.
What to do: store tightly covered; just before serving, stir in brisk flavouring such as liqueur.

CURDLED – milk separates, leaving egg curds.
Why: custard cooked too long or over too high a heat; milk was stale and soured on heating.
What to do: pour custard at once into cold bowl and whisk vigorously. If still curdled, see Quick Fix.

QUICK FIX

If custard is slightly curdled, with a thin, coarse texture, emulsify it with an immersion blender, or work it in a blender until smooth. Note: if custard is so overcooked that firm curds of egg yolk have formed, nothing can be done.

Pastry cream and thickened custard sauces

PASTRY CREAM IS ONE OF THE HALF DOZEN FOUNDATIONS OF THE DESSERT REPERTOIRE, indispensable in fruit tarts, for stabilizing cream fillings and as a base for hot soufflés. Without pastry cream we would have no éclairs, napoleons, cream horns and puffs, no classics such as *gâteau Saint-Honoré*, nor many versions of profiteroles. Pastry cream often acts as a medium to enrich and thicken other ingredients, so consistency is all-important. For almost all uses pastry cream should be thick enough to hold a shape but not so sticky as to be unpleasant on the tongue. Standard proportions are 3 egg yolks, 50 g/1¾ oz sugar and 10 g/1½ tablespoons flour or 7 g/1 tablespoon cornflour for each 250 ml/8 fl oz of milk. With more milk, pastry cream becomes a custard, a handy accompaniment for puddings and fruit desserts.

Constant whisking of both pastry cream and thickened custard sauce ensures they thicken evenly, and a heavy pan lessens the risk of scorching. Given the ingredients of egg yolk and milk, you might think pastry cream or thickened custard sauce would be liable to curdle. However, the mixture contains enough flour or starch to be boiled without danger of separating. When thickened with flour, pastry cream is smooth and soft; with cornflour it is glossy, but can be sticky; while with potato starch it is very light. Sometimes a mixture of flour and starch is used. No matter what the final flavouring, pastry cream and thickened custard sauce should be thoroughly imbued with vanilla, preferably by infusing the milk with vanilla pod.

QUICK FIX

When pastry cream or custard sauce is heavy, dull or tasteless, give it an edge by whisking in 2-3 teaspoons kirsch or other white fruit alcohol, with the grated zest of a lemon.

  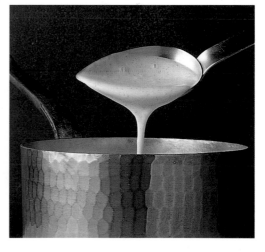

PERFECT PASTRY CREAM – glossy and very smooth; when hot, holds mark of whisk for 3-5 seconds but still falls easily from spoon; delicate golden colour dotted with vanilla seeds; flavour perfumed and rich, with no trace of flour or starch; when cooled thickens just enough to hold a shape.

PASTRY CREAM TOO THICK – when hot, pastry cream is sticky and holds a shape; when cold, it is stiff and glutinous; flavour is floury.
Why: too much flour or starch; reduced too much.
What to do: thin by whisking in milk or a flavouring such as liqueur or fruit juice.

PERFECT THICKENED CUSTARD SAUCE – glossy and very smooth; coats a spoon and pours off spoon in a steady stream; flavour delicate, usually of vanilla.

OTHER PROBLEMS

TOO THIN
Why: too little flour or starch; not fully cooked.
What to do: simmer, stirring constantly, until reduced.
LUMPY
Why: cooked too fast; not whisked as it thickened.
What to do: take at once from heat and whisk vigorously; if still lumpy, work through a sieve.
SKIN FORMS ON COOLING
Why: cream not covered with cling film.
What to do: whisk vigorously until smooth; if still

lumpy, work through a sieve.
CURDLED
Why: too little flour or starch to stabilize egg yolks and milk; milk stale; acid flavouring like lemon juice.
What to do: take from heat and whisk vigorously; re-emulsify using a blender or immersion blender.
BLAND
Why: lacks flavouring, particularly vanilla; flavouring evaporated from hot cream or custard.
What to do: when cold, add more strong flavouring

such as vanilla essence, rum, brandy or fruit liqueur.
TASTES OF FLOUR OR STARCH
Why: cream or custard not fully cooked.
What to do: if warm, bring to boil and simmer 2 minutes, whisking; if cold, add flavouring like coffee.
BROWN FLECKS
Why: scorched due to overheating or lack of whisking.
What to do: work through sieve into another pan, taking care not to scrape scorched pan surface.
Note: if badly burned, nothing can be done.

Mint custard sauce
Crème anglaise à la menthe
MAKES 500 ML/16 FL OZ

Mint is popular for flavouring custard, but other perfumed herbs such as lemon verbena are good too. Serve the sauce hot with a rich chocolate cake or chilled with Chocolate Caramel Terrine (page 245).

small bunch of fresh mint
500 ml/16 fl oz milk
5 egg yolks
50 g/1¾ oz sugar

Remove the sprigs from the top of the mint and reserve. Add the stalks and large leaves to the milk. Scald the milk. Cover and leave over a low heat to infuse for 10 minutes.

Beat the egg yolks and sugar until light and slightly thickened, 1-2 minutes. Whisk in half the milk, then stir this back into the remaining milk.

Heat gently, stirring constantly, until the sauce thickens slightly – do not allow to boil or it will curdle. Take from the heat at once and strain into a chilled bowl. If chilling, cover tightly to prevent a skin forming as it cools. Use the mint sprigs for decoration.

Phyllo millefeuille with raspberries and light pastry cream

SERVES 4-6

This contemporary recipe is a light version of classic millefeuille in which phyllo replaces puff pastry and the pastry cream is lightened with whipped cream. An accompaniment of raspberry coulis (page 136) would add a touch of colour. Any red berries can be substituted for the raspberries.

4 sheets of phyllo pastry	for the pastry cream	for the Chantilly cream
45 g/1½ oz butter	250 ml/8 fl oz milk	250 ml/8 fl oz double
3 tablespoons honey	1 vanilla pod, split	cream
175 g/6 oz raspberries	lengthwise	2 tablespoons icing sugar
	3 egg yolks	1 tablespoon brandy
	50 g/1¾ oz sugar	
	1½ tablespoons flour	

Make the pastry cream: scald the milk in a medium saucepan with the vanilla pod, cover and leave to infuse off the heat for 5-10 minutes. Meanwhile, beat the egg yolks with the sugar until thick and light. Stir in the flour. Whisk the milk into the egg mixture and return it to the saucepan. Cook over a low heat, whisking constantly, until the cream comes to the boil and thickens. Simmer, stirring, until done, 1 or 2 minutes. Strain the pastry cream into a bowl. The vanilla pod can be rinsed and used again. Rub the surface of the pastry cream with butter or press cling film on top to prevent a skin from forming and then chill the pastry cream thoroughly.

Preheat the oven to 230°C/450°F/gas8. Brush a baking sheet with butter. Heat the honey and remaining butter until melted. Lay a sheet of phyllo on the prepared baking sheet and brush with the honey butter. Lay a second sheet on top and brush again. Repeat until all four phyllo sheets are used, brushing the top of the last layer with honey butter. With a sharp knife or pastry wheel, cut the phyllo layers lengthwise in 3 strips, trimming the edges. Cut each strip in 6 pieces to make 18 small rectangles. Bake in the preheated oven until the phyllo is golden and the glaze on top begins to caramelize, 5-6 minutes. The layers will puff and separate slightly. Transfer to a rack and let cool.

Make the Chantilly cream: whip the double cream until it holds a soft peak. Add the sugar and brandy and continue whipping until the cream again holds a soft peak. Pick over the raspberries, rinsing them only if they are sandy, reserving the best for decoration.

When the pastry cream is cold, whisk it briefly to lighten the texture. Fold in the Chantilly cream. Spread 1-2 heaping tablespoons of this lightened pastry cream over one rectangle of phyllo. Top with a few raspberries and set a second rectangle of phyllo, slightly askew, on top. Add more pastry cream and raspberries and top with a last rectangle of phyllo, setting it askew also. Transfer the millefeuille to a serving plate and sprinkle a few reserved berries around the edge. Assemble the remaining millefeuilles in the same way and serve them chilled.

Phyllo millefeuille with raspberries and light pastry cream

Sweet sabayon sauce

SWEET SABAYON SAUCE IS CLOSELY RELATED to the fluffy Italian dessert *zabaglione*, made with egg yolks, sugar and Marsala. Various flavourings can be used, whether for warming desserts such as rum sabayon served with candied chestnuts, or muscat sabayon with fig and walnut pudding. Perhaps sabayon's most popular use is to coat fresh fruits, particularly berries and orange segments, then to brown them as a gratin (see opposite).

Given its generous content of liqueur or fruit juice (standard proportions are 1 tablespoon sugar and 2 tablespoons liquid for each egg yolk), sweet sabayon sauce is inclined to curdle. Whisk it vigorously, using very low heat so thickening does not even start for 2-3 minutes. With regret, I must admit that an electric mixer is not a good substitute for hard work by hand with a balloon whisk in a copper or metal bowl. Do not heat the sauce too much – the bottom of the bowl should never be very hot to the touch. Serve sabayon as soon as you can, preferably still warm.

CONSISTENCY TOO THIN – pours very easily and lacks richness.
Why: not cooked enough; cooked too quickly so egg does not froth and thicken to maximum; egg overcooked and about to curdle; too much liquid flavouring.
What to do: continue cooking if not cooked enough; if sauce starts to thin after thickening, it is about to curdle – cool bowl or pan at once by dipping base in cold water and whisk sauce constantly until tepid; see Quick Fix.

PERFECT – smooth, fluffy and rich, holds ribbon trail of whisk 10 seconds; flavour is delicate, aromatic with liqueur, wine or fruit juice. Note: if whisked until cool, sabayon will hold 10-15 minutes without separating, but not longer.

CURDLED – thin, coarse consistency with tiny curds of egg visible; texture is slightly granular on the tongue.
Why: cooked over too high a heat or for too long; kept warm for too long.
What to do: unfortunately, little can be done. For a face-saver, see Quick Fix.

OTHER PROBLEMS

LACKS TASTE
Why: too little flavouring.
What to do: whisk in more sugar or sweet liqueur.
SEPARATED AND LIQUID FALLS TO BOTTOM
Why: left to stand too long.
What to do: whisk vigorously and serve at once.

QUICK FIX

If sabayon overcooks and becomes granular, take it at once from the heat, set bowl in cold water and whisk sabayon until cool. Then transform it into a pleasant cream sauce. For every 250 ml/8 fl oz sabayon, whip 125 ml/4 fl oz double cream until it holds a soft peak. Fold the sabayon into the cream.

Berries and pears with sabayon sauce

SERVES 4

If you have heatproof serving plates, add a professional touch to this dessert by browning it under the grill.

2 ripe pears
125 g/4 oz mixed berries
30 g/1 oz plain chocolate, grated

for the sabayon sauce
5 egg yolks
60 g/2 oz sugar
150 ml/5 fl oz Sauternes or other sweet
   white wine

Peel, halve and quarter the pears. Discard the cores and slice the quarters. Spread the slices on heatproof individual plates. Pick over the berries, rinsing them only if they are sandy. Sprinkle them over the pears, cover the plates tightly with cling film and chill.

Make the sabayon sauce: put the egg yolks, sugar and wine in a bowl, preferably of copper or stainless steel. With a balloon whisk or hand-held electric mixer, whisk the ingredients just until mixed. Set the bowl over a pan of hot but not boiling water, and whisk until done,

5-8 minutes. Sabayon can be made 10-15 minutes ahead and kept at room temperature; whisk it until cool, then whisk it occasionally again to prevent it from separating.

To serve: spoon the sabayon over the fruits, coating them completely. If you like, brown the sabayon under the grill. Top with grated chocolate and serve at once.

Fruit coulis and purées

THE NAME COULIS COMES FROM THE FRENCH *COULER*, meaning 'to flow', and implies a puréed sauce, used to describe both savoury and sweet preparations. Consistency should be pourable but somewhat thicker than a coating sauce, perfect with pastries and cakes. A fruit purée is even thicker than a coulis, firm enough to hold a shape. It is usually mixed with other more delicate ingredients, such as the custard used in ice cream, or the whipped cream in a parfait.

Fruit coulis and purées may be fresh or cooked. Both should be vivid in flavour and colour, with a smooth or slightly chunky texture free of fibre. You need an assertive fruit, such as apricot, peach, mango, pineapple, cranberry, raspberry, blackberry or strawberry.

For both coulis and purée, I like to work the fruit pulp briefly in a processor or with an immersion blender so a bit of texture is left, but it is equally correct to strain them for a smoother finish. In any case, some fruits such as raspberries must be strained to remove seeds or fibre. Remember that sugar seasons any fruit and develops flavour, acting like salt in savoury dishes. Some fresh fruits discolour very quickly and must be generously doused with lemon juice.

Peppered strawberry coulis

MAKES 250 ML/8 FL OZ

You'll be surprised how freshly ground black pepper and balsamic vinegar pick up the taste of strawberries in this coulis, which is delicious with pastries and cakes such as Angel Food Cake (page 281).

500 g/1 pound strawberries, hulled
2 tablespoons icing sugar, or to taste
1 tablespoon balsamic vinegar
½ teaspoon freshly ground black pepper, or to taste

Purée the strawberries in a blender or food processor or work them through a food mill. Stir in the sugar, vinegar and pepper. Taste, adding more sugar or pepper if necessary.

CONSISTENCY TOO THIN – coulis or purée watery, lacks body; easy to pour; colour and flavour muted. *Why:* too much liquid added; too much sugar. *What to do:* purée and stir in more of same fruit, or a firm fruit such as fresh raspberries (for red fruit) or peach (for yellow fruit); treat purée as a coulis, or transform coulis into a cooked fruit sauce (opposite).

PERFECT COULIS – texture smooth, glossy but less emulsified than strained sauce; coulis generously coats a spoon but pours easily; colour vivid and flavour rich.

PERFECT PURÉE – texture even, possibly coarse but not fibrous; purée thick enough to leave a ribbon trail, but still just falls from spoon; flavour intense.

QUICK FIX

Pick up a coulis that is too thin, flat, pale or discoloured with chopped fresh fruit. For each 250 ml/8 fl oz red berry coulis, stir in 175 g/6 oz coarsely chopped strawberries and raspberries and chopped mint; for each 250 ml/8 fl oz mango or peach coulis, add 175 g/6 oz chopped orange, honeydew or cantaloupe, with chopped lemon balm and toasted slivered almonds. The perfect disguise!

OTHER PROBLEMS

TEXTURE COARSE OR FIBROUS
Why: fruit contains natural seeds or fibre; poorly puréed.
What to do: purée fruit thoroughly in food processor or blender, then work through a sieve.

FLAT TASTE
Why: poor or bland fruit; lacks sugar or flavouring.
What to do: whisk in sugar, lemon juice and lively flavouring such as kirsch or other white alcohol such as pear or plum brandy.

ACID
Why: unripe fruit; too little sugar.
What to do: whisk in sugar or other sweetener such as honey.

PALE OR DISCOLOURED
Why: poor or unripe fruit; sauce oxidized by air.
What to do: distract attention by adding bright whole or chopped fruit, particularly berries, or chopped herb such as mint; colour with food colouring.

Cooked fruit sauces

Berry fruit sauce

MAKES 500 ML/16 FL OZ

SIMILAR AS THEY ARE ON THE DESSERT PLATE, a cooked fruit sauce gives a different impression from a coulis. Where a coulis is vibrant, the flavour of a fruit sauce is more complex and mellow. Texture can be as thick as the apple sauce commonly served with pancakes, or semi-transparent and so thin that the sauce scarcely veils the food beneath. Fruits should be pungent: apricot, blackberry, cherry, cranberry, lemon, orange, plum, redcurrant and blackcurrant are typical. Often they are cooked in syrup and may or may not be puréed. When they need thickening, a starch which cooks to be transparent and glossy is best, such as cornflour, arrowroot or potato starch.

By no means all cooked fruit sauces are intended for dessert. Cranberry sauce with roast turkey springs to mind, and contemporary menus are alive with dishes like pan-seared snapper with orange ginger sauce or pepper steak with redcurrant glaze. The appeal of such sweet-and-sour combinations is timeless.

500 g/1 pound sweet blueberries, or tarter
  bilberries, raspberries or blackberries
250 ml/8 fl oz water
2 tablespoons brown sugar, or more to taste
2 strips of lemon zest
2 teaspoons arrowroot, mixed with
  1 tablespoon water
1 teaspoon ground allspice

In a heavy pan, mix the berries, water, sugar and zest. Cover, bring to the boil and simmer until the fruit is very soft, 5-7 minutes. Work through a fine sieve into another pan. Bring to the boil. Whisk in the arrowroot paste and allspice. Simmer for 1 minute. Add more sugar or lemon juice if necessary. Serve warm or cool.

CONSISTENCY TOO THIN – watery, almost transparent, lacks colour and taste.
Why: too much liquid; not enough fruit pulp or thickener to bind.
What to do: simmer until reduced to right consistency; thicken further with arrowroot or cornflour.

PERFECT – very smooth and lightly coats a spoon; colour brilliant and glossy; flavour concentrated and refreshing.

GRAINY – uneven, sometimes gluey texture, often muddy colour.
Why: fruit pulp poorly puréed; seeds or fibre not sieved out.
What to do: purée sauce more thoroughly in blender or use an immersion blender; if necessary work through a sieve.

OTHER PROBLEMS

CONSISTENCY TOO THICK, STICKY TEXTURE
Why: too little liquid; too much thickener, particularly cornflour.
What to do: thin with fruit juice, liqueur or water.
LACKS TASTE
Why: poor fruit; too little fruit with too much liquid; sauce stored too long and flavour faded.
What to do: add sugar; add strong flavour such as lemon juice, liqueur or chopped herb; simmer cooked

sauce to reduce until concentrated.
MUDDY COLOUR
Why: inferior fruit; fruit browned on exposure to air.
What to do: colour with liqueur such as cassis, fruit purée such as raspberry, or food colouring; disguise by adding chopped herb such as mint.

QUICK FIX

After cooking, the flavour of a fruit sauce may need a pick-me-up such as a few drops of almond essence (good with plums, apricots and other stone fruits), or a teaspoon of vanilla essence or orange flower water.

Chocolate sauces

YOU'LL FIND MANY RECIPES FOR SWEET CHOCOLATE SAUCE and they all should deliver the same result, a rich, dark, glossy sauce that is exuberant with flavour. Additions such as coffee, rum, brandy and spices, even chilli, play a supporting role to the chocolate itself. Whether a recipe calls for plain, dark, milk or white chocolate, look for reputable brands made without cocoa substitutes or additives (other than the milk added to milk chocolate). Suit your personal taste, trying different brands to find your favourite. Chocolates of lesser quality will produce insipid, thin-bodied sauces that can sometimes also be bitter.

A cold sauce to go with mousses, sponge or angel food cake or poached fruit, as in pears *belle Hélène*, should be thinner than a hot one for profiteroles, puddings and soufflés. Fudge sauce for ice cream and sundaes is thickest of all.

A reliable recipe for chocolate sauce will always call for enough liquid to melt the chocolate without danger of seizing (see opposite). In chocolate sauce this is caused by too little liquid – 1½ teaspoons of liquid per 30 g/1 oz chocolate is the bare minimum to keep melted chocolate smooth. When simmering a sauce to the right consistency for a given dish, you may by accident boil too far. Another mishap can occur if hot or cold liquid is poured on melted chocolate and stirred – the chocolate may briefly seize so the sauce looks lumpy and flecked. If simmered it will become smooth, so do not worry.

I've been talking here about sweet chocolate sauces. Chocolate also turns up in ethnic savoury sauces as in Mexican *mole poblano*, a labour-intensive sauce for roasted turkey made of chillies, nuts, spices and chocolate. Here the chocolate is one of many ingredients, rather than playing the dominant role.

Chocolate and stout sauce

MAKES 250 ML/8 FL OZ

'The flavour of chocolate', declared a journalist friend of mine one day, 'blends much better with beer than wine' – hence the inspiration for this sauce, delicious with freshly cut fruit, especially pear slices and orange segments.

175 g/6 oz plain chocolate, chopped
175 ml/6 fl oz stout or dark beer

Over a low heat, melt the chocolate with the beer, stirring gently until the sauce is smooth. Bring to the boil and simmer, stirring, to the consistency wanted, 1-2 minutes.

Remove the sauce from the heat and serve hot or cool.

QUICK FIX

There's nothing like a shot of alcohol for improving chocolate sauce: whisk in 1-2 tablespoons rum, whisky or brandy, adding it just before serving so the alcohol has no time to evaporate. Rather than throw the chocolate out you may want to dissolve it in milk or cream and serve it as hot chocolate – allow about 250 ml/8 fl oz milk for 175 g/6 oz chocolate. The drink will, however, never be completely smooth.

PERFECT – rich-flavoured, glossy; whether hot or cold, lightly coats a spoon.

PERFECT FUDGE – very thick and rich; sets on contact with cold surface such as ice cream.

OTHER PROBLEMS

CONSISTENCY TOO THIN
Why: too much liquid.
What to do: simmer until reduced to right consistency.

BITTER OR POWDERY TASTE
Why: too little sugar; not enough fat.
What to do: add a little more sugar and butter or oil, stirring gently until melted.

Melting chocolate

THERE ARE DOZENS OF TYPES AND FLAVOURS OF CHOCOLATE, each with varying amounts of cocoa butter. The higher the cocoa butter, the more easily chocolate softens and melts. Some recipes may call for couverture, often called dipping or coating chocolate. This is the ideal confectioners' chocolate as it has a high cocoa butter content, varying between 35 and 50 percent, with no padding of cheaper vegetable oil. Melting is also affected by sugar content, particularly in sweet and milk chocolates.

The main problem when melting chocolate is 'seizing', a term which describes chocolate which suddenly stiffens and becomes grainy. This will happen if a few drops of water come in contact with the chocolate – a damp bowl can be the cause, or steam from a water bath. Seizing can be reversed (below) but the chocolate will never be quite so glossy. More serious is the seizing caused by overheating, which makes the cocoa butter separate from the cocoa solids. It cannot be recombined. In fact, chocolate can be tricky stuff, so it needs some attention.

After chopping, chocolate can be melted by warming it in a double boiler or in a bowl or plate placed over hot water (about 48°C/120°F); a microwave also does a good job. Don't stir at once, but leave the warmth to penetrate and when you see the sharp outlines of the chocolate blur, it's nearly melted. Begin stirring gently every 15-20 seconds until the chocolate is smooth – consistency will vary, with unsweetened chocolate the thinnest, milk chocolate the thickest. Take particular care with milk and white chocolates – a lower heat of around 37°C/100°F is best. Once melted, chocolate may be tempered – a heating and cooling technique which makes it more malleable and glossy. You can also melt chocolate in generous amounts of liquid (see Chocolate and Stout Sauce, opposite).

PERFECT – chocolate just thin enough to pour, smooth, very glossy and even-textured when stirred; colour rich, varying with type of chocolate.

SEIZED – chocolate suddenly stiffens to rough, lumpy texture; oily cocoa butter may separate to surface; chocolate looks granular and lacks gloss.
Why: a few drops water or steam were in contact with chocolate; chocolate was heated above 48°C/120°F (less for milk and white chocolate), so cocoa butter separates.
What to do: see Quick Fix.

Chocolate-coated cherries
MAKES 36

Several fruits may be dipped in chocolate – fresh cherries, strawberries and strips of candied citrus peel spring to mind – but I think brandied cherries are the best. The cherries should ideally still have stems to make dipping easier. I suggest 'tempering' the chocolate here to keep its gloss, but you can just use melted chocolate.

36 cherries preserved in Cognac, with stalks
150 g/5 oz couverture chocolate, chopped

Drain the cherries (keep the Cognac for another use), set on paper towels and leave uncovered in the refrigerator to dry 5-8 hours.

To temper chocolate: put it in a small deep bowl and set over a pan of hot water or in a hot, but not boiling, water bath. Leave until outlines start to blur, indicating melting. Stir gently until completely melted and smooth; temperature should measure 45°C/115°F. Transfer bowl to a pan of cold water and let cool for 12-15 minutes, stirring often (temperature should be 32°C/90°F). The chocolate will stiffen slightly; melt it again over hot water or in a water bath.

To dip cherries: line a baking sheet with greaseproof paper, then take chocolate from heat, leaving over pan or in bath. Dip cherries one by one into chocolate, letting excess drain for 15-30 seconds before setting on paper. This prevents a 'foot' of chocolate forming at the base. If cherries have no stems, dip on a fork.

Leave in a cool place to set – if refrigerated the cherries will lose their gloss. They keep well 2-3 days provided they are completely coated with chocolate. Transfer to paper cases for serving.

QUICK FIX

If chocolate seizes and stiffens suddenly during melting, take it from the heat and dry any beads of steam on the bowl; stir in 1-2 teaspoons vegetable oil or white vegetable fat, adding it a little at a time until the chocolate is smooth again – it will never be as glossy. Note: if very overheated, chocolate may be scorched and unusable.

VEGETABLES

THERE'S MORE TO THE HUMBLE VEGETABLE than meets the eye. Living at Château du Feÿ, with a vegetable garden in full production, has been a revelation. Every year is different, with tomatoes a bumper crop one season, yet the next they scarcely manage to ripen. Leeks seem to flourish no matter what the weather, but garlic and shallots are timid and supply is always meagre. I've learned that produce varies also with the seasons – the same potatoes which are firm and waxy when first harvested, have dried six months later to the floury consistency that is perfect for purée.

The point is that cooking vegetables is not a matter of standard rules. Instructions on seasoning, cooking methods and timing can never be more than approximate. Therefore, being able to recognize when a vegetable is cooked to perfection is doubly important. In this chapter I've deliberately concentrated on tricky varieties such as asparagus, which is inedibly chewy if underdone but can overcook in a moment or two. Greens have at least two useful stages of cooking, blanched and lightly cooked. Roots, also, can be cooked until just tender, but if they are to be puréed or used for soup they must be very soft. Onions change flavour radically depending on how fast and how long they are cooked and whether or not they are allowed to brown and caramelize.

The vegetable tribe is so varied that only a few universal rules hold good. Some vegetables discolour easily when peeled, notably roots such as potato and celeriac, white asparagus, and globe artichokes, so cut them with a stainless knife and if necessary hold them in water acidulated with lemon juice. There's a move towards leaving the peel on vegetables both for flavour and nutrients, but be aware that fertilizers and pesticides also collect near the surface. In this case, organically grown produce is a good idea. When preparing vegetables, cut them in even-sized pieces so they cook evenly as well as look attractive.

This is just a beginning. I've learned so much more from the chefs at La Varenne. It was Chef Chambrette who introduced me to his buttered cabbage, made by blanching cabbage then slowly baking it with quantities of butter until it falls into a glistening rich confit. Pumpkin soup was Chef Claude's speciality – the whole pumpkin was filled with milk and baked in its skin until the flesh could be scooped out with a spoon, leaving a spectacular serving container. Demonstrations by Chef Bouvier introduced me to clouds of deep-fried ginger and leek julienne as a garnish for fish. Giant bouquets of herbs appeared in the kitchen, a reflection of the huge amounts which infuse contemporary cuisine.

Roasted tomato, mushroom, onion and
garlic bruschetta, page 163

Artichokes

A SPIKY BOILED ARTICHOKE IS A CONUNDRUM, its prickles and hairy choke bristling guardians of the rich flesh inside. I do so appreciate a cook who trims an artichoke before cooking, snapping the stem, trimming the top with a knife and snipping spines from the leaves. After cooking, spread back the leaves and scoop out the monster of a choke with a teaspoon to leave space for a filling of fresh tomato and goats' cheese, or a Provençal *barigoule* mixture of ground pork, garlic, wild thyme, olives and breadcrumbs, or simply serve it with the piquant *gribiche* mayonnaise (opposite). When cooking artichokes, it's important to keep the water at a steady simmer and to allow at least 1 litre/1⅔ pints of salted water per artichoke. A single garlic clove pushed inside the leaves perfumes the whole artichoke with great effect and a squeeze of lemon juice in the water helps preserve the green colour. Artichokes tend to float during cooking, acquiring an ugly 'tide mark' at water level, so I sink them firmly with a heavy heatproof plate.

QUICK FIX

When an artichoke is overcooked or discoloured, pull away large plump leaves and arrange in concentric circles on a large individual plate. Discard central leaves and small outer leaves as well as choke. Set artichoke bottom in centre of plate. Spoon a Salsa of Tomato and Coriander (page 129) or Brown Butter Hollandaise (page 119) into the bottom, serving remaining sauce separately.

PERFECT – artichoke an even olive green colour; a leaf pulled from near centre comes out easily; heart is tender when pierced with two-pronged fork; flavour is rich, intense but not bitter.

OVERCOOKED AND DRAB – leaves falling from artichoke; centre very soft when pierced with two-pronged fork; colour muddy.
Why: cooked too slowly; cooked too long; water not boiling when artichokes added; not enough water (see Blanching and boiling green vegetables on page 153).
What to do: drain artichokes upside down on a rack, squeezing them so water runs off leaves. Serve with a lively sauce such as pesto, a red pepper coulis or mustard and herb vinaigrette. If very overcooked, discard leaves and choke and cut up artichoke heart to mix with other vegetables as a salad – rice, broad beans, mushrooms and spring onions are traditional.

OTHER PROBLEMS

UNDERCOOKED, TOUGH AND FIBROUS
Why: cooked too slowly; not cooked long enough; old artichokes.
What to do: continue cooking until tender, if necessary increasing heat – I find that young artichokes cook in 20-30 minutes, but when large and mature they can take up to an hour. If they are very fibrous, nothing can be done.

PRICKLY, OR HAIRY FROM CENTRAL CHOKE
Why: poorly trimmed before cooking; not fully cleaned when cooked.
What to do: twist out central leaves to form a crown, scoop out choke with a teaspoon and replace crown of leaves, point down.
BITTER
Why: old; stem not trimmed; too little water used.
What to do: disguise with a tart lemon vinaigrette.

Artichokes with sauce gribiche

SERVES 4

This light version of mayonnaise, called *sauce gribiche*, is excellent with many cold cooked vegetables such as asparagus, broccoli or cauliflower. Here I suggest serving it with large artichokes, and it is also good with little ones, so small they contain no choke and are totally edible. Trim the tips of the leaves of little artichokes and peel the stem, as you can eat much of its centre. As this recipe uses raw egg, please read the notes about salmonella on page 9.

4 large globe artichokes
½ lemon
4 garlic cloves

for the gribiche sauce
2 hard-boiled eggs
1 raw egg yolk
salt and pepper

250 ml/8 fl oz vegetable oil
2 tablespoons white wine
1 teaspoon Dijon-style mustard
1 tablespoon chopped gherkins
1 tablespoon capers, rinsed and drained
2 tablespoons chopped parsley
juice of ½ lemon

Bring a large pan of salted water to the boil. Break off the stem from each artichoke so that any fibres are pulled out. Trim the bases with a knife so each artichoke sits flat and rub the cut surfaces with lemon to prevent discolouration. Add the lemon half to the pan. Trim the leaves with scissors to remove spines. With a large knife, cut off the pointed top of the artichoke, parallel to the base. Push a garlic clove into the leaves of each artichoke. Add them to the boiling water and lay a heavy heatproof plate on top to keep the artichokes submerged. Simmer uncovered until done, 30-50 minutes, depending on age and size. Drain artichokes upside down, so no water is trapped by the leaves. Let the artichokes cool.

Make the gribiche sauce: separate the hard-boiled egg whites from the yolks, coarsely chop the whites and set aside. Force the cooked yolks through a sieve into a bowl. Mix in the raw egg yolk with a large pinch of salt. Whisk in about 2 tablespoons of oil, very slowly at first, until the mixture thickens, as for mayonnaise. Whisk in the white wine. Continue whisking in the remaining oil in a slow steady stream. Stir in the mustard, reserved egg whites, gherkins, capers, parsley and lemon juice. Taste and adjust the seasoning.

To finish the artichokes: grasp the central cone of leaves and, with a quick twist, lift it out. Reserve it, discarding the garlic cloves. With a teaspoon or melon baller, carefully scoop out the fibrous choke and discard it. Set the cones of leaves upside down in the centre of each artichoke. Place the artichokes on individual plates and spoon some sauce into each cup of leaves. Serve the remaining sauce separately.

PREVENTING DISCOLORATION

Like many fruits, several types of vegetables oxidize very readily when they are peeled or cut, and the flesh exposed to the air will discolour dramatically in a fairly short time.

When preparing such vegetables, like artichokes, potatoes, parsnips, celeriac, jerusalem artichokes, salsify and avocados, it is preferable to use a stainless steel knife as contact with other types of metal can exacerbate the situation.

Acids like vinegar or lemon juice will prevent oxidation, so as soon as the vegetable is cut either rub any exposed surfaces of the vegetable with a cut lemon or brush it all over with vinegar or lemon juice. Root vegetables should immediately be immersed in cold water; for potatoes this is sufficient, but other roots need the water to be acidulated with a dash of vinegar or lemon juice.

It is also a good idea idea to add vinegar or lemon juice to the cooking water. Vegetables prone to oxidation like this, if cooked by steaming, are likely to lose their colour and it is difficult to prevent this from happening.

You may prefer to cook vegetables that discolour in a *blanc*, that is to say in water which is acidulated with lemon juice and whitened with a little flour. Bring a pan of salted water to the boil. Make a soft paste by stirring some cold water into flour, allowing 3 tablespoons water and 1 tablespoon flour for every 1 litre/1⅔ pints of cooking water. Stir this into the boiling water and add the juice of half a lemon. Add vegetables and cook for the usual time.

Asparagus

ASPARAGUS APPEARS IN TWO GUISES — GREEN AND WHITE. The most succulent size for green asparagus is a matter of debate. Personally I think it is at its best quite slim, particularly as very thin spears really do not need to be peeled. White asparagus, grown under the ground so the stems stay blanched, is another matter. Here the fatter the spears the better they are. They must always be peeled to remove the outer, woody skin, and even then you will sometimes run across fibrous white asparagus which cannot be reduced to tenderness by thorough boiling. In this case, use the stems of the asparagus for soup, reserving the tips for garnish.

Asparagus is usually boiled in salted water, either blanched (see page 153) for a salad or stir-fry, or lightly cooked as shown below, centre. Asparagus can also be grilled, taking care to brush it with oil or melted butter so it does not dry out. No matter how asparagus is cooked, to complement its fresh taste I prefer it served simply with melted butter or a vinaigrette dressing, particularly when made with walnut oil. An accompaniment of tarragon white butter sauce is another possibility, as is a Japanese miso dressing flavoured with mustard.

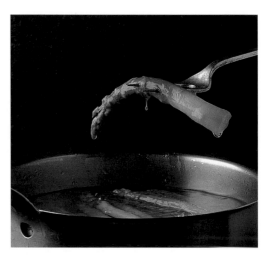

PERFECT BLANCHED – spears bend just slightly when lifted and are resistant when poked with a knife; texture is slightly crunchy but not fibrous; colour is vivid green. Slice blanched asparagus on the diagonal to stir-fry, or add to a sauce or salad.

PERFECT LIGHTLY COOKED – spears bend when lifted and are just tender when poked with knife; texture firm but not crunchy, and colour a clear green; flavour is fresh with no grassy overtones. Note: spears can vary in size; if necessary, sort and tie them by size so thin stems which cook more quickly can be removed first.

OVERCOOKED – spears are floppy when lifted and soft when poked with a knife; texture is soft, even slippery; colour tinged with yellow.
Why: cooked too slowly; cooked too long; if boiled, water not boiling when asparagus added, not enough water used (see Blanching and boiling green vegetables, page 153).
What to do: nothing can be done. Even trying to make a soup is disappointing as fresh flavour is gone.

OTHER PROBLEMS

FIBROUS
Why: undercooked; poorly peeled; old asparagus; if grilled, not basted often.
What to do: continue cooking, basting often if grilling; if very stringy, nothing can be done.

DISCOLOURED
Why: cooked too slowly; overcooked; pan covered with lid during cooking.
What to do: if boiled, refresh with cold water and drain thoroughly; disguise with colourful garnish such as chopped hard-boiled egg, red pepper, or herbs.

QUICK FIX

When asparagus is a bit overcooked, dress it as a vinaigrette salad. Cut spears diagonally into 1-cm/ ⅜-inch slices, reserving tips. For every 250 g/8 oz sliced asparagus, thinly slice 3 stalks of celery or ½ bulb of fennel. Add 3-4 tablespoons chopped fresh tarragon and vinaigrette dressing made with 1 teaspoon Dijon-style mustard, 2 tablespoons lemon juice, 75 ml/2½ fl oz olive oil, salt and pepper. Mix gently, taste and adjust seasoning. Pile on individual plates or in a serving bowl and top with asparagus tips. Serves 2-3.

Chicory, cardoon, celery, chard, fennel and leek

STALKS AND SHOOTS SUCH AS CELERY AND LEEKS turn up in many guises all over the world and several are edible raw. Where would Italy be without fennel, or China without bamboo shoots? Not necessarily related botanically, stalks and shoots share much in common in the kitchen. They are robust and crisp, lending themselves to a variety of cooking methods, from braising to grilling to steaming. However, many have a fibrous texture which is aggravated by improper cooking and they will turn tasteless or bitter if overcooked. These staple vegetables provide many favourite dishes, such as celery soup flavoured with caraway, braised chicory with ham in cheese sauce, leek vinaigrette and Italian fennel braised in milk with cinnamon, nutmeg and sugar. Tasty stalks like celery, leek and fennel also turn up in flavouring mixtures for soups and braises, often combined with onion, carrot and herbs.

PERFECT BLANCHED – vegetable opaque; crisp when poked with a knife; texture is crunchy, slightly fibrous and flavour grassy. Note: some stalks and shoots, such as fennel and chicory, are edible after blanching, but others such as leek and chard need further cooking.

PERFECT – vegetable slightly translucent; just tender when pierced with point of a knife, but holding shape well; flavour full-bodied.

PROBLEMS

OVERCOOKED AND WATERY
Why: cooked too long; vegetable pieces uneven so some cooked before others.
What to do: disguise by sprinkling with fried breadcrumbs, a hot bacon dressing or strips of prosciutto and shavings of Parmesan cheese.

FIBROUS
Why: poor or old vegetables; undercooked.
What to do: continue cooking until tender; when serving, cut across fibres to minimize toughness; for serving ideas, see Overcooked and watery.

TASTELESS OR BITTER
Why: poor or old vegetables; overcooked; underseasoned; if bitter, cooked with too little liquid (see Blanching and boiling green vegetables, page 153).
What to do: season well and add flavourings such as aniseed, coriander, anchovy or blue cheese.

DULL, GREYISH COLOUR
Why: poor or old vegetables; overcooked.
What to do: sprinkle with chopped hard-boiled egg, chopped tomato or sweet pepper.

Gratin of fennel with walnuts and raisins
SERVES 4

You may use a large bunch of celery in place of the fennel in this recipe.

2 fennel bulbs	75 g/2½ oz raisins
(about 375 g/¾ lb)	75 g/2½ oz pine nuts
60 g/2 oz butter	60 g/2 oz grated
salt and pepper	Parmesan cheese

Preheat the oven to 175°C/350°F/gas4. Trim the fennel and halve the bulbs. Set the halves cut-side down on a chopping board and cut into 6-mm/¼-in slices.

Melt half the butter in a frying pan. Add the fennel with some salt and pepper. Cover and sweat over a low heat until the fennel is tender, 10-15 minutes. Uncover, raise the heat and sauté, stirring, until the fennel is lightly browned, 3-5 minutes.

Stir in the raisins, pine nuts and half the Parmesan. Taste and adjust the seasoning. Spread the fennel mixture in a buttered gratin or baking dish. Sprinkle with the remaining Parmesan and dot with the remaining butter. Bake until very hot, 10-15 minutes.

QUICK FIX

All of these green vegetables are difficult to save when they've gone wrong. Simplest is to transform them into a creamed vegetable: to 375 g/¾ pound cooked, sliced vegetable add 45 g/1½oz butter, salt and pepper and a generous grating of nutmeg. Cover and sauté for 3-4 minutes. Uncover and cook until almost dry, 3-4 minutes. Add 125 ml/4 fl oz double cream and cook over a medium heat, stirring often, until soft and creamy, 7-10 minutes. Season to taste. Serves 4.

Green beans, sugar snap and mange-tout peas

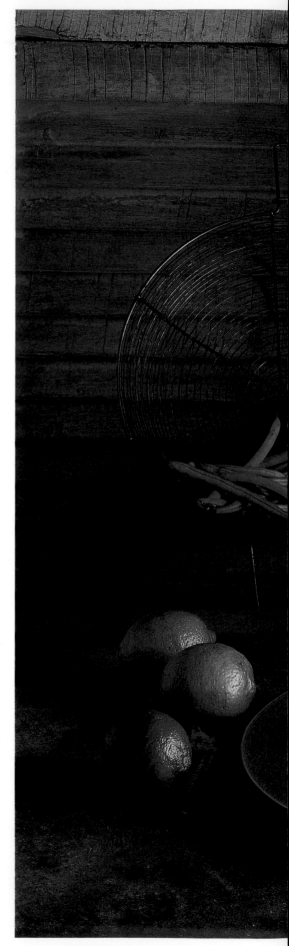

CONTROVERSY RAGES OVER THE COOKING OF GREEN BEANS. One school of thought likes them blanched, still crunchy. The other, to which I energetically subscribe, maintains that crunchy green beans taste of grass and need 1-2 additional minutes cooking to develop their flavour fully. Take your pick! All cooks reunite on sugar snap and mange-tout peas, whose pods become slippery and fall apart when overcooked. Brief cooking is essential here and one minute can make the difference between a mange-tout pea that is just right, and one gone too far. Don't forget that beans and pea pods have tops, stems and often strings that must be removed before cooking.

Being tricky to boil, mange-tout peas are popular crisply stir-fried, perhaps with beansprouts and black mushrooms as a colour contrast, or with red or yellow pepper strips or sliced red radishes. To ensure sugar snap peas live up to their name, I think they are best simply boiled or steamed, then tossed perhaps in a little butter. Green beans are more robust, good with *aïoli* or a Japanese sesame miso dressing. They are invaluable in salads, including the classic *Niçoise*, while older, more fibrous beans are candidates for puréeing or braising with bacon, tomato and whole peeled garlic cloves or baby onions.

PERFECT BLANCHED – still crisp enough to snap; slightly softened but crunchy, resistant to knife; flavour grassy, not fully developed; use blanched peas and beans in stir-fries and add to soups, sautés and stews.

PERFECT – tender enough to bend but still slightly crisp (here, string beans); easy to cut with knife; colour vivid and taste well-defined and fresh.

PROBLEMS

OVERCOOKED
Why: cooked too slowly (except braised); cooked too long; if boiled, water not boiling when vegetable added, not enough water used (see Blanching and boiling green vegetables, page 153).
What to do: if boiling, drain and rinse at once with cold water to stop cooking; drain very thoroughly. For serving, add a distracting flavouring such as lemon zest, ground cumin or coriander.

STRINGY
Why: old or inferior beans or peas; undercooked; strings not removed before cooking.

What to do: continue cooking until tender; if cooked, braise vegetables in the oven with diced onion, carrot, celery and a little stock. If very stringy, nothing can be done.

DISCOLOURED
Why: poor vegetables; cooked too slowly; too little water so vegetable not immersed; pan covered during cooking; overcooked.
What to do: drain and rinse at once with cold water to stop cooking; add lots of colourful chopped tomato or red pepper.

Indonesian salad, spicy peanut sauce

Gado gado

SERVES 4-6

A wide variety of vegetables in contrasting colours should be used for this Indonesian salad. They are usually blanched, but should remain crunchy. The tangy peanut dressing, *bumbu saté*, tastes better and better on standing.

250 g/½ pound mange-tout peas, trimmed

125 g/¼ pound beansprouts, cleaned

250 g/½ pound carrots, peeled and cut into julienne strips

175 g/6 oz green beans, trimmed

for the spicy peanut sauce
250 ml/8 fl oz crunchy peanut butter

½ onion, chopped

1 garlic clove

¼ teaspoon red pepper flakes, or more to taste

1 teaspoon ground ginger

½ teaspoon brown sugar

juice of ½ lime, plus more if needed

175 ml/6 fl oz hot water, plus more if needed

soy sauce

pepper

Make the spicy peanut sauce: in a blender or food processor, combine the peanut butter, onion, garlic, pepper flakes, ginger, sugar and lime juice. Purée until very smooth, adding hot water as necessary so the mixture churns well. Work in more hot water or lime juice, adding enough to make a sauce that is thick enough to coat the back of a spoon. Taste and adjust the seasoning with more lime juice, soy sauce and pepper. Set aside.

Bring a large pan of salted water to the boil. Add the mange-tout peas to the water and leave 30 seconds. Drain, refresh with cold water and drain again. Repeat the process for the beansprouts and carrots. Add the green beans to the boiling salted water and cook until perfectly blanched, 4-6 minutes. Drain, refresh with cold water and drain again.

Arrange the vegetables in individual mounds on a large serving platter. Serve the sauce separately in a bowl. The salad may be served at room temperature or chilled.

QUICK FIX

Revive tired vegetables with this Mediterranean-style yogurt dressing. For every 375 g/¾ pound of drained cooked vegetables combine 125 ml/ 4 fl oz plain yogurt, 1 tablespoon chopped dill, 1 tablespoon chopped mixed herbs such as coriander, mint, parsley or tarragon, large pinch of ground cinnamon, the juice of ½ lemon and a pinch of sugar. Mix well. Pour dressing over the drained vegetables and toss well. Season to taste. Serves 4.

Broccoli and cauliflower

*Broccoli and cauliflower
with lemon butter sauce*
SERVES 3-4

FROM THE COOKING VIEWPOINT, broccoli and cauliflower have two parts, the stem and the more delicate floret. There's no problem with trimmed florets, but when stem is included (and it's good) it must be pared down to cook as rapidly as the floret. Like most Englishwomen, I was brought up on cauliflower cheese and I much appreciate the modern version which includes broccoli. The Italian alternative of broccoli sautéed in olive oil and garlic is pretty tasty too, as is cauliflower in Spanish style with a garlic and paprika sauce.

PERFECT BLANCHED – stem resistant when poked with point of a knife and texture slightly crunchy; colour virtually unchanged; ideal for salads, stir-frying and serving in crudités.

PERFECT – stem is just tender when pierced with point of a knife; cut stems are slightly translucent, with florets still intact; colour vivid green or white, texture firm and just short of crunchy; flavour fresh.

PROBLEMS

OVERCOOKED AND FLORETS DISINTEGRATING
Why: stems too large, so florets cooked first; florets cut unevenly or too small; cooked too slowly or too long; if boiled, water not boiling rapidly when vegetable added or not enough water used.
What to do: if boiling, drain at once and rinse with cold water; if boiled or steamed, spread on baking sheet and dry for 3-5 minutes in a low oven; do not stir as pieces will break up; serve sprinkled with chopped hard-boiled egg, fried breadcrumbs or small croutons, or with chopped herbs for cauliflower; mask with a cheese or tomato sauce.

TASTELESS
Why: poor or stale vegetables; underseasoned; overcooked.
What to do: season with salt, pepper, lemon juice, anchovy, garlic, herbs such as dill and spices such as nutmeg and coriander.

DISCOLOURED
Why: stale vegetable (broccoli turns yellow, cauliflower brown); too little water, so vegetable not immersed; pan covered with lid during cooking; overcooked.
What to do: nothing can be done.

QUICK FIX

To save bland or overcooked broccoli or cauliflower, make them into a soup. Allow about 500 ml/16 fl oz chicken or vegetable stock for every 375 g/¾ pound cooked broccoli or cauliflower. Reserve a few small florets for garnish. In a large saucepan, fry 2 sliced onions in 30 g/1 oz butter until soft. Stir in 2 garlic cloves, add the stock and vegetables with salt and pepper to taste and bring to the boil. Purée the soup in a processor or with an immersion blender. Stir in 250 ml/8 fl oz double cream, bring back to the boil and season to taste again with salt and pepper. Serve hot with the reserved florets on top, or chilled with sour cream. Serves 4.

A bright lemon butter sauce dresses up these everyday vegetables, which make cheerful accompaniments to poultry and all sorts of fish. Using the baby cauliflowers now becoming so readily available can make this a very attractive dish.

1 head of broccoli (about 500 g/1 pound)
½ head of cauliflower (about 375 g/¾ pound)

for the lemon butter sauce
175 g/6 oz butter, cold and cut into pieces
2 shallots, chopped
1 tablespoon double cream
juice of 1 lemon, more if needed
salt and white pepper

Trim the broccoli and cauliflower and cut them into large florets, discarding the stems. Rinse and drain them separately. Bring 2 large pans of salted water to the boil. Add the cauliflower to one pan and the broccoli to the other and simmer, uncovered, until done, 5-7 minutes for the broccoli and 7-10 minutes for the cauliflower.

Meanwhile, make the sauce: in a medium saucepan, melt 30 g/1 oz of the butter, add the shallots and sauté them until soft but not browned, 1-2 minutes. Stir in the double cream and simmer until the liquid is reduced by about half, 1-2 minutes.

Whisk the remaining butter into the sauce, a few pieces at a time, working on and off the heat so the butter softens and thickens the sauce without melting to oil. Whisk in the lemon juice, taste and adjust the seasoning. Keep the sauce warm on a rack set over a pan of warm (not hot) water.

Thoroughly drain the cooked broccoli and cauliflower and arrange the pieces in a pattern of alternating colours on a warmed serving platter. Pour over the lemon butter sauce and serve at once.

Green peas, sweetcorn kernels

IF YOU ASK A FRENCHMAN ABOUT A FRESH GREEN PEA HE WILL WAX LYRICAL. In the late 17th century, Madame de Sevigné describes how courtiers of Louis XIV would deliberately go home hungry to feast on the sweet delicate green peas which had so short a season. Baby peas are still at their best quite plainly boiled, or possibly combined with rice in the famous Italian *risi e bisi,* see Quick Fix, below. They also make a memorable soup (see right). When older and tougher, I prefer to braise them, possibly with ham, or with little artichokes as you find in Greece and Italy.

Odd, however, how corn is still regarded in France as fit only for cattle. What a mistake! On a hot summer evening, ears fresh from the field and simply boiled or roasted in the husk are memorably sweet – primitive perhaps, but epicurean. Quality is all-important – it must be young and freshly picked. If in doubt, add sugar instead of salt to water for boiling, or include garlic cloves when roasting. The repertoire of dishes using fresh sweetcorn kernels begins with creamed corn, corn pudding, pancakes and soup, extending to succotash, the native American combination of corn kernels and lima beans, which share the same short season.

Though belonging to quite different botanical families, green peas and corn kernels are cooked alike. When boiling or steaming them, follow the guidelines for green vegetables (see Blanching and boiling green vegetables, page 153).

PERFECT BLANCHED – texture still crunchy but skins softened somewhat by light cooking; colours vivid, flavours not developed. Add blanched corn kernels and green peas to stir-fries, sautés and stews.

PERFECT – corn or peas are just tender, still slightly chewy; colours are vivid and flavours fresh.

OVERCOOKED AND SOFT – texture mushy and skins often bursting; fresh colour and flavour lost.
Why: cooked too slowly or too long; if boiled, water not boiling when added, or not enough water used to cook vegetables rapidly (see page 153).
What to do: if boiled, drain and rinse under cold water to cool quickly; drain very thoroughly; toss in oil or butter and plenty of chopped marjoram, thyme or parsley; a little sugar can help flavour.

QUICK FIX

Transform insipid sweetcorn kernels into creamed corn: purée about half of the kernels using a processor or immersion blender and combine with remaining kernels in a saucepan. Add just enough double cream so the creamed corn falls easily from the spoon, heat until very hot and season to taste with salt, pepper, nutmeg and sugar.

If tasteless peas are your problem, make a quick version of Italian *risi e bisi:* for every 375 g/¾ pound cooked peas,

bring an equal volume of chicken stock to the boil. Stir in 200 g/7 oz long-grain rice with salt and pepper. Cover and simmer 15-18 minutes or until all the liquid is absorbed and the rice is just tender.

Meanwhile sauté 2-3 slices bacon, diced, in 1 tablespoon olive oil. Add the peas and heat 1-2 minutes. Stir the peas and bacon into the rice with 2 tablespoons chopped parsley. Taste and adjust the seasoning. Serves 4-6.

OTHER PROBLEMS

TASTELESS
Why: old or inferior vegetables; cooked too slowly; not enough seasoning.
What to do: sauté a little chopped shallot or garlic in walnut or olive oil and toss with the vegetable.

My mother's pea soup

When I was a child, in early June I would be put to shelling peas. Some were plump and some were skinny, so my mother would solve the problem of cooking them all evenly by simmering them in a soup, flavouring it lavishly with fresh mint.

1.15 kg/2½ pound peas	1 teaspoon sugar
30 g/1 oz butter	salt and white pepper
1 onion, finely chopped	large bunch of fresh mint
1 garlic clove, finely chopped	125 ml/4 fl oz double cream, plus
1 litre/1⅔ pints chicken stock	more for serving (optional)

Shell the peas: there should be about 500 g/1 pound. Melt the butter in a large pan, add the onion and garlic and cook until soft but not brown, 3-4 minutes. Add the peas, chicken stock, sugar, salt and pepper. Cover and bring to the boil. Reduce the heat and simmer until done, 10-15 minutes, depending on the maturity of the peas.

Strip the mint leaves from the stems, reserving 4 sprigs for garnish. Chop the leaves. With a slotted spoon, remove the peas, onion and garlic from the stock. Purée them in a food processor with a little of the cooking liquid until smooth. Work the purée through a sieve into a large pan, strain in the cooking liquid and stir the soup until well blended.

To finish: bring the soup to the boil, stir in the cream and chopped mint. Taste and adjust the seasoning. Ladle the soup into 4 warmed individual bowls. If you like, add a spoonful of double cream to each bowl and stir to marble it. Top with mint sprigs and serve at once.

Corn on the cob

Every few years our garden produces a bumper crop of corn, and we delight in eating it with plenty of butter. Peeling off the husk and pulling away the silk is easy, and then in the pot of boiling water it goes. To roast or grill the ears in the husk, strip it back, remove the silk, brush the corn with butter or oil and seasoning and rewrap in the husk. An unpeeled garlic clove and a sprinkling of red pepper oil adds zip and you'll know when the corn is done by the fragrant aroma. When corn is elderly, no amount of cooking will make it tender, so cut it from the cob to add to soup or a salad. Perfectly cooked kernels can be pried easily from cob with the point of a knife; they will be tender but still slightly chewy with juicy, sweet flavour.

Hearty greens including spinach and cabbage

MOST GREENS GROW JUST ABOUT EVERYWHERE, but that doesn't prevent them from having strong ethnic overtones. Collard, mustard and turnip greens are signature dishes of the American South, yet the Brussels sprouts so popular in England are often regarded with derision in the USA. Escarole is a staple in Italy, while Greeks cling obstinately to their spinach. When tackling any green, the big question is its texture. If fibrous, it's a good idea to soften greens which are old or tough by blanching before cooking them further. Blanching also tempers bitterness and helps set bright colour (see opposite). Spinach and green and white cabbage are most versatile of the group, while more robust greens such as mustard, collards and red cabbage are best baked, braised or stewed to mellow their brash flavours. Red cabbage must always be cooked with vinegar or an acid ingredient to set its cheerful colour.

Favourite recipes of mine for greens include dandelion leaves in hot bacon dressing, green cabbage stuffed with pork and chestnuts, and the amazing *gumbo z'herbes* from Louisiana which includes at least seven different greens, plus okra to give it body. There are wonderful Oriental ways of cooking greens, too, like Chinese stir-fried spinach with charred garlic, and Indian braised greens with paneer (curd cheese).

PERFECT BLANCHED – colour vivid; greens softened but still very crunchy; resistant to the knife; flavour grassy and not fully developed.

PERFECT – colour still bright (here, cabbage); when boiled, sautéed, steamed or sweated, greens tender and translucent (for cabbage, chicory and escarole) but slightly crunchy, easy to cut with a knife; flavour is well defined and fresh; when baked, braised or stewed, greens are tender, moist but not watery and easy to cut with a spoon, but not chewy; flavour is full-bodied and rich.

OVERCOOKED AND SOFT – leaves limp and watery; colour yellowed or muddy and flavour flat, sometimes sour.
Why: cooked too slowly; cooked too long; if boiled, water not really boiling when greens added, not enough water used (see Blanching and boiling green vegetables, opposite).
What to do: if boiled, drain and rinse at once with cold water to stop cooking; drain very thoroughly, if necessary pressing between two plates or with your fists to extract water. For serving, add texture to greens with fried bacon dice or croutons, chopped walnuts or browned almonds or pine nuts; mix with lively flavourings such as onion or garlic fried in olive oil, season with hot red pepper, caraway, mustard seeds or grated lemon zest; transform into purée by chopping and cooking with white sauce or double cream; finely chop and mix with toasted nuts and cheese as a topping or stuffing for pasta.

OTHER PROBLEMS

STRINGY AND TOUGH
Why: old or inferior greens; undercooked.
What to do: continue cooking until tender; before or after cooking, slice greens across fibres to minimize toughness. Note: if in doubt, blanch first.
BITTER OR SOUR
Why: greens old; overcooked. Note: some greens such as escarole have naturally tart flavour.
What to do: add 1-2 teaspoons sugar to greens to take

edge off bitterness, then continue cooking for an hour or more so the greens meld and become a 'confit'.
DISCOLOURED
Why: poor greens; cooked too slowly; too little water so greens not immersed; pan covered with lid during cooking; overcooked.
What to do: drain and rinse at once with cold water to stop cooking and set colour; add lots of colourful chopped herbs such as chives and parsley.

Lettuce and salad greens

NOT UNTIL I LIVED WITH A VEGETABLE GARDEN did I realize the reason for cooking the delicate greens which are usually eaten raw in a salad. The annual cascade of overgrown, chewy lettuce about to bolt has led generations of cooks to save its life by braising, steaming or shredding lettuce to simmer as a surprisingly piquant soup. Flavour, never very strong in salad greens, gets a boost in dishes such as braised Boston or Cos lettuce with sliced onion, carrots and country ham, or sautéed escarole or frisée with brown onion, lemon juice, coriander and paprika. Recently, grilled greens, particularly radicchio, have become popular, at their best basted with a simple mix of virgin olive oil, salt and cracked black pepper. The key to cooking salad greens is to tenderize them (they can be quite stringy) without losing their pretty colour.

PERFECT BLANCHED – colour brilliant; texture wilted but still crispy, resistant to the knife; flavour still grassy. Blanching sets colour and helps remove bitterness before further cooking.

PERFECT – colour is bright (here, lettuce); greens just tender but retaining texture, easy to cut with a knife; flavour intense.

PROBLEMS

OVERCOOKED
Why: cooked too slowly; cooking time too long.
What to do: if simmered or steamed, rinse with cold water to stop cooking and set colour. Add texture with fried bacon dice or croutons, chopped sun-dried tomatoes or toasted sesame seeds.

FIBROUS
Why: old greens; undercooked.
What to do: continue cooking until tender; before or after cooking, slice greens across fibres to minimize toughness.

BITTER
Why: greens old; scorched during grilling.
What to do: if in doubt about bitterness, blanch before cooking; if scorched, nothing can be done.

PALLID OR DISCOLOURED
Why: poor greens; cooked too slowly; too little water so vegetable not immersed; pan covered during cooking; overcooked.
What to do: drain and rinse at once with cold water to stop cooking and set colour; add chopped peppers, or coat with cheese sauce and grill.

BLANCHING AND BOILING GREEN VEGETABLES

Green vegetables are blanched for several reasons: to set their colour, whether green or white, to temper strong flavour or to soften a hard or fibrous texture slightly. Boiling, by contrast, implies that the vegetable will be fully (albeit lightly) cooked.

When boiling green vegetables there's an ancient rule of thumb: green vegetables (which grow in the open air) go into boiling water and must cook as rapidly as possible, uncovered. This treatment, in fact, best preserves their vitamin content and fragile cellular structure; leaving the vegetables uncovered allows acids to vaporize which would otherwise turn them yellow. On the other hand, root vegetables (which grow under the ground) should go into cold water and be simmered slowly, covered with a lid.

When blanching or boiling green vegetables, they must be generously immersed in water. For each 375 g/¾ pound of vegetables, allow at least 4 litres/ 7 pints of water seasoned with 2 teaspoons salt. A bay leaf in the water helps sweeten strong-smelling vegetables such as cabbage and cauliflower. Be sure vegetables are of uniform size, or cut into even pieces. Bring water to a rolling boil, add the vegetables to the water and bring back to the boil as fast as possible, uncovered. Boil the vegetables rapidly to the stage wanted, then drain and immerse or rinse in cold water. This stops cooking instantly, so as much bright green colour as possible is retained. Finally, leave blanched or boiled vegetables to drain thoroughly.

QUICK FIX

Make soup with chopped cooked lettuce. For every 250 g/½ pound, fry 1 sliced onion in 2 tablespoons olive oil until soft. Add the greens with 2 chopped garlic cloves and sauté for 1-2 minutes. Add about 1 litre/1⅔ pints stock, season and simmer until tender, 10-15 minutes. Stir in drained 400-g/14-oz can of white kidney beans and bring to the boil. Stir in 30 g/1 oz shredded basil leaves. Serves 4.

Sautéed peppery greens

SERVES 4

Kale is a leafy member of the cabbage family with quite a peppery bite. If the leaves are very young and tender, they can be tossed in salads. More often, however, they must be cooked – a perfect side dish for grilled meats or roasted chicken. Other winter greens, such as collard, turnip, chard, mustard – even Savoy cabbage or curly endive – do well too.

500 g/1 pound kale
1 tablespoon vegetable oil
250 g/½ pound spicy Italian sausage meat
1 onion, chopped
3 garlic cloves, finely chopped
½ teaspoon red pepper flakes, more to taste
salt and pepper

Wash the kale well, discarding the tough stems. Drain and shake as much water as possible from the leaves. Heat the oil in a frying pan, add the sausage meat and sauté, stirring, until brown, 3-5 minutes.

Stir the onion and garlic into the pan and sauté with the sausage meat until lightly browned and fragrant, 4-5 minutes.

Stir in the kale with a little salt and pepper and cook over high heat until wilted, 2-3 minutes. Lower the heat, cover the pan and leave to sweat until the kale is done, 10-12 minutes. Sprinkle with red pepper flakes, taste and adjust seasoning. Serve at once.

Sautéed peppery greens

Lettuce packages au jus

SERVES 4

When the first excitement of baby spring lettuce leads to endless quantities of tougher autumn greens, I start cooking. I long ago discovered these lettuce leaf packages as a pretty way to bundle braised lettuce. Serve them as a garnish for roast chicken or fish.

1 kg/2 lb Cos or Boston lettuce
6 slices of bacon (about 125 g/4 oz), diced
500 ml/16 fl oz chicken or vegetable stock
salt and pepper
30 g/1 oz butter, cold and cut into pieces

Trim the lettuce stems and discard any wilted outer leaves. Select 8-12 perfect leaves, wash and dry them. Shred the remaining leaves, put them in a colander and rinse under cold water.

Bring a large pan of salted water to the boil. Add the whole lettuce leaves and blanch them, about 1 minute. Transfer the leaves to a bowl of cold water, then spread them out on paper towels, stem-sides down. Leave to drain.

Fry the bacon in a sauté or deep frying pan until browned. Pour off excess fat, add the stock and bring to the boil, stirring to deglaze pan juices. Stir in the shredded lettuce and simmer until wilted, 2-3 minutes.

Remove the lettuce and bacon with a slotted spoon and transfer to a large bowl. Strain the cooking liquid into a small saucepan and boil until reduced by half. Meanwhile, taste the lettuce mixture and adjust the seasoning. Place a spoonful of lettuce mixture in the centre of each blanched lettuce leaf. Fold the cut end up and over the filling, then fold in each side and roll into a package. Set the packages on a warmed serving dish, cover and keep warm.

Make the *jus*: whisk the butter into the reduced cooking liquid a few pieces at a time, working on and off the heat so butter softens and thickens the *jus* without melting to oil. Taste the *jus* and adjust the seasoning, spoon over the lettuce packages and serve at once.

Summer and winter squash including courgette and pumpkin

SUMMER SQUASH BELIES ITS NAME AND BRIGHTENS OUR PLATES for most of the year. The family includes crookneck, cucumber, vegetable marrow, pattypan, scallop, yellow squash and courgette. It's best to leave these soft-fleshed vegetables unpeeled, both for colour and to hold them together. Small size is important as overgrown summer squash bloat with water and lose flavour. Given so much moisture, they overcook easily, so avoid slicing thinly unless they are to be cooked rapidly by deep- or stir-frying. Mature summer squash also develop large seeds, best scooped out and discarded. Decorative miniature squash are one way of guaranteeing firm texture, though they can be bitter. Summer squash marry well with most foods, particularly shellfish, tomato, onion, and peppers, and herbs like bay and mint. I like them best with energetic seasonings like garlic and dried chilli flakes.

With their evocative shapes and brilliant interiors, winter squash such as acorn, butternut, Hubbard, pumpkin and turban are even more picturesque. Tough skin protects woody flesh, which can be tiresomely fibrous. However, winter squash are less watery than summer and so overcook less easily. For maximum flavour, baked winter squash is often spiced and sweetened to serve in the skin, or puréed for soup or as a side dish, while the Italian custom of baking squash with citrus zest and cinnamon harks back to the Renaissance.

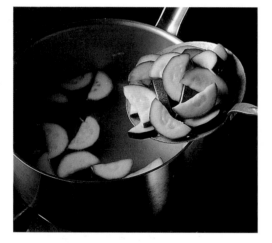

PERFECT BLANCHED – colour bright, still opaque; texture moist and slightly crunchy. Served as crudités, used in salads and stir-fries.

PERFECT LIGHTLY COOKED – translucent, just tender when pierced with a knife, firm but not crunchy; colour is vivid and edges lightly browned; flavour fresh for summer squash, smooth for winter types. Note: squash for soup or purée should be very tender, but not so soft as to be watery.

OVERCOOKED AND WET – colour faded, texture watery and very soft when pierced with point of knife; pieces often collapsed and very dark brown; flavour insipid. Note: summer squash overcook very easily, often in a minute or two.
Why: squash overgrown, coarse-textured and watery; cooked too long; heat too low; cooked with too much liquid. Note: mature squash are better steamed than boiled.
What to do: drain thoroughly, then sprinkle with sautéed chopped shallot, onion or garlic with chopped herbs such as dill, basil, thyme or parsley; for winter squash, go the spice route and sprinkle with ground cumin, coriander, nutmeg, cinnamon, allspice or ginger; top with grated cheese and grill.
Note: overcooked squash breaks up easily, so avoid stirring. Make into purée or soup.

OTHER PROBLEMS

FIBROUS
Why: poor or old squash; undercooked.
What to do: continue cooking until tender. If very fibrous, chop to toss with pasta and herbs, or stir into mashed potatoes, or work through sieve or food mill for purée or soup, see Quick Fix.
TASTELESS
Why: overgrown or poor squash; underseasoned; overcooked.

What to do: sprinkle with brown sugar and grill; see Overcooked and wet.
BITTER
Why: overgrown or stale squash, particularly cucumber.
What to do: add zesty seasonings such as soy sauce, Worcestershire sauce, dried hot red pepper, capers, pickles, olives or anchovy. If very bitter, nothing can be done.

Aubergine

VEGETARIAN COOKING WITHOUT AUBERGINE IS UNIMAGINABLE, so robust and meaty is its texture. During cooking, aubergine has the curious habit of absorbing liquid or fat like a sponge, then expelling it when the flesh shrinks under heat. It helps to salt aubergine before cooking by halving or slicing the flesh, then sprinkling it with salt to draw out moisture. Leave 15-30 minutes, then rinse and drain before continuing with the recipe. Sprinkling with salt can also counteract bitterness in mature aubergine (large seeds are a bad sign).

The flavour of aubergine blends agreeably with a wide range of other ingredients without losing its own identity. I think of it marinated with lemon as part of an antipasto, or sautéed with onion, pepper, tomato and courgette in Provençal ratatouille. Turkish stuffed aubergine *imam bayildi* means 'fainting priest' it is so rich, while in Italy aubergine is stewed with wine vinegar, tomato and rosemary. Perhaps it is best of all deep-fried, whether breaded or dipped in batter as in Japanese Deep-Fried Vegetables (page 173) – an outstanding appetizer.

PERFECT LIGHTLY COOKED – with or without skin, aubergine flesh is juicy and meltingly tender, somewhat translucent and lightly browned; flavour is rich, almost smoky.

PERFECT CRISP – deep golden crisp on outside, but still soft in centre; flavour is rich, smoky and sweet.

QUICK FIX

Providing the aubergine has not been mixed with too many other ingredients, give it new life by making Poor Man's Caviar. Scrape the pulp from 4 medium aubergines, (about 375 g/¾ pound) and discard the skins. Use a fork to mash up the aubergine with 1 finely chopped garlic clove, 3 tablespoons lemon juice, 3 tablespoons olive oil, 2 tablespoons double cream,

½ teaspoon ground cumin, ½ teaspoon ground coriander, ½ teaspoon Tabasco sauce, salt and pepper. Taste, adding more Tabasco if you like. The mixture should be full-flavoured and slightly chunky. Serve in a pretty pottery bowl with some salad greens or on toasted slices of country bread rubbed with garlic. Serves 4.

PROBLEMS

UNDERCOOKED
Why: heat too low; cooking time too short; not basted often.
What to do: continue cooking until tender, basting often if cooking with oil or sauce.

OVERCOOKED AND DRY
Why: cooked too long; heat too high; not basted often.
What to do: brush lightly with olive oil, then combine or layer with juicy ingredients such as tomato, fried onion, white or cheese sauce, or meat sauce as in moussaka. A sprinkling of grated cheese hides more shortcomings. Alternatively, sprinkle aubergine Turkish-style with cumin seeds, lemon juice, cayenne, chopped mint and a little sugar.

BLAND
Why: lack of seasoning; undercooked.
What to do: season with salt, pepper and one or two of the many flavourings which suit aubergine: coriander, cumin, allspice, paprika, thyme, oregano, rosemary, parsley, lemon juice and flavoured oils. Don't forget the garlic!

BITTER
Why: aubergine old or too mature.
What to do: sprinkle with salt to draw out bitter juices before cooking; combine with well-flavoured ingredients such as garlic, wine vinegar and nuts such as walnuts. If very bitter, nothing can be done.

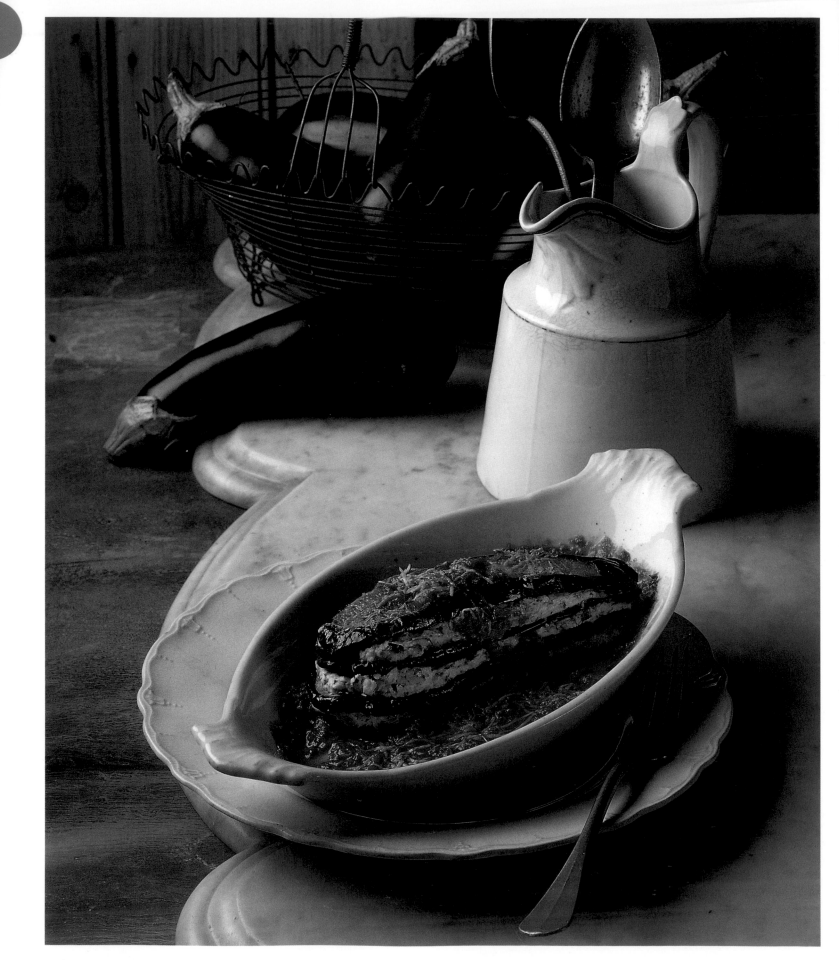

Aubergine stacks with three cheeses

SERVES 4

Sliced aubergine takes the place of bread in this sandwich of ricotta and goats' cheese, baked in a rich tomato sauce and sprinkled with Parmesan cheese. Be sure to use a fresh goats' cheese which is soft and creamy.

500 g/1 pound aubergine	for the fresh tomato, garlic and
salt and pepper	oregano sauce
60 ml/2 fl oz olive oil	75 ml/2½ fl oz olive oil
small bunch of basil	3 onions, chopped
small bunch of parsley	5 garlic cloves, finely chopped
250 g/½ pound ricotta cheese	1.5 kg/3 lb tomatoes, peeled,
175 g/6 oz goats' cheese	seeded and chopped
30 g/1 oz grated Parmesan cheese	90 ml/3 fl oz tomato purée
	3-4 tablespoons chopped oregano
	pinch of sugar
	4 individual gratin dishes

Preheat the oven to 190°C/375°F/gas5. Trim the aubergine and cut them across in sixteen 1.25-cm/½-inch rounds. If they are small, cut them diagonally. Lay the slices in a single layer on a tray. Sprinkle them generously with salt on both sides and leave 20-30 minutes to draw out excess juices.

Rinse the aubergine slices, drain in a colander and pat dry with paper towels. Arrange on oiled baking sheets and brush the tops with olive oil. Bake the slices until perfect crisp, turning once, 25-30 minutes. Let cool.

Meanwhile, make the tomato sauce: heat the oil in a large deep saucepan. Add the onions and fry over medium heat until soft and lightly browned, 4-5 minutes. Add the garlic and cook until fragrant, 1 minute. Stir in the tomatoes, tomato purée, oregano, sugar, salt and pepper. Cover and cook over low heat until the tomatoes are very soft, 10-15 minutes. Uncover the pan and continue cooking the tomato sauce, stirring occasionally, until slightly thickened but still falling easily from the spoon, 5-10 minutes. Taste the sauce and adjust the seasoning.

Strip the leaves from the basil and parsley stems and chop the leaves, reserving 4 basil sprigs for decoration. Beat the ricotta and goats' cheeses in a bowl until smooth. Stir in the chopped herbs, salt and pepper, then taste for seasoning. Brush the gratin dishes with olive oil and place an aubergine slice in each one. Spread about 2 tablespoons of the cheese mixture on the aubergine. Top each with a second slice. Repeat with remaining aubergine rounds and filling to make four-decker stacks.

Spoon the sauce over the stacks and sprinkle with Parmesan cheese. Bake in the oven until very hot and bubbling, 20-25 minutes. Serve at once.

Aubergine stacks with three cheeses

Pat's stuffed courgettes

SERVES 4

Ask a New Englander for a recipe for squash and you'll get a winner. Bostonian Pat Kelly has had much experience dealing with the annual glut of courgettes and yellow squash and suggests this simple recipe, equally good as an accompaniment to fish, meat or poultry. For a more substantial dish, add about 125 g/4 oz chopped cooked peeled prawns to the stuffing.

750 g/1½ pounds small courgettes	45 g/1½ oz grated Gruyère cheese
or yellow squash	3-4 tablespoons chopped thyme
2 slices of white bread	grated zest of 1 lemon
60 g/2 oz butter, melted	½ teaspoon freshly grated nutmeg
1 medium onion, chopped	salt and pepper
2 garlic cloves, chopped	
1 medium tomato, peeled, seeded	
and chopped	

Preheat the oven to 175°C/350°F/gas4. Bring a large pan of salted water to the boil. Trim the ends of the courgettes or squash and cut them in half lengthwise. Scoop out the seeds with a teaspoon. Add the courgettes or squash to the boiling water and blanch for 8-10 minutes. Drain, rinse with cold water and leave to drain thoroughly.

For the stuffing, tear the bread into pieces and work to crumbs in a food processor. Heat half the butter in a frying pan, add the onion and sauté until soft but not brown, 3-5 minutes. Stir in the garlic and continue cooking for 1 minute. Let cool slightly, then stir in the breadcrumbs, chopped tomato, grated cheese, thyme, lemon zest, nutmeg, salt and pepper. Taste and adjust the seasoning.

Fill this stuffing into the courgettes or squash, mounding it well. Set them in a buttered baking dish and moisten with the remaining butter. Bake in the preheated oven until done and the top is browned, 20-25 minutes.

Sweet peppers and chillies

FOR THE COOK, THE CAPSICUM PEPPER FAMILY FALLS INTO TWO GROUPS: sweet peppers, and hot peppers (chillies). Within these two categories, botanists identify hundreds of different kinds, their flavours depending not just on variety, but also on the soil in which they have been grown. So peppers are to some extent a lottery – you must taste and try. Flavour is also much altered when a pepper is roasted or grilled, charring the skin so it can then be peeled off, leaving only the tender flesh for a salad or for chopping or puréeing for a sauce.

For crunchy texture, you can leave peppers unpeeled before chopping or slicing to add to dishes such as the Spanish sautéed mixture of green peppers and pimientos (brick-red sweet peppers with a sweet flavour). When baking with a stuffing, peppers are often left unpeeled so they hold their shape better. Blanching is a halfway house, a way to soften the peppers and moderate their sometimes sharp taste.

PERFECT BLANCHED – colour vivid and texture lightly crisp, resistant when pierced with knife; flavour slightly grassy. Blanched peppers, particularly strips, are used in salads and for decoration.

PERFECT WHOLE PEPPERS FOR PEELING – if grilled or roasted, skin charred and flesh limp but still firm, juicy and colourful with smoky taste; if stuffed and baked or roasted in skin, still holding a shape but tender when poked with a knife.

PROBLEMS

UNDERCOOKED
Why: heat too low; time too short.
What to do: continue cooking, raising heat if necessary.
ACID TASTE
Why: poor or unripe peppers; undercooked.
What to do: continue cooking if vegetable not tender; temper acidity with olive oil, sautéed onions, raisins and other dried fruits, or mask with fresh or dried chilli.
FADED COLOUR
Why: poor or stale peppers; overcooked.
What to do: refresh blanched peppers with cold water to stop cooking at once and set bright colour; top green peppers with chopped tomato, and red peppers with chopped coriander or parsley.

OVERCOOKED AND WET – peppers are limp, faded and bland.
Why: cooked too long; too slowly.
What to do: rinse with cold water to stop cooking and drain thoroughly. Heat 1 tablespoon oil in a frying pan or wok and stir-fry peppers over very high heat to dry them, 30-60 seconds. Add a crisp topping of roasted sunflower seeds or coarsely chopped peanuts.

Tomatoes

WE USE TOMATOES SO OFTEN FRESH IN SALAD or mixed with other vegetables, that it's easy to overlook them as a cooked vegetable in their own right. There are dozens of ways of cooking a whole, halved or sliced tomato to serve as an appetizer or a cheerful accompaniment to grilled and roast meats. In France tomatoes come stuffed with sausage meat or topped with garlic, herbs and breadcrumbs *à la provençale*. In the American South you might find them still green, breaded and fried or baked with vinegar, walnuts and herbs. Have you thought of oven-drying your own ripe tomatoes, perhaps with a topping of thyme and Parmesan cheese?

When you cook a tomato thoroughly, its flavour will change radically, losing its fruity tartness and mellowing to be rich and concentrated. You'll find more about that in the chapter on Sauces.

Tomatoes often need to be peeled and blanching makes this easy. Bring a large pan of water to the boil. Cut out the cores and mark a small cross in the flower end of each tomato. Plunge them into boiling water and leave until the skin pulls away from the cross, 10 seconds or longer if the tomatoes are not very ripe. Transfer to cold water and peel when cool (see below left).

PERFECT BLANCHED FOR PEELING – skin pulls away from tomato and is very easy to peel; flesh is still uncooked and firm.

PERFECT BAKED – tomato hot, juicy, tender when pierced with point of a knife, but still holding shape; skin starting to split; colour vivid, flavour assertive.

QUICK FIX

Creative outlets for overcooked tomatoes are legion and here are just a few. First peel away as much skin from the tomatoes as possible but you can leave the seeds. Then, choose one of the following:

• Coarsely chop the tomatoes, mix with chopped basil or flat-leaf parsley and add with olive oil to hot pasta or pasta salad.

• Drain chopped tomatoes and add to cornbread batter.

• Blend chopped tomatoes with cooked polenta or grits as a savoury accompaniment to meats or poultry.

• Make fresh or cooked tomato salsa (see Sauces, pages 126-7).

• For a tomato sandwich, split a length of baguette, add tomatoes and drizzle with balsamic vinegar, salt and pepper; press sandwich between 2 heavy plates for at least 15 minutes, so all tomato juice is absorbed by the bread.

PROBLEMS

OVERCOOKED

Why: cooked too long; heat too low — tomatoes keep their shape better when cooked rapidly at high heat.

What to do: cover with chopped herbs, particularly oregano, basil or parsley; sprinkle with grated cheese and breadcrumbs and grill. See also Quick Fix.

PALE AND WOOLLY

Why: inferior tomatoes, not ripened on the vine.

What to do: revive with crisply fried onions, or a *gremolata* of chopped lemon zest, fresh garlic and parsley.

ACID

Why: poor or unripe tomatoes.

What to do: add a teaspoon of sugar – tomatoes are, after all, a fruit.

Mexican stuffed peppers
Chiles rellenos
SERVES 4

Classic *chiles rellenos* are stuffed with cheese then dipped in batter and fried, but when properly done they are not at all heavy. Anaheim peppers can be quite hot, so I suggest a mild, cooling salsa.

125-g/4-oz piece of
  Monterey Jack (or sharp
  Cheddar) cheese
8 Anaheim or New Mexico
  chilli peppers (about
  625 g/1¼ pounds), with
  stems attached
150 g/5 oz fine yellow
  cornmeal, more if
  needed
3 eggs, separated
salt and pepper
vegetable oil for frying

for the tomato and
  coriander salsa
500 g/1 pound tomatoes,
  peeled, seeded and
  chopped
2 garlic cloves, finely
  chopped
1 large onion, chopped
1 green or red sweet
  pepper, seeded and
  chopped
small bunch of coriander,
  leaves chopped
juice of 1 lemon

Make the salsa: mix together the tomatoes, garlic, onion, sweet pepper and coriander in a non-metallic bowl. Stir in the lemon juice and season to taste. Let stand at room temperature at least 30 minutes.

Preheat the grill. Cut the cheese into sticks just shorter than the length of the peppers. Rub the peppers with oil and roast over an open flame or under the grill, turning them until the skin chars and bursts, 10-12 minutes. Put them in a plastic bag to retain steam as this will help loosen the skins. Leave them to cool.

Peel the peppers, keeping any stems attached. Carefully make a slit in the side of each, stopping short of stem and pointed ends. With the tip of a knife or fingers, pull out the cores and seeds. Insert cheese sticks into the peppers.

Spread the cornmeal on a plate. Beat the egg yolks with salt and pepper. Whip the egg whites with a pinch of salt until soft peaks form and fold these into the beaten yolks. Holding the peppers by the stems, dip them into the egg mixture. Roll the peppers in cornmeal to coat them.

Heat 6 mm/¼ inch oil in a cast-iron skillet or frying pan until hot but not smoking. Fry the peppers until golden brown on all sides, 3-5 minutes. Drain them on paper towels and serve at once, with the salsa in a separate bowl.

Mexican stuffed peppers

Roasted tomato, mushroom, onion and garlic bruschetta
SERVES 4 as an appetizer   *pictured on pages 140-41*

These vegetables, particularly cherry tomatoes, fare very well in the high heat of an oven set for roasting, where flavours concentrate and sweeten. If you add tougher vegetables such as fennel, cut them into small pieces so they roast as quickly as the more tender ones. The rest is simple!

500 g/1 pound cherry
  tomatoes
2 onions
8 garlic cloves
125 g/4 oz chestnut or
  other brown mushrooms
3 tablespoons olive oil,
  more if needed
salt and freshly ground
  black pepper

8 small slices of Italian
  bread, cut 2 cm/¾ inch
  thick
1 tablespoon balsamic
  vinegar
1 tablespoon coarsely
  chopped flat-leaf parsley
2-3 tablespoons coarsely
  chopped basil

Remove the stems from tomatoes. Peel the onions, keeping the roots intact, and cut them in half, through root and stem. Thinly slice each half into crescents. Peel the garlic cloves and halve them lengthwise. Trim the mushroom stems and halve the mushrooms if small or quarter them if large.

Preheat the oven to 260°C/500°F/gas10 or its highest possible setting. Toss the tomatoes, onion, garlic and mushrooms with 1 tablespoon of the olive oil, salt and pepper. Spread them in a pan just big enough to hold the vegetables in a single layer. Roast them in the preheated oven until tender and browned, stirring once, 6-8 minutes. When done, toss the vegetables with the vinegar and chopped herbs. Taste, adjust seasoning and keep warm.

Meanwhile, toast the bread: brush both sides of the bread slices with the remaining olive oil. Lay them directly on an oven rack and toast in the preheated oven until golden, turning once, 6-8 minutes. Top the slices of bread with the roasted vegetables and serve at once.

Root vegetables including sweet potatoes

ROOT VEGETABLES USED TO GET ROUGH TREATMENT IN THE KITCHEN. Standard practice was to boil them to a watery, tasteless pulp, reviving all-too-vivid memories of school lunches from the steam table. Today's creative approach to roots is a constant, joyful surprise. Think of dishes like roasted winter roots with a topping of chopped walnuts, or Jerusalem artichokes stewed with ham and tomato in white wine, or Chinese carnelian carrots with star anise, ginger, sugar, soy sauce and rice wine. Beetroots taste much better in an orange vinaigrette, while parsnips and Jerusalem artichokes acquire a nutty sweetness when baked in butter.

For the cook, sweet potatoes and yams behave very like potatoes (see pages 166-7), though they belong to different botanical families. Their skin colours run the autumn gamut of golden-orange to pink to brown and even violet, though the flesh is often a pastel tint. They all do well with orange, cranberry and pecans. Yams, the darkest and sweetest of the bunch, are good with spices such as cinnamon, allspice and cloves, with a sprinkling of brown sugar or honey. Roots are not only versatile, they are inexpensive, and require little labour apart from peeling. Even that can be avoided if you're prepared to eat the chewy but tasty skin.

Take care to cut roots into even pieces so they all cook at the same speed, and watch out for fibres in large, old roots, particularly celery, swede and parsnip. When boiling, immerse roots in plenty of cold salted water and cook with the lid on, simmering gently so they do not break up. You'll find a touch of sugar in many recipes for roots – it's an old trick for developing their flavour.

PERFECT – tender but does not break up when pierced with point of a knife; when drained, flesh is moist not watery and slightly translucent; flavour is mellow, sometimes sweet as for carrots, or piquant as with turnip and artichoke. Note: vegetables for soup or purée should be more tender, but not so cooked as to be watery.

PROBLEMS

UNDERCOOKED AND FIBROUS
Why: cooking time too short; temperature too low; acid ingredients such as tomatoes added, which slow rate of cooking; if fibrous, poor or old vegetable.
What to do: continue cooking, raising heat if necessary; if tender and still fibrous, make a purée, working vegetable through a sieve or vegetable mill (see Quick Fix).

OVERCOOKED
Why: cooked too long; cooked too fast, so inside of vegetable remained firm and outside overcooked.
What to do: drain vegetable thoroughly, return it to pan and dry over low heat or spread on a baking sheet and dry in a low oven before continuing with recipe.

TASTELESS
Why: poor vegetables; underseasoned; overcooked.
What to do: pick up flavour with brown or white sugar, honey, warm spices such as cumin, coriander, ginger, cinnamon or cloves, or herbs such as thyme, oregano, mint or coriander; a few tablespoons of cream or butter can be helpful.

BITTER OR SHARP
Why: poor-quality or old vegetables.
What to do: peel off skin; balance vegetable with contrasting flavours: orange is good with carrot, apple with beetroot and parsnip, and toasted sesame seeds with Jerusalem artichoke; for sweet potatoes, add a sprinkling of brown sugar and breadcrumbs and grill.

DISCOLOURED
Why: inferior, old or poorly stored vegetables; peeled vegetables left in open air (particularly Jerusalem artichoke, parsnip, celeriac and salsify); too little cooking water, so vegetables not fully immersed.
What to do: trim vegetables well before cooking; store peeled vegetables in cold water acidulated with lemon juice; boil in generous amounts of salted water, with lemon juice if you like.

Root vegetable couscous

VEGETABLE STOCK

To make about 1.5 litres/2⅓ pints of vegetable stock: in a large pan combine 3 onions, sliced, 3 carrots, thinly sliced, 3 stalks of celery, sliced, and 2 garlic cloves, lightly crushed, with about 2 litres/3¼ pints water. Add a bouquet garni and 1 generous teaspoon black peppercorns. Bring slowly to the boil, skimming often. Simmer uncovered ¾-1 hour; until the liquid is reduced by about one-quarter. Strain, let cool and store in refrigerator.

QUICK FIX

The best solution for overcooked roots is puréeing. First spread on a baking sheet and heat in a 175°C/350°F/gas4 oven until dry, 5-10 minutes. Purée in a processor or with an immersion blender, for each 375 g/¾ pound of vegetable adding 60 ml/2 fl oz double cream and 2 tablespoons butter. If vegetable is fibrous, work it through a sieve or food mill. Heat purée in a saucepan, stirring, until very hot. It should fall easily from the spoon; if too stiff, add more cream. Season to taste with sugar, salt, pepper and spice of your choice. Serves 4.

For good luck, Moroccans add a combination of any seven vegetables to their couscous. In this version, I've chosen to use lots of roots but cabbage, aubergine or leek can be substituted. The key is to cut the vegetables into larger or smaller chunks, depending on their toughness, so they all finish cooking at the same time. Serve the couscous with Moroccan chilli paste (*harissa*), thinned with a little olive oil and lemon juice.

500 g/1 pound new potatoes
500 g/1 pound parsnips
500 g/1 pound carrots
250 g/½ pound celeriac
250 g/½ pound butternut squash
bunch of coriander
bouquet garni
2 tablespoons olive oil
1 onion, chopped
1 teaspoon ground turmeric
1 teaspoon ground ginger
1 cinnamon stick, broken into pieces
1 kg/2 lb tomatoes, peeled, seeded and chopped

2 litres/3¼ pints chicken or vegetable stock, more if needed
salt and pepper
30 g/1 oz raisins
2-3 fresh red chilli peppers, cored, seeded and chopped

for the couscous
50 g/1¾ oz flaked almonds
large pinch of saffron threads
625 g/1¼ pound precooked couscous
45 g/1½ oz butter
1.5 litres/2⅓ pints boiling water

Peel the potatoes and cut into 2 or 3 pieces. Peel parsnips and carrots and cut at an angle into 2.5-cm/1-inch slices. Trim and peel celeriac, and cut into 8 wedges. Halve squash lengthwise and scoop out the seeds. Lay flat side on a board and cut away skin. Cut flesh into 2.5-cm/1-inch chunks. Strip coriander leaves from stems. Chop and reserve leaves; add stems to bouquet garni.

Heat oil in a large pan and sauté onion until soft but not brown, 3-4 minutes. Stir in spices and sauté until fragrant, about 30 seconds. Stir in tomatoes and cook, stirring, until softened, 4-5 minutes. Stir in stock, potatoes, parsnips, carrots, celeriac, bouquet garni, salt and pepper. Cover, bring to the boil and simmer, stirring occasionally, 15-20 minutes. Stir in squash, raisins, chilli and enough stock to cover vegetables. Continue simmering until very tender, 10-15 minutes. Discard bouquet garni and cinnamon. Taste and adjust the seasoning.

Meanwhile, toast the nuts and prepare the couscous: preheat the oven to 175°C/350°F/gas4. Spread the almonds on a baking sheet and toast in oven until lightly browned, stirring once, 12-15 minutes. Pour 2-3 tablespoons of the boiling water over the saffron and leave to infuse. Put the couscous and butter in a large bowl, pour over remaining boiling water and add saffron and its liquid. Note: types of precooked couscous vary and may require more or less water, so follow packet instructions. Stir couscous quickly with a fork and let stand until plump, about 5 minutes. Taste and adjust seasoning.

Spoon the couscous into 8 warmed shallow bowls, making wells in the centre. With a slotted spoon, transfer vegetables to wells. Pour over broth, and sprinkle with toasted almonds and chopped coriander to serve.

Potatoes

Baked, braised, steamed, boiled

COMMON WHITE-FLESHED POTATOES FALL INTO TWO GROUPS: firm, waxy varieties which hold their shape during cooking; and floury or baking potatoes which purée easily. Waxy potatoes are good for boiling, steaming, sautéing or simmering in liquid, when the potato needs to stay firm. When boiling potatoes, remember to start them out in cold water (as with other root vegetables). Cover the pan, bring to the boil and simmer, so the potato cooks gently without falling apart. Waxy potatoes are right for potato salad, whether dressed with vinaigrette, mayonnaise or simply with white wine and oil (right), and they hold up well in potatoes stewed Greek-style with tomatoes and feta cheese, or with a Spanish flavouring of onion, chilli pepper, garlic and cumin. Floury potatoes are good for everything else – for baking in the oven, for mashing, for deep-frying (opposite), for British roast potatoes cooked in drippings to accompany a roast, and for baking in liquid to melting tenderness as a gratin. A dish of scalloped potatoes baked in milk is the simplest of gratins; with onion, veal stock and Gruyère cheese, a gratin becomes *savoyarde*, while *gratin dauphinois* baked with cream and topped with cheese is perhaps the most famous of all.

The limited selection of potatoes in the average market gives little clue to their diversity. We're seeing more and more 'boutique' potatoes, perhaps coloured a dusky purple or pink, or in odd shapes like the cylindrical French la ratte. Most behave like standard potatoes, whether waxy or floury, but have flavour superior to the average supermarket varieties.

OTHER PROBLEMS

UNDERCOOKED
Why: time too short; heat too low; potato variety very firm. *What to do:* continue cooking, raising heat if necessary.

TASTELESS
Why: inferior or old potatoes; underseasoned; overcooked. *What to do:* sprinkle with or beat in salt, pepper and nutmeg, with chopped herbs such as sage, thyme, chives or parsley; top with butter, olive oil, sour cream or crisp bacon.

SHARP FLAVOUR
Why: inferior, old or poorly stored potatoes, often with green patches and sprouted eyes. Note: green patches are toxic and must be trimmed off. *What to do:* add powerful seasoning such as crisp bacon, sautéed onion or garlic, or cut sharp taste by adding cream, sour cream or plain yogurt.

DISCOLOURED
Why: inferior, old or poorly stored potatoes; peeled potatoes left in open air; potatoes not fully immersed. Note: under frost or too much refrigeration, potatoes blacken. *What to do:* trim potatoes well; store peeled potatoes in cold water; boil in generous amounts of salted water.

PERFECT – potato tender but does not break up when pierced with point of a knife; if boiled, flesh is moist not watery when drained; flavour has earthy overtones. Note: this stage is right for steamed and boiled potatoes, or potatoes cooked to serve in a sauce.

PERFECT WELL-COOKED – skin peels very easily and when drained, outside of peeled potato is floury. Note: oven-baked potatoes and potatoes steamed or boiled for potato purée should all be cooked to this stage.

OVERCOOKED – very floury; waterlogged if cooked in liquid, or shrivelled if baked. *Why:* cooked too fast, so inside firm but outside overcooked; cooked too long. *What to do:* drain thoroughly, spread on a baking sheet and dry in a low oven. If very overdone, see Quick Fix.

left to right
UNDERCOOKED – potato hard when pierced with point of a knife; when cut, centre is translucent.
PERFECT – when cut, potato opaque not translucent.
PERFECT WELL-COOKED – potato very tender, almost falling apart.
OVERCOOKED – potato very soft and disintegrating.

QUICK FIX

If potatoes are falling apart, take all the way by mashing with herbs. Drain well, return to pan and dry over low heat, 1-2 minutes. For each potato, add 3 tablespoons milk or cream, 15 g/½ oz butter and 1 tablespoon chopped herbs like chives or parsley. Beat over low heat until fluffy (see opposite). Season to taste.

Warm potato salad with tarragon and white wine

SERVES 4

Potatoes have more flavour when they are cooked in their skins and, when peeled while still warm, they absorb more dressing. Served warm, the salad is a classic accompaniment to hot garlic sausage. Flat-leaf parsley can be substituted for the tarragon.

750 g/1½ lb waxy potatoes, scrubbed but unpeeled
60 ml/2 fl oz white wine
salt and freshly ground black pepper
bunch of tarragon
125 ml/4 fl oz olive oil

Put the potatoes in a large pan of cold salted water. Cover, bring to the boil, and simmer until done, 15-20 minutes. Drain.

When cool enough to handle, peel and cut into 2.5-cm/1-inch chunks. Sprinkle with the wine, season and stir gently. Leave to cool until tepid.

Meanwhile, strip the tarragon leaves from stems and coarsely chop the leaves. Sprinkle the tarragon and oil over potatoes and toss gently to mix. Taste, adjust the seasoning and serve while still warm.

MASHED POTATOES

With its soft texture and adaptable taste, the potato is the ideal vegetable for mashing and puréeing. For a classic potato purée, rich yet fluffy and falling easily from the spoon, the guidelines are clear. First choose the right floury type of potato (see opposite). Cut into even 2.5-cm/1-inch chunks. (I leave the peel as it adds flavour and helps hold the potato together during cooking.) Immediately immerse potatoes in a pan of cold salted water, cover and bring to the boil. Simmer until very tender when pierced with a knife, 15-20 minutes, then drain. Let cool slightly and remove skin. To dry, warm gently in the pan or spread on a baking sheet in a low oven.

Potatoes are full of starch and the aim when puréeing is to expand and fluff the grains without letting them glue together. Work the potatoes through a ricer or a coarse strainer, or simply mash thoroughly in the pan. To lighten and smooth the purée, it is beaten over heat with a wooden spoon, adding hot milk or cream and generous amounts of butter. (Overbeating, typically in a processor, will make the purée heavy, almost stringy.) Proportions depend to some extent on the type of potato, but are mainly a matter of taste. Lastly season with salt and white pepper (to avoid speckling).

Potatoes

Sautéed, pan-fried, deep-fried

HERE I CONCENTRATE ON FRYING, a cooking method well suited to potatoes, especially floury types. Their hard, starchy texture stands up well to high heat, whether sautéed, pan- or deep-fried. The challenge is to brown the exterior in the same time as cooking the interior until tender. Not always easy, and as usual the French are masters of the art. Here are a few points to bear in mind. First of all, the potatoes must be cut uniformly in small or thin pieces. Think of the delicate round slices used for a *pommes Anna* potato cake, or the matchstick cut of *pommes allumettes*, not forgetting the balls of *pommes Parisienne*. Secondly, once cut, rinsing or soaking removes some of the starch, keeping deep-fried potatoes from sticking together and helping to crisp them. A ten-minute soak will do. Lastly, cooking temperature must be closely watched. Sautéed and pan-fried potatoes need a brisk but not scorching heat, so they cook to the centre while becoming very brown and crisp on the outside. For deep-fried wafer-thin potato crisps and matchsticks, fat should be very hot so the slivers of potato brown in a minute or so. When deep-frying larger chunks of potato, including the classic *frites*, or chips which much of the world calls French fries, potatoes are cooked twice, first at 160°C/325°F so they soften and cook through, then at 190°C/375°F so they darken to a triumphant golden crisp.

UNDERCOOKED AND PALE – scarcely browned; floppy rather than crisp; flavour fatty. *Why:* cooking time too short; fried too slowly, pan overcrowded, too many added all at one time.
What to do: if deep-fried, drain potatoes, heat fat to 190°C/375°F, then fry potatoes rapidly until brown and crisp; if pan-fried, increase heat and fry potatoes briskly until browned and crisp on one side, then flip or stir and brown them further.

PERFECT – golden (if deep-fried) with darker edges (if pan-fried or sautéed); crisp outside, tender, almost floury texture inside; flavour nutty with no trace of grease. Note: to keep potatoes crisp, be sure to brown them really thoroughly, especially when pan-frying.

OTHER PROBLEMS

SOGGY
Why: undercooked; fried too slowly; poorly drained after frying; not served at once; salt added too long before serving.
What to do: if deep-fried, fry again briefly (see Undercooked); if pan-fried, dry on paper towels and heat in warm oven to remove excess fat. In potato pan, fry a sliced onion until golden and sprinkle over potatoes with some chopped parsley.
BURNED
Why: cooked too long; at too high a heat; fat or oil scorched before potatoes added.
What to do: discard worst burnt pieces and sprinkle rest with chopped chives or parsley.

Onions

ONIONS ARE THE FOUNDATION OF SO MANY SAVOURY DISHES that doing without them is unimaginable. It is important not only to choose the right type of onion for the job, but also to cook them to the right stage. Yellow onions are the most versatile. Their flavour can vary from harsh when raw, to mild and sweet when sliced and sweated gently in oil or butter and their own juices – perfect for serving with grilled chicken breasts or peppered steaks. When onions are cooked further, juices darken slowly to caramel, a rich flavouring for a quiche (right). Yellow varieties become pungent, the basis of the best onion soup. Do not let onions scorch, however, as they will turn unpleasantly acrid.

Other types of onion have more specific uses. The first white onions of spring, mild and sweet, are wonderful glazed in butter and sugar, or simmered in chicken stock with a touch of honey. Spring onions are tangy and crisp, in my opinion better raw than cooked though they do well in stir-fries. Full-grown white and yellow onions may be stuffed with minced beef to bake in white wine, herbs and cream, or baked to a dark glaze with raisins, chocolate and vinegar. Decorative red onions, valued for their mildness, are also a choice for salads and sandwiches.

PERFECT SOFT – sliced or chopped onions are translucent, moist and meltingly tender with no trace of browning; whole onions are plump, juicy, tender when pierced with a skewer but still holding shape; for all types, flavour is sweet and rich.

PERFECT LIGHTLY BROWNED – sliced or chopped onions are rich golden brown, slightly crisp, with moisture evaporated; flavour is savoury and mellow.

PERFECT VERY BROWN AND CARAMELIZED – sliced onions have become a *confit*, cooked down to a dark purée with no trace of scorching; flavour is intense, mellow and sweet with caramel.

PROBLEMS

TASTELESS
Why: wrong type of onion; not enough seasoning; undercooked so caramelized flavour not developed.
What to do: season with salt, pepper and sweetener such as port, brown sugar or honey, and continue cooking to right stage. When done, add contrasting hot, sour or sweet ingredients such as dried red pepper or chilli, vinegar or wine, raisins and other dried fruits.

BURNT
Why: cooked too long; cooked too fast.
What to do: if partly scorched, transfer unburnt onions to another pan and continue. If very burnt, nothing can be done.
COLLAPSED (whole onions)
Why: cooked too long.
What to do: disguise with chopped tomato, walnuts, or a herb such as thyme, sage or parsley.

Caramelized onion quiche

SERVES 6-8

Here an intense confit of onions cooked in red wine gives a contemporary twist to quiche. Serve it warm as a starter, or for lunch or brunch with a seasonal green salad.

30 g /1 oz butter

500 g/1 lb yellow onions, thinly sliced

salt and pepper

2-3 tablespoons sugar

75 ml/2½ fl oz red wine

1 tablespoon chopped thyme

for the French pie pastry

200 g/6½ oz flour

100 g/3¼ oz butter

1 egg yolk

½ teaspoon salt

3 tablespoons water, more if needed

for the custard

3 eggs, plus 3 extra egg yolks

500 ml/16 fl oz milk

125 ml/4 fl oz double cream, or more milk

pinch of nutmeg

white pepper

25-cm/10-inch tart pan with removable base

Make the French pie pastry: sift the flour on to a work surface and make a well in the centre. Pound the butter with a rolling pin to soften it. Put the butter, egg yolk, salt and water into the well. With your fingers, work the moist ingredients until thoroughly mixed. Draw in the flour with a pastry scraper and work in the other ingredients with the fingers of both hands until coarse crumbs form. If the crumbs are very dry, add 1-2 tablespoons more water. Press the dough into a ball.

Lightly flour the work surface. Blend the dough by pushing it away from you with the heel of your hand, then gathering it up until it is very smooth and peels away from work surface in one piece, 1-2 minutes. Shape into a ball, wrap and chill until firm, at least 30 minutes.

Meanwhile, make the confit: heat the butter in a frying pan and add the onions with some salt and pepper. Press a piece of buttered foil on top, cover and sweat the onions, stirring occasionally, until soft, 10-15 minutes. Sprinkle with the sugar, turn up the heat and cook until golden brown, 5-10 minutes. Stir in the wine and cook, stirring often, until the liquid has evaporated and onions are deep brown, 15-20 minutes. Stir the thyme into the confit, adjust the seasoning and let it cool.

Use the pastry to line the tart pan (see page 295) and chill until firm, about 15 minutes. Preheat the oven to 220°C/425°F/gas7 and blind-bake the pastry shell (see page 295). Leave oven at 190°C/375°F/gas5.

Make the custard: in a bowl, whisk the eggs, egg yolks, milk, cream, nutmeg, salt and white pepper just until mixed. Spread the cooled onions evenly in the base of the pastry shell and pour over the custard. Bake in the oven until the custard is browned on top and just set, 30-35 minutes. Let cool slightly before unmoulding.

Serve the quiche warm or at room temperature.

Whole garlic and shallot

For centuries, garlic and shallots have been used as flavourings, but recently they've taken centre stage in dishes like confit or roasted garlic and shallot. Twin garlic and shallot purées regularly appear on our table with roast lamb, a contrast of pungent and sweet. To temper the flavour of winter garlic (which can be harsh), discard any green sprout from the centre of the clove and blanch the garlic in boiling water for 1-2 minutes. When roasting garlic or shallots, I like to squeeze the cooked flesh from skins, then chop or purée it with herbs such as thyme or oregano and a little oil. Season the purée to taste and spread it on crusty bread. If the garlic or shallot has been cooked too long, cut away any charred portions, then chop and use the flesh to flavour other dishes.

PERFECT – flesh can easily be squeezed in pieces from a whole bulb; whether peeled or still in skin, garlic clove or shallot bulb is tender when pinched or pierced with point of a knife; flesh is moist and very aromatic.

Mushrooms

IT SEEMS TO ME THAT MUSHROOMS can be one of the very best cultivated vegetables, comparable to the elusive wild mushrooms that I can just remember gathering in the fields as a child. Apart from the ubiquitous common mushroom, today the half dozen so-called exotic varieties which are commonly available include cep, chanterelle, cloud ear, enokitake, chestnut, hedgehog, morel, oyster and shiitake. All can be relied upon to bring colour and meaty flavour to a dish – though at a certain price. I'm happiest when mushrooms are tart with lemon juice or red wine, or liberally laced Italian-style with garlic, tomato and oregano. Thanks to modern methods, almost all mushrooms now have clean caps and very little to trim off the stem – the woody stems of shiitake are an exception, as they must be trimmed level with the cap. Most mushroom caps have tender skins, though you may want to peel some chestnut mushrooms.

I find this earthy combination of toasted nuts and wild mushrooms irresistible, outstanding with roast game. A mixture of mushrooms, such as ceps with orange and black chanterelles, is ideal.

125 g/4 oz chopped hazelnuts
500 g/1 pound mixed wild mushrooms
60 g/2 oz butter
2 shallots, finely chopped
1 garlic clove, finely chopped
salt and pepper
2 tablespoons chopped parsley
squeeze of lemon juice

Preheat the oven to 175°C/350°F/gas4. Spread the hazelnuts on a baking sheet, and toast in the preheated oven until lightly browned, stirring once, 12-15 minutes.

Clean the mushrooms: trim the stems and brush off any twigs and dirt. Rinse them quickly with cold water. Note: do not soak the mushrooms or they will soften to pulp. Drain thoroughly. Leave small mushrooms whole and cut large ones in half or quarter them.

Melt half the butter in a large sauté pan. Add shallots and sauté until soft but not brown, 1-2 minutes. Add the mushrooms, garlic, salt and pepper and sauté briskly until done, tossing and stirring so the mushrooms cook evenly, 3-5 minutes. Add remaining butter, nuts and parsley and continue to sauté 1-2 minutes. Sprinkle with lemon juice, taste, adjust seasoning and serve.

UNDERCOOKED AND WOODY – flesh is firm and resistant to a fork, with juices not yet developed; colour pale and flavour not yet released.
Why: cooking time too short; cooked too fast; too little liquid.
What to do: lower heat and continue cooking, adding liquid or fat if necessary. Note: do not add too much as eventually mushrooms will render their own juices.

PERFECT – texture tender and juicy, soft enough to cut with a fork; colour striking (pale cream for common mushrooms) and flavour intense.

OTHER PROBLEMS

DRY AND OVERCOOKED
Why: inferior or old mushrooms; cooked too long; cooked too fast; too little liquid.
What to do: add stock, cream or water and cook 1-2 minutes longer. Note: mushrooms are still very edible when overcooked.
WET
Why: inferior mushrooms; mushrooms stored in plastic; not sufficiently cooked. Note: some varieties, notably common and oyster mushrooms, yield a lot of juice when they soften.

What to do: if necessary, drain off excess liquid then continue cooking over high heat until moisture has evaporated.
TASTELESS
Why: inferior or old mushrooms; not enough seasoning.
What to do: sauté chopped onion, shallot or garlic and add to mushrooms with salt, pepper and spices such as nutmeg, coriander, cumin and celery seed or herbs including tarragon, chives, thyme and parsley.

QUICK FIX

If mushrooms are dry or underflavoured, pour over some stock and simmer a minute or two until moist. Sprinkle with salt or soy sauce, pepper or fresh herbs, if you like. Makes a delicious filling for omelettes and sandwiches.

Braised and glazed vegetables

WHEN BRAISING VEGETABLES I USUALLY SIMMER THEM WITH WINE, stock or water and flavourings such as tomato or dried fruits to develop their natural mellow flavours. They may first be browned in oil or butter to concentrate the taste. Carrots, celeriac, leek, sweet potato, turnip, onion and fennel are top choices. For glazing with oil or butter in their own juices, the same robust vegetables hold their shape well. For either method, aromatic herbs – rosemary, thyme and bay leaf – add character, and if you include diced bacon or sausages, the vegetable becomes almost a main dish in itself.

PERFECT – vegetable tender but does not break up when pierced with point of a knife; butter and sugar pale golden-brown and colours bright; flavours robust and sweet.

OVERCOOKED – vegetables soft, almost falling apart when poked with a knife; sugar starting to caramelize, flavour often bitter.
Why: cooked too long; cooked too slowly.
What to do: cover with a blanket of chopped walnuts, spring onions or parsley; revive flavour of braised vegetables with 2-3 teaspoons tomato purée; for glazed vegetables, sprinkle with a little brown sugar and grill.

OTHER PROBLEMS

UNDERCOOKED AND FIBROUS
Why: cooking time too short; temperature too low; acid ingredients used such as tomatoes which slow rate of cooking; if fibrous, poor or old vegetable.
What to do: continue cooking, raising heat if necessary.
TASTELESS
Why: poor vegetables; underseasoned; overcooked.
What to do: season with chopped garlic, salt, pepper and a little sugar; see also Overcooked.

QUICK FIX

When braised or glazed vegetables are soft or tasteless, top them with crispy deep-fried ginger or leek: Thinly slice a 7.5-cm/3-inch piece of fresh ginger, cutting across the fibres. Taking a few at a time, stack the slices and cut into the thinnest possible strips. For leek, cut 1 large leek into julienne strips. Heat deep fat to 190°C /375°F and fry ginger or leeks until crisp, 1-2 minutes. Lift out with draining spoon, dry on paper towels and scatter over vegetables.

Glazed root vegetables

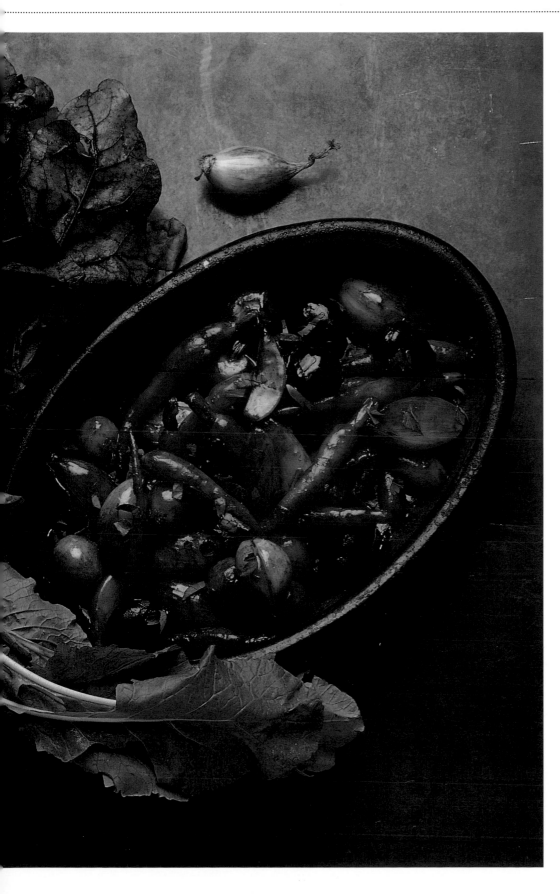

Common roots, such as the carrots, turnips and onions used here, are transformed by glazing. Baby vegetables can be left whole. Larger vegetables should be cut to small even shapes and preferably 'turned', with sharp edges trimmed so they roll in the bottom of the pan and glaze evenly.

500 g/1 pound baby carrots, or larger carrots, peeled and cut into even pieces
500 g/1 pound baby beetroots, or larger beetroots, peeled and cut into even pieces
500 g/1 pound baby onions, trimmed and peeled
60 g/2 oz butter
2 tablespoons sugar
salt and pepper
500 ml/16 fl oz water, more if needed
3-4 tablespoons chopped parsley

Put the raw vegetables in separate pans large enough for each of the vegetables to form an even layer on the bottom of pan. For 500 g/1 lb vegetables, add 1-2 tablespoons butter, 2 teaspoons sugar, with salt and pepper to taste. Pour over just enough water to cover the vegetables halfway. Cover with lids. Bring to the boil and simmer until the vegetables are almost tender, 10-25 minutes depending on type and size of vegetable.

Remove the lids and boil each pan until the liquid has evaporated to a syrupy glaze and the vegetables are done, shaking the pan occasionally to turn the vegetables and coat them evenly.

Sprinkle the vegetables with parsley and toss to mix. Taste and adjust the seasoning. Serve each vegetable separately or mix them together, if you like – the beetroots will, however, tend to bleed slightly.

Puréed vegetables

VEGETABLE PURÉES ARE MORE OF A CHALLENGE THAN THEY SEEM. It's no good simply mashing a vegetable and sending it to the table. First, be sure to choose one which purées easily, such as carrot or pumpkin; fibrous types like leek do not do well. The starch in dried vegetables, particularly kidney beans, is helpful in lightening and binding a purée, and some puréed vegetables such as celeriac need some potato added for starch.

Be sure the vegetable is thoroughly cooked (usually boiled or steamed) so it breaks up smoothly. Long cooking means that bland vegetables like pumpkin and squash become even blander, needing plenty of seasonings. To soften and lighten them, most purées are beaten over the heat with butter and cream in generous quantities. Finally a bright-coloured vegetable is a bonus, though the white of turnip or celeriac has its own appeal.

There's a trend towards mixing puréed vegetables, for instance beetroot with apple, or pumpkin with swede, but my own preference is for a single, well-defined taste highlighted with appropriate seasonings. Then a purée moves beyond a mashed vegetable to a gourmet dish, a worthy accompaniment to veal, game and the most expensive of shellfish.

QUICK FIX

Any purée is improved by adding butter and cream. For every 250 ml/8 fl oz purée, add 1-2 tablespoons butter and 2-3 tablespoons double cream. Set the purée over medium heat and work with an immersion blender or beat by hand with a wooden spoon until the purée is light and smooth, 2-3 minutes. Add any of the flavourings suggested under Lacks flavour.

TOO THIN — purée watery, almost thin enough to pour; colour is pale and flavour flat.
Why: unsuitable or immature vegetable, lacking in starch; vegetable not thoroughly drained before puréeing; undercooked so no starch leached from vegetable to thicken liquid.
What to do: simmer over medium heat to evaporate liquid, stirring constantly to prevent scorching.

PERFECT — purée (here, sweet potatoes) is smooth, light and falls from spoon; holds a clear shape without being sticky; colour is clear, usually pastel; flavour fragrant.

TEXTURE LUMPY OR COARSE — consistency of purée uneven, watery at edges, often sticky on the tongue; colour may be dull.
Why: unsuitable vegetable; undercooked; insufficiently puréed.
What to do: work through a sieve or food mill.
Note: fibrous vegetables such as celeriac or leek cannot be puréed effectively in a food mill or using a potato masher.

OTHER PROBLEMS

TOO THICK
Why: vegetable very starchy; cooked with too little liquid.
What to do: thin with cream, milk, stock or water.

STICKY OR GLUTINOUS
Why: starchy vegetable such as potato or lentil was overworked, often in food processor.
What to do: stir in chopped nuts or raw celery to break up texture.

LACKS FLAVOUR
Why: poor vegetable; overcooked; underseasoned.
What to do: add salt, pepper and dry spices — nutmeg; coriander, cumin and cardamom particularly develop the taste of lentils, split peas and the kidney bean family; allspice and cinnamon go well with chestnut, pumpkin and squash, while summer vegetables such as courgette, tomato and green beans are best with garlic and fresh herbs such as oregano, basil and parsley.

MUDDY COLOUR
Why: vegetables cooked too slowly; vegetables overcooked; purée not beaten over heat to develop and whiten starch.
What to do: beat purée over low heat, 1-2 minutes, then stir in chopped herbs for colour.

Carrot purée with cardamom

SERVES 4

Because of their sweetness, root vegetables have a natural affinity with warm, sweet spices like cinnamon, nutmeg and cloves. Carrot and cardamom is a particularly good combination. I like to crush cardamom seeds myself to extract their delicate floral flavour, but if you are in a real rush, use ground cardamom.

1 kg/2 pounds carrots, peeled and
    thickly sliced
1 teaspoon cardamom pods
15 g/½ oz butter
½ teaspoon sugar
salt and pepper
60 ml/2 fl oz double cream, more if
    needed

Bring a large pan of salted water to the boil. Add the carrots, cover and simmer until they are very tender, 15-20 minutes.

Meanwhile, break open the cardamom pods and remove the seeds, discarding the shells. Crush the seeds in a mortar with a pestle or on a board under a heavy pan.

When the carrots are done, drain them and purée them in a food processor, or work them through a sieve.

Melt the butter in a pan. Add the carrot purée and stir in the crushed cardamom, sugar, salt and pepper. Beat in the cream. Heat the purée, stirring, until very hot and thickened to the right consistency. If too thick, add more cream. Taste and adjust the seasoning. Transfer the purée to a warmed serving bowl, smooth the top and mark in waves with a rubber spatula or knife.

Grilled and roasted vegetables

GIVEN THE DRY HEAT OF GRILLING AND ROASTING, it is only logical to choose robust vegetables, preferably with plenty of natural juice. First choice are vegetable fruits – tomatoes, sweet peppers, and both summer and winter squash. Roots such as carrot, turnip and celeriac roast well, and green vegetables like asparagus, chicory and radicchio are good grilled, providing this is done with care. Beware of charring vegetables and overwhelming their, often mild, flavours.

Constant basting is the key to all these grilled and roasted vegetables, though the need for basting in the oven can be reduced by covering with foil or a lid. Before cooking begins, moisten the vegetables well with oil or butter, salt, pepper and seasonings such as lemon juice, soy sauce, flavoured vinegars, or simply with vinaigrette dressing. You'll find that if left to marinate for just 5-10 minutes the vegetables will do even better.

To obtain the attractive lined pattern on vegetables which is left by a hot grill, preheat the grill rack thoroughly, then brush it with oil before adding the vegetables. Leave them until they are well toasted with score marks before moving or turning over.

PERFECT – vegetables moist, tender but still holding shape; surface lightly browned and edges charred; flavours intense, slightly smoky, colours bright.

OVERCOOKED AND DRY – vegetables dry and shrivelled; colours faded and flavour often harsh.
Why: unsuitable or old vegetable; cooked too long; heat too high; not basted enough.
What to do: moisten by brushing with olive oil, melted butter or vinaigrette dressing; sprinkle with red wine vinegar, lime or lemon juice and chopped aromatic herbs such as basil and thyme; if scorched, nothing can be done.

OTHER PROBLEMS

FIBROUS AND UNDERCOOKED
Why: unsuitable vegetable; cooking time too short; heat too low.
What to do: if fibrous, cut vegetables across grain into smaller pieces; continue cooking, raising heat if necessary, basting often.
BLAND
Why: poor or stale vegetables; not basted often.
What to do: brush with vinaigrette dressing, or sprinkle with olive or nut oil and lemon juice; brush lightly with an Oriental mix of 1 crushed garlic clove, 2 tablespoons rice wine, 1 teaspoon each of fish sauce, soy sauce and dark sesame oil, juice of 2 lemons and ½ teaspoon sugar.

QUICK FIX

Employ bland or overcooked vegetables as the filling of a giant submarine sandwich in a baguette loaf: brush loaf with olive oil or vinaigrette dressing, and add vegetables, layering them with sliced Gruyère or goats' cheese. Press sandwich firmly together and cut diagonally in lengths for serving.

Vegetable terrines and moulds

COLOURFUL VEGETABLES SUCH AS CARROT, green beans, broccoli, turnip, spinach, artichoke and peas look best in terrines. Those with a high natural moisture content, for instance tomato or squash, are not suitable, nor are fibrous vegetables such as leeks which could tear the terrine apart when sliced. Vegetable purées to be moulded in a terrine should be stiff, more so than if served alone (see Puréed vegetables, page 176).

Vegetable terrines divide into two basic types: simple moulds made of vegetable purée bound with egg, and more complicated terrines with whole or very coarsely chopped vegetables arranged in layers and held together with a separate mixture, often an egg custard. In both, the vegetables are lightly precooked, then cooked again in the terrine. The challenge is to maintain colour and taste while setting the vegetables firmly enough to slice. During precooking, usually boiling or steaming, the vegetables should be seasoned very well. Most importantly, maximum moisture must be extracted if the finished terrine is to hold its shape.

Whole eggs are the usual binder for vegetable terrines and moulds, perhaps with a starch in the form of white sauce, breadcrumbs, or aspic if the terrine is cold. Sometimes a veal or chicken mousseline may be added. When moulding a layered terrine, put the softest vegetables on the bottom, so that when unmoulded, the stiffer ones form a firm base. Baking in a water bath ensures moist, even heat so the vegetables do not overcook and the egg custard does not curdle.

PERFECT – mould is just set with moist surface; mixture is firm when pressed and a skewer inserted in centre is hot to the touch when withdrawn after 30 seconds; vegetable colours are vivid and flavours distinct.

OVERCOOKED – mixture shrinks from sides of mould, with cooking juices expelled around edges; flavour is flat. *Why:* heat too high; cooked too long. *What to do:* if firm enough to unmould, conceal poor texture with chopped herbs and a butter sauce (if hot) or mayonnaise (if cold); if collapsed see Quick Fix.

left to right
UNDERCOOKED – mould soft in the centre when pressed, collapses when unmoulded.
PERFECT – tall and with straight sides, the mould is light-textured when cut.
OVERCOOKED – mould is coarse-textured, lightly browned and tending to crumble.

Two-colour vegetable timbale with red pepper sauce

SERVES 4 as an appetizer or 8 as a side dish

OTHER PROBLEMS

UNDERCOOKED AND SOFT – mould is soft and liable to collapse, especially near centre; a skewer inserted in centre of mould is warm, not hot, to the touch when withdrawn after 30 seconds; when cut, terrine or mould is too soft to hold shape; flavour is underdeveloped.

Why: cooking time too short; heat too low; too much moisture in vegetables; too little binding agent.

What to do: if undercooked (terrine or mould will be soft in centre, not throughout) continue cooking, raising heat if necessary; if too much moisture or too little binding agent, see Quick Fix as further cooking will not help.

COLLAPSED

Why: vegetables unsuitable with too much moisture or fibre; vegetables wet after cooking; not enough binding agent; terrine or mould overcooked.

What to do: see Quick Fix.

LACKS TASTE

Why: lack of seasoning; poor or unsuitable vegetables.

What to do: sprinkle each mould or slice of terrine with salt and pepper. Serve with well-flavoured sauce, such as horseradish cream sauce or herb vinaigrette; add a crisp relish such as sweetcorn kernels with shallot and coriander.

DULL COLOURS

Why: poor choice of vegetable; vegetables overcooked.

What to do: serve with green mayonnaise or a tomato coulis; top with a colourful garnish such as chopped tomato, sweet pepper or herbs.

QUICK FIX

When a terrine or mould is seriously collapsed, bring bread to the rescue. Pack the mixture in pitta pockets with lots of crispy beansprouts. For a party, pile the mixture on rounds of garlic bread and top with curls of Parmesan cheese or slivers of sun-dried tomato.

Almost any vegetable that is in season can be used in a vegetable mould, you just need a combination of vibrant colours. Serve the moulds as an appetizer or as an accompaniment to grilled fish or chicken.

1 kg/2 lb cauliflower	for the red pepper sauce
2 tablespoons double cream	2 red sweet peppers
1 kg/2 lb spinach	1 tablespoon butter
salt and white pepper	1 onion, chopped
pinch of nutmeg	2 garlic cloves, chopped
2 eggs	2 tomatoes, peeled, seeded and chopped

eight 125-ml/4-fl oz dariole moulds or ramekins

Preheat the oven to 175°C/350°F/gas4. Trim the cauliflower and cut it into florets, discarding the stems. Rinse and drain. Bring a pan of salted water to the boil. Add the florets and simmer, uncovered, until very tender, 8-12 minutes. Drain very well. Purée the cauliflower with the double cream until smooth and set aside.

Meanwhile, tear the stems from the spinach leaves. Wash the leaves well in plenty of cold water and drain most of the water from the leaves. Pack the spinach in a large heavy-based saucepan, cover and cook just until wilted, stirring occasionally, 3-4 minutes. Let the spinach cool, then squeeze it in your fists to extract water. Purée the spinach.

Transfer the vegetable purées to two saucepans. Cook over low heat, stirring constantly, until nearly all liquid has evaporated and the purées pull away from the sides of the pans, 5-7 minutes. Let cool, then taste and adjust the seasoning, adding nutmeg to the spinach.

Meanwhile, make the red pepper sauce: preheat the grill; roast the peppers under the grill, turning them until the skins char and burst, 7-10 minutes. Put them in a plastic bag to retain steam and loosen skins. Let cool. Peel the peppers, discard their cores and seeds, and chop the flesh. Melt the butter in a frying pan. Stir in onion and garlic and sauté until soft but not brown, 3-4 minutes. Put in a food processor with the peppers, tomatoes, salt and pepper. Purée the vegetables, transfer to a small saucepan and cook over low heat until hot and slightly thickened, 1-2 minutes. Taste and adjust seasoning.

Butter the moulds. Half-fill a roasting pan with water for a water bath and bring to the boil on the stove. Whisk 1 egg with salt and pepper in a small bowl and stir into the cooled cauliflower purée. Repeat for the spinach purée. Spoon some cauliflower purée into each mould, then top with some spinach purée. Note: spinach goes in last to form a firm base for the mould when it is turned out. Place the moulds in the water bath and bring the water back to the boil. Bake in the preheated oven until done, 15-20 minutes.

Reheat the pepper sauce and spoon a little on some warmed plates. Run a knife around the edge of the moulds, turn out on the plates and serve at once.

PASTA, GRAINS &

MY FATHER, BRITISH-BORN AND TRADITIONAL to the core, would never touch pasta or rice if he could avoid it – 'foreign frippery' he said. How different we are today! Pasta has become a staple, from simple spaghetti to homemade ravioli filled with luxuries like lobster and wild mushrooms. Half a dozen robust grains are routinely available, while long-ignored beans and lentils are back in style.

Oddly enough, pasta – which is no more than a plain paste of wheat flour and water, with or without eggs – is in its way more versatile than any of the grains, being shaped in dozens of different string or hollow shapes as well as being stuffed for ravioli or cannelloni, or layered with sauce as in lasagne. Pasta dishes have developed far beyond Italian classics like *tagliatelle con ragù bolognese* and *penne al pesto* to contemporary creations such as fettuccine with braised garlic and balsamic vinegar or Prawn-stuffed Ravioli in Fragrant Broth (page 187). You'll find advice on kneading and rolling your own pasta dough on page 183.

Grains offer a wide palette of tastes and plenty of chew – be sure to cook them thoroughly as when undercooked they are crunchy and indigestible. In the West, grains are invariably treated one of three ways: boiled or steamed to be light and fluffy, simmered as a pilaf, or cooked with quantities of liquid as a creamy, soft risotto. The grain may be whole, cracked or coarsely ground as a meal, when it is simmered to purées familiar as polenta and grits. When cooked to be fluffy, the flavour of a grain comes through clearly as with nutty buckwheat or fragrant white basmati rice. In pilaf and risotto the intrinsic taste of the grain blends with vegetables and spices, sometimes with the addition of fish, shellfish or meats. However, it must never be overwhelmed.

As for beans, peas and lentils, it's the choice of flavourings which gives the ethnic twist, as in Portuguese broad beans with pork, cumin and coriander, or French *salade de lentilles* with a vinaigrette dressing. These pulses are prime sources of hearty winter soups, and spicy purées, many of Asian ancestry.

We rely on grains, pasta and pulses for so many simple, everyday dishes. Given their low cost, it is well worth buying the best and seeking out a reliable, fresh supply. Grains, pasta and pulses are high in carbohydrates and turn bland and powdery when stale – debris in the bottom of the package is a bad sign. All offer excellent nutritional value. And all, even pasta, remain stubbornly, refreshingly ethnic.

PULSES

Spaghetti and string pasta; macaroni and shaped pasta

THERE'S SOME ASTONISHINGLY GOOD PASTA AROUND THESE DAYS in the local grocery, from top-quality dried spaghetti and string pasta like angel hair to reliable 'fresh' noodles (in fact, lightly dried) such as tagliatelle and linguine. Start with good raw materials and all you have to do is add character. String pasta can be tossed simply with oil or butter and herbs, or with a sauce that dresses the strands – classics include *spaghetti alla carbonara* with pancetta, Parmesan and egg, *spaghetti alla puttanesca* with anchovies, capers, olives and tomatoes, and spaghettini with little clams, garlic, parsley and olive oil.

Shaped pastas, particularly hollow ones such as penne or rigatoni, hold more sauce and invite coarser, more moist mixtures such as a traditional *ragù*. Shells suggest shellfish to me, and other shapes like snails, a rustic, earthy approach with lots of herbs and garlic. Other nations chip in with recipes like Thai rice noodles with beansprouts and long beans in a curry coconut sauce, or Alsatian saddle of hare with noodles and wild mushrooms in cream. A few tiny pasta shapes – alphabet letters and stars for instance – are designed for soup, and the rice-shaped pasta called orzo can be served like a true grain. If you're interested in making your own fresh pasta, you'll find some tips opposite.

An Italian friend of mine adds a few comments on cooking pasta: use plenty of salted water, allowing 4 litres/7 pints of water and 1 tablespoon salt per 500 g/1 lb of pasta. A spoonful of oil will discourage the water from boiling over after the pasta is added. Once boiling, stir the pasta to separate the strands, then let it simmer until done (rapid boiling can break up pieces before they are cooked).

TYPICAL STRING PASTA

bucatini, capelli d'angelo, fettuccine, linguine, pappardelle, spaghetti, tagliatelle, vermicelli

TYPICAL HOLLOW AND SHAPED PASTA

boccolotti (tubes), conchiglie (shells), farfalle (butterflies), fusilli (twists), lumache (snails), maccheroni, orecchiette (little ears), penne (quills), rigatoni, ruote (wheels)

PROBLEMS

UNDERCOOKED WITH HARD STARCHY CENTRE

Why: cooking time too short; water not simmering briskly.

What to do: continue cooking, turning up heat if necessary.

OVERCOOKED

Why: pasta cooked too long; if fresh, pasta not dried before cooking; if dried, poor pasta with low gluten content.

What to do: drain pasta, rinse with hot water to remove starch; toss briefly with oil to keep strands separate then serve at once, spooning sauce on top to avoid stirring pasta further. If very overcooked, nothing can be done.

HEAVY AND STICKY

Why: too little water used for boiling; pasta not stirred while cooking, so strands stuck together; pasta overcooked; sauce too thick; pasta left to stand before or after adding sauce.

What to do: if no oil, butter or sauce already added, immerse pasta in hot water, stir to separate strands and drain; after adding sauce, mix in a few spoonfuls of oil, red or white wine, or simply a little cooking liquid or water and reheat gently. See also Overcooked.

FLAVOUR BLAND

Why: lacks seasoning; sauce tasteless; poor-quality pasta.

What to do: add a little salt, then season generously with fresh black pepper, dried red pepper flakes and Italian herbs such as basil, thyme and oregano; for fish and vegetable sauce add grated lemon zest and juice; serve with grated Parmesan (not for fish).

PERFECT – pasta tender but still firm to the bite (*al dente*); string pasta can be cut with your thumbnail; pieces show no tendency to stick together and the flavour is nutty.

PERFECT *left* – pasta firm, almost slippery and pieces separate easily.
OVERCOOKED *right* – pasta swollen, limp and soft; pieces sticky, especially string pasta.

QUICK FIX

When pasta is seriously overcooked, start again – don't bother saving it as you'll always be disappointed. However, if the pasta is only slightly overdone, it's worth proceeding with the recipe. So the pasta does not tear, spoon sauce on top rather than tossing the two together, and don't forget the grated Parmesan!

Cannelloni, lasagne and layered pasta

ONLY THE ITALIANS HAVE FULLY EXPLORED STUFFED AND LAYERED PASTA, and what masters they are! Plain pasta sheets, cooked to be slightly chewy, are the perfect foil for the meat sauce and béchamel in familiar lasagne bolognese, or for the wild mushrooms, prosciutto and herbs in *cannelloni al funghi*. Leave out the prosciutto and we enter vegetarian territory, an invitation to sweet peppers, squash, tomato, pumpkin and aubergine with a backing of olives, garlic, herbs and Parmesan cheese.

For the pasta itself, you have a choice: you can buy dried or fresh commercial pasta, or make your own fresh pasta sheets (see right). I've had good luck with commercial pasta, particularly given the complex sauces and stuffings which are used with layered pasta, but I have to admit that cannelloni or lasagne with homemade dough are incomparable.

Before layering or stuffing, the pasta must, of course, be boiled and drained on paper towels. Simmer the sheets or tubes in plenty of salted water so they don't stick together and undercook them slightly as they will cook further with the filling. To make filling cannelloni tubes easy, use a pastry bag, leaving the tip open without a tube. For cannelloni of homemade pasta, cut flat sheets in rectangles and roll them around your filling.

As you proceed, be sure to strike a good balance of pasta, filling and sauce: with too much pasta the finished dish will be heavy, with too much filling it will be overly rich, and with too little sauce it will be dry. Finally bear in mind the balance of flavourings – discreet, mellow or forceful – so there'll be no surprise when you taste them all together after baking. *Buon appetito!*

PERFECT – pasta just tender when cut with knife; filling is rich, moist and hot; flavour hearty and colours contrasting and bright.

QUICK FIX

If baked cannelloni or lasagne are overcooked and dry, pour 250 ml/8 fl oz milk, stock or water over the pasta, then cover and continue baking briefly until the liquid is absorbed. Just before serving, sprinkle generously with freshly chopped herbs such as chives, basil or parsley.

PROBLEMS

UNDERCOOKED AND PASTA HARD
Why: pasta undercooked: baking time too short; oven heat too low.
What to do: if pasta hard but sauce already absorbed, moisten with stock, cream or water and continue baking; if sauce thin, continue baking; if top pale, increase oven heat or brown under grill.

OVERCOOKED AND DRY
Why: baked too long; oven heat too high; too little filling or sauce.
What to do: serve small portions and moisten with more sauce or a warm walnut or hazelnut vinaigrette.

HEAVY
Why: too much pasta; sauce or stuffing too thick; overcooked.
What to do: serve with more sauce and a light, crisp accompaniment such as sweetcorn kernel and sweet pepper relish, thinly sliced fennel, celery or cucumber marinated in vinegar, or a green salad of rocket.

KNEADING AND ROLLING FRESH PASTA DOUGH

For egg-rich pasta dough, plain flour is best. Add a minimum of liquid – classic proportions are 100 g/3¼ oz flour to 1 large egg and a pinch of salt, with no water at all. The dough should be so firm that kneading it is hard work.

To knead and roll dough by hand: lightly flour the work surface and push the ball of dough away from you with the heel of one hand, holding it with the other. Lift dough from the work surface, give it a half turn and push it away from you again. Continue kneading until the dough is elastic and peels from the surface in one piece, 5-10 minutes. Let the dough rest, covered with an upturned bowl, at least 30 minutes to lose elasticity. Flour the work surface and pat the dough flat into a round with the rolling pin. Roll the dough, turning and moving it so it does not stick, to the thickness of a postcard.

Purists insist that pasta is best when hand-kneaded and rolled, but I find it much easier to use the pasta rolling machine. Divide the dough into 2-3 pieces and cover all but one with a cloth. Set the machine at its widest setting and work the dough through it. Fold the dough in two or three and continue working through the machine until the dough is satin-smooth and elastic, 8-10 minutes, dusting with flour if it seems sticky. Pasta dough should always be firm, so don't hesitate to work in extra flour during kneading.

When the dough is very smooth, start reducing the machine settings until the dough is rolled to a 15-cm/6-inch strip the thickness of a postcard, the thinnest setting. Continue with the remaining dough. Use the strips as directed in the recipe, cutting them to size for tagliatelle, lasagne or cannelloni, or filling them for ravioli or turnovers.

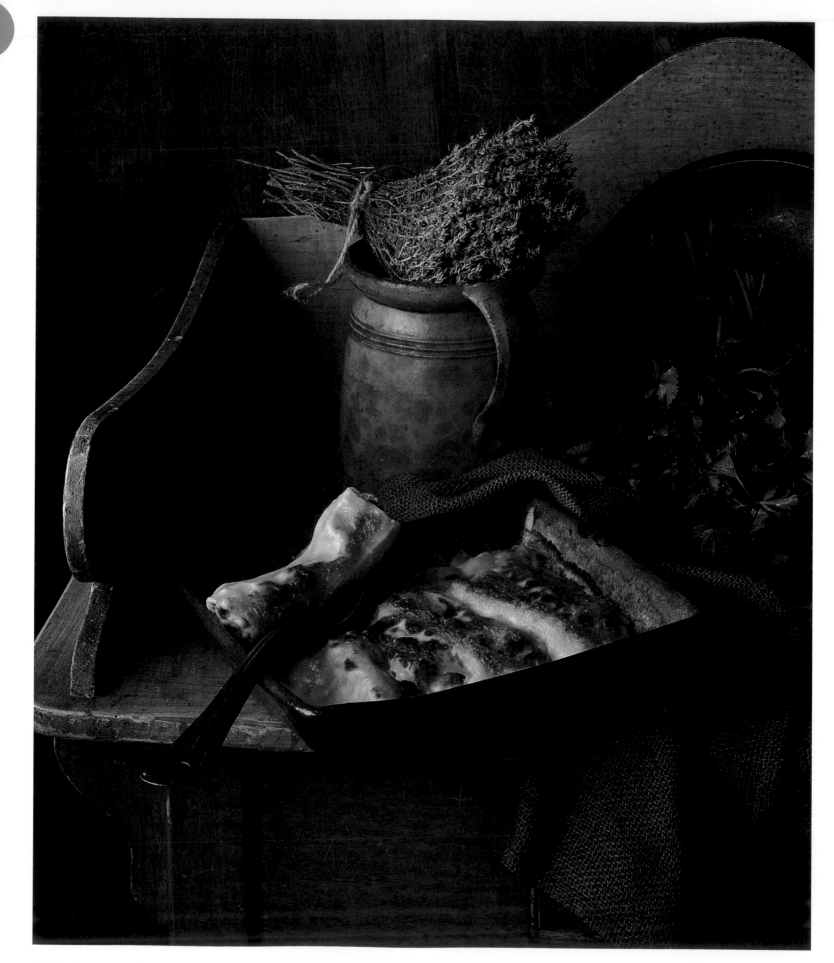

Cannelloni stuffed with veal and fresh herbs

SERVES 4

Cannelloni means 'big pipes' in Italian, reflecting their tubular shape. Don't be surprised by the stuffing of raw veal in this recipe – it bakes to be deliciously light and delicate.

375 g/¾ pound minced veal
8 dried cannelloni (about 150 g/5 oz)
60 g/2 oz chopped mixed herbs,
    such as sage, thyme and parsley
60 g/2 oz grated Parmesan cheese
1 egg
125 ml/4 fl oz milk

pastry bag without tube

for the béchamel sauce
500 ml/16 fl oz milk, more if
    needed
1 large slice of onion
1 bay leaf
½ teaspoon black peppercorns
45 g/1½ oz butter
20 g/¾ oz flour
salt and white pepper
generous pinch of nutmeg

Preheat the oven to 175°C/350°F/gas4. Brush a medium baking dish with butter. Bring a large pot of salted water to the boil.

Make the béchamel sauce: scald the milk with the onion, bay leaf and peppercorns. Cover and leave to infuse off the heat, 10-15 minutes. In a heavy-based saucepan, melt the butter, whisk in the flour and cook, stirring, until the flour is foaming but not browned, about 1 minute. Off the heat, strain in the hot milk. Whisk well, then bring to the boil, whisking constantly until the sauce thickens. Season to taste with salt, pepper and nutmeg, and leave to simmer for 1-2 minutes. Take off the heat, cover the sauce and leave to cool.

Add the cannelloni to the boiling water and simmer until done, 8-10 minutes or according to packet instructions. Using a slotted spoon, transfer them to a bowl of cold water to cool, then drain the cannelloni quite thoroughly.

Make the filling: in a bowl, stir together the veal, half the cooled béchamel, the chopped herbs and half the Parmesan cheese. Season well with salt and pepper. Beat in the egg. Using the pastry bag, pipe the filling into the cannelloni and set them in the baking dish.

Whisk the milk into the remaining béchamel and bring just to the boil. The sauce should lightly coat a spoon – if necessary, thin it with more milk. Taste and adjust the seasoning. Spoon over the cannelloni to coat them completely. Sprinkle with the remaining Parmesan cheese. Bake the cannelloni in the preheated oven until done, 40-50 minutes.

Spaghetti with bacon, tomatoes and chilli *Spaghetti all'amatriciana*

SERVES 4-6

This is a great dish for those evenings when time and energy are short. Tomatoes are the focus, so be sure they are perfectly ripe – as a time saver, you'll find that plum tomatoes really do not need to be peeled.

500 g/1 pound spaghetti
8 slices of bacon
    (about 175 g/6 oz), diced
1 onion, thinly sliced
125 ml/4 fl oz dry white wine
1 kg/2 pounds tomatoes, peeled,
    seeded and chopped

¼ teaspoon red chilli pepper flakes,
    more to taste
salt and pepper
75 g/2½ oz grated Parmesan
    cheese

Heat a large frying pan. Add the bacon and cook until the fat runs and the bacon starts to brown, 3-5 minutes. Add the onion and sauté until soft and lightly browned, 4-5 minutes.

Add the wine and boil until reduced by half. Stir in the tomatoes and red pepper flakes, bring to the boil and simmer until the sauce is thickened, 12-15 minutes. Taste and adjust the seasoning.

Meanwhile, bring a large pan of salted water to the boil. Add the spaghetti and stir to separate the strands. Simmer until *al dente*, tender but still firm to the bite, 7-10 minutes. Drain, return to the pan and add the tomato sauce and half the Parmesan cheese. Toss until the spaghetti is thoroughly coated with sauce. Taste, adjust the seasoning and transfer to warmed individual bowls. Serve at once, with remaining grated Parmesan cheese in a separate bowl.

Spaghetti with olives, tomatoes and chilli

For a vegetarian version of this spaghetti, omit the bacon and fry the onion in 2 tablespoons olive oil. Add 60 g/2 oz black olives to the sauce with the red pepper flakes, stoning the olives first if you like.

Cannelloni stuffed with veal and fresh herbs

Ravioli and stuffed pasta

Here I'm looking at delectable homemade packages — ravioli, tortellini and their cousins — which were once the province of Italian grandmothers but have now invaded the international table. We begin by making the dough. For egg-enriched pasta dough, plain is best. Add a minimum of liquid — classic proportions are 100 g/3¼ oz flour to 1 large egg and a large pinch of salt, with no water at all.

The dough should be so firm that kneading it by hand, in the manner of bread, is hard work. I strongly recommend you use the pasta rolling machine, running the dough through ever-finer settings until it is satin-smooth and elastic. By the time you finish, you'll have long ribbons of dough, ready to shape at once into packages. For noodles, let the dough dry for 10-15 minutes before cutting it.

Shaping the packages is a matter of patience, as they must be cut and sealed with care. Be sure the filling is assertive to offset the neutral dough, and don't be tempted to add too much — my usual failing — or the package will burst. Ravioli and pasta packages are best cooked in plenty of water at a brisk simmer to keep the pasta moving so it does not stick together. For fragile packages, steaming can be safer — but don't overlap them as they cook.

Italian cooks like to base their fillings on fresh cheese or ricotta, with herbs and vegetables like spinach or pumpkin as cheerful alternatives. From Asia come seafood stuffings of prawn and crab with the pasta served in a fragrant broth (opposite) or a contemporary spiced tomato coulis. The best sauces for packages are simple, the better to display the pasta and filling. Often a moistening of cream or vinaigrette dressing, or a bowl of Oriental dipping sauce is enough.

TYPICAL STUFFED PASTA
cappelletti, pansoti, pot-stickers, ravioli, steamed dumplings, tortellini, wontons

QUICK FIX

Here are three easy cover-ups for stuffed pasta that's less than perfect. Depending on the problem and the pasta, take your pick:
- Coat with a layer of tomato sauce.
- Fold in a few spoonfuls of double cream or crème fraîche.
- Top with crumbled crispy fried bacon.

PERFECT — parcels (here, ravioli) clearly shaped, with filling tightly sealed; when cut with a thumb nail or knife, pasta feels tender with no hard core; when tasted, pasta is tender but still firm to the bite (*al dente*); flavour is hearty and fresh.

OVERCOOKED — parcels swollen and often leaking; pasta is limp and sticky; texture soft and flavour pasty.
Why: dough too wet or not dried before cooking; cooked too long.
What to do: drain pasta carefully so as not to break packages; do not toss packages with sauce, but arrange on plates and spoon sauce on top; to balance soggy texture, sprinkle with crunchy topping such as chopped spring onion, celery, browned pine nuts or browned flaked almonds. If very overcooked, nothing can be done.

OTHER PROBLEMS

UNDERCOOKED AND STARCHY
Why: cooking time too short; water not simmering briskly.
What to do: continue cooking, turning up heat if necessary.

PACKAGES FALL APART
Why: too much stuffing; package edges not well sealed; overcooked; water boiled too vigorously.
What to do: see Overcooked.

LACKS TASTE
Why: dough lacked salt; stuffing underseasoned; sauce or topping bland.
What to do: season sauce highly, also adding spices such as nutmeg, allspice, cinnamon, hot red pepper flakes, saffron or anise seed; sprinkle packages with chilli or other flavoured oil, or with very finely chopped garlic, shallot, capers, lemon or lime zest, chilli or sweet pepper.

LACKS COLOUR
Why: sauce is pale with no bright garnish.
What to do: add colourful garnish such as chopped herbs or tomato, ribbons of Parmesan or a *sofrito* of mixed vegetables.

Prawn-stuffed ravioli in fragrant broth

SERVES 6

Although time-consuming, these delicious ravioli are well worth the effort. I use a pasta machine to knead as well as roll out the dough (page 183), but you can, of course, do this by hand. Substitute crab or lobster for the prawns if you like.

375 g/¾ pound medium raw
    prawns, in their shells
white of 1 egg
1 tablespoon double cream
pinch of cayenne pepper
2 spring onions

for the pasta dough
300 g/10 oz flour, more if needed
3 eggs
2 teaspoons vegetable oil
1 teaspoon salt

for the fragrant broth
2 tablespoons vegetable oil
1 shallot, chopped
125 ml/4 fl oz dry white wine
2.5 litres/4 pints chicken
    or vegetable stock
3 star anise
7.5-cm/3-inch piece of cinnamon
    stick
salt and pepper

pasta machine (optional)

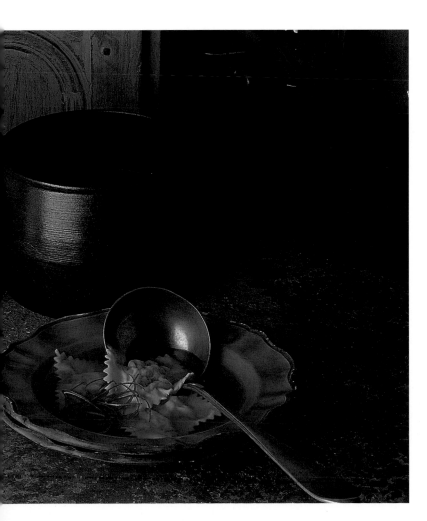

Peel and devein the prawns, reserving the shells. Make the fragrant broth: heat the oil in a saucepan. Add the shallot and sauté until soft and lightly browned, 4-5 minutes. Add the prawn shells and sauté, stirring, until bright pink, 2-3 minutes. Add the wine, stock, star anise and cinnamon and bring to the boil. Reduce the heat and simmer, uncovered, until well-flavoured, about 30 minutes.

Meanwhile make the pasta dough: sift the flour on to a work surface and make a well in centre. Add the eggs to the well with the oil and salt and work together with fingers until well mixed. Gradually draw in the flour with the fingers of both hands to make crumbs. Continue working until the crumbs are sticky, then press the dough together in a ball (work in more flour if it seems too sticky). Cover the dough with an upturned bowl and let rest for 30 minutes.

Make the prawn stuffing: strain the broth, season to taste with salt and pepper and bring to the boil. There should be about 2 litres/3½ pints of broth. Add the prawns and bring just back to the boil. Remove the prawns with a slotted spoon and coarsely chop them; set the broth aside. Beat together the egg white, double cream, salt and pepper until mixed. Stir in the chopped prawns. Finely chop the white part of the spring greens and stir them into the stuffing. Cut the green tops into fine julienne strips and set aside.

Knead and roll the dough (see page 183).

Brush half the dough strips lightly with water. Arrange teaspoonfuls of stuffing on half of the moistened dough, spacing them about 5 cm/2 inches apart and leaving a 1-cm/⅜-inch border at the sides and ends. Flip the dry strip of dough over the filling and press the dough with your fingers to seal between the mounds of filling, pushing out any pockets of air.

Using a fluted pasta wheel or chef's knife, trim the edges of dough and cut between the mounds to make 6-cm/2½-inch square ravioli. Transfer the ravioli to a floured tray and lightly sprinkle them with more flour. Chill for 1-2 hours, uncovered, so the dough dries slightly.

Bring a large shallow pan of salted water to the boil. Add the ravioli, a few at a time, stir to separate them and simmer until done, 3-4 minutes. Using a slotted spoon, transfer the ravioli to paper towels to drain. Simmer and drain the remaining ravioli. They can be cooked up to 30 minutes ahead.

To finish, bring the broth to the boil. Taste and adjust the seasonings. Add 3-4 ravioli to each of 6 warmed soup bowls. Ladle over some broth, decorate with the reserved strips of spring onion and serve at once.

Fluffy whole and cracked grains

FOR FLUFFY GRAINS, WATER — AND LOTS OF IT — is the usual cooking medium. The grains may be boiled, simmered or steamed and the key to lightness is to limit the effects of dissolved starch. Much depends on the type of grain and whether it is whole or cracked. Clearly whole grains give off much less starch than when they are cracked and their structure is cut open.

Thorough rinsing of the grain with cold water before cooking launches the process and cleans the grains as well. When boiling, allow generous quantities of water — at least four times the volume of the grain — and boil rapidly to keep the grains bubbling and separate. When steaming, spread the grain in a shallow layer so moisture is absorbed and penetrates evenly.

Grains form a delicious, nutty background for all sorts of dishes and seasonings. Boiled or steamed grains may be served plain, or tossed with herbs, spices or cooked vegetables such as sautéed onion and mushrooms. Rice, by far the most common whole grain, turns up often in ethnic dishes such as stir-fried Indonesian rice with chicken, garlic, egg, hot red pepper, or Iranian crispy baked rice cake with saffron.

TYPICAL WHOLE GRAINS
(also called berries and kernels)
brown rice, buckwheat groats, hominy, long-grain white rice, millet, oat groats, pearl barley, quinoa, rye, triticale, wild rice

TYPICAL CRACKED GRAINS
bulghur, cracked wheat, rolled oats

UNDERCOOKED — grains (here boiled white rice) separate but densely packed with hard, starchy core.
Why: grain very dry; cooking time too short; heat too low.
What to do: continue cooking, adding more water or other liquid and turning up heat if necessary.

PERFECT — boiled grains fluffy and separate; large grains can be cut with thumbnail; tender but still firm to the bite when tasted; flavour earthy, colour clear.

OVERCOOKED — grains soft, often burst and falling into mush when stirred; when tasted, grains pulpy offering no resistance; flavour mealy, colour dull.
Why: cooked too long; cooked too fast.
What to do: spread on oiled tray and dry in low oven 10-15 minutes; if very overcooked, see below.

OTHER PROBLEMS

GRAINS COOKED UNEVENLY
Why: grains of different sizes; grain from different crops, so some drier than others.
What to do: continue cooking, adding more water or other liquid if necessary.

LACKS FLAVOUR
Why: not enough seasoning; grain poor-quality or stored too long.
What to do: first taste and adjust salt and pepper; add piquant flavourings, such as cayenne, Tabasco, soy sauce, chilli or sesame oil and/or spices such as

ground allspice, coriander, nutmeg, paprika, saffron, curry powder or garam masala.

COLOUR MUDDY
Why: grain a dull colour; too many multicoloured ingredients added, particularly mixtures of ground spices.
What to do: stir in brilliant ingredient, such as turmeric (with spices), tomato paste (with vegetables) or chopped herbs.

QUICK FIX

When fluffy whole or cracked grains are overcooked or tasteless, save the day with savoury baked rice. Preheat the oven to 220°C/425°F/gas7. For every 500 g/1 pound cooked grain, add 1 lightly beaten egg, 1 finely chopped garlic clove, 1 tablespoon chopped parsley, and plenty of freshly ground black pepper. Spoon mixture into a buttered gratin dish and sprinkle with 2 tablespoons breadcrumbs. Dot with 30 g/1 oz butter and bake in preheated oven until very hot and lightly browned, 12-15 minutes. Serves 2.

Risottos

FOR RISOTTO, THE GRAIN (almost always short-grain rice, arborio being the most famous variety) is simmered quite rapidly. It is essential to stir constantly for the 25 minutes or so of cooking. As with pilaf, rice for risotto is toasted first in butter or oil (or a combination of the two). This process encourages the grains to separate, yet still allows them to release starch and make the risotto creamy.

The longer you toast the rice, the longer it will take to cook to its creamy finale. Some wine, usually white, is added for flavour and stirred until evaporated. Then boiling liquid, typically a light stock, is ladled in little by little so the temperature of the rice does not drop. Constant stirring helps keep the rice moving as it cooks; in time, the rice will soften and thicken the liquid to a creamy consistency, absorbing 4-5 times its own volume. In Venice a risotto is served *al onda*, soft enough to pour, but elsewhere in Italy it's preferred *al dente*, somewhat firmer to the bite. Either way, risotto should be creamy without being soupy or dry, and never mushy. No small task! You may have noticed that good risotto is always prepared to order, so don't be tempted to reheat it as it will turn heavy.

PERFECT SOFT – grain falls easily from spoon, with liquid thickened to a creamy consistency; flavour mellow and colour clear.

PERFECT FIRM – grain lightly thickened, just holds a shape with no trace of stickiness; flavour earthy.

OTHER PROBLEMS

UNDERCOOKED AND CHEWY
Why: cooking too short; heat too low; insufficient liquid.
What to do: continue cooking, adding more liquid and raising heat if necessary.

LACKS TASTE
Why: not enough seasoning; grain poor-quality or stored too long; flavourings added were bland.
What to do: adjust seasoning; add warm spices such as nutmeg, cumin and ground coriander, stir in chopped spring onion or celery, caramelized fried onions or coarsely chopped nuts; flavour with grated citrus zest.

QUICK FIX

Turn overcooked/sticky risotto into *arancini*, rice croquettes. Stir into 1 litre/1⅔ pints of the cold grain 2 lightly beaten eggs, 90 g/3 oz grated Parmesan cheese and 1 tablespoon chopped parsley. Divide the mixture into 12 equal portions and shape them into cylindrical croquettes. In a large frying pan, heat 2 tablespoons olive oil. Fry half the croquettes until golden brown, 2-3 minutes. Turn and brown other sides. Fry the remaining croquettes in the same way. Serves 4-6.

Risotto deserves the best short-grain rice – look for arborio, carnaroli or maratelli – and Parmigiano reggiano, the aged Parmesan cheese that is only made from April to November, when the grass is lush and the cows' milk is at its richest.

2 litres/3½ pints chicken or vegetable stock,
more if needed
60 g/2 oz butter
1 small onion, very finely chopped
2 shallots, very finely chopped
400 g/14 oz short-grain rice
125 ml/4 fl oz dry white wine
90 g/3 oz grated Parmesan cheese

for the spring greens
750 g/1½ pound spring greens or turnip tops
3 tablespoons olive oil
1 garlic clove, lightly crushed
salt and pepper

Prepare greens: discard any tough stems; wash and drain in a colander. Heat oil in a large frying pan. Add garlic and sauté just until fragrant, about 30 seconds. Discard garlic and add greens, salt and pepper. Cover and sweat until tender, stirring occasionally, about 5 minutes. Taste, adjust seasoning and keep warm.

Make risotto: bring stock to the boil. Reduce heat to simmer. Meanwhile, heat all but 1 tablespoon of butter in a large, heavy-based pan. Add onion and shallots and cook, stirring, until soft but not brown, 3-4 minutes. Stir in rice and sauté, stirring, until it begins to go translucent, 2-3 minutes. Stir in wine and reduce until almost dry. Over medium heat, ladle in 250 ml/8 fl oz of stock. Simmer, stirring constantly, until almost completely absorbed. Ladle in more stock, working with smaller quantities as rice becomes tender, and continue cooking until done, 20-25 minutes.

Remove from heat and stir in remaining butter and half the cheese. Taste and adjust seasoning. Spoon some risotto into warmed soup bowls, top with greens and spoon over more risotto. Sprinkle with remaining cheese and serve at once.

Grain pilafs

WHEN COOKING BY THE PILAF METHOD, grains are fried in hot fat before being simmered until a measured amount of liquid has been absorbed. Be sure to brown the grains thoroughly first in order to seal the surface as this helps to keep them separate. In one recipe for cooking whole kasha (roasted buckwheat groats), the grains are first cooked with a whole egg, stirring constantly over high heat to separate them and to encourage lightness.

One-and-a-half to twice the volume of liquid to grain is usual. Less liquid means drier, fluffier grains, but some tough varieties such as wild rice and barley need more time and a larger amount of liquid to cook completely.

When a pilaf is cooked, the grains should have absorbed all the liquid, but taste to make sure they also are tender. Leave the pilaf to cool for at least 10 minutes so the grains contract slightly, then stir gently with a fork to separate them without crushing. A pilaf lends itself to spices such as cardamom, cumin and saffron, particularly with white rice. The way is also open to more substantial additions like the ham, prawns and tomato of American jambalaya, or the lamb, tomato and onion of Russian *plov* (opposite).

PERFECT – WHOLE GRAIN PILAF (here, brown rice pilaf) grains separate, liquid absorbed so rest is lightly thickened and creamy; when tasted, grains are soft but still resistant; flavour full-bodied and rich.

PERFECT – CRACKED GRAIN PILAF (here, bulghur) grains separate when stirred with fork; texture fluffy and light, slightly chewy; flavour full-bodied, colour clear.

PROBLEMS

UNDERCOOKED
Why: cooking time too short; too little liquid.
What to do: continue, adding more liquid if necessary.
OVERCOOKED
Why: cooked too long; cooked too fast.
What to do: see Quick Fix.
BLAND
Why: not enough seasoning; grain poor-quality or old.
What to do: season; stir in chopped spring onion, celery, caramelized onions or nuts; add grated citrus zest.

QUICK FIX

When a grain pilaf is sticky or bland, transform it into spiced cakes. For 1 litre/1⅔ pints pilaf, combine a 2.5-cm/1-inch piece of finely chopped fresh ginger, 2 finely chopped garlic cloves, 1 teaspoon aniseed and ½ teaspoon each of ground cinnamon and cardamom. Stir in 125 ml/4 fl oz plain yogurt and grated zest and juice of 1 lemon. Stir this mixture into the cold pilaf. Shape into 12 cakes. Brown the cakes in 2 tablespoons hot vegetable oil, allowing 2-3 minutes on each side. Serves 4-6.

Russian rice pilaf with lamb

Plov

SERVES 4-6

There are as many versions of *plov* as there are former Russian republics. I enjoyed this recipe in the home of an Uzbeki family in Moscow. It can be made with chicken, fish, eggs or, my favourite, lamb. For flavour, the meat is cooked with the bones, which are discarded at the end of cooking. I've tried cutting down on the amount of oil, but *plov* doesn't taste the same without it, so I leave the decision to you.

500 g/1 pound long-grain white rice
175 ml/6 fl oz vegetable oil
1 kg/2 pounds lamb shoulder on the bone, boned and meat cut into 3.75-cm/1½-inch pieces
2 onions, coarsely chopped
2 carrots, diced
3 garlic cloves
500 g/1 pound tomatoes, peeled, seeded and chopped
1 litre/1⅔ pints water, more if needed
2 tablespoons paprika
1 tablespoon tomato paste
salt

large heavy-based casserole

Rinse the rice with cold water and drain thoroughly. Heat the oil in the casserole until very hot. Add the lamb bones and brown thoroughly, 10-15 minutes. Reduce the heat, add the onions and cook until soft but not brown, 3-4 minutes. Add the carrots and garlic cloves and cook until slightly softened, 4-6 minutes. Remove the bones and vegetables with a slotted spoon.

Add the lamb pieces to the pan and brown them on all sides, 5-7 minutes. Do not crowd the pan and, if necessary, brown in two batches. Return the bones and vegetables to the pan with the tomatoes and water. Cover and simmer for 1 hour, stirring occasionally. Discard the lamb bones. Stir in the rice, paprika, tomato paste and a large pinch of salt.

Add more water, if necessary, to cover the rice. Bring back to the boil, cover the pan, turn the heat to medium and simmer until the water has evaporated and the rice is done, 20-25 minutes. Leave to stand 10 minutes before stirring. Taste and adjust the seasoning with salt and paprika. Serve from the casserole. The flavour of *plov* mellows if it is made a day or two ahead and reheated.

Polenta and ground grains

COARSELY GROUND GRAINS ARE ALSO CALLED MEALS, the most common example being the cornmeal used to make polenta and the quick breads and savoury puddings so popular in the southern USA. The crunchy bite and vigorous taste of stoneground cornmeal is startlingly different from bland commercial types, well worth a search of your market shelves. Other meals include buckwheat grits, hominy grits and spelt. Semolina, made from wheat, and tapioca, made from dried yuca root, also behave like meals.

Ground grains are usually cooked by whisking a steady stream of grain into simmering water or milk. Use a heavy saucepan which sits firmly on the stove so one hand is free to trickle in the grain while you whisk or stir with the other. Cooking time depends mainly on the coarseness of the meal. Seasoning is important – be generous to avoid an effect of nursery pap. Ground grains are often served like boiled rice as a background for savoury stews. Polenta, for instance, may come as a soft purée, falling easily from the spoon, or it may be left to set and then grilled or fried in cakes to serve *alla piemontese* with meat, or baked with wild mushrooms in a savoury pie called *pasticciata*. In the American South, grits usually appear as a savoury pudding flavoured with butter and cheese, though contemporary chefs add anything from greens or tomato, to prawns, cream and Parmesan.

PERFECT – mixture (here, polenta) is smooth, thick but not sticky and falls easily from spoon; flavour is full-bodied, colour clear.

OVERCOOKED – texture dense and sticky, clinging to spoon; flavour dull.
Why: cooked too long; too little liquid.
What to do: if overcooked, nothing can be done; if dry, stir in more liquid and cook to right consistency.

OTHER PROBLEMS

UNDERCOOKED AND THIN
Why: cooking too short; heat too low; too much liquid.
What to do: continue cooking to right consistency.
CHEWY
Why: grain not fully cooked.
What to do: add more liquid and continue cooking.
LUMPY
Why: ground grain added too quickly; mixture not constantly stirred during cooking.

What to do: take from heat and whisk vigorously; if still lumpy, work in food processor and reheat.
BLAND
Why: too little seasoning; grain poor-quality or stored too long.
What to do: season with salt and pepper; add spices such as cayenne or hot red chilli pepper, nutmeg, cumin, ginger and mustard; beat in grated cheese.

Cornmeal dumplings baked with parmesan
Gnocchi alla romana

SERVES 4-6

These simple gnocchi are made with polenta which is left to set, then cut into shapes. Rounds are traditional, but squares are more economical. Coarse yellow cornmeal or semolina may be used for the polenta. In Italy, the polenta for gnocchi is flavoured only with Parmesan, but I've found that Dijon-style mustard really picks up the taste.

45 g/1½.oz butter, melted
1 litre/1⅔ pints milk, more if needed
1 onion, spiked with a clove
bay leaf
1 teaspoon peppercorns
pinch of grated nutmeg
salt and pepper

150 g/5 oz coarse yellow cornmeal
    or semolina
3 egg yolks
1 teaspoon Dijon-style mustard, more to taste
125 g/4 oz grated Parmesan cheese

5-cm/2-inch pastry cutter or glass tumbler (optional)

Thickly butter a baking sheet. In a saucepan, heat the milk with the onion, bay leaf, peppercorns, nutmeg and a little salt. Cover, bring just to the boil and leave to infuse over a low heat for 10-15 minutes. Strain and return the milk to the saucepan.

Gradually whisk the cornmeal or semolina into the hot milk. Bring to the boil and simmer, whisking constantly to prevent lumps, until the mixture is thick enough to pull from the sides of the pan, 8-10 minutes.

Remove the pan from the heat and beat in the egg yolks one at a time – they will cook and thicken slightly. Stir in the mustard and half the cheese and taste for seasoning – the polenta should be highly seasoned.

Spread the polenta to form a 1-cm/⅜-inch layer on the prepared baking sheet. Brush with the melted butter and chill until set, 1-2 hours. Preheat the oven to 230°C/450°F/gas8.

When the mixture is set, use the pastry cutter or glass to cut out 5-cm/2-inch circles, or cut 5-cm/2-inch squares. Overlap the shapes in the baking dish and sprinkle with the remaining cheese. Bake the gnocchi in the preheated oven until very hot and browned, 5-10 minutes. Serve at once.

Dried beans, peas and lentils

DON'T BE CONFUSED BY THE HUGE NUMBER OF DIFFERENT DRIED BEANS – red, white, green, purple, black or striped. They all behave similarly and many taste alike too, so can easily be substituted for each other. Add to dried beans the large and varied family of dried whole and split peas and lentils, and you have a wide range of possibilities. Common combinations include Mexican pinto beans and rice and picturesque 'hoppin' John' of black-eyed peas (actually a bean), bacon and rice from the southern USA. Split peas and lentils are often braised to serve with ham and other pickled meats, or they may be puréed for Indian *dhal* or for soup (see Dried Bean, Pea and Lentil Purées, opposite).

At the market, dried beans, peas and lentils should look plump and brightly coloured, never shrivelled. Rinse them and pick them over – I've never understood why lentils, in particular, come with a few bits of gravel, but it's a hazard. Beans and whole peas have a thick skin, so must be soaked for several hours in cold water – to speed the process, you can pour boiling water over them and leave them for half an hour or so. Time needed to soften peas and beans varies with type and age – if you cut short the soaking time, cooking will take longer. So-called 'pre-soaked' pulses are also commonly available – what you gain in time, you lose in depth of flavour.

When cooking dried beans, peas and lentils, it's good to flavour them with a whole onion stuck with a clove and a bouquet garni of bay leaf, thyme and parsley stems. Whole or ground spices such as black pepper, coriander, nutmeg and cloves are helpful, too. However, do not add salt or any acid such as vinegar or tomato until cooking is well advanced as the skins of the beans will toughen for good. If your tap water is high in minerals, it too can toughen the skins of pulses, so use filtered water. Note that some pulses contain toxins in the skin, easily dissolved during cooking. To be sure, boil beans rapidly for at least 10 minutes. Lentils and split peas need only to be brought to the boil.

Cooking time varies enormously depending on age and variety. If you have a batch which cooks unevenly, with some remaining tough when others are fully cooked, they are probably from different harvests and hence unevenly dried. This is especially true of beans.

TYPICAL DRIED BEANS
black, red and white kidney, black-eyed peas, cannellini, broad, flageolet, lima, navy, pinto

TYPICAL OTHER DRIED PULSES
brown, green, red and yellow lentils, chickpeas, green and grey split peas

QUICK FIX

If beans are overcooked or tasteless, transform them into a version of Mexican fried beans. Drain the beans and coarsely crush them. For every 1 litre/1¾ pints of beans, dice 6 thin slices of bacon. Fry in a large frying pan until the bacon fat runs. Add 1 chopped onion, 2 crushed garlic cloves and, if you like, 1 small green chilli pepper, peeled, seeded and chopped. Continue frying, stirring, until both bacon and onions are brown. Stir in the crushed beans and cook, stirring constantly, until very hot, 5-7 minutes. Serves 6.

OTHER PROBLEMS

OVERCOOKED
Why: cooked too long.
What to do: purée beans, peas or lentils for soup or to serve as a purée.

JUICES WATERY
Why: too much liquid; undercooked.
What to do: if pulses are not tender, remove lid and continue cooking; if already tender, thicken juices lightly with cornflour or potato starch or kneaded butter.

TASTELESS
Why: stored too long; not enough flavourings.
What to do: season with chopped herbs, particularly marjoram, savory or thyme; add sautéed onion and garlic; flavour with lemon juice or red wine vinegar, plus 2-3 tablespoons tomato purée for beans and 1-2 teaspoons sugar for peas.

UNDERCOOKED AND TOUGH – texture chewy, especially skins on beans or peas; juices watery; flavour not yet developed.
Why: pulses dry and stored too long; not cooked long enough; salt or acid ingredients toughened skins during cooking.
What to do: continue cooking, using plenty of liquid.

PERFECT – beans (here, navy beans), peas or lentils soft and tender; for beans or peas, a few skins starting to burst; most liquid absorbed, so rest is lightly thickened; colour clear not muddy and flavour mellow.

French white bean soup with vegetables

Potage garbure

SERVES 6-8   *pictured on pages 180-81*

This substantial soup from south-western France generally forms the main dish of a peasant supper, backed up by bread croûtes topped with the local Cantal cheese, which resembles sharp Cheddar. Beans and roots are a basis to which other vegetables, such as peas, green beans and courgettes, are added in season. The recipe makes generous quantities, and it is even better reheated.

75 g/2½ oz butter

2 turnips, peeled and cut into
    1-cm/⅜-inch dice

2 large carrots, peeled and cut into
    1-cm/⅜-inch dice

500-g/1-pound head of cabbage, shredded

white parts of 3 leeks, thinly sliced

2-3 stalks of celery, cut into small dice

2 potatoes, peeled and cut into
    1-cm/⅜-inch dice

2.5 litres/4 pints water, more if needed

bunch of parsley, chopped

for the beans

200 g/6½ oz dried white haricot beans
    or navy beans

1 onion spiked with 2 cloves

1 carrot, peeled and quartered

bouquet garni

salt and pepper

for the croûtes

1 baguette, cut into 1-cm/⅜-inch slices

2 tablespoons olive oil, bacon or goose fat

60 g/2 oz grated Cantal or Cheddar
    cheese

Soften the beans: soak the dried beans overnight in plenty of cold water and drain. Alternatively, put them in a saucepan with enough water to cover them generously. Bring to the boil, cover the pan and remove from the heat. Leave the beans to stand for 1 hour, then drain them.

Place the softened beans, onion spiked with cloves, carrot and bouquet garni in a pan with water to cover. Cover with the lid and simmer until the beans are done, 1½-2 hours – if the beans get dry during cooking, add more water. Season with salt and pepper when the beans are almost tender. When the beans are done, discard the onion, carrot and bouquet garni.

In a large heavy-based pot, melt 30 g/1 oz of the butter, add the turnips, carrots, cabbage, leeks, celery, potatoes, salt and pepper and press a piece of buttered foil on top. Cover with lid and sweat, stirring occasionally, until the vegetables are nearly tender but not browned, 15-20 minutes.

Add the beans and their cooking liquid, with water to cover and salt and pepper. Cover and simmer until the vegetables are very tender, 20-30 minutes. Taste the soup and adjust the seasoning.

Meanwhile, make the croûtes: preheat the oven to 200°C/400°F/gas6. Set the bread slices on an oiled baking sheet and brush the slices with oil. Bake in the preheated oven until brown, 8-10 minutes. Turn them over, sprinkle the croûtes with grated cheese and bake until well browned, 8-10 minutes.

If necessary, bring the soup back to the boil. Stir in the chopped parsley and ladle into individual bowls. Float the croûtes on top and serve at once.

Dried bean, pea and lentil purées

Dried beans, peas and lentils are a fertile source of earthy soups and full-flavoured purées, since they fall easily into a mush when thoroughly cooked. Long simmering will not spoil their flavour (how different from fresh vegetables!). In fact, the key is to cook the beans or peas so long they start to fall apart. By this stage most of the water should have been absorbed; split peas or lentils will now be ready for puréeing in a food processor or with an immersion blender until smooth. However the skin of beans and whole peas spoils the creamy texture of a perfect purée or soup, so they should be worked through a sieve. By all means, if you like a coarse-textured soup, simply crush the beans or peas to a chunky paste. For tips on vegetable purées, see Vegetables.

All these purées and soups cry out for spicing, for the fragrance of coriander, cinnamon and clove. Think of Indian *dhal* with cumin, garlic, chilli and turmeric, and American senate bean soup flavoured with ham, onion and bay. Pork and beans have a natural affinity – try simmering beans and peas for soup with a ham hock or bones, or adding chopped ham or bacon to the finished dish.

PERFECT FOR PURÉES – very soft and falls from the spoon with no trace of stickiness; purée has texture but is smooth on the tongue; flavour is full-bodied and fragrant.

FRUIT

THE LESS YOU DO TO A FINE FRUIT, THE BETTER IT IS.
What can equal the heady aroma of pears poached in sugar syrup
with vanilla and spices or an apple baked with honey or sautéed in
a bit of butter and sugar to a rich caramel brown? Firm fruits such
as apple are also good deep-fried as fritters, but only the juiciest
like peach or pineapple grill well. I find that a fruit's flavour can be
quite transformed by cooking – a poached or baked apricot, for
example, can be a revelation. Always buy the ripest and most
aromatic fruit you can. Good cooking cannot compensate for lack
of taste in fruit picked too soon.

For many dishes, a fruit is cooked when it is tender but still
holds its shape. With further cooking, fruits often collapse naturally
into purée – this may be deliberate, so don't think of them as
necessarily being overcooked. They'll be perfect to serve with ice
cream, to flavour cream desserts and sauces or to cook down as
preserves. (A small range of fruit preserves is also included at the
end of this chapter.)

Sugar, or another sweetener such as honey, is the first and
often the only ingredient needed when cooking fruit. Consider its
role like that of salt in savoury foods, developing and highlighting
taste. The amount you want to add will vary, depending not just on
the acidity of the fruit itself but also on its role, whether as an
accompaniment to meat or poultry, or as a traditional dessert.
Under individual fruits, you'll find suggestions for other flavourings,
with spices, sweet wines and liqueurs featuring large. Use your
judgement when adding liquid as juicy fruits will need less.

The characteristic shape and colour of a fruit is decoration in
itself, so I like to leave them whole whenever possible. Portions
are easy to judge by eye and intuition. Cut pieces should suit a
fruit's personality – crescents for apples, hemispheres for apricots
and plums, and flower-petal slashes for figs to display their pretty
pink interior. The dullest day must surely be cheered by a pile of
fruit on the kitchen table, so I hope you'll read on with pleasure.
Life, after all, is just a bowl of cherries.

Upside-down apple pie,
page 199

Apples

CLOSE YOUR EYES AND THINK BACK. Surely we all have memories involving apples? Whether it be gathering windfall fruit in the wet autumn grass, or that clear vision of the perfect apple pie topped, *à la mode*, with vanilla ice cream. My own childhood image is of greedily biting into a crisp Newton Pippin, filched from the store my mother kept for winter, only to find the apple had taken with it one of my first teeth.

How an apple behaves in the kitchen depends on the variety. By and large, apples fall into three categories: there are those which hold their shape during cooking and so are good for baking in their skins, sautéing in slices or poaching in syrup – Golden Delicious is the most common. Other varieties such as Granny Smith fall apart quickly when heated and are ideal for purée and apple sauce. In pies, either firm or soft apples can be used. A few apples are good only for the table, losing their taste and crisp texture all too easily if they are subjected to heat – Fuji, Gala and Red Delicious for instance. We're lucky to have more and more varieties of apple appearing in the markets now, some new and others a revival of old, half-forgotten favourites. How they will behave in the kitchen can be a mystery, so look out for information from the grower.

Apples are by far the most useful dessert fruit. Apple pie comes in dozens of guises, hidden under a top crust and flavoured with blackberries or cloves or arranged in a flower pattern in a glazed open tart. An apple pie may be caramelized and then turned upside down as a *tarte Tatin* (opposite), or the fruit juices may be trapped inside a crumbly double crust. Apples are good baked, sautéed, poached, simmered to a purée or baked in a pudding. I think of apples with cinnamon, ginger, sage, orange, raisins, vanilla, chocolate, almonds and cheese – after all I come from Wensleydale, home of a fine hard cheese. Natural savoury marriages include ham, bacon, roast pork and goose. Take care to remove every bit of the core – fingernail shreds left behind do not dissolve during cooking. To obtain thin, even slices instead of the usual crescent wedges, halve the apple, scoop out the core, set it cut-side down on the board and slice it like an onion.

UNDERCOOKED AND PALE – resistant when pierced with point of a knife; if cut, centre is hard and opaque; whether whole, sliced or chopped, apple holds a firm shape.
Why: fruit underripe; apple variety very firm; cooking temperature too low; cooking time too short; lacking liquid to moisten fruit.
What to do: if dry, sprinkle fruit with liquid such as sugar syrup, water, apple or orange juice or white wine; continue cooking until done, raising temperature if necessary.

PERFECT – tender when pierced with point of a knife; flesh looks translucent, not opaque; if sliced or chopped, pieces hold shape; if baked in skin, apple is slightly puffed, still holding shape; colour is pale or caramelized, depending on recipe; flavour tangy and fresh.

OVERCOOKED – very soft, shape disintegrating into purée; if sautéed or grilled, edges often scorched; if whole, apple collapses; fresh flavour mellowed.
Note: for purée or apple sauce, apples should be cooked to this stage.
Why: wrong type of apple; fruit cut too small or too thin; cooked too fast; cooked too long.
What to do: if disintegrating, transform into purée in food processor or through a sieve, then flavour with grated citrus zest, ground cinnamon or allspice or Calvados; if scorched, moisten with apple or orange juice and Calvados or port.

Upside-down apple pie
Tarte des Demoiselles Tatin

SERVES 8-10   *pictured on pages 196-7*

COBBLERS AND OTHER FRUIT PUDDINGS

Crumble, streusel, gratin, cobbler, when you think about it there are a multitude of toppings designed to be baked on a layer of fruit. That's because the results are so delicious. The topping, whether crisp, crumbling or cake-like, is invariably rich and sweet. Crumble (also called a crisp) is typical, a combination of butter, sugar and flour (see Quick Fix, page 203), often with chopped nuts or oatmeal added, that is baked on top of fresh or stewed fruit.

Streusel is the German version of crumble, often with a cake base beneath the fruit, resulting in a three-layered finish. In France, the term *gratin* covers any browned fruit pudding, while cobbler is a catch-all indeed. The finish of a cobbler is juicy, rather than crisp. Cobbler may be topped with a dough resembling a sablé biscuit, or with scone dough, or with a cakey batter, or even with pie pastry though I would call this a top-crust pie.

Cobbler is just the start of the toppings created by American cooks, who are the virtuosi of the field. A betty is topped with buttered breadcrumbs, a buckle uses cake batter, and a grunt is covered with scone dough soft enough to drop in loose mounds from the spoon. As for pandowdy, this refers to a pie pastry topping which is partially baked, then slashed and pushed down into the fruit so it finishes to be crisp and flavoured with juice.

How about the fruit? Here I hold strong views: fruit to be baked with a topping must be tart and juicy to balance the sweet crust. Plums, tart apples or cherries, rhubarb and blackberries make outstanding crumbles and cobblers. Peaches, apricots, pears and blueberries are suggested too, but it's important they have some acidity – if necessary add plenty of lemon. Personally I add little or no sweetener or flavouring to the fruit unless the topping is plain (scone dough for instance). Vanilla, grated orange or lemon zest, spices like cinnamon and nutmeg, or a splash of fruit liqueur or Cognac are another matter – go ahead by all means.

For fruit pies, see page 299, and page 229 for fruit batter puddings.

OTHER PROBLEMS

TASTELESS
Why: poor or unripe apples; wrong type of apple; too little sugar added.
What to do: adjust flavouring with sugar, lemon juice, Calvados or liqueur; sprinkle with sugar and caramelize using blow torch or grill.
FLAVOUR ACID
Why: apples unripe; wrong type of apple; too little sugar.
What to do: add sugar or sweet ingredient such as honey or apple juice to taste.

DISCOLOURED, OFTEN SHRIVELLED
Why: apples lacking juice; peeled too soon before cooking; cooked with too little liquid; cooked too fast.
What to do: when peeled, rub apples at once with lemon juice and slice them only just before using; after cooking moisten by brushing generously with sugar syrup, melted butter, fruit juice or water; brush with apricot glaze. If you like, disguise brown colour by sprinkling with sugar and caramelizing with blow torch or grill.

The secret of this upside-down apple pie is to cook the butter and sugar with the apples in a heavy pan so the juice caramelizes and flavours deep inside the fruit. Use a firm apple such as Golden Delicious, which holds its shape well during long cooking. The tart should be served warm, with a bowl of whipped cream or crème fraîche if you like.

175 g/6 oz butter
400 g/14 oz sugar
2.8 kg/6 pounds firm apples

30-35-cm/12-14-inch heavy-based deep frying pan

for the French pie pastry
200 g/6½ oz flour
100 g/3¼ oz butter
1 egg yolk
½ teaspoon salt
45 ml/1½ fl oz water, more if needed

Make the French pie pastry: sift the flour on to a work surface and make a well in the centre. Pound the butter with a rolling pin to soften it. Put the butter, egg yolk, salt and water into the well. With your fingers, work the moist ingredients until thoroughly mixed. Draw in flour with a pastry scraper and work in the other ingredients with the fingers of both hands until coarse crumbs form. If the crumbs are very dry, add 1-2 tablespoons more water. Press the dough into a ball. Lightly flour the work surface. Blend the dough by pushing it away from you with the heel of your hand, then gathering it up until it is very smooth and peels away from work surface in one piece, 1-2 minutes. Shape into a ball, wrap and chill until firm, at least 30 minutes. Preheat the oven to 220°C/425°F/gas7.

Melt the butter in the pan and sprinkle with sugar. Cook over medium heat until the sugar starts to brown and caramelize. Stir, then continue cooking to a medium caramel. Let cool. Note: the butter may separate.

Peel, halve and core the apples. Arrange the halves upright, cut side at right angles to the edge of the pan, in concentric circles on top of the caramel; they should fill the pan completely and be snugly packed. Cook the apples over high heat until deep golden caramel, 15-20 minutes. Note: the apples will make juice, which must evaporate before they will caramelize. With a two-pronged fork, turn the apples so the upper surfaces are now down in the caramel and continue cooking 10-15 minutes more.

When the apples are cooked, let them cool slightly. Roll out the pie pastry to a circle slightly larger than the diameter of the pan. Set the dough on the apples so that they are completely covered, tucking the pastry in at the edges. Note: work fast so the dough does not soften from the heat of the apples. Bake until the pastry is firm and slightly browned, 20-25 minutes. Let the tart cool in the pan.

Not more than a half hour before serving, if necessary, warm the tart on top of the stove. Turn it out on a tray or a large plate. If any apple sticks to the bottom of the pan, transfer it to the top of the tart with a spatula.

Fruit 199

Pears and quinces

ACCORDING TO MY MOTHER, A RIPE PEAR SHOULD BE EATEN IN THE BATH. I've never gone quite that far, but it's true that a good table pear should be dripping with juice. All too few of them achieve such perfection but many varieties of pear cook well, holding their shape in gentle heat and developing a mellow, aromatic taste when you give them time. Common cooking pears include Anjou and Williams. The only one I'd avoid is the juicy Comice as its melting texture does not hold up well. All sorts of flavourings are a help in the pan with pears, notably honey, vanilla, lemon and spices such as anise, cardamom, cinnamon and ginger. A kick of pepper does not go amiss. Pears have an affinity for chocolate – remember the classic pear *belle Hélène* with vanilla ice cream and chocolate sauce – and also caramel and red wine.

Looking like a craggy yellow pear, the quince is an old fruit which is coming back into style. It cannot be eaten raw and needs very thorough cooking for up to three or four hours with plenty of sugar until the crunchy flesh softens and turns a beguiling deep pink. I think of quince in time-honoured recipes like quince jelly and butter, but you'll also come across contemporary dishes such as confit of duck with quince, or puff pastry tarts with poached quince and mascarpone. Both pears and quinces are delicious with cheese.

Whatever the flavouring, pears and quinces must be peeled for cooking and moistened generously with liquid (sautéed pears are an exception). They discolour quickly, so a rub with lemon is a necessity. Pears are fragile and easily bruised: if picked too soon, the flesh around the core may darken before or after cooking. When poaching a pear whole, scoop out the core from the base with a pointed teaspoon; for easier handling, leave the stem. When quartering or slicing quince or pear, be sure to remove the fibrous internal stem.

PERFECT – tender when pierced with point of a knife; flesh looks opaque, with no translucent centre when cut (texture of quince always remains slightly granular); fruit pieces hold shape; colour is pale or lightly caramelized depending on recipe; flavour fresh (for pears) or fragrant (for quinces). Note: tests for under- and overcooked pear and quince are the same as for apple (page 198).

PROBLEMS

UNDERCOOKED
Why: fruit underripe; variety very firm (for pears); temperature too low; time too short; lacking liquid.
What to do: if dry, soak in liquid such as sugar syrup, apple or orange juice or white wine; continue cooking until done, raising temperature if necessary.
OVERCOOKED – very soft, disintegrating into purée; if whole, fruit collapses; fresh flavour lost. Note: for purée or butter, fruit should be cooked to this stage.
Why: wrong variety of fruit (for pears); cut too small or too thin; cooked too fast; cooked too long.
What to do: turn into purée in processor or by sieving, then flavour with grated citrus zest and ground cinnamon or ginger. Serve with ice cream and crisp biscuits.
TASTELESS
Why: underripe; too little sweetener; cooked too fast.
What to do: sprinkle with sugar and citrus juice, fruit vinegar, pear brandy or kirsch. Serve with chocolate sauce, raspberry coulis or tart sorbet such as mango.
DISCOLOURED
Why: peeled too soon; if poached, not fully immersed (tide mark); undercooked (core of whole fruit brown).
What to do: sprinkle with chopped herb such as mint; top with tiny rosettes of whipped cream; coat with custard.

Poached pears in sweet wine with ginger
SERVES 4

Many variations can be played on this basic recipe. I'm fond of using cinnamon stick or crushed peppercorns instead of ginger, and substituting red for white wine to give a pink blush to the pears. For poaching, it is important to use firm pears which hold up.

4 pears (about 750 g/1½ pounds)
1 lemon
1 bottle (750 ml/1¾ pints) Sauternes or other sweet white wine
250 ml/8 fl oz water
2.5-cm/1-inch piece of fresh ginger, thinly sliced
50 g/1¾ oz sugar

Pare zest from lemon and squeeze juice from one half. Peel pears, leaving stems intact, and rub with the remaining lemon half to prevent discoloration. Using a vegetable peeler or pointed teaspoon, scoop out fibrous cores without breaking open pears. Cut a thin slice from base of each pear so they sit upright.

Combine wine, water, lemon zest and juice, ginger and sugar in a small deep pan. Heat mixture, stirring occasionally, until sugar has dissolved, then bring to the boil. Add pears and press a piece of greaseproof paper on top to keep them submerged. Bring just to the boil, reduce heat and poach until done, 25-35 minutes.

Lift pears from pan, using stems as handles, and stand them upright in a serving bowl or individual bowls. Discard lemon zest and ginger and boil liquid until syrupy and reduced by about half, 10-15 minutes. Spoon syrup over pears. Cover and leave to cool. Serve at room temperature or chilled.

QUICK FIX

If pears or quinces are bland or overcooked, take advantage of their affinity with peppy flavourings:
• Sprinkle them with freshly ground black pepper.
• Serve them with hot chocolate sauce (page 138).
• Make a quick fresh mint sauce: in a processor, purée 30 g/1 oz fresh mint leaves with 3 tablespoons raspberry vinegar and 3 tablespoons sugar. Using the pulse button, add 375 ml/12 fl oz double cream. Serve the sauce chilled for 4-6 people.

Apricots and plums

APRICOTS AND PLUMS CAN BE THE BEST OR THE WORST OF FRUIT – juicy, perfumed, brilliantly coloured, or a dreadful disappointment. We've all had apricots that are tasteless from lack of sun, or plums that pucker the mouth. Plums are the easier to remedy, as sugar will at least add sweetness if not depth of flavour. Apricots are more difficult; if they are bland I'd suggest poaching them in a lively syrup with plenty of lemon, vanilla and a splash of liqueur. Another route is to spice them in Arab style with cinnamon, cardamom or cloves, rose water and honey (apricots are a Middle Eastern favourite). Plums are more aggressive – with no extra help you can rely on them to assert their flavour in all manner of pies and puddings. Both apricots and plums make charming open tarts, halved or quartered to arrange in a flower pattern, and then baked cut-side up so the juices evaporate and the pastry remains crisp. Ripe fruits are easy to halve with a knife, following the indentation, then twisting the halves apart, but unripe they tend to cling to the stone. Sprinkle apricots with lemon juice or they discolour rapidly.

Austrians make dumplings by wrapping plums in potato dough and topping them with butter-fried breadcrumbs and sugar. Both apricots and plums bake and grill well. Their acidity makes them fine accompaniments to rich meats like pork and duck, and I've baked pumpkin with plums and bacon with success as a side dish for the Christmas turkey.

PERFECT – tender when pierced with a two-pronged fork; flesh translucent; whether whole or pieces, fruit holds shape; colour bright and flavour strong.

PERFECT FOR PURÉE – flesh disintegrating into purée; very soft if pierced with a two-pronged fork; flavour mellowed; colour slightly faded.

PROBLEMS

UNDERCOOKED AND HARD
Why: fruit underripe; cooking temperature too low; time too short; for apricots, too little liquid added.
What to do: continue cooking until done, raising heat and adding more liquid if needed.

OVERCOOKED
Why: fruit overripe; cooked too fast; cooked too long.
What to do: distract by topping with ice cream if hot, or rosettes of whipped Chantilly cream if cold; if very soft, purée in food processor or work through sieve to make a sauce for ice cream, cake or other fruit such as poached pears (for plums) or bananas (apricots).

TEXTURE WOOLLY
Why: fruit poor or underripe, especially apricots.
What to do: add zest by sprinkling with fruit brandy such as plum, cherry, or kirsch; top with caramelized nuts, or purée for sauce (see Overcooked).

FLAVOUR ACID
Why: fruit underripe; too little sugar, especially plums.
What to do: add sugar or honey.

Apricot snow

SERVES 6

This recipe can be adapted for many different fruits. Apricots colour the snow pale orange, while red plums make it rosy. Serve the snow with crisp biscuits.

750 g/1½ pounds apricots, halved and stoned
200 g/6½ oz sugar, more if needed
250 ml/8 fl oz water
pared zest and juice of 1 orange
white of 1 egg
6 mint sprigs

six 250-ml/8-fl oz parfait glasses

In a sauté pan or shallow saucepan, add sugar to water, reserving 3-4 tablespoons sugar. Heat, stirring, until sugar dissolves. Bring just to the boil, take from heat and add apricot halves and orange zest. Cut a round of waxed paper the size of pan and press on fruit. Return to heat and poach fruit over low heat until just tender, 5-7 minutes. Using a slotted spoon, remove half apricots and reserve.

Continue cooking remaining apricots until soft enough to purée, 3-5 minutes longer. Let cool to tepid, discard orange zest and purée them with the syrup in a food processor or blender. You should have about 375 ml/12 fl oz. Chill purée.

Beat egg white just until foamy, 1-2 minutes. Beat in the reserved sugar, a tablespoonful at a time, then continue beating until egg white is glossy and forms a long peak when whisk is lifted, about 1 minute more. Beat in the chilled apricot purée and orange juice. Continue beating until the snow is smooth, light and slightly thickened, 3-5 minutes. Taste and add more sugar if needed.

Spoon snow and reserved whole apricots into parfait glasses in 2-3 alternating layers. Top each glass with a slice of poached apricot and a mint sprig. Chill for at least 1 hour before serving.

QUICK FIX

Top disappointing, baked plums or apricots with spiced yogurt. Mix 1 teaspoon ground cardamom with 250 g/8 oz plain yogurt and 2 tablespoons brown sugar. Spoon over fruit and sprinkle with 3-4 tablespoons browned sliced almonds.

Nectarines and peaches

A FRESH RIPE PEACH, WARM FROM THE SUN, is so good absolutely plain that I tend to forget they perform equally well in the kitchen. Peaches are delicious flambéed with Cognac, simmered in a lemon and vanilla syrup or baked with candied pumpkin, citrus peel and white wine, as in Italy. They have an affinity for almonds and Amaretto liqueur as their kernels (like those of apricots and cherries) carry a whiff of almond flavour. Any recipe for peaches can be used with nectarines but I think they fare less well when cooked – their rich flavour loses its bite and texture can be mushy.

Handle nectarines and peaches carefully as they bruise easily. Once cut they discolour rapidly, so rub with lemon juice and then immerse them in liquid or cook them at once. Europeans tend to like tangy, white-fleshed peaches but in the USA richer, yellow-fleshed varieties are preferred. Look out for the designation 'freestone' or 'clingstone', a key to how peaches behave when you try to halve them (cut along the indentation and around the fruit, then give a quick twist). The skin also clings more firmly to clingstone fruit. To loosen the skin of peaches, immerse them for 10-15 seconds in boiling water, then transfer to cold water and peel. When poaching in syrup, peaches are peeled after cooking and you'll find a pretty pink blush has formed under the skin. Nectarines can be hard to peel even when blanched, but their skin is thin so I often don't bother.

PERFECT – tender when pierced with two-pronged fork, but fruit still firm enough to be lifted; if whole or halved, fruit still holds shape; surface shiny with juice; fruit is translucent, with no opaque centre when cut; colour clear and flavour fresh and fruity.

OVERCOOKED AND WOOLLY – shape slumped; juices run into pan; fruit is very soft if pierced with fork, and falls apart when lifted; colour and flavour dull.
Why: fruit overripe; cut too small or too thin; cooked too fast; cooked too long.
What to do: to add texture, sprinkle with chopped walnuts, browned pine nuts, or sliced almonds; see also Tasteless.

OTHER PROBLEMS

UNDERCOOKED
Why: fruit underripe; cooking temperature too low; time too short; lacking liquid to moisten fruit.
What to do: if dry, add liquid such as syrup, liqueur, red or white wine, or water; continue cooking until done, raising temperature if necessary.

TASTELESS
Why: fruit poor or underripe; too little sweetener.
What to do: sprinkle with lemon juice, peach liqueur, Amaretto or kirsch; add topping of grated lemon zest, chopped mint and browned almonds; sprinkle with grated nutmeg, cloves or cinnamon.

Grilled peach and strawberry kebabs
SERVES 4

Fruit kebabs can be grilled indoors, or they make the ideal dessert for a summer barbecue. I don't bother to peel the peaches, as high heat softens the skins in any case. Serve the lightly caramelized kebabs warm with the Salty Caramel Sauce on page 240.

4 large peaches (about 500 g/1 pound)
12 large strawberries
45 g/1½ oz melted butter
100 g/3¼ oz sugar

four 25-cm/10-inch wooden skewers

Preheat the grill. Put the skewers in a dish of cold water to soak so they do not scorch during grilling.

Cut the peaches in half, using the indentations on one side as a guide. With both hands, give a quick, sharp twist to the halves to loosen them from the stones. Cut each half in half again, or in thirds if the pieces are large. Hull the strawberries, rinsing them only if they are sandy.

Drain the skewers. Thread 3 strawberries and 4 peach quarters alternately on each skewer. Brush the kebabs generously with melted butter and roll in sugar so the fruit is thoroughly covered. Arrange the kebabs on a grill rack lined with foil.

Grill about 7.5 cm/3 inches from the heat, until the fruit is tender and caramelized, turning once, 4-6 minutes on each side. Serve on the skewers.

QUICK FIX

Top overcooked, woolly or tasteless peaches or nectarines with a crisp crumble. For 500 g/1 pound fruit, in a food processor (or with your fingers) work 90 g/3 oz butter to fine crumbs with 125 g/4 oz flour. Stir in 60 g/2 oz sugar. Drain the fruit, cut it in large chunks and spread it in a baking dish to form a 2.5-cm/1-inch layer. Spread the crumble on top and bake in a 230°C/450°F/gas8 oven until light golden and the fruit juice bubbles at the edges, 25-35 minutes. Serves 4.

Cherries

Cherries jubilee

CHERRIES ARE ONE OF THE FEW FRUITS WHICH REMAIN SEASONAL, an instant evocation of the summer sun to come. Varieties divide into cookers and eaters and you'll know which by tasting – cooking cherries are almost inedibly acid. They are often, though not necessarily, bright red. These are the best for classics such as cherry pie, duck with cherries and sweet-and-sour Middle Eastern meatballs, as their tang is potent even when laced generously with sugar. Other recipes like black cherry jam and Cherries Jubilee (right) rely on sweeter fruit for a more mellow taste – Bing cherries are the most common variety.

Stones are a nuisance when cooking with cherries. If you leave them the fruit has more taste as the stones contain a trace of almond flavour. Removing them takes time, even with the tool designed for the purpose, and the fruit then tends to disintegrate. In many recipes, the choice is yours. When stoning cherries, use a bowl to catch the juice.

Cooking time for cherries varies greatly with the variety and its ripeness. Undercooking is rarely a problem, but be warned that cherries, like berries, can overcook and fall apart in a minute or two if the heat is high.

PERFECT – cherries tender, just starting to lose shape; juices running generously; colour bright and flavour tart.

QUICK FIX

For tasteless or overcooked cherries, add a tablespoon or two of red wine vinegar or balsamic vinegar to the dish – a sweet-and-sour approach suits cherries very well.

Flambéed cherries are most famous served over ice cream as a 'jubilee' celebration, but if you reduce the sugar they are also delicious with duck or pork. Dark sweet cherries such as Bing are best for flambéing.

750 g/1½ pounds dark sweet cherries
1 litre/1⅔ pints vanilla ice cream, for serving
30 g/1 oz butter
45 g/1½ oz sugar
1 tablespoon redcurrant jelly
175 ml/6 fl oz brandy

Scoop the vanilla ice cream into 6 chilled coupe glasses or attractive serving bowls and store them in the freezer. Stone the cherries.

Melt the butter in a sauté pan, stir in the sugar, and heat gently until the sugar dissolves completely, stirring occasionally, about 1 minute. Add the cherries and sauté over high heat for 1 minute. Add the redcurrant jelly and stir until dissolved. Simmer until the cherries are almost tender, 3-5 minutes.

To flame the cherries: warm the brandy in a small saucepan, then set it alight. Pour it, flaming, over the cherries and baste them.

When the flames have died down completely, spoon the hot cherries and their delicious sauce over the ice cream and serve at once.

Marinated cherries jubilee

If you'd rather not have the theatrics of flambéing, simply marinate the cherries in the brandy sweetened with the sugar overnight, stirring from time to time. You can serve these cold or warm them gently in a saucepan. For an even stronger flavour, spoon 2 tablespoons of kirsch over the cherries just before serving.

PROBLEMS

OVERCOOKED
Why: cherries very ripe; heat too high; cooked too long.
What to do: strain off excess juice and thicken lightly with arrowroot or potato flour to make a sauce; if very overcooked, purée to make

sauce or soup (see page 207).
TASTELESS
Why: wrong type of cherry for cooking method; fruit underripe; too little sugar.
What to do: adjust flavouring with sugar, lemon juice and port or kirsch. If you like, add

ground cinnamon, and grated lemon or orange zest. See also Quick Fix.

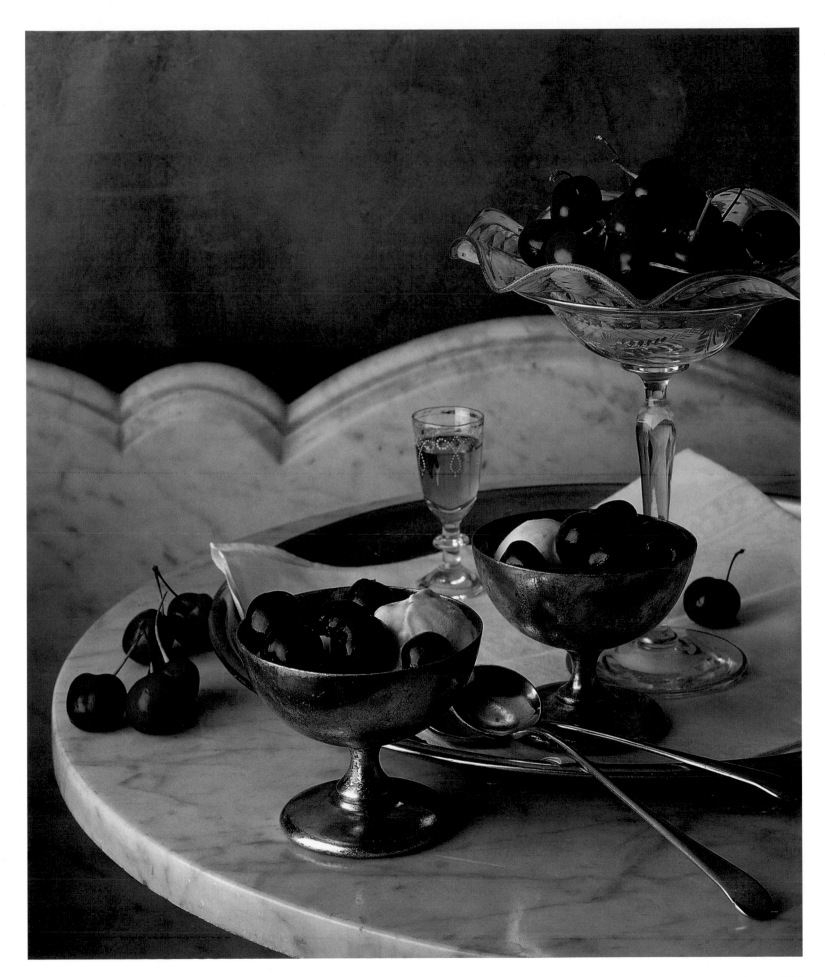

Berries

FOR BERRIES, RIPENESS IS ALL-IMPORTANT, whether in the pan or on the plate. No sleight of hand will substitute for the natural sweetness and juice of a perfectly ripe strawberry. I'm constantly astonished by the difference a few days' sun makes to the redcurrants in our garden, coaxing them from stringency to a tartness that pleasantly shocks the tongue. Of the dozen or more berries commonly available to the cook, strawberries and redcurrants lie at opposite ends of the cooking spectrum. Fragile types such as strawberries and raspberries scarcely hold up to cooking at all – often brief maceration in sugar and wine or fruit juice is enough. At the other end of the scale, currants and gooseberries are almost always improved by some gentle simmering with sugar, while cranberries are quite simply inedible when raw. Other berries range between the two extremes.

The sugar content of berries can vary enormously with variety and ripeness, so taste one to judge its quality before you start. At the same time, you can decide if the flavour needs help, such as a squeeze of lemon. You'll find red wine goes well with strawberries, rose geranium herb with gooseberries, orange with blueberries and cranberries. Many berries are so full of juice that they need no added liquid for cooking. I simply pick over and trim them, avoiding washing if I can. If berries are sandy, rinse them gently with water in a colander, but never leave them to soak. Be aware that they all overcook easily: plump and tender one minute, they can burst or collapse the next, so watch them carefully and use gentle heat.

One of the great joys of berries is their colour, so don't hesitate to add them when cooking other fruits – the classic combinations of rhubarb with strawberry and blackberry with apple are just a beginning. Red gooseberries are delicious with peaches, blueberries with baked bananas, and currants with pear.

TYPICAL FIRM BERRIES – bilberries, blackcurrants and redcurrants, blackberries, blueberries, cranberries, gooseberries

TYPICAL SOFT BERRIES – loganberries, raspberries, strawberries (rarely cooked except in preserves)

PROBLEMS

UNDERCOOKED AND HARD
Why: berries underripe; cooking time too short.
What to do: cook until done, raising temperature if necessary.

OVERCOOKED
Why: berries overripe; cooked too fast; cooked too long.
What to do: handling berries carefully, strain off excess juice and thicken lightly with arrowroot or potato flour to make a sauce; if very overcooked, purée in food processor to make a sauce or soup (see opposite).

FLAVOUR HARSH AND ACID
Why: berries underripe; too little sugar.
What to do: add sugar or honey; balance with a contrasting flavour such as ice cream, vanilla custard or whipped cream.

FLAVOUR BLAND, COLOUR PALE
Why: berries poor or underripe.
What to do: bolster flavour by sprinkling with brown sugar, grated orange or lemon zest, or juice, fruit vinegar or liqueur such as Grand Marnier; for colour, add red wine or port.

PERFECT – berries just tender when tasted, but still holding shape; juices running generously; colour vivid; flavour biting, usually softened by sugar.

PERFECT WELL-COOKED – berries very soft and shapes disintegrating to purée; flavour less biting, more concentrated; colours muted. Note: this stage is perfect for berry purées.

QUICK FIX

When berries are overcooked or acid, make a quick 'trifle' topped with whipped cream browned under the grill. You'll need 250 g/8 oz sponge cake or biscuits, such as chocolate chip or oatmeal. Cut or break them into large chunks and spread in a soufflé dish or deep baking dish. Top with the berries and juice and leave until juice is absorbed. Stiffly whip 750 ml/24 fl oz double cream and spread over berries to cover them completely. Grill very close to heat for 3-4 minutes until cream melts and starts to brown. Serve at once for 4.

Danish berry soup

Rødgrød

SERVES 4-6

Practically a national dish in Denmark, the dessert soup called *rødgrød* is popular throughout Scandinavia. I like to make it with a combination of firm berries that need to be simmered, such as redcurrants or blueberries, and softer fruits like strawberries and raspberries, which should be scarcely cooked at all. Always serve the soup with the thickest possible double cream.

175 g/6 oz strawberries
250 g/½ pound raspberries
250 g/½ pound redcurrants or
*   blueberries*
50 g/1¾ oz sugar, more to taste
500 ml/16 fl oz water
2 tablespoons arrowroot mixed to a
*   paste with 60 ml/2 fl oz water*
juice of 1 lemon (optional)
double cream and caster sugar for
*   serving*

Pick over and trim or hull the berries. Rinse and drain them only if sandy. Cut the strawberries in pieces about the same size as the raspberries.

Combine the sugar and water in a pan and heat gently, stirring occasionally, until the sugar dissolves. Bring this syrup to the boil and simmer 2 minutes. Add the redcurrants or blueberries and simmer until very soft, 8-12 minutes depending on the fruit.

Let fruit and syrup cool slightly, then purée in a food processor or with an immersion blender. Return purée to pan and bring just to the boil. Whisk in arrowroot paste – the purée will thicken at once. Stir in the raspberries and strawberries and simmer, stirring gently, until soft, 3-5 minutes.

Take from heat and taste. Add lemon juice or more sugar if needed. Let cool, then pour into a glass serving bowl or 4 individual bowls and chill thoroughly. It will thicken considerably on standing but should remain pourable. If necessary, thin with a little cold water. Serve chilled, passing cream and sugar separately.

COOKING WITH BERRIES

Many varieties of berry are improved by cooking, particularly firm ones (see opposite). Simplest is to simmer them in a light sugar syrup, perhaps flavoured with strips of lemon or orange zest and a split vanilla pod. Honey is an alternative sweetener. The amount needed varies very much with the fruit – redcurrants and cranberries need much more sugar than blueberries, for instance. If you're looking for more concentrated flavour, many berries do well simply baked with sugar and flavourings in a covered casserole in the oven. I like to do this when cooking berries for ice cream and cream desserts such as mousses and Bavarian creams.

Beware of overcooking, as many juicy berries burst from their own steam when the heat reaches their centres – gooseberries and cranberries are particularly vulnerable in this respect. Of course, if the berries are to be puréed, this is the result you want. Berries lend themselves well to baking in a batter, perhaps for muffins (page 289) or a pudding (page 229). Be sure they are ripe, as if still firm they may not cook through and they will certainly taste acid. You'll do best to poach or bake them instead.

Candied fruits

Fruit is candied by simmering and soaking it in sugar syrup. The boxes of multicoloured candied whole fruit that appear at Christmas time demand multiple soakings and can sometimes take several months to candy. However, with a simple candying process you can still have colourful candied slices of fruit such as figs, oranges and pineapple which will keep up to a week. Semi-translucent, fragrant strips or julienne of citrus fruits, useful for decoration, are even easier to achieve at home.

Slow, gentle cooking ensures that the syrup reaches the centre of the fruit, sweetening and preserving it. Keep the pieces even and small enough for the syrup to soak the fruit thoroughly – whole fruit like cherries must be pricked with a cocktail stick. Fruit that tends to be bitter, such as citrus peel, should be blanched in boiling water before candying. If the syrup is too thick, it will not penetrate thoroughly; if too thin the fruit scarcely candies to the ideal soft, almost translucent finish.

All the rules for cooking with sugar apply to candying. When making the syrup, be sure the sugar has completely dissolved before bringing it to the boil. Sugar loves to crystallize; it will tend to do so if a syrup is stirred or if crystals from the side of the pan or top of the fruit fall into it. A spoonful of glucose or honey, a squeeze of lemon juice or a pinch of cream of tartar added to the syrup helps prevent this. Keep a close eye on the pan; if sugar syrup cooks too fast or too long, it will caramelize and your lovely colourful fruit will darken and scorch. For maximum effect, let the fruit cool in the syrup before lifting it out to dry.

UNDERCOOKED *top* – fruit opaque, with glaze not yet formed on surface; texture firm; flavour raw, not candied.
PERFECT *bottom* – fruit translucent, with an even, shiny glaze.
OVERCOOKED *right* – colour dark and surface of fruit hard; texture very chewy; flavour caramelized.

Rhubarb

EARLY IN THE SEASON, RHUBARB MAY BE BRIGHT PINK AND TENDER, raised in a hot house, but garden rhubarb is likely to be tougher, with thick, bright green stems that must be peeled like those of celery. It is never bland – the acidity of rhubarb can rival that of cranberries, needing plenty of added sugar. Any flavouring must be pungent to make an impact. Watch out for overcooking, as once it is done, rhubarb softens very quickly to become a stringy pulp.

I bake rhubarb simply with raspberry or strawberry jam, as it develops plenty of its own juice. In the USA it is also known as the pie plant, and makes a favourite filling for a double crust pie when mixed with strawberries. Rhubarb compote (opposite) can be a dessert or a pleasant contemporary accompaniment to roast duck and game dishes. I thought such savoury dishes with rhubarb a new idea until I tasted Hungarian beetroot and rhubarb soup and Iranian *khoreshe rivas*, a stew of lamb with rhubarb. Both of these are well worth a try.

PERFECT – tender when pierced with a fork; juices running and pieces just starting to lose shape; colour bright and flavour tart but fresh.

OVERCOOKED – pieces shrivelled and falling apart when touched with fork; juices running very freely; colour faded and flavour pungent.
Why: rhubarb cut too thinly; cooked too fast; cooked too long.
What to do: purée in a food processor or work through a coarse sieve and flavour with fruit liqueur or chopped candied ginger for a sauce or sorbet.

OTHER PROBLEMS

TOO ACID
Why: underripe; too little sweetener.
What to do: add sugar, honey, raspberry or strawberry jam.

QUICK FIX

When rhubarb is overcooked or unpleasantly acid, mix each 500 ml/16 fl oz of cooked fruit with 175 g/6 oz crushed meringues or macaroons. Whip 175 ml/6 fl oz double cream. Spread the fruit in a deep baking dish and top with the whipped cream. Serve chilled for 4-6.

Rhubarb compote

Other fruit leaves and herbs to use in this compote include elderflowers, rose geranium, comfrey or lemon balm. If fresh leaves are not available, you can use herbal tea bags. Almond Tile Biscuits (page 317) make a pleasant accompaniment to the compote.

1 kg/2 pounds rhubarb stalks
250 ml/8 fl oz water
250 ml/8 fl oz white wine
400 g/14 oz sugar
2 tablespoons fresh blackberry leaves
2 tablespoons fresh strawberry leaves
2 tablespoons fresh raspberry leaves
1 Ceylon tea bag
500 g/1 pound strawberries

Peel the outer skin from the rhubarb. Slice the stalks thinly and put in a stainless steel bowl. Combine the water, wine and sugar in a saucepan. Heat the mixture, stirring occasionally, until the sugar has dissolved, then bring to the boil. Add the blackberry, strawberry and raspberry leaves and the tea bag. Remove from the heat, cover, and let infuse for 15 minutes.

Strain through a fine sieve and bring back to the boil. Add the rhubarb and bring back to the boil again. Pour into a bowl, cover with cling film and then aluminium foil. Note: the rhubarb continues to cook in the insulated bowl. Let stand until cool. Chill the fruit for at least 6 hours – the flavour improves on standing.

Hull and halve the strawberries, rinsing them only if they are sandy. Just before serving, add the strawberries to the compote and taste, adding more sugar if necessary. Spoon into coupe glasses and serve chilled.

Bananas

WE DON'T COOK BANANAS OFTEN ENOUGH in Europe and North America. Heat develops their taste and allows their somewhat sticky flesh to turn more juicy and fruit-like. First choice is often to bake the fruit with brown sugar and rum (aptly, where bananas grow you also find sugar cane, not to mention rum). More adventurous treatments include batter-coated fritters or banana kebabs baked with chunks of orange and pineapple and a topping of cinnamon and orange. In Brazil, bananas are baked in a pie with sugar, white wine and nutmeg, while Thais simmer bananas in coconut milk with raw palm sugar.

For cooking, it's important that bananas be firm rather than fully ripe and soft. When choosing the fruit, the skin should be lightly freckled with brown spots, but never brownish and yielding to your touch. Don't be misled by plantains, which are larger and firmer than bananas and lack the sugar. (Plantains should be treated as a starchy vegetable, and are good baked or deep-fried.) When preparing bananas, leave them whole or cut them in big chunks so they hold their shape. After peeling, they discolour quite quickly, so cook them immediately – for once lemon juice is no remedy as it spoils the rich sweet taste of the fruit.

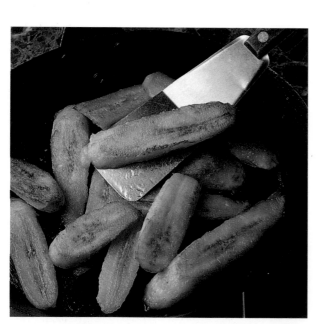

PERFECT – flesh very tender but still holds shape; colour light gold or dark with caramel, depending on recipe; flavour full-bodied and mellow.

QUICK FIX

For bananas which are dry, pasty or overcooked, prepare the following sauce: in a small bowl, whisk together 4 tablespoons lime juice, 1 tablespoon finely chopped fresh ginger and 2 tablespoons brown sugar. Gradually whisk in 250 ml/8 fl oz double cream. Spoon sauce over bananas or serve separately. Makes 375 ml/12 fl oz sauce to serve 4.

PROBLEMS

UNDERCOOKED AND HARD
Why: bananas underripe; wrong type of banana; cooking temperature too low; cooking time too short; lacking liquid to moisten fruit.
What to do: if dry, sprinkle with liquid such as orange juice, apricot nectar, or water; continue cooking until done, raising temperature if necessary.
OVERCOOKED AND MUSHY
Why: bananas too ripe; cut too small or too thin; cooked too fast; cooked too long.
What to do: top bananas with one or more of the following: sliced browned almonds, toasted shredded coconut, coarsely crumbled chocolate biscuits, sliced strawberries, or plain yogurt.

Baked banana pudding

SERVES 6

This dessert can stand alone, but is even better with Coconut Ice Cream (page 250).

8 bananas	gratin dishes
(about 1.4 kg/3 pounds)	for the pastry cream
1 tablespoon sesame seeds	175 ml/6 fl oz milk
1 teaspoon lemon juice	1 vanilla pod, split
2 tablespoons rum	2 eggs, separated
1 tablespoon sugar	2 tablespoons sugar
	1 tablespoon flour
6 individual 15-cm/6-in	

Preheat the oven to 220°C/425°F/gas7. Brush the gratin dishes with butter. In a small frying pan, toast the sesame seeds on a low heat, stirring them until browned, 2-3 minutes. Peel 6 of the bananas and split them lengthwise. Set the banana halves cut side down around the edge of the dishes.

Make the pastry cream: scald the milk in a medium saucepan with the vanilla pod, cover and leave to infuse off the heat, 5-10 minutes. Meanwhile, beat the egg yolks (reserving the whites) with the sugar until thick and light. Stir in the flour. Whisk the milk into the egg mixture and return it to the saucepan. Cook over a low heat, whisking constantly, until the cream comes to the boil and thickens. Simmer, stirring, for 1-2 minutes. Remove the vanilla pod and set the pastry cream aside. The vanilla pod can be rinsed and used again.

Make the pudding: peel the remaining 2 bananas and purée them in a food processor with the lemon juice, rum and vanilla. Stir the purée into the pastry cream.

Stiffly beat the reserved egg whites, preferably in a copper bowl. Add the sugar and continue beating until the whites are glossy and hold a long peak, 30-60 seconds.

If necessary, heat the banana mixture until hot to the touch. Stir in about a quarter of the egg whites. Add this mixture to the remaining egg whites and fold them together as lightly as possible. Spoon the mixture into the prepared gratin dishes, piling it inside the bananas.

Bake in the preheated oven until the pudding is puffed and the bananas are done, 12-15 minutes. Sprinkle with the toasted sesame seeds and serve at once.

Figs

Fig toasts

FIGS ARE A FAVOURITE WITH CONTEMPORARY CHEFS, valued for their pretty shape and deep pink interior in dishes such as pork medallions with figs in red wine, and foie gras with roast figs. More traditional ideas include figs simmered in rum syrup or orange juice and ginger. The simplest way to cook them is to bake or poach them, whether whole, quartered or thickly sliced. The two common types of fig – black- or green-skinned – are interchangeable. Leave the skin, both for colour and to hold the soft flesh in place.

Fresh figs, with their deep red flesh and delicate flavour, call for the simplest treatment. Here, they are sautéed briefly in butter and sugar, then topped with browned almonds to make a perfect summer dessert. For a luscious treat substitute mascarpone for the yogurt.

*12 medium figs
   (750 kg/1½ pounds)
4 slices of brioche
   or challah (page 264),
   cut 2.5-cm/1-in thick
100 g/3¼ oz sugar*

*45 g/1½ oz butter
125 g/4 oz plain yogurt,
   stirred until smooth
45 g/1½ oz slivered
   almonds*

Preheat the oven to 260°C/500°F/gas10 or its highest possible setting. Toast the bread: lay the bread slices directly on the oven rack and toast in the preheated oven until golden, 4-5 minutes. Place the slices of toast on 4 warmed plates.

Meanwhile trim the stems off the figs. Slice the figs in half and dip the halves in sugar, turning them so they are well coated. Set aside.

In a frying pan, heat 1 tablespoon of the butter, add the almonds and sauté until golden brown, 2-3 minutes. Set them aside.

Heat the remaining butter in the pan until foaming. Add the figs, cut-side down, and sauté until done, turning once, 3-5 minutes.

Set the figs on the toast and spoon over the pan juices. Top each toast with yogurt and a sprinkling of toasted almonds. Serve at once so the toast stays crisp.

PERFECT – fruit flexible but still holding shape; tender when pierced with point of a knife; juices starting to run; flavour mellow.

PROBLEMS

UNDERCOOKED AND DRY
Why: figs underripe; cooking temperature too low; cooking time too short; liquid lacking to moisten fruit.
What to do: add liquid and continue cooking until juice runs, raising heat if necessary.

OVERCOOKED
Why: figs overripe; heat too high; cooked too long.
What to do: revive with a topping of chopped walnuts mixed with grated orange zest and coarse or brown sugar; in a savoury dish, substitute celery for the sugar.

WOOLLY AND TASTELESS
Why: figs under- or overripe; overcooked.
What to do: sprinkle with balsamic vinegar, crumbled goats' cheese or a tart fruit such as raspberries or seeds of passion fruit.

QUICK FIX

Grill overcooked or tasteless figs with brown sugar and cloves. For every 250 g/½ pound figs, mix 2 tablespoons sugar and ¼ teaspoon ground cloves. Place the figs in a shallow flameproof baking dish and top with the sugar mixture. Grill until caramelized, 3-4 minutes. Serves 2.

Fruit fritters

FRUITS ARE TRICKIER TO FRY AS FRITTERS THAN VEGETABLES because of their juice, but they are all the more delicious. Cut the fruit (which should be firm, even slightly underripe) into quite generous slices or chunks so they overcook less easily, and be sure they are well dried before coating. Fruits are invariably fried in batter as a breadcrumb coating is too heavy and a simple coating of flour does not offer sufficient protection. You'll find a light, tempura-style batter is good, or a frothy mix like the champagne batter opposite. Don't be tempted to add much sugar to fritter batter, however, as it scorches quickly in the high heat. I always try a test fritter to gauge fat temperature, thickness of coating and behaviour of the fruit itself. If fritters are acid after frying, there are plenty of remedies (below). Try to keep flavourings to a minimum as deep-frying wonderfully develops that of the fruit itself. A sprinkling of lemon juice, sugar, liqueur or rum just before the fritters are rushed to the table is often enough. And always, always, serve them at once.

TYPICAL FRUITS FOR FRITTERS — apple, apricot, banana, pineapple, plum, strawberry

PERFECT – fritters a pale to deep gold, crisp and light when drained; fruit evenly coated with batter; fruit flavour is vivid, texture soft or firm but not soggy.

left to right
UNDERCOOKED – coating pallid, soggy when drained; when cut, fruit often raw and has absorbed fat.
PERFECT – coating crisp and golden; when cut, fruit is tender.

COATING DISINTEGRATING – coating unevenly browned and breaks off into fat; fruit not thoroughly coated, so exposed parts scorch.

QUICK FIX

A few fast ideas:
• In a food processor or blender, coarsely chop 2 tablespoons blanched whole or sliced almonds or walnuts and 2 tablespoons brown sugar; sprinkle over fritters.
• Make a piquant dipping sauce by mixing 125 ml/4 fl oz white wine, 2 tablespoons lemon juice and 2 tablespoons honey. Stir in 2 tablespoons chopped raspberries or chopped dried cherries or cranberries. Serves 4.
• For soggy or undercooked fritters, spread fritters in a shallow baking dish, sprinkle with sugar and grill until tops are crisp and caramelized; serve with lemon wedges.

PROBLEMS

UNDERCOOKED
Why: heat too low, often because too many fritters in pan; fruit pieces too large; cooking time too short.
What to do: lift out fritters and heat fat to 190°C/375°F. Re-fry until coating is browned and crisp, if necessary in two batches so as not to crowd pan.
COATING DISINTEGRATING
Why: batter too thin; heat too low, often because too many fritters in pan at once.
What to do: nothing can be done; add more flour to coating for next batch.

OVERCOOKED AND HEAVY
Why: cooked too long; cooked too fast; coating too thick.
What to do: sprinkle with lemon juice and icing sugar; serve with raspberry, citrus or other tart sauce.
SOGGY
Why: fruit inappropriate or overripe; poorly drained after frying; undercooked; coating too moist; fritters not served at once; softened by sprinkling with lemon juice or sugar.
What to do: keep fritters warm in oven

with door open and serve within 15 minutes; sprinkle with flavouring just before serving; see also Overcooked.
BLAND
Why: poor or inappropriate fruit; too little sugar.
What to do: see Quick Fix.
FLAVOUR ACID
Why: fruit underripe.
What to do: sprinkle with sugar, top with honey, or serve with a sweet sauce of fruit jam or marmalade.

Champagne fruit fritters

MAKES ABOUT 18 FRITTERS

This recipe features two fruits which fall neatly into rings – apple and pineapple. Apples are easily cut, but fresh pineapple takes time to prepare unless you're lucky like me – our local market has a contraption that removes peel and core with the stroke of a lever. If not, you'll find instructions here. There's no need to use real champagne for the batter as any sparkling white wine will do. You'll get the same lightness with soda water – though not, of course, the same taste!

1 pineapple, about
   750 g/1½ pounds
2 tart apples, about
   500 g/1 pounds
2 tablespoons sugar
1 tablespoon ground cinnamon
vegetable oil, for deep-frying
icing sugar, for sprinkling

for the champagne fritter batter
250 g/8 oz flour
½ teaspoon salt
375 ml/12 fl oz champagne,
   more if needed

Make the champagne fritter batter: sift the flour and salt into a bowl and make a well in the centre. Pour the champagne into the well and stir gently with a whisk, gradually drawing in the flour, to make a smooth batter. Note: the batter should fall easily from the spoon, so add more champagne if necessary. Do not whisk vigorously or the batter will be heavy. Cover and let stand at room temperature for 30-60 minutes.

Peel and core the pineapple: slice off the plume and stem ends of the pineapple. Cut away the peel in strips, following the curve of the fruit and cutting deep enough to remove the eyes with the pineapple peel. Slice the pineapple into 1.25-cm/½-inch thick rounds. Core the rounds with a small pastry cutter or knife to make rings.

Peel the apples and scoop out their flower and stem ends. Remove the seeds and centre core with an apple corer or small knife. Slice each apple into 1-cm/⅜-inch thick rings, discarding the thin end slices.

Combine the sugar and cinnamon in a small bowl. Lay the apple slices on a tray, sprinkle with the sugar and cinnamon mixture, turn the slices and sprinkle the other sides. Repeat with the pineapple rings.

In a wok or deep-fryer, heat the oil to 190°C/375°F. Dip the apple slices in batter one by one so they are completely coated. Lift out and let excess batter drain for 1-2 seconds. Lower the pieces into hot oil and deep-fry until done, turning once and stirring gently with a draining spoon so the fruit cooks evenly, 3-4 minutes. Note: fry the rings in 3-4 batches so the pan is not crowded. Drain on paper towels and keep warm, uncovered, in a low oven with the door open. Fry the remaining apple rings in the same way, followed by the pineapple rings.

Sprinkle the warm fritters with icing sugar and serve at once.

DIPPED AND COATED FRUITS

I said at the beginning of this chapter that, with their lively colours and shapes, fruits are their own decoration. So what better way to display them than with a light coating which still reveals their underlying character? Dipped or coated fruits are delicious with coffee, and form elegant decorations for cakes and desserts.

Half a dozen ideal fruits include cherries, strawberries, grapes and segments of orange and tangerine. Cape gooseberries are particularly pretty, with their papery 'cape' folded back to reveal the golden fruit. The main criterion when choosing fruit for dipping is a firm skin so that juice does not come into contact with the coating – leave stems on cherries and grapes, hulls on strawberries and divide citrus fruits carefully so juice does not leak. Stems are handy for dipping the fruit, or use a toothpick.

Sugar syrup is a popular coating, setting to be clear and crisp. The syrup is boiled to the hard-crack stage (a sugar thermometer should register 146°C/295°F) or to a light caramel at the slightly higher temperature of 160°C/320°F. To coat about 200 g/6½ oz of fruits, you'll need syrup made with 300 g/9¾ oz sugar and 250 ml/8 fl oz water. Have ready a baking sheet lined with greaseproof paper and a bowl of warm water. When the syrup reaches the right temperature, immerse the base of the pan in the water to stop cooking. Dip the fruits one by one into the hot syrup, letting the excess drain off so a 'foot' does not form when the fruit is set on the paper to harden. Sugar-coated fruits soften after 3-4 hours, particularly in a moist atmosphere. Serve them in paper candy cases.

Fondant icing is an alternative to sugar syrup as a coating, easy to use and readily available commercially – don't think of making your own. Simply warm the fondant with a little sugar syrup so it lightly coats the fruit and dip as for sugar syrup. However the colour of the fruit is veiled by the white fondant coating. White or dark chocolate has the same disadvantage and is rich as well, so often fruits are half-dipped as a compromise.

For an attractive, frosted coating, fruits may be dipped in lightly beaten egg whites, then rolled in caster sugar and left to dry for an hour. Bunches of redcurrants or blackcurrants and baby grapes are favourites for this treatment and can hold up for 12 hours in an airtight container.

Fruit jams

WHY DOES SUCH AN AIR OF MYSTERY SURROUND MAKING JAM? The process is really very simple, a matter of achieving the right balance of acid, sugar and pectin so the jam sets just right, with a vivid colour and taste. Acid content is easy to judge by tasting the fruit: if low, you can add more in the form of lemon juice or perhaps a tart apple or two – allow 2 tablespoons juice per 500 g/1 pound of fruit. As for sugar, much depends on the type of fruit and its ripeness – anything from two-thirds to equal parts by volume of sugar to fruit is a good rule of thumb. (Some recipes specify another sweetener such as honey.) Pectin level can be judged by a simple test (see page 217).

When talking about jams and preserving, I cannot do better than refer to Roseline Fontaine, one of France's finest artisan jam makers, who makes more than 200 types of conserve each year. First, Madame Fontaine insists on prime fruit that, above all, is not too ripe, so it contains plenty of pectin and acid. She likes to macerate the raw fruit with sugar for a day before cooking and scorns added pectin, saying it leads to insipid jams which never develop full, concentrated flavour because they scarcely need cooking. In her kitchen, 4 kg/9 pounds of fruit is the maximum batch so the jam cooks rapidly, maintaining fresh taste and colour. If the fruit is soft, she may leave it whole or cut it in chunks; if firm, it is cooked before adding sugar, which is warmed separately in a low oven to reduce boiling time.

Once sugar is added to the fruit it must be allowed to dissolve before the jam is brought to the boil. Then it is kept at a rolling boil. Towards the end of cooking, you must skim often and stir so the jam does not boil over or scorch on the base of the pan. When nearly done, Madame Fontaine is careful to taste and adjust flavourings. For storage, she underlines the importance of sterilizing the jar, sealing the contents and keeping the jam in a cool, dry place. Her method of sealing is startlingly simple and works every time (see page 217).

TYPICAL FRUITS FOR JAM – apple, apricot, blackberry, blueberry, cherry, cranberry, redcurrants and blackcurrants, gooseberry, grapefruit, lemon, lime, orange, peach, pear, plum, quince, raspberry, rhubarb, strawberry

TYPICAL FRUITS FOR JELLY *opposite* – apple, blackberry, blackcurrant, citrus, crab apple, grape, quince, raspberry, redcurrant

QUICK FIX

When jam is thick or dull: just before using, stir in some chopped fresh raspberries, blackberries or peaches with a few tablespoons of raspberry or strawberry liqueur to soften the texture and pick up the taste.

UNDERCOOKED – jam runs quickly from spoon and froths in pan; sugar thermometer registers under 106°C/220°F.
Why: cooking time too short; heat too low.
What to do: continue cooking as fast as possible until it is done.

PERFECT – jam sheets in even drops from side of spoon on a chilled plate, a few drops of jam set in 3-5 seconds when pushed with a finger; bubbles break more slowly and no longer froth in pan; sugar thermometer registers 106°C/220°F; colour rich, flavour full-bodied with good balance of tart, fruity and sweet.

OVERCOOKED – jam dark and sticky, clinging to spoon; thermometer registers above 106°C/220°F; colour has brownish tinge; flavour is dense, often smoky with caramel and pan base scorched.
Why: cooked too long; cooked too slowly; if scorched, jam not stirred often.
What to do: little can be done. When using, see Quick Fix.

Fruit jellies

OTHER PROBLEMS

JAM NOT SET
Why: not enough pectin; not enough acid; not enough sugar; undercooked; boiled too slowly.
What to do: if only slightly soft, leave pots of jam unsealed in a sunny place a few days so some moisture evaporates; if runny, use at once; if very runny, reboil jam to 110°C/220°F.

TOO STIFF
Why: overcooked; too much added pectin; fruit full of fibre.
What to do: use for filling or sauce, where texture is not so obvious.

TASTES BLAND OR FLAT
Why: poor or overripe fruit; bland type of fruit such as figs; too much pectin added, allowing too short a cooking time; jam boiled too slowly or too long; too much sugar.
What to do: while still hot, add assertive flavouring such as lemon juice, fruit brandy or liqueur, aromatic herb such as mint, thyme or rosemary (chopped or in sprigs) or spice such as ground ginger or cinnamon.

ACID OR BITTER
Why: poor or unripe fruit; not enough sugar; jam scorched.
What to do: if acid, take jam from heat, stir in sugar or honey and boil again to setting point; if bitter or burned, nothing can be done.

COLOUR PALE OR DULL
Why: poor or unripe fruit; too little fruit; cooked too slowly or too long; stored too long or in a warm place; poorly sealed (dark layer at top of jar).
What to do: use to flavour fresh fruit or in a sauce with other bright ingredients.

JAM CRYSTALLIZES IN JAR
Why: sugar not dissolved before jam boils.
What to do: scrape off crystals from surface of jam; melt rest to use for cooking.

FRUIT SEPARATES IN JAR
Why: fruit not ripe or undercooked; cut too large.
What to do: let jam cool before pouring into jars, 15-20 minutes, sealing when cold; if in jars, stir gently when tepid.

JAM MOULDY OR FERMENTED
Why: undercooked; too little sugar; poorly sealed; sealed when tepid, not hot or cold; stored in warm or damp place.
What to do: if fermented or very mouldy, discard jam.

JELLY IS MADE BY STRAINING THE JUICE FROM COOKED FRUIT, then boiling it with sugar, just like jam. All the same guidelines apply, particularly the need to balance acid, sugar and pectin. Fruits for jelly must have plenty of flavour and preferably colour too (see opposite) – blackcurrants, redcurrants and raspberries are generous in this regard and you'll find the pale flesh of apple and quince boils down to be pleasantly pink. If the fruit tastes good, sufficient acid is not usually a problem. Sugar depends on the type and ripeness of the fruit; anything from two-thirds to equal parts by volume sugar to fruit juice is a reliable measure. Pectin content is particularly important – only high-pectin fruits should be used; be sure to test the juice before boiling. (With jam, you can fall back on the fruit fibre to hold it together, with jelly you will have no such luck.) One important rule: never squeeze juice from the cooked fruit, but leave it free to drain naturally, if possible overnight, so it does not cloud. Then you'll have clear, sparkling jelly.

UNDERCOOKED AND CLOUDY *left* – jelly too thin to hold a shape on a chilled plate; jelly thin and opaque, not translucent.
PERFECT *centre* – on a chilled plate, in 3-5 seconds a few drops of jelly set when pushed with a finger; sugar thermometer registers 106°C/220°F; bubbles break more slowly and no longer froth in pan; colour deep but vivid, flavour fruity with good balance of tart and sweet.
OVERCOOKED *right* – jelly dark, sticky and too thick to spread; if very overcooked, flavour is caramelized.

QUICK FIX

When jelly is bland or flat, put 2-3 leaves of a fresh herb in the jars, pour hot jelly on top and seal. The herb flavour will infuse the whole jar. Bay leaf, lemon verbena, mint, rosemary, sage and thyme are particularly good in this respect.

OTHER PROBLEMS

UNDERCOOKED
Why: cooking time too short; heat too low.
What to do: continue cooking as fast as possible until done.

OVERCOOKED
Why: cooked too long; cooked too slowly; if caramelized, not stirred often.
What to do: nothing can be done.

CLOUDY
Why: fruit forced through jelly bag or strainer.
What to do: when jelly is cooked, take from heat and stir in chopped herb such as mint, lemon verbena or basil.
See also Quick Fix. For other problems, see Jams.

Old-fashioned raspberry jam

MAKES ABOUT I LITRE/I ⅔ PINTS

Ripe berries can be quite low in pectin, so to be sure this jam sets I always add a few unripe berries or a sliced tart apple.

I kg/2 pounds ripe raspberries
600 g/I ¼ pounds sugar
handful of unripe raspberries or I tart apple

Pick over the ripe and unripe raspberries, rinsing them only if they are sandy. Put alternating layers of the raspberries and sugar in a bowl. Cover and leave to macerate at room temperature at least 8 hours or overnight.

Transfer the berries and sugar to a large pan. If using an apple, peel, core and thinly slice it and add to berries. Heat gently, stirring occasionally, until sugar dissolves. Bring to a rolling boil and cook to the setting point, 20-30 minutes. Stir often and towards the end of cooking, skim off scum.

Let the jam cool 4-5 minutes, then ladle into a heatproof measuring cup. Pour jam into sterilized jars and seal as described below.

TESTING FOR PECTIN CONTENT

The natural pectin content of fruit varies with its ripeness – ripe fruit has less pectin – and the type of fruit. For instance, tart apples and plums are high in pectin, most ripe berries contain a medium amount, and apricots, peaches, figs and pineapple are low. Pectin can be judged from the fruit juice or pulp after it is cooked and before sugar is added. Mix I tablespoon of cooked fruit juice with I tablespoon of 70 percent rubbing alcohol; fruit rich in pectin forms a large clot, a medium amount of pectin forms a few small clots, and fruit low in pectin deposits a bit of flaky sediment. If need be, liquid or powdered pectin can be added to fruit, but don't overdo it or the jelly or jam will be glutinous.

PACKING AND SEALING PRESERVES

This is just one of the various methods of packing jams, jellies and other preserves. You can use any size jar you like, though I find small (250 ml/8 fl oz) jars with screw-top lids are most practical as the contents are eaten quickly and do not spoil.

To sterilize jars and lids, bring a large pan of water to the boil. Add jars and lids and boil 10 minutes. Remove them from water and leave to dry on clean paper towels – don't wipe them dry. Arrange jars on wooden board. I ladle preserves into jars while still very hot, using a funnel for jellies and thin jams, pouring others from a heatproof measuring cup. Fill to within I cm / ⅜ inch of the rim and while still hot, cover with lid, fastening tightly. Cover with a cloth in case of leakage and turn jars upside down so preserves are in contact with lid; leave to cool. When cold, turn jars upright. You'll find a vacuum has been created under the lid and enough air has been expelled to prevent any moulding. No further seal is necessary.

Apple rosemary jelly

MAKES ABOUT I LITRE/I ⅔ PINTS

Jelly needs an apple which is high in both pectin and in acid, and with that in mind I'd recommend you pick from the many interesting varieties now available. As I like a tart jelly, perfect with pork and duck, I add a minimum of sugar.

1.8 kg/4 pounds apples
about 2 litres/3⅓ pints water, more if needed
I large bunch of rosemary (about 90 g/3 oz)
3 tablespoons black peppercorns
2 tablespoons cumin seeds
2 tablespoons coriander seeds
juice of 2 lemons
about 800 g/I¾ pounds sugar

jelly bag (optional)
muslin

Scoop out the stem and flower ends of apples and quarter them, leaving peel and cores. Put them in a large saucepan and cover with water (there should be just enough almost to cover the fruit). Simmer, uncovered, stirring often, until fruit is very soft and falling apart, I-I¼ hours.

Prepare a jelly bag by dampening it and wringing it out. Alternatively, line a fine sieve with a clean damp cloth. Pour the apples into the jelly bag or sieve and let drip overnight into a large bowl. Note: squeezing the fruit clouds the jelly.

Meanwhile, prepare the herb and spices: coarsely chop the stalks and leaves of the rosemary. Put the peppercorns, cumin seed and coriander seeds in a thick plastic bag and crush with a rolling pin. Tie the rosemary and crushed spices in a piece of muslin.

Measure the apple juice and pour it into a large pan. Simmer the juice uncovered, skimming off any froth, 5 minutes. Meanwhile, measure 135 g/4⅓ oz sugar for each 250 ml/8 fl oz of apple juice. Add the sugar to the juice and heat gently, stirring occasionally, until the sugar dissolves. Add the lemon juice and the bag of herb and spices.

Bring to a rolling boil and cook to the setting point, 30-45 minutes, stirring often. Towards the end of cooking, skim off scum. Remove the herb bouquet, squeezing it against the side of the pot to extract all the flavours.

Let the jelly cool for 4-5 minutes, then ladle it into a heatproof measuring cup. Pour the jelly into sterilized jars and seal (see left).

Old-fashioned raspberry jam and Apple rosemary jelly

Fruit chutneys, confits and cooked relishes

I WAS BROUGHT UP WITH CHUTNEYS — wonderful dark sweet-and-sour mixtures of fruits, vegetables and spice to accompany cold meats, poultry and cheese. They were one of the few exotic touches recognized by my father, who was deeply conservative in food as in everything. When I came to France I encountered savoury confit (the word means 'preserved') usually of single fruits and vegetables, cooked with butter, wine or vinegar and a bit of sugar, less complex but no less pungent than chutney. Finally, I think of the USA as the home of cooked relishes such as green tomato pickle and persimmon relish with onions, white wine, cinnamon and brown sugar. Chutneys, confits and relishes are much less tricky than jams and jellies, thanks to spices and the acid in vinegar, which act as preservatives as well as flavourings. Far more than in other preserves, fruit and vegetables play a secondary role to seasonings and they must hold up well to the long cooking needed for flavours to mellow. In chutneys and confits, sugar is also a factor, toasting to a rich dark caramel — towards the end of cooking scorching is a danger, so watch out!

UNDERCOOKED — thin, often watery, lacking body; some ingredients still crisp; flavours not yet thoroughly blended; colours relatively pale.
Why: undercooked; too little sugar (chutney and confit).
What to do: continue cooking over low heat; more sugar often helps chutney and confit.

PERFECT — thick enough to hold mark of spoon but still soft enough to fall from the spoon; all ingredients soft (for chutney and confit) or tender (for relishes); colour deep and rich; flavour intense with good balance of acid, sweet and savoury.

OTHER PROBLEMS

OVERCOOKED AND HEAVY
Why: cooked too long.
What to do: when using, add a fresh ingredient such as peeled, seeded and chopped tomato, chopped celery or sweet onion, or chopped fruit such as mango or peach.

ACID OR BITTER
Why: too many acid ingredients; not enough sugar; undercooked; scorched.
What to do: add more sugar or other sweetener such as honey and continue cooking until dissolved, 2-3 minutes; if scorched, nothing can be done.

COLOUR PALE OR DULL
Why: pallid ingredients; fruit poor or underripe; undercooked (especially chutney and confit).
What to do: for chutney, add colour with peeled, seeded and chopped tomato, red or green pepper, cooking until fully incorporated; for confit, add more sugar, increase heat and cook until caramelized; for relish, stir in chopped herb such as parsley or chive.

MOULDY OR FERMENTED
Why: undercooked; too little sugar; poorly sealed; sealed when tepid, not hot or cold; stored in warm or damp place.
What to do: if fermented or mouldy, discard.

Apple and tomato chutney

Here's a great way to use the abundance of two autumn fruits!

1.8 kg/4 pounds ripe tomatoes	1 tablespoon ground ginger
750 g/1½ pounds onions, sliced	2 tablespoons salt
400 g/13 oz dark brown sugar	2 teaspoons peppercorns
1.25 litres/2 pints white wine vinegar	1.8 kg/4 pounds tart apples

Bring a large saucepan of water to the boil. Core the tomatoes and score an 'x' on each base. To peel them, immerse them in boiling water until the skin starts to split, 8-15 seconds. Transfer to a bowl of cold water. When cool enough to handle, peel the tomatoes and cut them into thick slices.

In a large bowl, combine the tomatoes, onions, sugar, vinegar, ginger and salt. Tie the peppercorns in a cheesecloth bag and add to tomato mixture. Cover and leave to macerate overnight in a cool place.

Peel, core and slice apples. In a large pan, combine the apples with the tomato mixture. Heat gently, stirring occasionally, until the sugar is dissolved. Bring the chutney to the boil and simmer until done, stirring often, about 1½-1¾ hours.

Let the chutney cool for 4-5 minutes, then discard the peppercorn bag. Ladle the chutney into a heatproof measuring cup, pour it into sterilized jars and seal (see page 217).

QUICK FIX

When chutney, confit or relish is bland, add a sweet-and-sour gastrique: for every 750 ml/24 fl oz conserve, heat 50 g/1⅔ oz sugar with 60 ml/2 fl oz water over low heat until dissolved. Bring to the boil and boil without stirring to a dark golden caramel.

Take from the heat, let bubbles subside and add 75 ml/2½ fl oz red wine vinegar. Note: stand back as the vinegar vapour will otherwise sting your eyes. Heat gently, stirring until the caramel dissolves. Let cool, then stir the gastrique into the conserve.

TYPICAL FRUITS FOR CHUTNEYS, CONFITS AND COOKED RELISHES — apple, fig, mango, peach, pear, pineapple, plantain, plum, quince, rhubarb, tomato

DESSERTS

HOW CONSERVATIVE WE ARE IN OUR EATING HABITS! A chef once told me that his dessert menu was almost impossible to change as customers clamoured for the same old favourites year after year. Certainly this collection bears him out. In this entire chapter only half a dozen dessert flavourings dominate – vanilla, chocolate, coffee, caramel, citrus and red berries. The ingredients are scarcely more varied, as most desserts rely on eggs, sugar, milk or cream, and possibly flour or a grain. Yet with this narrow palette we create a huge variety of firm favourites. We beat eggs for hot and cold soufflés and meringue, we set them in baked custards and use them to enrich many traditional hot puddings. We cook sugar to caramel or toast it with nuts to a praline, while chocolate is the common foundation of a dozen rich confections. Gelatine helps to set a series of cold desserts, and ice cream, sorbet and parfait form their own little group.

A dessert can be as simple as the crispy brown top of a baked pudding or as fanciful as the fluffy tower of a moulded cold soufflé. However, each one must make an impact, signalling the end of the meal – its last hurrah. Flavours must be vivid and colours dramatic, with the white of whipped cream and meringue, the gold of caramel and the darkness of chocolate. Think of the stained-glass window colours of a molded jelly set with fruit, or the instant appeal of sorbet scooped into a frosted glass, or arranged in careful ovals on a plate.

So traditional are all these desserts that a quick glimpse tells you what is to come. Where does innovation enter? It appears in new flavours such as cape gooseberry, rose hip, or macadamia oil, and new combinations such as bread pudding made with panettone or a custard flavoured with lime. It comes with unexpected decorations such as a pointed spike of chocolate, or a sprig of basil instead of mint. The old custom of flaming a festive dessert is reappearing – why not? Here's where experiment is up to you.

Red wine and berry terrine,
page 247

Whipping cream

WHEN WHIPPING CREAM, THE IMPORTANT POINT TO REMEMBER is that it turns to butter if you go too far. I learned this the hard way. When overwhipped, the butterfat in cream starts to separate and curdle. This happens more easily and rapidly if the cream is warm, so be sure to chill it, together with the bowl and whisk. To stiffen satisfactorily, cream must contain enough butterfat – 30 percent is a minimum, and 40 percent ('whipping cream' is about 35 percent and double cream about 45) is better. Very high butterfat cream, over 50 percent, can be heavy when whipped, so thin it with a little cold water. Sterilized cream, which contains stabilizer, stiffens more reliably than pasteurized cream but has much less taste.

Most commercial cream is bland stuff, I think, so after whipping I usually flavour it as Chantilly cream unless it is to be mixed with other ingredients. Chantilly is whipped cream flavoured with vanilla or Cognac and sweetened with caster or icing sugar – icing sugar gives a smooth result and the small amount of cornflour in the sugar helps stiffen the cream. Note that crème fraîche (page 109), with its nutty, slightly sour taste, is not usually whipped for desserts.

When whipping cream, you'll find two distinct consistencies useful. At the first stage, the cream holds a fluffy, soft peak, just right for folding into other mixtures such as meringue or pastry cream. Continue whipping and the cream will become stiff enough to hold the firm peak needed for piped decorations. Take care, as if the cream is very stiff it may curdle slightly when forced through a star tube – we've all seen ragged rosettes of cream weeping at the edges. At any stage of whipping, a yellowish tinge signals that butterfat is coagulating and the cream is about to curdle; stop at once and chill the cream again before use. On standing, even stiffly whipped cream may separate slightly – simply beat it to recombine and stiffen it again.

QUICK FIX

If cream curdles, you can always make butter: continue whipping it until butter separates in clumps, 1-2 minutes. Transfer butter pieces with a draining spoon to a bowl of cold water and squeeze with your fist to wash off whey, until butter comes together into a single cake, 1-2 minutes. Lift out and dry on paper towels. If you like, sprinkle with up to ½ teaspoon salt. Shape into a neat cake, wrap and chill; 500 ml/16 fl oz cream with 40 percent butterfat yields about 150 g/ 5 oz butter.

PERFECT FOR FOLDING – cream is light and just holds a soft peak when whisk is lifted; colour pale cream.

PERFECT FOR PIPING – cream is fluffy and holds a stiff, well-defined peak when whisk is lifted; colour slightly deeper cream.

CURDLED – cream wet and granular; colour yellowish from butter curds.
Why: whipped too long so butterfat coagulated; cream, bowl and whisk not sufficiently chilled; butterfat content of cream too low for cream to thicken satisfactorily; acid ingredient such as lemon juice added.
What to do: nothing can be done. If you like, make butter, see Quick Fix.

OTHER PROBLEMS

TOO SOFT
Why: butterfat in cream too low; not sufficiently whipped; overwhipped and about to separate; too much liquid flavouring or sugar added; cream softened on standing.
What to do: continue whipping until cream stiffens, watching for yellow look which signals curdling.

TASTELESS
Why: cream of poor quality, often sterilized; cream low in butterfat; flavouring lacking.
What to do: for savoury dishes, flavour with salt, white pepper, Cognac or ground spices such as cardamom or cinnamon; for desserts, flavour with sugar and vanilla, Cognac, powdered coffee or liqueur such as Grand Marnier.

Beating egg whites

QUICK FIX

When beaten egg whites have separated: for every 2 whites, add 1 unbeaten egg white and whisk very vigorously until smooth and light, about 45 seconds. Use at once.

IN THE EARLY 1960S, I BASED MY BRIEF CAREER AS A CATERER IN PARIS on my success with soufflés. Armed with copper bowl, whisk, and boundless energy, I could guarantee a light, fluffy soufflé which would rise even in the most primitive oven lacking a thermostat. I had hit on the key to soufflés, meringues and many sponge cakes – nothing is more important than correct beating of the egg whites to a fine, even texture incorporating the maximum of air. Since then, I am happy to say, many kitchens have been equipped with heavy-duty electric mixers which do the hard work for you. Constant beating with a balloon whisk is needed, gradually increasing speed to maximum as the whites froth and break up. Do not stop whisking before the whites are stiff. The whites themselves should be at room temperature, with no trace of moisture or fat, particularly any trace of egg yolk. (Fish out any egg yolk with nature's tool, the egg shell.) For once, very fresh eggs are not an advantage as they contain more moisture.

The type of mixing bowl also has an influence – the efficiency of copper is not just an illusion. A copper surface stabilizes egg whites so they can be beaten more easily to a smooth, close texture which holds well when folded with other ingredients. Stainless steel is the next choice, with glass and ceramic bowls a poor substitute. A copper bowl must be cleaned before use by rubbing it with 1 or 2 tablespoons of salt and 1 or 2 tablespoons vinegar or a cut lemon. Rinse the bowl with water, dry it thoroughly and use within 15 minutes.

Overbeating is the greatest danger when whipping egg whites, particularly in a machine – they seem to coagulate suddenly and the texture coarsens, making them hard to fold smoothly into other ingredients. For savoury recipes, a pinch of cream of tartar slows stiffening and lessens the danger of overbeating. For sweet recipes, a tablespoon of sugar per egg white, whipped in when the whites are already stiff, acts as a stabilizer. If beaten egg whites do separate, they can usually be reconstituted, see Quick Fix.

TOO SOFT – peak long when whisk lifted; whites floppy.
Why: whites not beaten long enough; bowl or whites contaminated with water or egg yolk; bowl or whites too cold; eggs very fresh; beaten too slowly.
What to do: add pinch of cream of tartar or sugar and continue beating vigorously; if still not stiff, warm bowl 30-40 seconds over very low heat, beating constantly.

PERFECT – stiff enough to hold crisp peak when whisk is lifted; whites very smooth, appearance matt and clinging to sides of bowl with no trace of granular 'curdling'; bowl can be turned upside down without whites spilling.

SEPARATED – texture of whites granular, particularly at edges; whites pull away from sides of bowl and no longer hold clear, stiff peak.
Why: whites beaten too long; ceramic or glass rather than metal bowl used; whites beaten too slowly; beating not done continuously, so whites separated when beating resumed; whites not used immediately.
What to do: for meringue and desserts, make light meringue by adding a tablespoonful of sugar for each egg white and beating until smooth and glossy, about 1 minute. See also Quick Fix.

OTHER PROBLEMS

POOR VOLUME
Why: beaten too slowly; whisk too small, whites very fresh.
What to do: see Too soft.

GREY OR GREENISH COLOUR (in copper bowl)
Why: bowl not properly cleaned; whites left too long in bowl.
What to do: discard, as whites are now toxic.

Mango and lime fool

The English dessert of 'fool', based on whipped cream, is ancient, dating back to the Renaissance. This tropical version is delicate and airy – perfect for a warm summer evening. Be sure to use very ripe mangoes.

1 kg/2 pounds mangoes
3 limes
1 tablespoon sugar, or more to taste
250 ml/8 fl oz double cream

Prepare the mangoes: cut a vertical slice about 6mm/ ¼ inch from either side of each mango stem, clearing the flat stone inside. Set each of these thick slices skin-side down and score the flesh in a lattice pattern, cutting through the flesh but not the skin. Holding the mango flesh upward, push the centre of the skin with your thumbs to turn it inside out, opening the cut flesh to reveal cubes. Cut the cubes from the skin. Trim the remaining flesh from the stone with a knife, discarding the skin.

Grate the zest from the limes. Halve the limes, cut 4-6 thin slices from one half, and reserve these for decoration. Squeeze the juice from the remaining lime halves. Purée the mango flesh with the lime zest and juice in a food processor, or work the mango through a sieve and stir in the zest and juice. Stir in sugar to taste.

Whip the cream until it holds a soft peak. Stir a little into the mango purée to lighten it. Add the purée to the remaining cream and fold together. Taste again, adjusting the amount of sugar and lime juice. Pile the mixture in stemmed glasses and chill for at least 2 hours or overnight – the flavour mellows on standing.

Just before serving, top each fool with a lime slice.

Hazelnut and pear soufflé

Toasted hazelnuts both add flavour and stabilize the juice in fruit, so this soufflé mixture holds well and doesn't lose volume when the egg whites are added.

75 g/2½ oz hazelnuts	*for the thick pastry cream*
1 ripe pear	*150 ml/5 fl oz milk*
½ lemon	*1 vanilla pod, split*
whites of 4 eggs	*2 egg yolks*
1½ tablespoons caster	*1½ tablespoons caster*
* sugar*	* sugar*
icing sugar	*2 tablespoons flour*
* (for sprinkling)*	
	1.25-litre/1¼-quart
	soufflé dish

Preheat the oven to 175°C/350°F/gas4. Brush the dish well with melted butter. Spread the nuts on a baking sheet and toast in the oven until lightly brown, 12-15 minutes, stirring once. Let cool slightly, then rub in a cloth to remove the skins. Grind in a processor (do not overwork or they will be oily). Increase oven to 220°C/425°F/gas7.

Make the thick pastry cream: scald milk with vanilla pod, cover and leave to infuse off the heat for 5-10 minutes. Meanwhile, beat egg yolks with sugar until thick and light. Stir in flour. Whisk milk into mixture and return to pan. Cook over low heat, whisking constantly, until cream comes to the boil and thickens. Simmer, stirring, for 1-2 minutes. Strain pastry cream into a bowl. The vanilla pod can be rinsed and used again. Let cream cool slightly and stir in hazelnuts.

Peel, quarter and core the pear. Rub with cut surface of the lemon and purée until smooth. Stir into hazelnut mixture.

Stiffly beat the egg whites, preferably in a copper bowl. Add the sugar and continue beating until the whites are glossy and hold a long peak, 30-60 seconds.

If necessary, heat hazelnut mixture until hot to the touch. Stir in about a quarter of egg whites. Add this to remaining egg whites and fold together as lightly as possible. Spoon mixture into prepared soufflé dish and smooth top. Run thumb around edge of dish so soufflé rises in a hat shape.

Bake in the preheated oven until the soufflé is puffed and brown, 15-18 minutes. It should be slightly soft in the centre. Sprinkle the soufflé with icing sugar, set the dish on a plate lined with a napkin, and serve at once.

Hazelnut and pear soufflé

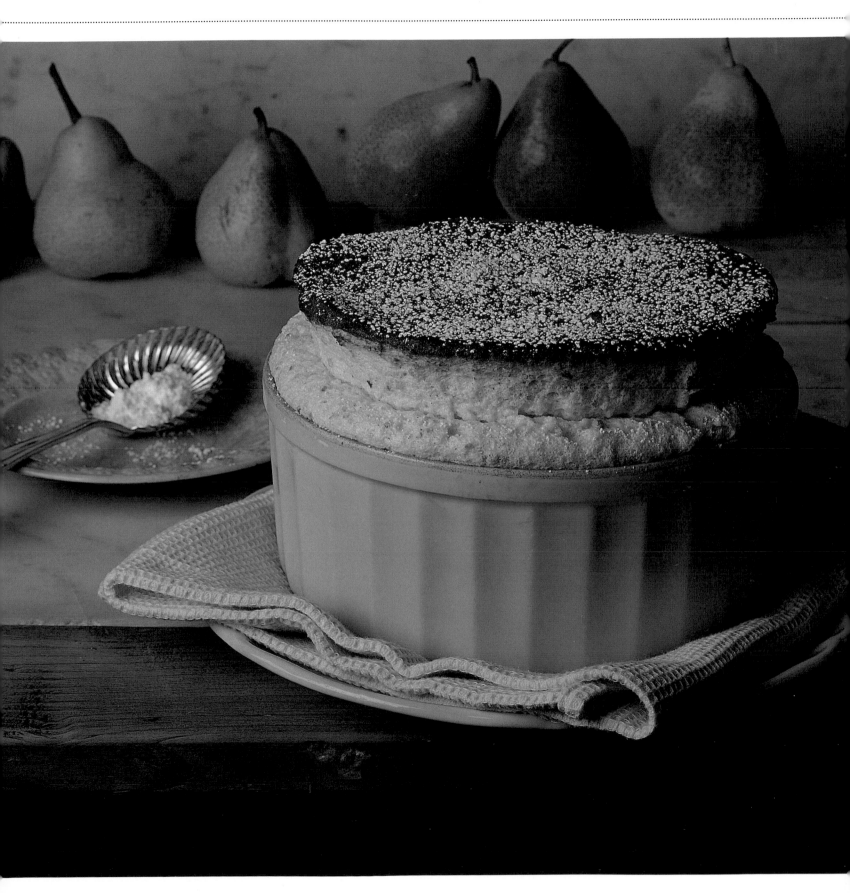

Meringue

THERE ARE THREE TYPES OF MERINGUE — simple, Italian and cooked — all of which are made with egg whites beaten with sugar. For a simple meringue, the only one made without heating the ingredients, the sugar is added to the beaten egg whites in two parts, first by beating thoroughly to dissolve the sugar and stabilize the whites, then by mixing more gently. This last stage used to be my downfall until I learned to stir until the meringue formed a long shiny peak, almost a ribbon. It should still, however, be stiff enough to pipe. Under- or overmixed meringue invariably weeps during baking, sticking, scorching and creating general havoc for the harried cook.

Once mixed, simple meringue should be cooked very slowly so it dries rather than bakes — traditional cooks like to leave it in a low oven overnight. To achieve the right crisp texture, at least 45 g/1½ oz of sugar is needed per egg white — with less, the meringue never becomes crisp, even after thorough baking. One hazard when working with meringue is humidity — a steamy kitchen or a damp day can seriously affect texture. Since even well-mixed meringue has a tendency to stick when baking, I suggest you use non-stick silicone paper or baking sheets, or give a regular baking sheet an even coating of butter and flour.

Liquid breaks down the structure of beaten egg whites, so flavourings for meringue are limited to powdered coffee, cocoa, dry spices or a few drops of vanilla essence. Even ingredients such as ground nuts, as in the classic *gâteau progrès*, soften the texture of meringue. One oddity is the dessert of *oeufs à la neige (*snow eggs), huge spoonfuls of simple meringue which are poached rather than baked, and served floating in a pool of egg custard — here too the meringue is soft rather than crisp.

Simple meringue is sometimes made with a smaller amount of sugar, 1-2 tablespoons per egg white. This yields a light meringue which is useful for combining with other ingredients, for example in a sweet soufflé or sponge cake batter. Light meringue is also piped as a topping for lemon and other fruit pies, but it does not hold up well after baking so must be served within an hour or two.

I've already confessed my shortcomings in making simple meringue. I feel much safer with Italian and cooked meringues, which in most recipes are interchangeable with simple meringue, though both are stiffer in texture. If stored in the refrigerator, they have the great advantage of holding up for several days before baking. Both Italian and cooked meringue bake and dry easily, to be smooth and dense but crisp. You'll find some recipes specify a relatively high temperature (150°C/300°F/gas2), so the meringue dries on the outside while the centre remains soft. Petits fours, for instance, are often based on cooked meringue. Italian meringue is sometimes used as cake frosting and acts as a handy sweetener for whipped cream and iced parfaits.

Italian meringue is made by whisking boiling hot sugar syrup, cooked to the hard-ball stage (120°C/248°F), into beaten egg whites. The process is easy with a heavy-duty electric mixer — make sure the whisk is turning fast when you pour in the hot syrup so it cannot coagulate on the bowl. For cooked meringue, egg whites and sugar are beaten together in a bowl over hot water until they froth and finally thicken to a firm white meringue. This process is foolproof but surprisingly hard work by hand, so I advise a hand-held electric mixer.

PERFECTLY BEATEN SIMPLE MERINGUE — meringue mixture stiff and glossy; holds a long trailing peak when whisk is lifted; no trace of separation at edges.

PERFECTLY BEATEN ITALIAN MERINGUE — very stiff and glossy with an almost glassy sheen; consistency tight, holding a sharp, very stiff peak.

Lemon meringues

OTHER PROBLEMS

UNEVEN, SUGARY TEXTURE
Why: coarse granulated sugar used; egg whites underbeaten; meringue underbeaten after sugar added.
What to do: see Quick Fix.

STICKY CENTRE
Why: meringue underbeaten after sugar added; underbaked; baked too quickly.
What to do: don't worry, many people prefer sticky meringues.

QUICK FIX

A few ideas for imperfect meringues:
• Crumble meringue to layer with fresh fruit and sour cream flavoured with vanilla essence.
• Crumble meringues, top with crushed strawberries and hide them under a blanket of Sabayon Sauce (page 134) flavoured with Grand Marnier and grated orange zest.
• Layer crushed meringues with ice cream as a moulded bombe.
• If meringues are too dark, hide colour by dusting with icing sugar or cocoa.

The very first meringues are attributed to François Pierre de la Varenne, the founder of French classical cooking and after whom I named La Varenne Cooking School. I've adjusted the recipe slightly as the original circa-1650 batter was thick enough to shape by hand and therefore very sweet.

200 g/6½ oz sugar
grated zest of 1 lemon
whites of 4 eggs

Preheat the oven to 110°C/225°F/gas¼ and line a baking sheet with non-stick baking paper.

Stiffly beat the egg whites, preferably in a copper bowl. Add 3 tablespoons of the sugar and continue beating until the whites are glossy, 1-2 minutes. Add the remaining sugar and beat 1-2 minutes until the meringue is perfectly beaten. Stir in the lemon zest.

Using 2 teaspoons, drop rounded spoonfuls of the mixture on the baking sheet, leaving room for them to spread slightly. Bake in the oven until the meringues are done, 1-1½ hours. Transfer them to a rack and let them cool completely. They will crisp as they cool.

WEEPING – meringue weeping syrupy liquid around edges; crust may be puffed and shattered; inside gluey and lacks lightness.
Why: egg whites under- or overbeaten (see Beaten Egg Whites); meringue under- or overbeaten after sugar added; too little sugar to stabilize whites; meringue underbaked; after storage, if surface of baked meringue moist, atmosphere too humid.
What to do: dry meringues in a very low oven, preferably several hours; store in an airtight container.

PERFECTLY BAKED – meringue white or very pale cream; evenly coloured on top and bottom; inside airy, crisp throughout, with no soft centre.

TOO DARK – surface of meringue colour of milky coffee, with scorched edges; inside paler, often with sticky centre.
Why: oven heat too high; baked too long.
What to do: trim any scorched parts and use in dishes where colour does not show. For individual meringues, drizzle surface with melted bittersweet chocolate, or dip small meringues in chocolate.

Orange, lemon and lime custards

SERVES 4-6

Classic *pots de crème* come in threes, flavoured variously with vanilla, coffee and chocolate. Here I'm suggesting a Californian touch of citrus. Two pots form a modest serving; with three, everyone tastes each flavour.

3 oranges	for the candied zest
4 lemons	150 g/5 oz sugar
4 limes	175 ml/6 fl oz water
1 litre/1⅔ pints milk	
12 egg yolks	12 individual mousse pots with lids, or small ramekins
150 g/5 oz sugar	

Preheat the oven to 175°C/350°F/gas4. For a water bath: line a roasting pan with a folded dish towel, add about 4 cm/1½ inches water and bring to the boil on the hob. Pare 2-3 wide pieces of zest from each type of fruit and slice into julienne strips. Grate the remaining zest into three separate bowls. Scald the milk.

Meanwhile, beat the egg yolks and sugar until thickened and light, 3-5 minutes. Whisk hot milk into the egg mixture, then divide mixture evenly into the three bowls of grated citrus zest. Leave to infuse 10-15 minutes.

Strain the custards into individual pots or ramekins – there should be four pots of each flavour. Set the pots in the water bath and cover with lids or a sheet of cardboard. Bring the water bath back to the boil on the hob and transfer to the preheated oven. Bake until the custard is done, 15-20 minutes. Remove the pots from the water bath and let them cool.

Meanwhile, candy the citrus julienne: blanch the julienne strips one fruit at a time in a small pot of boiling water for 2 minutes, then drain. In a separate pan, gently heat the sugar and water until the sugar dissolves to make a syrup. Pour off and reserve two-thirds of the syrup. Add one batch of blanched zest to the remaining syrup in the pan and simmer until all the water has evaporated and the zest is translucent, 8-10 minutes. Lift the zest out with a fork, spread on greaseproof paper and leave to cool. Repeat with the remaining syrup and zests.

Just before serving, top each pot or ramekin with a few strips of candied zest to identify the flavour. Serve the custards chilled.

Cherry batter pudding
Clafoutis limousin

SERVES 6

So as to extract the most flavour from the fruit, this pudding from central France is generally made without stoning the local tart black cherries. To safeguard everyone's teeth, however, I usually do remove the stones with a cherry or olive stoner or the point of a vegetable peeler. You can substitute other seasonal fruits, such as apples, apricots, plums and prunes.

500 g/1 pound tart cherries	60 ml/2 fl oz Cognac or
30 g/1 oz flour	3 tablespoons kirsch
60 g/2 oz granulated sugar	icing sugar for sprinkling
pinch of salt	
4 eggs	1.5-litre/1½-quart shallow baking dish
250 ml/8 fl oz milk	

Preheat the oven to 175°C/350°F/gas4. Butter the baking dish and sprinkle it with granulated sugar. Stone the cherries if you prefer. Spread the cherries in the dish.

Make the batter: sift the flour, sugar and salt into a bowl and make a well in the centre. Add the eggs to the well and stir with a whisk until mixed. Stir in half the milk, then continue stirring to draw in the flour and make a smooth mixture. Stir in the remaining milk to make a smooth batter.

Pour the batter over the cherries and bake in the preheated oven until the clafoutis is done, 35-45 minutes. Sprinkle the Cognac or kirsch over the hot pudding and serve hot or warm. The clafoutis will sink slightly as it cools. Sprinkle with icing sugar just before serving.

Cherry batter pudding

Bread puddings

IN A WELL-RUN KITCHEN, STALE BREAD DOES NOT GO TO WASTE – hence the dozens of versions of bread pudding, most based on a sweetened custard of eggs and milk. A pudding is only as good as the bread you use to make it. Firm-textured breads are best, preferably a day or two old, so if the bread is moist, let it dry out in a low oven. Some cooks like to bake bread pudding in a water bath, but I find the brown crust – which is one of its attributes – to be less crisp. You can enrich bread pudding with ground almonds or coconut, or you can butter the bread, or layer the bread with dried fruits (don't sprinkle them on top as they will scorch). Many recipes add a wine such as port or Marsala. That's basically it – a quick family dessert which has recently hit the bistro circuit.

OVERCOOKED – texture dry and chewy; top often very brown and dry.
Why: baked too long; heat too high; too little custard; bread very dry.
What to do: moisten with milk and warm gently 5-10 minutes; serve with ice cream or vanilla custard or warm fruit sauce (see pages 132 and 137).

PERFECT – pudding lightly set, golden brown especially around edges of bread; holds shape of spoon when scooped, but is not heavy; flavour mellow, lightly perfumed; colour creamy not grey.

OTHER PROBLEMS

SOGGY AND BLAND
Why: baking time too short; oven temperature too low; bread too fresh or too soft.
What to do: if custard not set, continue cooking; if custard set, sprinkle surface of pudding with sugar and grill until caramelized. Serve with honey or tart fruit coulis.

QUICK FIX

To enliven bread pudding, make rum or brandy butter. Cream 90 g/3 oz of unsalted butter. Then add 75 g/2½ oz sugar and beat until very soft and light, 2-3 minutes. Gradually beat in 3 tablespoons of rum or brandy. If the sauce separates, set the bowl over warm water and beat again until smooth. Beat in the grated zest of 1 lemon. Chill the sauce in the freezer until firm. Scoop it into balls for serving. Makes 175 g/6 oz to serve 4-6 people.

Panettone bread pudding

I first had this delicious pudding, made with rich, fruit-studded panettone, at one of London's finest Italian restaurants. When I tried it myself, to follow the Italian theme I added some grappa, a pungent eau-de-vie – Cognac is an alternative. Serve the pudding with chilled double cream if you like.

500 g/1 pound panettone
3-4 tablespoons butter
500 ml/16 fl oz double
  cream
125 ml/4 fl oz milk
75 ml/2½ fl oz grappa

4 eggs, lightly beaten
2 tablespoons sugar
pinch of salt

2-litre/3¼ pint soufflé dish

Preheat the oven to 160°C/325°F/gas3. Generously butter the soufflé dish. Cut the panettone into quarters lengthwise, then cut each quarter across in 2.5-cm/1-inch fan-shaped slices. Spread one side of each slice with butter. Line the bottom and sides of the soufflé dish with the panettone, buttered side inwards. Arrange the remaining slices in layers in the centre of the dish.

In a medium bowl, whisk the cream, milk, grappa, eggs, sugar and salt until foamy. Pour this mixture over the panettone. Press the slices down so they are submerged and let stand for 10 minutes so the bread soaks up the liquid. Cover the dish loosely with foil and bake in the preheated oven for 30 minutes. Uncover and continue baking until done, 30-40 minutes more. Serve warm.

Rice and grain puddings

RICE AND GRAIN PUDDINGS CAN BE SIMMERED ON THE HOB, or baked very slowly in the oven. They will absorb four or five times their own volume of liquid (usually milk) while still remaining whole and plump. The amount of liquid absorbed depends very much on the type of grain. Round-grain rice, for instance, absorbs more liquid than long-grain varieties, at the same time yielding starch which thickens the cooking liquid to a rich cream. Sugar is normally added only near the end of cooking as it scorches easily. Grain puddings need more stirring on the hob than in the oven so, to avoid extra work, I usually bake rather than simmer them. If left uncovered in the oven without stirring at all, puddings with milk bake to an attractive brown crust.

The same principle of simmering or baking in the oven holds good for puddings made with cracked or rolled grains such as oatmeal. The mixture may be savoury (see Pasta, Grains and Pulses) as well as sweet, and served hot or cold like the Indian Creamed Rice (see opposite). Remember a grain pudding will thicken considerably as it stands and cools.

QUICK FIX

If rice or a grain pudding is heavy or bland, top it with a thick layer of dark brown sugar and grill it until melted and caramelized.

UNDERCOOKED AND THIN – pudding watery, lacking richness; often grain is still chewy; flavour not yet developed.
Why: time too short; heat too low; wrong grain.
What to do: continue cooking, raising heat if necessary; just before serving, stir whisked egg yolks or whole egg into hot pudding.

PERFECT – liquid absorbed and grain creamy, falling easily from the spoon in a lightly thickened sauce; if baked, top forms a deep golden skin; when tasted, grains are very soft; flavour full-bodied and fragrant.

OVERCOOKED AND HEAVY – pudding is sticky, scarcely falling from spoon; rice grains have burst and fallen apart; if baked, pudding looks shrivelled; when tasted, pudding is pasty, flavour faded.
Why: cooked too long; too little liquid; stirred too much, especially at end of cooking.
What to do: if grains still intact, stir in more liquid and reheat gently. If grains disintegrating, serve pudding with double cream, whipped cream or custard sauce. When cold, heavy rice pudding makes delicious fried cakes, see Quick Fix for Pilafs, page 190.

OTHER PROBLEMS

CURDLES IF USING MILK
Why: acid ingredients such as lemon or molasses included; heat too high; milk stale.
What to do: stir in 1-2 tablespoons cornflour mixed to a paste with 4-5 tablespoons milk or water and simmer until thickened.

BLAND
Why: too little flavouring; not enough sugar.
What to do: add sugar or honey to taste with vanilla and flavourings such as grated lemon or orange zest, ground cinnamon, nutmeg or allspice.

SCORCHED
Why: pudding not stirred often, especially towards the end of cooking; heat too high. Note: milk and sugar burn easily.
What to do: transfer pudding to another pan without disturbing scorched layer on the base; add full-bodied flavourings such as dried raisins or apricots, grated lemon zest, ground cloves, cinnamon or allspice or herbs such as mint. If very scorched, nothing can be done.

Indian creamed rice

Kheer

SERVES 6

Not to be confused with rustic rice puddings, *kheer* is a dessert deemed worthy of royal banquets and newlywed brides. *Vark*, silver or gold leaf, is available at Indian speciality shops and adds the appropriate touch of ceremony.

1.5 litres/2⅓ pints milk, or more if needed
75 g/2½ oz short-grain rice
4 cardamom pods, crushed
2.5-cm/1-inch piece of cinnamon stick
2 whole cloves
75 g/2½ oz sugar
45 g/1½ oz sultanas
2 tablespoons rose water
60 g/2 oz sliced almonds, toasted
45 g/1½ oz blanched pistachios, chopped
silver leaf (optional)

muslin

In a large saucepan, bring the milk to the boil. Stir the rice into the milk. Cook, uncovered, over low heat, stirring often, 15 minutes.

Tie the cardamom, cinnamon and cloves in a piece of muslin and add to rice. Continue simmering, uncovered, stirring occasionally for 1 hour. Add the sugar and raisins and continue cooking until the raisins are plump and the rice is done, 45-60 minutes.

Remove the rice from the heat and discard the bag of spices. Stir in the rose water together with three-quarters of the almonds and taste, adding more sugar if you like. Transfer to a bowl, cover and chill, at least 12 hours or overnight. The flavour will improve and the pudding will thicken on standing.

To serve: if the pudding is thick, stir in a little milk. Spoon it into individual dishes and sprinkle with the reserved almonds, chopped pistachios and silver leaf, if using.

Steamed puddings

ANYONE BROUGHT UP IN ENGLAND, as I was, has surely enjoyed a moist steamed pudding redolent with spices and topped with golden syrup or honey. Variants often feature chocolate, dried and candied fruits. In Ireland, steamed pudding is laced with Guinness and in the USA steamed carrot pudding dates from pioneering days. Batter for steamed puddings ranges from pound cake to gingerbread and age-old mixtures based on breadcrumbs and suet. During steaming, the pudding must be covered with paper and a cloth so humidity does not dilute the batter. For serving, be sure to include a topping of honey, golden syrup, custard, chocolate sauce or brandy butter. Steamed puddings reheat well and the most famous of all, Christmas pudding, is cooked twice: the first time so its dried fruits and nuts can be left to mature, the second time to reheat it before it goes, flaming in triumph, to the table.

PERFECT – centre firm when pressed with a fingertip and a skewer inserted in centre comes out clean; pudding well risen in mould; when cut, texture is even and light; flavour warm.

QUICK FIX

When steamed pudding is heavy or undercooked, add a caramel topping: preheat the grill. Cut the pudding into 2-cm/¾-inch slices and set them on a buttered baking sheet. Sprinkle generously with granulated or brown sugar, spreading it evenly to the edge of the pudding. Grill until lightly caramelized, 3-5 minutes.

PROBLEMS

UNDERCOOKED AND SOGGY
Why: cooking time too short; water for steaming not boiling; water leaked into pudding.
Note that a large or rich pudding such as a Christmas pudding can take several hours.
What to do: if undercooked, continue steaming, raising heat if necessary; if water leaked, drain off as much as possible with paper towels; serve with a tart fruit sauce (see page 137); see also Quick Fix.

HEAVY
Why: too few eggs or raising agent; batter poorly mixed; undercooked.
What to do: cut into thin slices or wedges and moisten with plenty of topping or sauce; see also Quick Fix.

OVERCOOKED AND DRY
Why: batter too dry; cooked too long; water evaporated so steam was not constant.
What to do: before unmoulding, moisten with orange or apple juice, piercing pudding with a skewer so juice penetrates; serve with brandy butter (see Quick Fix on page 232).

Caramel

CARAMEL IS SIMPLY TOASTED SUGAR — the tricky part is toasting it just right. For some purposes caramel should be light — for coating fruits for instance, or shaping those intriguing latticed cages to cover a dessert plate (the melted caramel is trailed over an oiled ladle, left to cool and set, then detached in one piece). When caramel is used as flavouring for a sauce or to line moulds for crème caramel, it should be darker. Just how dark is a matter of taste — personally I like caramel well done, almost piquant, but I don't have a sweet tooth. Many people like it paler, the colour of golden honey.

Caramel is usually made by boiling sugar syrup, though it is also possible to melt and then cook dry caster sugar (see the Italian Iced Praline Mousse, overleaf). When boiling syrup, the danger is crystallization. Be sure the sugar dissolves completely before the syrup reaches the boil; do not stir during boiling and do not let any crystals dry on the side of the pan and fall back into the syrup. A spoonful of glucose or honey, a squeeze of lemon juice or a pinch of cream of tartar will deter the formation of crystals.

Cook the syrup at a steady rolling boil — take good care throughout the cooking process as the temperature of boiled sugar rises to 165-175°C/330-350°F when it caramelizes and it can cause serious burns. As the water evaporates, bubbles in the syrup will break more slowly until it starts to colour. Then it caramelizes rapidly, so turn the heat down a bit. Swirl the pan from time to time, so the syrup colours evenly and take it from the heat shortly before it reaches the right shade. Remember caramel burns quickly and irremediably and it will keep cooking in the heat of the pan. To stop it cooking, at once plunge the base of the pan in cold water, or if making a sauce add the liquid. For crisp caramel, pour it on an oiled baking sheet where it will set to a glassy sheet. For a contemporary decoration, break the sheet into slivers and stick them in your dessert. Use caramel at once — it cannot be stored as it quickly softens in the air.

QUICK FIX

When a sugar syrup starts to crystallize before it caramelizes, add a tablespoon of honey and swirl pan to mix. If still crystalline, take pan from heat and let cool slightly. Stir in a little water until crystals dissolve, then continue boiling without stirring. If crystals have formed a solid mass, start again with fresh sugar.

OTHER PROBLEMS

TOO PALE
Why: cooking time too short.
What to do: bring back to boil without stirring and cook until done.

SYRUP CRYSTALLIZED
Why: sugar not dissolved before syrup boiled; syrup stirred during boiling; sugar crystals formed on pan side and fell into syrup.
What to do: see Quick Fix.

CARAMEL SETS
Why: caramel cools too quickly before use.
What to do: if set, warm over low heat until melted; to keep warm and liquid, immerse base of pan in warm water.

CARAMEL STICKY ON STANDING
Why: absorbed water or humidity in air.
What to do: nothing can be done, so use as soon as possible.

PERFECT LIGHT – syrup well-coloured, showing pale golden when base of pan is tilted; sugar thermometer registers about 160°C/320°F.

PERFECT DARK – syrup dark, showing chestnut brown on base of pan; starting to smoke; sugar thermometer registers 165-175°C/330-350°F.

BURNED – syrup black, with thick, acrid smoke.
Why: cooked too long; pan too hot, so caramel continued cooking off the heat.
What to do: nothing can be done, so start again.

Praline

COOKING SUGAR

When sugar syrup is boiled, water evaporates until the syrup reaches its saturation point and the temperature starts to rise. The higher the temperature the more concentrated the syrup and the less moisture it contains; therefore the harder it will set when cooled. Stages are tested either with a sugar thermometer or by hand, and even a degree or two of temperature can make the difference between a sugar syrup that is malleable when set and can be used to make a light smooth butter cream, for example, and one that is too stiff to use.

Dip the tip of a teaspoon into the syrup to take a small ball, then dip this straight into a bowl of iced water. Knead the ball between your thumb and forefinger:

• If when you pull finger and thumb apart the ball forms a fine thread, this is the 'thread stage' (110°C/230°F) used for making fruit paste and sweets.

• If it forms a soft ball, this is the 'soft ball' stage (115°C/239°) used for fondant, buttercream and fudge.

• If it forms a firm pliable ball, this is known as 'hard-ball' stage (120°C/248°F) used for Italian meringue (see page 226) and almond paste.

• If it is brittle but sticks to the teeth, this is called 'soft-crack' stage (125°C/257°F) and is used for soft nougat, some caramels and taffy.

• If it is very brittle and does not stick to the teeth this is the 'hard-crack' stage (146°C/295°F) used for pulled and spun sugar, glazed fruits and sweets.

Caramel (opposite) is the final stage, when the sugar changes rapidly from translucent golden to deep brown. It is too hot to judge by hand.

PRALINE IS ONE OF THOSE HAPPY EXAMPLES of two ingredients adding up to more than the sum of their parts. It is made of equal weights of nuts (usually unblanched almonds) and sugar cooked to a caramel. The caramel may be made by boiling sugar syrup (see Caramel, opposite), or by cooking dry sugar as in the Italian Iced Praline Mousse recipe overleaf. Either way, the caramel should be well browned and the nuts must be toasted to develop their flavour.

Once cooled and hard, praline is crushed for sprinkling or for using as a flavouring, often in pastry cream, buttercream or ice cream. I like to leave it coarse for crunch, but you can also grind it finely in a processor or blender. Either way, the caramel in praline dissolves quickly when added to a liquid – this is why it softens custards and creams, particularly whipped cream, when left to stand. Even when stored in an airtight container, praline reduces to a sticky paste but this does not affect its flavouring qualities.

PERFECT – syrup evenly cooked to dark caramel; almonds pop in heat of caramel, showing they are well toasted; if an almond is removed and cut, it is brown and toasted inside.

PROBLEMS

FLAVOUR BITTER
Why: cooked too long; cooked too fast, so sugar scorched before nuts toasted.
What to do: nothing can be done.

FLAVOUR FLAT
Why: praline undercooked; caramel browned but nuts not toasted; ground praline is stale.
What to do: see Quick Fix.

QUICK FIX

If a praline-flavoured mixture lacks flavour, the best approach is to boost the taste of almond. Add Amaretto liqueur or just a few drops of almond essence (which is very concentrated).

Italian iced praline mousse
Semifreddo al croccante
SERVES 8

The high cream and sugar content of this confection prevents really hard freezing, thus giving the sensation of it being *semifreddo*, or 'half frozen'. If you prefer, the praline can be made with sugar syrup rather than dry sugar – dissolve the sugar in 3 tablespoons/45 ml/1½ fl oz water, boil to caramel, then stir in and toast the almonds.

500 ml/16 fl oz double cream	for the praline
200 g/6½ oz sugar	100 g/3¼ oz sugar
whites of 6 eggs	100 g/3¼ oz whole unblanched almonds

2-litre/3⅓ pint bombe mould

Oil a baking sheet or marble surface. For the praline: heat the sugar and almonds in a small heavy-based frying pan over medium heat. When the sugar starts to melt, stir very gently with a wooden spatula until it is liquid – it will start to caramelize at once. Continue cooking, stirring gently, until the sugar is quite dark and the nuts make a popping sound, showing they are toasted. Note: do not stir briskly or the caramel may crystallize.

Remove the pan from the heat and pour the praline mixture on the prepared baking sheet or marble surface. Spread it out and leave it to cool until quite crisp. Crack the praline in pieces and coarsely grind it in a food processor. Note: do not overwork, or the oil in the almonds will make the praline heavy.

Make the *semifreddo*: whip the cream until it holds a soft peak. Add three-quarters of the sugar and continue beating until the cream holds a stiff peak. Fold in the ground praline. Stiffly beat the egg whites, preferably in a copper bowl. Add the remaining sugar to the egg whites and beat until glossy, 30-60 seconds more. Fold the egg whites into the praline mixture. Spoon the mixture into the mould, smooth the surface and freeze until firm, at least 6 hours.

To unmould: dip the frozen mould in cool water for 10-20 seconds. Lift it out, wipe dry and run the point of a knife around the edge of the mixture. Set a chilled serving platter on top and turn the mould and platter over together to unmould the *semifreddo* on the platter. Cut the semifreddo in wedges and serve at once.

Salty caramel sauce with peaches and ice cream
SERVES 4

It was a renowned Burgundian chef who first thought of adding salted butter to caramel sauce, giving it a subtle, piquant edge. Delicious hot or cold, you can keep this sauce on hand in the refrigerator. Pull it out at the last minute as a cold dip for grilled peaches, oranges or strawberries, or serve it hot with ice cream or pound cake.

6 whole peaches
3 tablespoons dark brown sugar
3 tablespoons butter
vanilla ice cream (for serving)

for salty caramel sauce
200 g/6½ oz sugar
125 ml/4 fl oz water
250 ml/8 fl oz double cream
60 g/2 oz salted butter

Preheat the grill. Halve the peaches, discarding stones, and set them cut sides up in a buttered baking dish. Sprinkle them with brown sugar and dot with the butter. Grill about 7.5 cm/3 inches from the heat until the peaches are tender and starting to brown, 7-10 minutes.

Meanwhile make a dark caramel syrup: in a heavy-based saucepan, heat the sugar and water, stirring only once or twice, until the sugar is dissolved. Boil rapidly without stirring until the syrup begins to brown around the edge of the pan. Continue cooking over medium heat until done, 1-2 minutes, swirling the pan occasionally so the syrup colours evenly. Once it starts to brown, it colours quickly.

When the caramel is dark, remove the pan from the heat and let the bubbles subside. Add the butter, stir until smooth and then pour in the cream. Note: stand well back, as the caramel will sputter and foam when butter and cream are added.

To serve: transfer hot peaches to individual plates and spoon over any juice. Add a scoop of vanilla ice cream. If necessary, reheat the sauce, stirring, until the caramel is completely dissolved and the sauce is hot. Spoon it over the peaches and serve at once.

Salty caramel sauce with peaches and ice cream

Ganache

GANACHE IS MADE BY MELTING CHOPPED CHOCOLATE WITH CREAM, either by pouring boiling cream over the chocolate, or by heating chopped chocolate with the cream. It's as simple as that. Flavour depends on the quality of the chocolate you use and I'd strongly recommend investing in the very best dark chocolate – the cost is justifiable as ganache is so rich you'll be using it in small quantities. The consistency of ganache depends on the proportions of cream to chocolate – for truffles and other firm confectionery, allow 125 ml/4 fl oz double cream per 250 g/½ pound of chocolate. More is needed for a ganache which is soft enough to spread as filling or frosting. One word of caution: with too little cream (less than 1½ teaspoons per 30 g/1 ounce of chocolate), ganache can seize and suddenly stiffen (see Melting Chocolate, page 139), so be sure your recipe has adequate liquid. Ganache can be used quite plain, or flavoured with the classic chocolate partners of rum, Cognac, orange, coffee or praline. I've come across it with cinnamon, cloves and rose water, too. It's very adaptable.

PERFECT FOR FROSTING AND PIPING – glossy and very smooth; stiff enough to hold a firm shape when piped, but still easy to spread; flavour mellow and rich; colour varies with type of chocolate.

PERFECT FOR SHAPING – dark, pliable and stiff enough to hold a moulded shape; flavour dense.

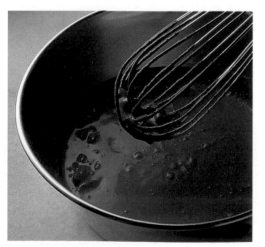

PROBLEMS

HEAVY OR GRANULAR
Why: chocolate not completely dissolved; too little cream so ganache 'seized'.
What to do: if seized, beat in a few spoonfuls of cream; to distract from granular texture add chopped nuts.

left
LUMPY – when cool, ganache is still liquid, with lumps at bottom.
Why: cream was not hot enough to melt chocolate smoothly.
What to do: warm bowl of ganache over hot water, then stir until smooth, leave to cool and set.

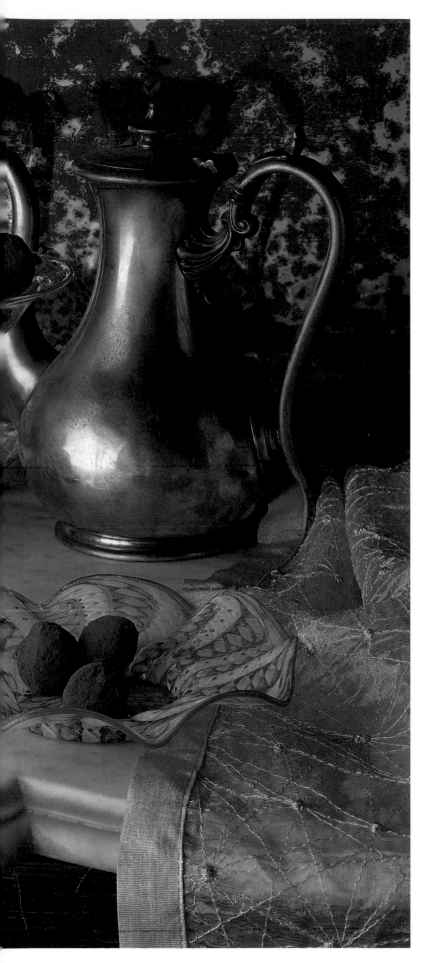

Pecan truffles

MAKES ABOUT 50 TRUFFLES

A chocolate truffle should be the ultimate rich mouthful, intense but not too sweet. Here, I've added a few chopped pecans to the ganache and then rolled the truffles in cocoa powder for a slightly bitter finish.

for the ganache
45 g/1½ oz pecans
125 ml/4 fl oz double cream
175 g/6 oz best dark chocolate,
    finely chopped
1 tablespoon butter, softened

for the coating
250 g/½ pound plain chocolate,
    finely chopped
90 g/3 oz unsweetened cocoa
    powder, or more if needed

Preheat the oven to 175°C/350°F/gas4. Spread the nuts on a baking sheet, and toast in the preheated oven until lightly brown, 12-15 minutes, stirring once. Let cool slightly and then chop the nuts with a large knife or in a food processor, taking care not to overwork or they will be oily.

Make the ganache: bring the cream just to the boil and pour it over the dark chocolate in a bowl. Leave to melt 2-3 minutes, then stir until smooth, if necessary warming for a few seconds over low heat. Chill without stirring until the ganache is cool but still soft, 8-12 minutes. Gently stir in the pecans and butter. Note: do not beat or the mixture will separate. Cover and chill until firm, 30-60 minutes.

Divide the ganache into 4 equal parts. Lightly dust a work surface with cocoa powder and roll the ganache into 15-cm/6-inch logs about 1.25 cm/½ inch in diameter. Set the logs on a baking sheet lined with greaseproof paper. Chill until firm, 1-2 hours.

To coat and finish the truffles: melt the plain chocolate in a bowl over a pan of hot but not boiling water. Spread the cocoa in a shallow tray. Cut the logs into bite-size pieces. Dip the palms of your hands in cocoa and roll the ganache pieces into balls. With two forks, dip the balls in the melted chocolate, drain off excess and roll them in cocoa. Transfer to a tray lined with greaseproof paper and sprinkle with more cocoa. Chill the truffles until firm, 1-2 hours. Store in a cool place in an airtight container, layered with greaseproof paper.

QUICK FIX

If ganache is bland, beat in a few teaspoons of rum, Cognac or grated orange zest with sugar to taste, taking care not to soften texture with too much liquid. If ganache seems bitter, add a generous spoonful of two of ground cinnamon. If bland ganache has already been rolled into shapes, add cinnamon to the sugar or powdered cocoa used for coating.

Chocolate mousse

ONE OF THE FIRST DESSERTS I EVER MADE AS A CHILD was chocolate mousse. It had two ingredients, melted chocolate and beaten egg whites – even without any flavouring it tasted pretty good. That's the joy of chocolate mousse and other fluffy chocolate desserts lightened with egg white – no matter what you do to them they remain edible, often delicious. You can angle them towards your audience, using milk chocolate for children or almond chocolate for lovers of nuts. My adult taste now inclines to dark chocolate enriched with cream and sharpened with rum or coffee. As well as a dessert, chocolate mousse is a lighter alternative to ganache as a filling for cakes and layered desserts, for instance of meringue. (See pages 248-9 for mousses set with gelatine.)

PERFECT – texture smooth, fluffy and rich, set but not sticky; colour a glossy brown; flavour mellow.

SEPARATED – texture granular and solid, speckled with egg white; on standing, liquid may separate to bottom of mousse; colour lacks gloss.
Why: egg whites or cream added when chocolate too hot; mixture overfolded; stored too long – after a few hours some mixtures may separate slightly but remain light.
What to do: sprinkle mousse with a crispy topping of chopped walnuts, browned almonds or crushed macaroons; for lightness, serve with whipped cream or Mint Custard Sauce (page 132).

QUICK FIX

When chocolate mousse does not set, or you are pressed for time, treat it as a rich chocolate sauce:
• Spoon it over vanilla ice cream.
• Layer it with fresh orange segments or chunks of pear in stemmed glasses and top with candied orange zest or a mint sprig.
• Serve it as a dipping sauce for strawberries.
• Make a Swiss Roll (page 282) and use the chocolate mousse as the filling.

OTHER PROBLEMS

DOES NOT SET
Why: chocolate melted with too much liquid; egg whites or cream added when chocolate too hot; not chilled long enough.
What to do: freeze mixture as a chocolate parfait. See also Quick Fix.

Chocolate mousse with raspberries

SERVES 4

Chocolate mousse can be cloyingly sweet, so I like to add a surprise layer of tart fresh raspberries. For best results, use the finest dark chocolate and leave the mousse to mellow at least 6 hours before serving.

250 g/8 oz raspberries
175 g/6 oz best dark chocolate, chopped
125 ml/4 fl oz water
3 eggs, separated
1 tablespoon raspberry liqueur or Cognac
3 tablespoons sugar

for the Chantilly cream
125 ml/4 fl oz double cream
1 tablespoon sugar
2 teaspoons raspberry liqueur or Cognac

four 125-ml/4-fl oz mousse pots or ramekins; pastry bag with medium star tube

Pick over the raspberries, rinsing only if they are sandy. Reserve 4 berries for decoration.

Heat the chocolate with the water, stirring until melted. Simmer until slightly thickened, but still falls easily from the spoon, 1-2 minutes. Take from heat and let cool 1-2 minutes. Beat the egg yolks into chocolate, one by one, so they cook and thicken slightly. Beat in liqueur or Cognac.

Stiffly beat the egg whites. Add the sugar and continue beating until the whites are glossy, about 30 seconds. Fold the egg whites into the warm chocolate mixture.

Pour half of the mousse mixture into pots or ramekins. Spread the raspberries in a layer on top of the mousse and cover with the remaining mousse. Chill until set, at least 2 hours.

Shortly before serving, make the Chantilly cream: whip cream until it holds a soft peak. Add sugar and liqueur or Cognac and continue whipping until stiff enough to pipe. Transfer cream to pastry bag fitted with star tube. Pipe one large rosette of cream on top of each mousse and top with a raspberry. Serve chilled.

Chocolate terrines

By DEFINITION, A CHOCOLATE TERRINE IS FIRM ENOUGH TO SLICE; by common accord it is also the richest, densest, lushest dessert you will ever encounter. Most often a terrine is based on dark chocolate, but layers of milk or white chocolate may be added. The mixture is set with butter or eggs, and nuts may be included, particularly chestnut purée. Mixing poses few problems, provided you respect the rules for melting chocolate (page 139). While I think of chocolate mousse as a family dessert, a chocolate terrine invites opulent decorations, such as chocolate curls, chocolate leaves, a spray of sugared redcurrants, a fan of pear poached in wine – possibly all at once. To contrast the richness, a sauce is mandatory, whether a coffee, pistachio or mint custard, an orange and Grand Marnier cream, or novelties such as the red wine sauce with prunes that I came across at an English country inn.

PERFECT – smooth, rich texture, melting in the mouth rather than heavy; dense enough to slice; colour varies with chocolate used; taste of chocolate intense with undertones of flavouring such as liqueur or citrus zest.

GRANULAR – texture coarse, slightly gritty; terrine may be heavy and solid, or moist and scarcely holding shape if eggs used; colour matt; flavour cloying.
Why: chocolate incompletely dissolved or melted; chocolate seized (see Melting Chocolate, page 139); eggs added when chocolate too hot.
What to do: disguise texture by sprinkling with chopped browned almonds, pistachios or crushed praline (page 239).

QUICK FIX

If a terrine crumbles, make truffles: cut into rough chunks. Dip the palms of your hands in icing sugar or cocoa and roll chunks into rough balls. Drop into chopped browned almonds or walnuts and toss with forks until coated. Transfer to a baking sheet and chill.

When a terrine is too soft to slice, scoop on crisp cookies and set on individual plates. Top with whipped cream and set another cookie flat on top to make a sandwich.

OTHER PROBLEMS

NOT FIRM ENOUGH TO SLICE
Why: too many liquid ingredients, not enough chocolate or butter; terrine not thoroughly chilled.
What to do: transfer terrine to freezer; when firm, slice it, arrange on plates and let thaw before serving. See also Quick Fix.

Chocolate caramel terrine

SERVES 8-10

In an odd way, caramel complements the richness of chocolate despite the added sugar – be sure the caramel is dark so the flavour has a hint of bitterness.

250 g/8 oz sugar
125 ml/4 fl oz water
250 ml/8 fl oz double cream
500 g/1 pound dark chocolate, chopped
250 g/½ pound butter, softened

for the coffee cream sauce
500 ml/16 fl oz double cream
2-3 tablespoons dry instant coffee, or more to taste
1-2 tablespoons sugar, or more to taste
2 tablespoons Kahlúa or Cognac

1-litre/1⅔-pint terrine mould or loaf pan

Line the mould or loaf pan with cling film. Put the chopped chocolate in a bowl.

Make a dark caramel syrup: in a heavy-based pan, heat the sugar and water, stirring once or twice, until sugar is dissolved. Boil rapidly without stirring, until syrup begins to brown around edge of pan. Continue cooking over medium heat, swirling pan occasionally so syrup colours evenly. When caramel is dark, remove pan from heat and let the bubbles subside. Pour in the cream. Note: stand well back as the caramel will sputter and foam when cream is added. Reheat sauce, stirring, until caramel is completely dissolved.

Make caramel ganache: pour the hot caramel cream sauce over chopped chocolate and leave to melt, 2-3 minutes. Cream butter in a bowl. Stir the ganache until smooth, then place bowl in a bath of ice water and stir constantly until ganache is cooled and thickened, 5-8 minutes. Beat creamed butter into the cool chocolate caramel mixture, a little at a time. Note: if the mixture is too warm, the butter will melt to oil. Pour the chocolate mixture into the lined mould and chill until firm, at least 4 hours. The terrine will keep for up to a week and its flavour matures.

Make the coffee cream sauce: heat about a quarter of the cream with the coffee and sugar, stirring until dissolved. Stir into the remaining cream with the Kahlúa or Cognac. Add more coffee and sugar to your taste and chill.

To serve: turn the terrine out on a board and remove the cling film. Cut very thin slices using a knife dipped in very hot water. Lay the slices on individual plates and spoon the sauce around the edge.

Moulded jellies

SCHOOL LUNCHES HAVE BROUGHT A BAD REPUTATION to moulded jellies, but they have possibilities far beyond the familiar cube of rubber in luminous colours. It's easy to start from scratch yourself by setting fresh fruit juice or puréed poached fruit with unflavoured gelatine, laced if you like with wine or liqueur. Be sure to check the flavour before the jelly starts to set. Winter brews of eggnog can be moulded with or without a layer of fruit, and one Chinese dessert calls for litchis and loquats to be set in almond milk. The way to use gelatine is standard (see Using Gelatine, opposite) and, in general, it will set just about anything. However, watch out for an enzyme found in certain raw fruits such as fig, pineapple and kiwi which destroys the setting properties of gelatine, with disastrous results.

TOO SOFT moulded jelly trembles easily when shaken, even in the mould; when turned out, jelly splits and collapses.
Why: too little gelatine; fresh fruits added which inhibited action of gelatine; mould left too long in a warm room; mould overchilled so jelly froze and separated when thawed.
What to do: chill moulded jelly until just before serving. If too soft to unmould, chop it coarsely and serve in bowls, topped with candied citrus zest or mint sprigs.

PERFECT – jelly firm enough to hold a stiff shape when pulled from side of mould with fingers after chilling; when unmoulded, jelly trembles if shaken but remains firm enough to cut, melting quickly on the tongue; colour vivid; flavour refreshing.

PERFECT *right*
TOO STIFF *left* – moulded jelly holds a stiff, straight shape which does not move when shaken; when cut, texture is rubbery, chewy on the tongue.
Why: stored too long in refrigerator; too much gelatine.
What to do: let moulded jelly warm to room temperature, up to 1 hour; if still stiff, not much can be done. See Quick Fix.

OTHER PROBLEMS

TEXTURE UNEVEN, WITH CHEWY STRINGS
Why: gelatine not fully softened before melting; gelatine overcooked to strings during melting; melted gelatine added to cold mixture, setting before it could be smoothly combined.
What to do: if strings form before mixture sets, strain them out and continue; if moulded jelly contains strings, see Quick Fix.

TASTES OF GELATINE
Why: gelatine incorrectly melted, usually overheated; basic mixture bland; too much gelatine.
What to do: if mixture not yet set, add a few tablespoons of vivid flavouring such as lemon or lime juice, rum, Grand Marnier or other liqueur; if set, serve with robust sauce such as a fruit coulis.

QUICK FIX

When a jelly is stiff or has strings when unmoulded, transfer it to a large sheet of wet greaseproof paper. Using a wet knife so the jelly does not stick, very coarsely chop it. For 1 litre/1⅔ pints chopped jelly whip 250 ml/8 fl oz of double cream until it forms a soft peak (see page 222). Fold the chopped jelly into the cream and spoon into parfait glasses. Chill thoroughly. Serves 4-6.

Red wine and berry terrine

When sliced, this colourful and tasty fruit terrine reveals a vivid mosaic of fruit held together with a red wine jelly. A fruity red wine such as a Zinfandel or a Beaujolais is best. For a winter version, substitute sliced poached pears, figs, grapes and segmented oranges for the berries. Serve the jelly with a bowl of whipped Chantilly cream.

250 g/½ pound strawberries
125 g/4 oz blueberries
125 g/4 oz raspberries
125 g/4 oz blackberries

1.5-litre/2⅓-pint terrine mould

for the wine jelly
15 g/½ oz powdered gelatine
250 ml/8 fl oz water
100 g/3¼ oz sugar, or more to taste
1 bottle (750 ml/1¼ pints) fruity red wine

Make the wine jelly: sprinkle the gelatine over half the water in a medium bowl and leave until softened and spongy, about 5 minutes. In a small pan, heat the sugar and the remaining water, stirring occasionally, until the sugar is dissolved. Bring the syrup just to the boil, pour over the gelatine and stir until melted. Stir in the wine.

Assemble the terrine: put the terrine mould in a roasting pan half filled with ice and water. Pour a 1-cm/⅜-inch layer of the gelatine mixture into the mould and leave it to set.

Meanwhile, hull the strawberries and halve them if large. Pick over the blueberries, raspberries and blackberries. Rinse the berries only if they are sandy, drying them well. Mix the berries in a bowl.

When the layer of jelly is set, spread the berries on top. Add the remaining gelatine mixture, shaking and tapping the mould so the mixture fills all the spaces between the fruit. Note: be sure the fruit is completely covered with jelly, so the terrine sits flat when unmoulded. Cover and chill until set, at least 6 hours.

Unmould the terrine: dip the mould in a bowl of warm water 5-10 seconds. Using the point of a knife or your fingers, gently ease the terrine away from the edges of the mould. Set a baking sheet or small chopping board on top, turn over and lift off the terrine mould. With a serrated knife, cut the terrine into 1.25-cm/½-inch slices and transfer to individual plates. The colourful berries, highlighted by the red jelly, are their own decoration.

USING GELATINE

Unflavoured gelatine comes as a powder or in sheets, and a little goes a long way – to set a litre/1⅔ pints of liquid you will need only 2 tablespoons/ 15 g/½ oz gelatine, less for a creamy mixture or fruit purée. Both powdered and sheet gelatine must first be soaked for a few minutes in cold water; sheet gelatine is then drained. Some cooks use a water bath to melt gelatine after soaking it, but personally I find a heavy pan works fine over low heat.

Temperature is important when dealing with gelatine, as it sets quite suddenly at around 20°C/68°F. Hence, when melted gelatine is added to another mixture, that mixture should be warm, or at least not so cold that the gelatine sets before it can be incorporated. Gelatine has a tendency to settle to the bottom of a mixture, so it must be stirred constantly until the mixture starts to stiffen. When the gelatine reaches setting point, pour it at once into the mould.

Filled jelly moulds should be stored in the refrigerator, but do not let them get too cold as the jelly will freeze and crystallize. Once set, gelatine holds well if kept cool, but in a warm room you shouldn't risk more than a half hour. How I sympathize with the legendary French chef, Antonin Carême, who 200 years ago lamented that his moulded charlottes, set with gelatine, had collapsed in the hot sun of an outdoor buffet!

Cold soufflés and mousses

Cold soufflés and mousses based on beaten eggs and set with gelatine are the stars of the buffet table. A ring of creamy mousse filled with macerated fruit, a fluffy soufflé towering high above its mould and crowned with chocolate leaves, a fruit charlotte walled with sponge cake, all are guaranteed to catch the eye. To please the palate as well, these delicate desserts need bold flavourings such as caramel, tart fruits like citrus, or liqueurs such as anise and pear. If a vivid ingredient such as raspberry or blood orange is available, so much the better, as soufflés and mousses are always lightened with whipped cream or beaten egg whites and can lack colour. Decorations of whipped cream, fresh or candied fruits, herbs sprigs and curls of chocolate are *de rigueur*, plus a contrasting sauce.

When making cold mousses and soufflés, you need to be organized. Prepare the mould, measure the ingredients, whip the cream and soften the gelatine before you start beating the eggs. Assembly moves quickly and is dictated by the setting of gelatine (see Using Gelatine, page 247). Whipped cream and beaten egg whites, folded in last of all when the basic mixture is about to set, must be ready at hand as most problems are caused by the mixture setting before all additions have been made. If the mixture does not fill the designated mould, this is a sign it is heavy and close-textured; be prepared to take remedial action as described opposite!

Of course, some mousses are not necessarily set with gelatine, especially if their principal ingredients have a solid enough consistency. The best example of this is, of course, Chocolate Mousse, which merits a whole entry of its own, see pages 244-45.

COARSE-TEXTURED — mixture lumpy and dense, often showing strings of gelatine when spooned; texture is coarse on the tongue. *Why:* gelatine not fully softened before melting; gelatine overcooked to strings during melting; mixture not beaten enough; melted gelatine added to cold mixture, setting before it could be smoothly combined; mixture too firm to fold smoothly with whipped cream or egg whites; mixture almost set before pouring into mould.
What to do: layer or sprinkle with crushed macaroons or chocolate biscuits; see also Quick Fix.

PERFECT — soufflés (here cold lemon soufflé) are very light and airy, just holding a shape; mousses are fluffy, just firm enough to unmould; flavour is delicate but lively; colour a clear pastel.

Pink grapefruit soufflé

SERVES 4-6

Pink grapefruit and the Italian aperitif Campari colour this dessert a delicate pink. Campari marries well with grapefruit, but you can substitute more grapefruit juice and a squeeze of lemon juice if you prefer. Decorate this pretty dessert with citrus zest or mint leaves to set off the colour.

1 tablespoon/10 g/⅓ oz powdered gelatine
60 ml/2 fl oz Campari
1 pink grapefruit
4 eggs, separated
200 g/6½ oz sugar
250 ml/8 fl oz double cream

for the Chantilly cream
125 ml/4 fl oz double cream
2 teaspoons sugar
1 teaspoon brandy

1-litre/1⅔-pint soufflé dish
pastry bag with star tube

Prepare the soufflé dish: cut a piece of foil about 5 cm/2 inches longer than the circumference of the dish; fold this lengthwise to double it. Wrap the foil around the dish, it should extend to at least double the height of the dish. Secure the foil with tape.

Sprinkle the gelatine over the Campari in a small pan and leave until softened and spongy, about 5 minutes. Grate the zest and squeeze the juice from the grapefruit – you will need 3 tablespoons of zest and 125 ml/4 fl oz juice.

In a large bowl, beat together the egg yolks and two-thirds of the sugar. Gradually beat in the grapefruit zest and juice. Set the bowl over a pan of simmering water and beat until the mixture is light and thick enough to leave a ribbon trail, 8-10 minutes. Melt the gelatine over very low heat and beat it into the grapefruit mixture. Take the bowl from the heat and continue whisking until the mixture is cool.

Whip the cream until it holds a soft peak. Stiffly beat the egg whites, preferably in a copper bowl. Add the remaining sugar to the egg whites and beat until glossy.

Set the grapefruit mixture over a pan of ice water to chill. Stir constantly until the mixture begins to set. Take it off the ice and immediately fold in the whipped cream, followed by the egg whites. Pour the mixture into the prepared mould. Note: work fast as the mixture sets quickly. Tap the dish on the table to eliminate any air bubbles; it should be filled about 5 cm/2 inches above the rim of dish. Chill until firmly set, at least 3 and up to 12 hours.

Not more than 2 hours before serving, make the Chantilly cream: whip the cream until it holds a soft peak. Add the sugar and brandy and continue whipping until the cream is stiff enough to pipe. Transfer to the piping bag fitted with the star tube. Trim the foil collar level with the soufflé mixture and pipe rosettes of cream on the soufflé. Chill for up to 2 hours. Just before serving the soufflé, remove the collar, peeling it back carefully from the soufflé mixture.

Lemon vodka soufflé

The many flavoured vodkas that are available come in handy in the kitchen. Try substituting lemon vodka (or plain vodka) for the Campari in Pink Grapefruit Soufflé, with the grated zest and juice of 2 large lemons (125 ml/4 fl oz juice) for the grapefruit.

OTHER PROBLEMS

HEAVY AND CLOSE-TEXTURED, DOES NOT FILL MOULD
Why: mixture under- or overbeaten; mixture overfolded when adding gelatine, beaten egg whites or whipped cream.
What to do: add tall decorations such as berries, herb sprigs or edible flowers.

BLAND
Why: too little flavouring.
What to do: serve with robust sauce such as caramel, chocolate or fruit coulis; at a pinch, baste with liqueur like Grand Marnier.

TOO STIFF
Why: too much gelatine; mixture not sufficiently beaten and light; stored too long in the refrigerator.
What to do: let soufflé or mousse come to room temperature up to one hour; scoop into individual portions and serve with a sauce and plenty of whipped cream.

TOO SOFT
Why: too little gelatine; fresh fruits added which attacked gelatine, see Moulded Jellies; soufflé or mousse left too long in a warm room; overchilled so gelatine froze and separated when thawed.
What to do: chill soufflé or mousse until just before serving; if necessary, serve in the mould, or scoop into stemmed glasses and top with candied citrus zest, grated chocolate or a mint sprig.

TASTES OF GELATINE
Why: gelatine incorrectly melted or overheated; too much gelatine.
What to do: if mixture not yet set, add a few tablespoons of vivid flavouring such as lemon or lime juice, rum, Grand Marnier or other liqueur. If set, serve with a tart fruit coulis.

Ice creams

SO MANY MACHINES MAKE HOME-MADE ICE CREAM EASY, from inexpensive hand-cranked tubs with containers of coolant to electric churns which do all the work of chilling and stirring. No wonder cooks have strayed into a fantasy land of ice creams flavoured with toasted spice bread (see Quick Fix, page 288), maple syrup, avocado and vanilla, red wine and prunes, green tea, or mango and muscat wine. I like to experiment too, particularly with summer fruits from the garden. The ice cream itself can be just a beginning, the start of a sundae or coupe such as St Jacques with fruit salad, or a chilled filling for profiteroles or ice cream cakes. Think, too, of ice cream bombes, moulded in multicoloured layers.

I find ice cream mixtures more flexible than sorbet, less likely to form ice crystals from inadequate churning or too many watery ingredients. All that's needed is a base of egg custard or a similar rich cream. Yogurt-based mixtures and ice milk are alternatives. The richer an ice cream is with sugar, the lower its freezing point and the longer it takes to freeze, so chill the mixture thoroughly before churning; alcohol also has the same effect. Very rich, double cream has been known to separate if overchurned so I usually add it halfway, when the ice cream is at the slushy stage. Rich ice cream should hold well for a couple of weeks in the freezer. Flavour will mellow, but the texture hardens after a few hours, so be prepared to let ice cream soften in the refrigerator before serving. And don't forget to chill the serving bowls or plates.

PERFECT – smooth, creamy and rich, but not cloying; soft enough to scoop with a spoon yet firm enough to hold a definite shape; flavour lively; colour clean.

PROBLEMS

HARD OR GRAINY
Why: too little egg, cream or other stabilizer in mixture; not churned constantly during freezing; stored too long.
What to do: let ice cream soften in the refrigerator for 1 or 2 hours before serving;

serve with warm chocolate, caramel or fruit sauce (see Quick Fix).
TOO SOFT
Why: ice cream not fully frozen.
What to do: continue freezing, if possible at lower temperature.

Coconut ice cream

When making ice cream, for maximum taste I like to leave flavourings to infuse in the custard until the last possible moment. Here the grated coconut is strained out after the custard has thickened.

1 vanilla pod, split lengthwise, or ½ teaspoon vanilla essence	500 ml/16 fl oz milk
	7 egg yolks
	100 g/3¼ oz sugar
200 g/6½ oz sweetened shredded coconut	250 ml/8 fl oz double cream
	ice-cream freezer

If using a vanilla pod, scrape the seeds from pod and add pod and seeds, with the coconut, to the milk. Scald the milk, cover it and leave it over a low heat to infuse for 10-15 minutes.

Beat the egg yolks with the sugar until light and slightly thickened, 1-2 minutes. Whisk in half the hot milk, then stir this mixture back into the remaining milk. Heat the custard gently, stirring constantly with a wooden spoon, until it thickens slightly. Note: do not allow custard to boil or it will curdle. Take from heat at once and strain custard into a bowl. Stir in the vanilla essence, if using. Cover tightly to prevent a skin forming and leave custard to cool.

Pour cool custard into ice-cream freezer and churn until partially set. Whip the cream until it holds a soft peak. Add whipped cream to custard and continue churning until stiff. Transfer ice cream to a chilled bowl, cover and store in the freezer. If making ahead, allow ice cream to soften in refrigerator before serving, 1-2 hours.

QUICK FIX

If ice cream is grainy or bland, make a simple version of profiteroles with chocolate sauce – almost any flavour of ice cream will do. For sauce, chop 175 g/6 oz dark chocolate and place in a pan. Bring 250 ml/8 fl oz double cream just to the boil and pour it over the chocolate. Leave to melt for 2-3 minutes, then stir until smooth. Bring to the boil, stirring constantly, and simmer until lightly thickened, 1-2 minutes. Place three small scoops of ice cream in a triangle on 4 chilled plates (about 500 ml/16 fl oz ice cream). Prop 3 wafer biscuits upright between the scoops of ice cream. Trail warm chocolate sauce over the ice cream and wafer and serve at once for 4.

Parfaits

PARFAIT IS INDEED 'PERFECT' SO FAR AS I AM CONCERNED. A simple mixture of egg mousse and whipped cream, parfait can be frozen without any of the churning needed for ice cream and sorbet. Flavourings may be plain, like chocolate, macerated dried or candied fruits, or the classic coffee, or as fanciful as caramel pecan, dried cherry with orange, or spiced apple sauce. When the children were small, I would add crushed Smarties. If you have leftover egg whites, you can use them in a parfait by substituting Italian meringue (see page 226) for the egg yolk and sugar mixture described in the recipe on the right.

PERFECT – just soft enough to scoop with a spoon; light but not fluffy, and very rich; flavour concentrated; colours clean, often with contrasting layers. Note: the classic parfait glass is heavy enough to withstand the cold of the freezer.

TOO HARD – too stiff to scoop with a spoon; texture buttery on the tongue; flavour often bland.
Why: parfait too cold; too much whipped cream; mixture overfolded and lost air; too much heavy flavouring.
What to do: let soften 1-2 hours in refrigerator.

QUICK FIX

When parfait is heavy or tasteless, top it with flambéed bananas. For 4 people, slice 2 bananas. Spoon the parfait into individual bowls. Melt 30 g/1 oz butter in a frying pan, add the bananas and sprinkle with 1 tablespoon sugar. Turn over the fruit and sprinkle with 1 more tablespoon of sugar. Sauté briskly until the sugar browns and caramelizes and the bananas are tender, stirring occasionally, 2-3 minutes. Add 60 ml/2 fl oz rum or Cognac and flambé with a lighted match or by tipping the pan towards a gas flame. Baste the bananas, spoon over the parfait while still flaming and serve at once.

OTHER PROBLEMS

TOO SOFT
Why: parfait not fully frozen.
What to do: continue freezing, if possible at lower temperature.

TEXTURE CRYSTALLINE
Why: too much liquid in mixture, such as fruit juice or purée.
What to do: serve with a warm chocolate sauce.

TASTELESS
Why: flavouring too mild; too little added.
What to do: before freezing, taste mixture and if necessary fold in strong flavouring such as vanilla, ground cinnamon or allspice, powdered coffee dissolved in hot water, rum, Cognac or kirsch. If frozen, see Quick Fix.

Coffee and rum raisin parfait

SERVES 4

The original parfait was flavoured with coffee and, despite the many variations, it remains the most popular. Here I've added a few raisins soaked in rum.

75 g/2½ oz raisins	for the Chantilly cream
90 ml/3 fl oz rum	125 ml/4 fl oz double cream
100 g/3¼ oz sugar	1 tablespoon sugar
90 ml/3 fl oz water	1 teaspoon rum
3 egg yolks	
3 tablespoons dry instant coffee dissolved in 3 tablespoons hot water	four 250-ml/8-fl oz parfait glasses or freezerproof dishes
300 ml/½ pint double cream	pastry bag with large star tube

Chop the raisins and mix with the rum in a small pan. Bring to the boil. Take from heat, cover and let stand for 30 minutes, until the rum is absorbed. Chill the parfait glasses.

In a small saucepan, heat the sugar with the water until dissolved, bring to the boil and boil without stirring, until the syrup reaches soft-ball stage, 115°C/239°F on a sugar thermometer. Let the bubbles subside. Meanwhile, beat the egg yolks just until mixed. Gradually pour in the hot sugar syrup, beating constantly. Continue beating as fast as possible until the mixture is thick and light and has cooled completely, 3-5 minutes.

Beat the dissolved coffee into the egg yolk mixture then stir in the raisins and rum. Whip the cream until it holds a soft peak and fold into the egg yolk mixture. Note: if the egg mixture is still warm it will melt the cream.

Spoon the mixture into individual parfait glasses or dishes and freeze until very firm, 3-5 hours. If freezing longer, transfer the parfaits to the refrigerator for 1-2 hours to soften before serving.

Make the Chantilly cream: whip the cream until it holds a soft peak. Add the sugar and rum and continue whipping until the cream is stiff enough to pipe. Transfer it to the piping bag fitted with the star tube. Pipe large rosettes of cream on top of parfaits.

Sorbets

THE FIRST SORBET I EVER TASTED, a children's party treat, was a solid lump of iced fruit juice. Some poor mother had not realized that constant churning is vital to break up the crystals which form as water freezes; we youngsters were ruthless in condemnation. I'm sure your guests would be kinder. Constant churning apart, much depends on the composition of the mixture itself. Sugar adds smoothness, though it lowers the freezing point and makes a mixture more difficult to set. A little lightly whisked egg white lightens and also discourages ice crystals, but a mere teaspoon per 1 litre/1⅔ pints of mixture is enough – too much makes it pasty on the tongue. Before you freeze a mixture, taste and adjust the flavouring. If the sorbet is to cleanse the palate in the middle of the meal, it needs less sugar.

In any case, the flavour of a sorbet should be assertive – citrus, and acid fruits such as raspberry or passion fruit are favourites. Centuries-old herb sorbets of lavender, rosemary and thyme have recently been revived, an alternative to sweet wines, Champagne and spirits such as Calvados and grappa. Don't be tempted, however, to add too much alcohol as it lowers freezing point, making it all the more difficult for the mixture to stiffen. If in doubt, spoon a spirit or liqueur over a sorbet just before serving.

You'll find that a sorbet's flavour mellows after a few hours in the freezer. If frozen more than 12 hours, however, texture will harden and you'll need to let the sorbet soften in the refrigerator before serving. Unlike ice cream, which complements so many other elements, I think a sorbet is best served very plain in a chilled glass or bowl. For me, this is enough, though I must admit that a selection of home-made sorbets, scooped into ovals on the plate beside slices of fresh fruit, can be the perfect end to a fine meal.

PERFECT – (here lemon tea sorbet) smooth and firm enough to hold a clear shape when scooped with a spoon; flavour intense and refreshing; colour clean.

GRAINY – texture gritty with ice crystals; shape jagged when scooped with spoon; colour cloudy.
Why: too much water in mixture; insufficiently churned during freezing; frozen too quickly; container was too full; sorbet stored too long.
What to do: not much can be done. If there's time, thaw and refreeze the mixture. See also Quick Fix.

QUICK FIX

If a sorbet is crystalline, serve it as granita: leave it to stiffen in the freezer, then stir with a fork to break up crystals. Pile in chilled stemmed glasses, layered with berries or sliced peaches if you like, and top with a mint sprig or twist of lemon zest.

Camomile rose hip sorbet

MAKES I LITRE/ I ⅔ PINTS

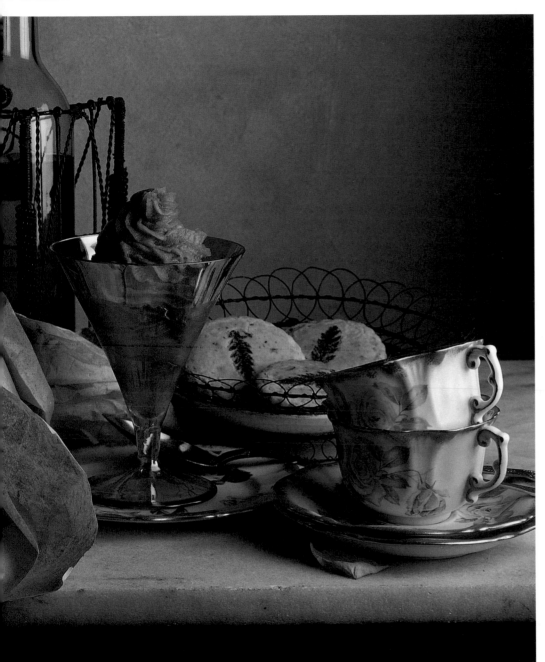

Adjust the quantity of sugar in this sorbet according to its role, using less to cleanse the palate between courses and more for a soothing sweet dessert. You'll find the rose hips colour it an appealing pink.

750 ml/1¼ pints water
10 camomile rose hip tea bags

for the lemon syrup
500 ml/16 fl oz water
400 g/13 oz sugar, or more to taste
grated zest and juice of 2 lemons,
*   or more if needed*

ice-cream freezer

Make the lemon syrup: heat the water with the sugar over low heat, stirring occasionally, until dissolved, then boil 1-2 minutes. Stir in the lemon zest and juice and leave to cool.

Make the tea: bring the water to the boil, and add the tea bags. Remove from the heat and leave the tea to infuse for 5-10 minutes before removing the bags.

Stir together the lemon syrup and the tea and leave to cool. Taste, adding more sugar or lemon juice if necessary. Pour into the ice-cream freezer and churn until stiff. Transfer to a chilled bowl, cover and store in the freezer.

If making ahead, allow the sorbet to soften in the refrigerator before serving, 30-60 minutes.

OTHER PROBLEMS

TOO HARD
Why: too much water in mixture; hardened during storage.
What to do: transfer to refrigerator to soften an hour before serving.
TOO SOFT
Why: not frozen long enough; too much sugar or alcohol in mixture.

What to do: continue churning. With luck the mixture will be slushy enough to serve over ice as a frozen daiquiri or fruit cooler. See also Quick Fix.
TASTELESS
Why: original mixture tasteless; too little sugar; too much egg white.
What to do: when serving, moisten with kirsch (for fruit sorbet) or Cognac (for wine sorbet).

BREADS & PANC

WHEN WE HAD A HOUSE IN NORMANDY, the first errand our children learned was fetching the bread. They followed the example of the boys down the road, part of a *famille nombreuse*, who went twice a day with a wheelbarrow to collect the vast, brown-crusted loaves still warm from the baker's oven. Bread is still very much the staff of life.

Nothing is more typical of a nation's diet than the bread it bakes from the local grain. The French repertoire of baguette, *pain de campagne* and croissants depends on the medium gluten wheat flour found in France. In Portugal, cornmeal and olive oil are added to wheat flour for chewy *broa*; Scandinavia and central Europe are famous for rye breads and pumpernickel. Further south in Morocco the flour is soft, making light, delicate bread often flavoured with aniseed or sesame. None of them are difficult or require rare ingredients. Success is all in the hands and eye.

There are dozens, even hundreds, of variations on the basic bread dough of wheat flour, yeast, salt and water, and by far the most bread is made from these four ingredients. That's why I've devoted so much space to the first entry in this chapter on Plain Yeast Breads. Sourdough and French Breads earn separate billing because sourdough and *levain* starters used for raising dough have their own quirks and techniques. The addition of eggs, milk or butter to yeast breads transforms their behaviour, leading to brioche, kugelhopf, *panettone*, Swiss *birnbrot*, some of the most famous breads of all. Only croissants outdo them in popularity and in complexity.

These breads are the classics. The rest of this chapter is a total change of pace, a look at lively ethnic breads like pitta and naan, at pizza, and the amusing range of tea breads, crêpes and pancakes which can be mixed and baked in minutes thanks to baking powder and bicarbonate of soda. They can accommodate many of the grains such as corn, buckwheat, barley and oats which have little or no gluten and therefore cannot be raised with yeast. Quickly made, most of these breads are best eaten while still warm.

*Skillet cornbread with herbs,
page 271*

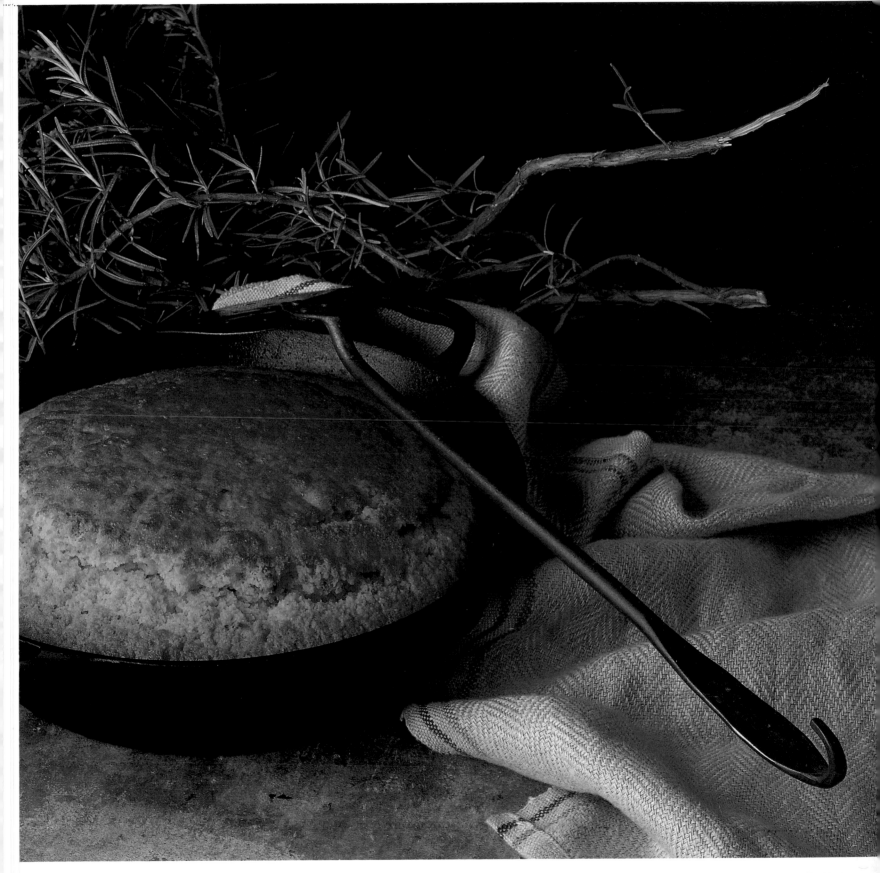

Chocolate rolls

Pains au chocolat

MAKES 15

These fluffy rolls filled with sticks of chocolate are the traditional French reward for an obedient child, bought at the *pâtisserie* on the way home from school.

7 g/¼ oz dried yeast	125 ml/4 fl oz lukewarm milk
175 ml/6 fl oz lukewarm water	250 g/8 oz butter
500 g/1 lb strong white flour	500 g/1 lb dark chocolate
45 g/1½ oz sugar	1 egg beaten with ½ teaspoon salt
1½ teaspoons salt	for glazing

Sprinkle the yeast over half the warm water in a small bowl and let stand, stirring once, until dissolved, about 5 minutes. Sift the flour with the sugar and salt on a marble slab or work surface and make a well in the centre. Pour the yeast mixture, the milk and the remaining water into well. Work together with your fingers until well mixed, then gradually draw in the flour with your hand and a pastry scraper to make crumbs. Work just until the dough is mixed, adding more flour if it is sticky. Shape the dough into a rough ball, cover and let rest in the refrigerator 15 minutes.

Lightly flour the butter, put it between 2 sheets of greaseproof paper and flatten it with a rolling pin. Fold it, wrap and continue pounding and folding until pliable but not sticky – the butter should be the same consistency as the dough. Shape the butter into an 20-cm/8-inch square and flour it lightly. Roll out the dough to a 40-cm/16-inch square, set the butter diagonally in the centre, and fold the dough around it like an envelope, pinching the edges to seal the package.

Flatten the package of dough slightly with the rolling pin and turn it over. Roll out the package to a 60x20-cm/24x8-inch rectangle. Fold over one of the short sides of the dough, then the other, so the rectangle is folded in three layers, like a business letter, and forms a square. Press the open ends lightly with the rolling pin to seal them.

Turn the package of dough 180 degrees to bring the open edges towards you. Roll out again and fold in three. Keep a note of these 'turns' by marking the dough lightly with appropriate number of fingerprints. Wrap the dough and let it rest in the refrigerator until firm, 20-30 minutes. Give the dough two more turns and let it rest again for 20-30 minutes.

Break or cut the chocolate into fifteen 13-cm/5-inch sticks. Roll the dough to an 45x50-cm/18x20-inch rectangle and cut it in three 15-cm/6-inch wide strips. Cut each strip into four 13-cm/5-inch squares. Lay a stick of chocolate in the centre of each square, brush one side with water and fold the dough over the chocolate. Transfer the rolls, seam-sides down, to baking sheets. Cover the rolls with a damp cloth and let rise in a cool place until almost doubled in bulk, 45-60 minutes.

When the rolls are nearly risen, preheat the oven to 220°C/425°F/gas7. Brush them with the egg glaze and bake in the preheated oven until done, 25-30 minutes. Transfer to a rack to cool.

Jewish egg bread

Challah

MAKES 1 LARGE LOAF

This Jewish bread is ancient, baked to bring to temple on holidays and the Sabbath – *challah* means 'offering.' The bread is usually, but not always, plaited.

10 g/⅓ oz dried yeast	550 g/18 oz strong white flour,
250 ml/8 fl oz lukewarm water	or more if needed
60 ml/2 fl oz vegetable oil	1 egg yolk mixed with 1 tablespoon
50 g/1¾ oz sugar	water for glazing
2 eggs, beaten until mixed	1 teaspoon poppy seeds for
2 teaspoons salt	sprinkling

Sprinkle the yeast over 3-4 tablespoons of the water and let stand until dissolved, stirring once, about 5 minutes. Add the oil and sugar to the remaining water and stir until the sugar dissolves.

In a large bowl, combine the eggs with the salt, dissolved yeast and the water, oil and sugar mixture. Stir in half the flour and mix well with your hand. Work in the remaining flour, a little at a time, adding enough to make a dough which pulls away from sides of bowl in a ball. It should be soft and slightly sticky.

Brush a large bowl with oil. Turn the dough out on a floured work surface. Knead the dough by picking it up and slapping it down on the work surface. Continue kneading the dough until it is smooth and very elastic, 5-8 minutes. Alternatively, the dough can be mixed or kneaded in a heavy-duty electric mixer. Put the dough in the oiled bowl and flip so the surface is oiled. Cover with a damp cloth and let the dough rise in a warm place until doubled in bulk, 1-1½ hours.

Brush a baking sheet with oil. Turn the dough out on the work surface and knead lightly to knock out air. Cut the dough into 3 equal pieces. Roll each piece under the palms of your hands to form a long strand, stretching and tapering each end. Line the strands up next to each other. Starting in the centre and working towards one end, braid the strands, stretching them as you move towards the end to accentuate the taper. Turn the dough and braid the other half. The loaf should be fattest in the centre. Pinch the ends and tuck them under the braid. Transfer the braided loaf to the baking sheet. Cover with a dry cloth and let rise in a warm place until doubled in bulk, 45-60 minutes.

Preheat the oven to 190°C/375°F/gas5. Brush the loaf with egg glaze and sprinkle with poppy seeds. Bake in the preheated oven until done, 35-40 minutes. Transfer the bread to a rack to cool.

Jewish egg bread

Indian wholemeal flat bread

Naan

MAKES 6

Naan is the basic bread of the Indian subcontinent, its ingredients varying only slightly from region to region. Though traditionally baked in a *tandoor* oven, the dough still puffs well in a standard oven set on the highest heat. *Naan* can be served hot or at room temperature.

1 teaspoon sugar	175 g/6 oz wholemeal flour,
2 tablespoons warm water	or more if needed
7 g/¼ oz dried yeast	175 ml/6 fl oz lukewarm milk
175 g/6 oz plain flour	175 ml/6 fl oz plain yogurt
1 teaspoon salt	

Combine the sugar and water and stir until sugar dissolves. Sprinkle the yeast over the sugar mixture and let stand until dissolved, stirring once, about 5 minutes. Brush a bowl with vegetable oil.

Sift the plain flour and salt into a large bowl, stir in the wholemeal flour and make a well in the centre. Stir the milk and yogurt into the yeast mixture and pour into the well. Mix with your hand, gradually drawing in the flour, to make a soft dough. The dough should be wet and slightly sticky. If necessary, work in more wholemeal flour. Turn the dough out on a floured work surface and knead until it is smooth and elastic, 5-8 minutes. Alternatively, the dough can be mixed and kneaded in a heavy-duty electric mixer.

Put the dough in the oiled bowl and flip so the surface is oiled. Cover with a damp cloth and let the dough rise in a warm place until doubled in bulk, 2-3 hours.

Turn the dough out on a work surface and knead lightly to knock out air. Shape the dough into a cylinder with your hands and cut it into 6 equal pieces. Roll each piece into a ball, place on an oiled plate, cover with lightly oiled cling film and let rest for 10-15 minutes.

Preheat the oven to 260°C/500°F/gas10 or its highest setting and place a baking sheet near the top of the oven. Roll and stretch each ball of dough into a tear-drop shape about 25 cm/10 inches long and 13 cm/5 inches at its widest.

Set 2-3 shaped *naan* on the hot baking sheet and bake in the preheated oven until puffed, with brown spots, 5-8 minutes. Remove from the oven and stack, covered with a cloth so the bread steams and softens. Continue baking the remaining breads. Serve hot or at room temperature.

Indian wholemeal flat bread

Three cheese and red pepper pizza

SERVES 4

Smooth Mozzarella, nutty Fontina and tart goats' cheese — three cheeses may sound like overkill, but you'll miss any one of them in the finished pizza.

3 red sweet peppers	for the dough
125 ml/4 fl oz olive oil	7 g/¼ oz dried yeast
2 onions, thinly sliced	175 ml/6 fl oz lukewarm water
2 garlic cloves, crushed	250 g/½ lb plain flour, or more if
salt and pepper	needed
60 g/2 oz chopped fresh sage	1 teaspoon salt
½ teaspoon ground hot red pepper	2 tablespoons olive oil
125 g/4 oz goat cheese, crumbled	1-2 tablespoons cornmeal for
125 g/4 oz Fontina cheese,	sprinkling
coarsely grated	
250 g/½ lb Mozzarella cheese,	
thinly sliced	

Make the dough: sprinkle the yeast over 3-4 tablespoons of the water in a small bowl and let stand until dissolved, stirring once, about 5 minutes. Brush a large bowl with vegetable oil. Sift the flour and salt on a work surface and make a well in the centre. Pour the yeast mixture, the remaining water and the olive oil into the well. Gradually draw in the flour with your hand and a pastry scraper to make a slightly sticky dough; if necessary, work in more flour. Knead the dough on a floured work surface until it is smooth and elastic, 5-8 minutes. Put the dough in the oiled bowl and flip so the surface is oiled. Cover with a damp cloth and let the dough rise until doubled in bulk, 1-1½ hours.

Meanwhile, roast the peppers over an open flame or under the grill, turning them until the skin chars and bursts, 7-10 minutes. Put them in a plastic bag to retain their steam (this loosens the skins) and let cool. Peel the peppers, discard the cores and seeds, and cut the flesh into strips.

Heat 2 tablespoons of the olive oil in a frying pan and sauté the onions until soft but not brown, 3-4 minutes. Add the garlic, salt and pepper, and continue cooking gently 1-2 minutes. Remove from the heat, and stir in the roasted peppers and sage. Taste and adjust the seasoning. Mix the ground hot red pepper with the remaining olive oil and set aside.

Preheat the oven to 200°C/400°F/gas6. Turn dough out on a work surface and knead lightly to knock out air. Lightly flour the surface and roll out the dough to a 30x35-cm/12x14-inch rectangle (the size of most baking sheets).

Sprinkle the baking sheet with cornmeal and transfer the dough to it. Brush the dough with the hot pepper oil and spread with the red pepper mixture, leaving a 2-cm/¾-inch border. Sprinkle the peppers with the goats' and Fontina cheeses and top with Mozzarella slices. Let the pizza rise in a warm place until almost doubled in bulk, 20-30 minutes. Bake the pizza in the preheated oven until done, 15-18 minutes.

Savoury tea breads and scones

SAVOURY BREADS SUCH AS CORNBREAD AND SCONES are in dramatic contrast to yeast breads. Raised with baking powder or bicarbonate of soda (see page 271), they can be made in just a few minutes. For best effect, the dough or batter should be very lightly worked so the gluten in the flour is not developed – the opposite principle from that of yeast breads. Doughs should have a rough, shaggy appearance and batters should be scarcely smooth.

Tea breads often use low-gluten wheat flour such as the soft winter wheat popular in the American South, or flour from other grains such as corn, which add greatly to their taste. Most tea breads have pleasant, floury overtones, best on their own so the taste of the grain stands out – typical are Irish soda bread and American corn sticks. Scones, too, are usually kept plain to serve with with tea or coffee. Their counterparts in the USA are confusingly known as 'biscuits'. American biscuits really differ little from their British cousins, though scones are served with tea or coffee rather than with a main meal. British bakers may add a touch more sugar to scones, and like to flavour them with currants or candied peel. By common consent, the outstanding partners for a fluffy, floury scone are clotted cream and strawberry jam. Americans, however, serve their biscuits with thinly sliced country ham, or with gravy or a stew of chicken or rabbit. Scone or biscuit dough can also form the topping for a cobbler, or a chicken pot pie.

PERFECTLY BAKED – crust (here a scone) crisp and golden brown or darker, depending on sugar content; flavour fresh with hint of flour and acidity (for scones), or sweeter and mellower (for tea breads).

UNDERBAKED *left* – surface pale (here a scone); inside moist, sticky in centre; tastes of uncooked flour. **PERFECT** *centre* – inside is light and crumbles easily; texture is floury (for scones) or more crumbly (for tea breads).

HEAVY AND UNDERRISEN *right* – crust thick; inside, crumb is close-textured, often moist; flavour cloying.

Skillet cornbread with herbs

BICARBONATE OF SODA AND BAKING POWDER

When bicarbonate of soda (baking soda) is mixed with an acid, such as buttermilk or lemon juice, it releases bubbles of carbon dioxide which will raise and lighten a dough. Baking powder, a mix of bicarbonate of soda plus an acid, functions the same way. Almost all brands of baking powder are 'double acting', activated partly by contact with liquid, partly by oven heat. Therefore double-acting baking powder can be left to stand before use, for instance when making pancake batter. The leavening action of bicarbonate of soda, however, is relatively rapid, best for recipes cooked at once. Normal proportions for tea bread dough are for each 125 g/4 oz flour, 1½ teaspoons of baking powder or ½ teaspoon bicarbonate of soda and 1 tablespoon lemon juice or vinegar. Though pancake batters need more leavener, too much raising agent gives a sharp, chemical taste to both bread and pancakes. Too much bicarbonate of soda in proportion to acid leads to a coarse texture, with a soapy flavour and yellowish colour (chocolate cake looks chestnut and blueberries are tinged with green).

PROBLEMS

HEAVY AND UNDERRISEN
Why: dough or batter too dry or too wet; overworked; too little raising agent; too many heavy ingredients such as cornmeal or dried fruits; not cooled on rack so steam could escape; wrapped before cool; stored too long.
What to do: if batter is stiff, add more liquid; if dough is dry or overworked, nothing can be done; slice breads thinly for serving; see also Quick Fix.

UNDERBAKED
Why: cooking time too short; oven temperature too low; baked in too large a mould, so outside done before centre.
What to do: continue baking until done, raising heat if necessary.

CRUST HARD
Why: dough or batter dry; overbaked.
What to do: brush surface with milk or melted butter during baking or when still warm.

CENTRE FALLEN (batter breads)
Why: batter too wet; too little or too much raising agent; batter not baked at once; oven too low.
What to do: cover with herb sprigs.

CENTRE PEAKED (batter breads)
Why: too much raising agent; oven temperature too high.
What to do: nothing can be done, but bread still tastes good.

TEXTURE HEAVY
Why: underbaked; too much acid (soda breads).
What to do: if underbaked, continue baking; if too much acid, see Flavour acid or sour.

TEXTURE COARSE
Why: too much raising agent.
What to do: cut into chunks rather than slices to distract from texture.

FLAVOUR ACID OR SOUR
Why: too much raising agent, particularly bicarbonate of soda; dough not baked immediately.
What to do: serve with contrasting topping such as cream cheese, jam or apple butter.

For colour I usually use yellow cornmeal for cornbread, but white cornmeal tastes equally good. For a sweeter cornbread, simply double the sugar in this recipe. For a rich and savoury cornbread, fry some bacon in the pan and substitute the drippings for butter to coat the pan. Pouring the batter into a hot pan makes for a crispy crust.

125 g/4 oz plain flour
1 tablespoon baking powder
175 g/6 oz fine yellow
   or white cornmeal
1 tablespoon sugar
1½ teaspoons salt
2 eggs
60 ml/2 fl oz melted butter

300 ml/½ pint milk
2 tablespoons mixed chopped
   herbs such as rosemary, sage
   and thyme

25-cm/10-inch skillet
or deep ovenproof frying pan

Preheat the oven to 220°C/425°F/gas7. Thoroughly butter the skillet or frying pan and heat it in the oven.

Sift the flour and baking powder into a large bowl. Stir in the cornmeal, sugar and salt and make a well in the centre. In another bowl, whisk the eggs, melted butter, milk and herbs until mixed and pour into the well. Stir together just until smooth.

Pour the batter into the hot skillet or frying pan and tap the pan on the work surface to smooth the top of the batter. Bake in the preheated oven until done, 20-25 minutes. Brush the bread with melted butter while hot to soften the crust. Serve at once.

Crêpes

THE PERFECT CRÊPE BRINGS A SMILE TO THE FACE OF THE MOST JADED COOK. It all happens so fast, with a quick twist of the wrist to swirl the hot pan so the batter spreads quickly and evenly. A minute later the crêpe is done to a patterned golden brown. Now we can go on to fill a nutty buckwheat crêpe with creamed mushrooms or chopped ham and an egg. We can spread a delicate wheat crêpe with orange butter and flambé with Grand Marnier for crêpes Suzettes, or stuff it with apples and Calvados for *crêpes Normande*. A lemon or praline soufflé even rises nicely inside a loosely rolled crêpe.

A good crêpe originates in a good frying pan and nothing beats the traditional shallow black steel *poêle*, available in several sizes. Don't be tempted to wash it after use, but clean it while still warm with a wipe of a damp cloth. A non-stick pan is an alternative, but I think the crêpe browns less well. Fry over high heat with a minimum of fat, preferably butter; a brush with butter every fifth or sixth crêpe should be sufficient. Stir rather than beat the batter, as you don't want to develop the gluten and make the crêpes tough. Don't stint on the eggs, however, as they lighten the crêpe and hold it together. Leaving batter to stand also helps lightness, as starch in the flour expands and protein relaxes.

When frying, the first crêpe is almost always a failure, before you get the right heat and amount of butter in the pan. Don't hesitate to throw it away and try again. The first side of your crêpe will be lightly speckled with brown; the underside is spotted and less attractive, so take care it is folded to the inside. As the crêpes come from the pan, pile them on top of each other so they stay warm and moist. Stacked crêpes can be kept for several hours, or up to a day in the refrigerator. Depending on the dish, 2-3 crêpes is an average serving.

Crêpes are so thin they are almost always folded, the shape being dictated by the dish: flambéed crêpes are folded in quarters, the point placed on the plate facing away from the diner. Firm or creamy fillings are rolled in a cylinder, and looser mixtures are contained by turning in the sides of the crêpe, then rolling it as a package called a *pannequet*. Crêpes can be used to line a ramekin, echoing a pastry case but with a frilled edge, or left flat and sandwiched with filling like a cake (see Quick Fix).

OTHER PROBLEMS

PALE
Why: heat too low; cooking time too short.
What to do: increase heat and continue cooking, turning crêpe several times if necessary.

DARK OR SCORCHED
Why: heat too high; cooked too long; butter scorched; too much sugar in batter.
What to do: lower the heat; use clarified butter.

STICKS TO PAN
Why: pan surface not seasoned; too little fat; too much sugar.
What to do: try another crêpe, being sure pan is lightly but thoroughly buttered; if still sticking, re-season pan by heating a generous layer of vegetable oil and coarse salt in it until smoking, then leaving to cool before wiping out for use.

THIN – crêpe full of holes, even lacy; breaks easily when handled; texture dry.
Why: batter too thin; too few eggs to bind crêpe.
What to do: whisk in 1 or 2 more eggs.

PERFECT – crêpe very thin and flexible, without holes; colour a patterned golden brown on one side, golden spots where batter had risen on reverse; shape a perfect round; flavour delicate, not doughy.

HEAVY – crêpe thick and rubbery, often dark brown; flavour pasty.
Why: batter too thick; too few eggs in batter; too much batter in pan; crêpe cooked too slowly.
What to do: if heat was low, increase heat and try again; if crêpe still heavy, thin batter with milk.

Belgian apple crêpes

Crêpes aux pommes caramelisées

MAKES 12 CRÊPES, TO SERVE 4-6

There's a back-street restaurant in Brussels which serves huge pots of steamed mussels, followed by these tantalizing crêpes, each set with a ring of caramelized apple. Use firm apples which hold their shape, such as Golden Delicious.

3 medium apples	*for the crêpes*
(about 500 g/1 lb)	*60 g/2 oz flour*
2-3 tablespoons sugar	*2 teaspoons sugar*
1 tablespoon ground cinnamon	*¼ teaspoon salt*
2 tablespoons butter	*3 eggs*
icing sugar for sprinkling	*250 ml/8 fl oz milk*
	grated zest of 1 lemon
18-cm/7-inch crêpe pan	*75 g/2½ oz melted butter*

Make crêpe batter: sift flour, sugar and salt into a bowl and make a well in centre. Add eggs and half milk to well and whisk until mixed. Continue stirring, gradually drawing in flour to make a smooth batter. Stir in half remaining milk, cover and let stand at room temperature for 15-30 minutes.

Peel and core the apples and cut each in 4 rings, discarding the thin end pieces. In a small shallow bowl, combine the sugar and cinnamon. Dip the apple rings in the sugar and cinnamon mixture. Heat half the butter in a large frying pan. Add half the apple rings and fry briskly on both sides until caramelized. Transfer the rings to a plate and caramelize the remaining rings in the same way.

Fry the crêpes: stir the lemon zest and 2 tablespoons of the melted butter into the batter. The batter should be the consistency of thin cream, but if thicker stir in the remaining milk. Heat 2-3 teaspoons more butter in the crêpe pan until very hot. Add 2-3 tablespoons batter, turning and rotating the pan so the base is covered. At once set an apple ring in the centre of the crêpe and drizzle over a little batter to cover it.

Fry the crêpe until browned, 1-2 minutes. Toss the crêpe, or turn with a palette knife and brown the other side. Transfer to a serving plate and keep warm. Continue frying the crêpes, overlapping 2-3 per plate per person. Sprinkle the crêpes lightly with icing sugar and serve at once.

Pancakes

A PANCAKE IS THICKER AND MORE SUBSTANTIAL THAN A CRÊPE, playing the lead role rather than acting as a background for other ingredients. A plain pancake is a pleasant foil for toppings of maple syrup, honey and melted butter. Add cornmeal and you've a robust breakfast dish or an accompaniment to savoury roast chicken. Colourful additions such as purées of green bean or pumpkin offer further possibilities. Look further afield and you'll find Chinese mandarin pancakes flavoured with sesame oil, Vietnamese rice flour pancakes with spring onion and turmeric, and Russian *blini* based on buckwheat flour (right). Some pancakes are raised with yeast, others with baking powder or bicarbonate of soda and, at the whim of the cook, they may vary from the size of a large coin to 20-cm/8-inch platters. For a sophisticated finish, cut your pancake to a perfect round with a fluted cutter.

As with crêpes, leaving pancake batter to stand helps lightness. For yeast batters this also allows the yeast to rise. Batter for small pancakes should fall easily from the spoon, and for larger ones, should pour easily. A heavy pan or griddle is important for even heat. Always fry a trial pancake before adjusting the batter – a thick batter is easy to thin with liquid but adding flour to thicken is more complicated. At the same time, taste the flavouring of your pancake. Small even bubbles bursting on the top indicate a pancake is ready to flip; if the heat of the pan is right, the underside will be an appetizing golden brown. Unlike crêpes, pancakes don't keep well and are best eaten at once, while fluffy and warm.

PERFECT – pancakes fluffy and thick enough to have body; shaped in neat rounds; attractively browned on top, with centre as firmly set as edges; texture porous and tender; taste mild or nutty, depending on type of flour, with no trace of acid raising agent.

QUICK FIX

When plain breakfast pancakes seem dreary, here are some quick toppings to pick them up:
• Make orange butter: cream 125 g/4 oz butter with 1 tablespoon icing sugar, 1 tablespoon orange juice and 1 tablespoon grated orange zest.
• For a creamy fruit sauce: whisk 3-4 tablespoons raspberry jam or redcurrant jelly until soft. Whisk in 125 ml/4 fl oz double cream until smooth and thick.

PROBLEMS

HEAVY
Why: batter too thick; too little raising agent; batter not risen (for yeast).
What to do: thin batter with milk or water and try again; if still heavy, stir in a little more raising agent; if yeast, leave to rise longer in a warm place.

THIN
Why: batter too thin; too little raising agent; heat too low, so batter spread rather than setting at once.
What to do: raise heat and try again; if still thin, put 60 g/2 oz flour in a small bowl, stir in a few spoonfuls of batter until smooth, then pour this into remaining batter. If pancake is also heavy, add more raising agent or, for yeast, leave longer to rise.

DISINTEGRATES
Why: batter too thin; cooked too fast, so underneath scorched before batter set.
What to do: if batter thin, stir in a lightly whisked egg; if browned very fast, lower the heat.

DARK OR SCORCHED
Why: heat too high; cooked too long; butter scorched; too much sugar in batter.
What to do: lower the heat; use clarified butter.

FLAVOUR ACID OR SOUR
Why: too much chemical raising agent; if yeast, batter raised too long.
What to do: flavour batter with curry or hot red pepper for savoury pancakes, or ginger or clove for sweet.

Buckwheat pancakes
Blini
MAKES 12

Traditional Russian *blini* are made only with buckwheat flour, but I find they're lighter with a mixture of buckwheat and plain flours. On the other hand, the time-honoured accompaniments of caviar or smoked salmon with lemon wedges, sour cream and possibly melted butter can't be bettered. Buckwheat contains no gluten, so *blini* batter takes a long time to rise, but the wait is amply repaid in richness of flavour.

500 ml/16 fl oz milk, or more if needed
10 g/⅓ oz dried yeast
125 ml/4 fl oz lukewarm water
125 g/4 oz plain flour
200 g/6½ oz buckwheat flour
½ teaspoon salt
3 eggs, separated
45 g/1½ oz melted butter
45 ml/1½ fl oz sour cream

griddle, skillet or heavy frying pan

Scald milk and cool to lukewarm. Sprinkle yeast over water and let stand until dissolved, stirring once, about 5 minutes. Sift flours and salt into a bowl. Make a well in centre and pour yeast mixture with half the milk into it. Mix with your hand, gradually drawing in flour to make a smooth batter. Beat well for 2 minutes, cover with a damp cloth and let rise in a warm place until batter is light and full of bubbles, about 2 hours.

With your hand, beat mixture to knock out air. Beat in the remaining milk, followed by the egg yolks, melted butter and sour cream. The batter should be the consistency of double cream, but if too thick stir in more milk. Stiffly beat the egg whites and fold them into the batter. Cover and leave to stand 30 minutes longer.

Preheat griddle, skillet or frying pan and brush lightly with butter. Pour in batter to make a 15-cm/6-inch round. Cook for 2-3 minutes until underside is lightly browned and top is bubbling, then turn and cook until done. Pile *blini* on top of each other and keep warm while cooking rest. Serve at once with accompaniment of choice.

AS I WROTE THIS CHAPTER, I found my attention constantly slipping back to childhood – to Thursday, baking day, when our cook Emily stoked up the kitchen fire and, little by little, beat, rolled, folded and baked her way through an array of fragrant pastries and cakes which lasted through the following week. She was a champion pastry cook, light-handed and a perfectionist, and she set my standards for life.

It was she who taught me that beating a batter meant doing a thorough job, never mind the effort involved. Folding, on the other hand, called for a light touch and I was rarely allowed to participate. She was clever at making the most of a few ingredients – this was during the Second World War – and at wheedling eggs and the occasional bowl of curd cheese from the neighbouring farmer. I later realized that Emily followed many of the dicta of professional pastry chefs, taking care to shape each individual cake or pastry exactly to size so they baked evenly, and insisting on the right size of pan. She kept a constant eye on the oven, shifting the baking sheets when necessary.

In this chapter I've tried to pass on some tricks of the trade, the little techniques which make so much difference to cakes and pastry – how to line and bake tartlet moulds with a minimum of fuss, for instance, and a quick way to fix wafer biscuits which have flopped on a damp day. You'll find that salt is an important but often overlooked ingredient, without which cakes and pastries lose their subtle edge. In pastry, a half teaspoon of salt per 500 g/ 1 pound of flour is usual; for cakes, often a pinch is enough. The refrigerator is less of a friend in baking than you might think. It is useful, of course, for storage and for chilling pastry before baking. However, cold butter must often be brought to room temperature for creaming or for mixing pastry, and chilled eggs whisk less well. Very fresh eggs (less than three days old) whisk less well, too – I wish that were a more common complaint!

Looking at cakes, I've started with basic sponge – it's amazing how much there is to say – and you'll find some general advice on preparing cakes there as well. Next there's a run through half a dozen other cakes, including Swiss roll, Madeira cake, fruit cakes, batter breads, tortes and cheesecakes. All have their own quirks. After that come a clutch of open-faced, top-crust and double-crust pies and tarts, all of them specialities of Emily's. However, she never ventured into the realms of puff and choux, I had to go to cooking school for that. Finally we have a handful of biscuits, a friendly ending which for me evokes a time when I had to reach up to the tabletop to capture a biscuit when I hoped no one was looking.

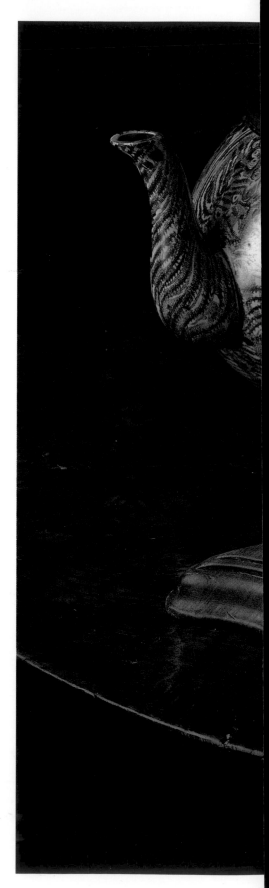

Cranberry orange bread,
page 289

Sponges and whisked cakes

'AIR IS IN PLENTIFUL SUPPLY', REMARKS ONE OLD COOKBOOK, 'the trick is to incorporate it into your sponge.' The writer goes on to describe the energetic whisking, followed by gentle folding, which are the keys to a perfect sponge. The classic génoise is made with whole eggs, sugar and flour, with or without butter; a variant is biscuit in which the egg yolks and whites are beaten separately with sugar, then combined with the flour. The finished cake has a slightly firmer, drier texture than génoise – ladyfingers are the most familiar use. For both cakes, standard proportions are 3 eggs to 100 g/3¼ oz flour and 90 g/3 oz sugar.

I'd strongly recommend using a heavy-duty electric mixer for making sponge cakes, particularly for génoise. (If you whisk génoise by hand you will need to warm it over a bowl of hot water.) After thorough beating, the whole eggs and sugar used in génoise develop to an even-textured, fluffy mousse which should hold a ribbon trail for 10-15 seconds; the disappearance of frothy, uneven bubbles is also a sign the mousse is ready. No other leavening is used, only eggs.

A light touch is needed to fold flour into the egg batter – sifting is vital – and adding butter demands even more delicacy as it quickly knocks out air. Techniques vary but I like to soften the butter over warm water until it is soft enough to pour (but not melted to oil). I add a few spoonfuls of the batter to the butter, stir thoroughly, and then fold this mixture back into the remaining sponge. When batter is poured into the pan, it should be about two-thirds full; tap the pan on the worktop to expel any large air bubbles, which can leave white patches on the bottom crust. By now the oven will be hot (see Preparing to Bake Cakes, page 287), so the cake can be baked at once; 175°C/350°F/gas4 is the customary temperature.

When done, run a knife carefully around the cake so the crust is not crushed and turn it out to cool on a rack so steam escapes. If slicing the sponge into layers, let it cool completely first to minimize crumbs. Plain sponges are best eaten as soon as they are cool; butter in the batter helps keep them moist and so do rich fillings, which mellow and improve on standing.

A sponge cake by itself is plain stuff. Good flavourings for the batter include vanilla, grated citrus rind, rose or orange flower water and perfumed spices such as cardamom and anise. Ground nuts, cocoa, cornflour or potato flour may take the place of some flour, but sponge cake batter is delicate and cannot support heavy additions such as dried fruit. On the baked cake, a sprinkling of icing sugar is customary, if not a more formal sugar glaze or icing. Why not fill the cake with strawberries and cream? The classic English Victoria sponge is a sandwich filled with whipped cream and raspberry jam. In France you are more likely to find buttercream, even chocolate mousse.

This leads us to some of the triumphs of the pastry cook's art – grand gâteaux such as French *marronnier*, flavoured with chestnuts and rum, and Spanish *pastel Sant Jordi* with chocolate buttercream. Black forest cake, with its chocolate sponge, whipped cream and cherries, has travelled far beyond its birthplace. Israel offers an orange fig sponge cake, and Japan a sponge cake flavoured with honey.

PERFECTLY BAKED – cake springs back when lightly pressed; edge just starts to shrink from pan; batter nearly doubled in volume; surface golden-brown and top is level; a skewer inserted in centre of cake comes out clean; flavour fresh and fragrant.

PERFECT TEXTURE – when cut, cake is fluffy and even, slightly crumbly.

QUICK FIX

If a sponge cake is heavy, dry, or unevenly baked:
- Split cake horizontally and brush with syrup made with 60 g/2 oz sugar dissolved in 3 tablespoons water and flavoured with 2 tablespoons Cognac; add a fruit mousse or other filling of fruit and cream.
- Serve cake with this orange sauce: with a serrated knife, cut skin and pith from 3 oranges; cut out orange segments, discarding membranes and reserving any juice. Melt 4 tablespoons of orange marmalade in a small saucepan. Stir in 125 ml/4 fl oz orange juice, including the reserved juice from the oranges. Let cool, then stir in orange segments and 1 tablespoon Grand Marnier. For greater effect use blood oranges; makes 250 ml/8 fl oz sauce.

OVERBAKED, HEAVY AND SHRIVELLED — batter poorly risen and cake shrunken and pulled from side of pan; crust dark; cake very firm when pressed with a fingertip; flavour lacks freshness.

SPOTTED TOP — surface crusty and flecked with white spots.

UNEVEN POROUS TEXTURE — top crust dry and uneven; bubbles and poorly mixed flour may be visible on surface; cake may draw tightly in from side.

OVERBAKED, HEAVY AND SHRIVELLED — when cut, cake is dry; texture is tight.
Why: baked too long; egg mixture overwhisked; too much butter in batter; overfolded; pan wrong size; left to cool in pan, or wrapped before completely cool.
What to do: sandwich with a generous filling of buttercream, or whipped cream and red berry jam; frost top or dust with icing sugar.

SPOTTED TOP — when cut, crust may have separated from crumb.
Why: too much sugar in batter; sugar not completely dissolved in eggs during whisking.
What to do: serve cake base upwards, particularly if top crust separated from crumb; alternatively, cover with buttercream frosting or light sugar icing (see Lemon Génoise overleaf).

UNEVEN POROUS TEXTURE — when cut, texture has large holes and unmixed ingredients are visible.
Why: eggs not whisked enough; batter insufficiently folded; too much raising agent, if used.
What to do: cut horizontally in 2-3 layers and sandwich with colourful fruit jam or jelly. See also Quick Fix.

OTHER PROBLEMS

UNDERBAKED
Why: cooking time too short; temperature too low.
What to do: continue baking.
PEAKED TOP
Why: oven heat too high.
What to do: if adding a pourable icing, trim cake level and turn upside-down to coat with icing; if using a stiff icing or leaving plain, a peak can be attractive.

SUNKEN CENTRE
Why: too many eggs, not enough flour in batter; eggs not whisked enough; batter overfolded; batter not baked immediately; oven heat too low.
What to do: brush cake with melted apricot or redcurrant glaze, fill sunken centre with fruits such as peeled sliced peaches, berries, seeded grapes or poached pears, brushing them also with glaze.

DRY
Why: no butter used in batter; batter overfolded; overbaked; not stored in airtight container; cake stale.
What to do: serve with fruit coulis or custard sauce.
FLAVOUR FLAT
Why: not enough flavouring; overbaked; cake stale.
What to do: add a well-flavoured cream filling; top with frosting or sprinkle with vanilla sugar.

Lemon génoise with lemon icing

SERVES 6-8

The classic pan for génoise is a *moule à manqué*, with sloping sides. Unlike cakes baked in straight-sided pans, this cake is turned bottom up, so the warm icing runs evenly down the sloping sides. Lemon is my favourite flavouring, but orange zest and juice can be used as well.

60 g/2 oz butter
125 g/4 oz flour
pinch of salt
4 eggs
125 g/4 oz granulated sugar
grated zest of 1 lemon

for the lemon icing
pared zest and juice of 1 lemon
200 g/6½ oz icing sugar, or more if needed

23-cm/9-inch moule à manqué cake pan

Preheat the oven to 175°C/350°F/gas4. Butter the base and sides of the cake pan, line the base with greaseproof paper and butter the paper. Sprinkle the pan with flour, discarding excess. Warm the butter in a bowl over hot water until it is soft enough to pour, but do not melt it to oil. Leave it to cool. Sift flour with the salt.

Put the eggs, sugar and grated lemon zest in the bowl of a heavy-duty electric mixer and whisk until mixed. Turn the speed to high and continue whisking until the mixture is light and thick enough to leave a ribbon trail when the whisk is lifted, 8-10 minutes. Note: if whisking by hand, set the bowl over a pan of hot but not boiling water, whisk mixture to the ribbon, stage then take the bowl from the heat and whisk until cool.

Sift the flour over the egg mixture in 3 batches, folding in each as lightly as possible. Stir a little batter into the softened butter, then fold this mixture into the remaining batter. Note: the batter quickly loses volume after the butter is added. Pour the batter into the prepared pan and bake in the preheated oven until done, 35-40 minutes. When the cake is done, run a knife around the sides to loosen it and turn out on a rack. Leave it to cool.

To make the icing: cut the pared lemon zest into very fine julienne strips. Put the strips in a small pan of cold water, bring to the boil, simmer for 1 minute and drain. Sift the icing sugar into a small bowl. Stir in the lemon juice to make a stiff paste. Set the bowl in a bath of hot water and stir the icing until quite warm to the touch. It should lightly coat the back of a spoon. If too thick, thin it with a little water; if too thin, stir in more sifted icing sugar. Stir in the lemon zest and keep warm.

Pour the warm icing over the cake on the rack and spread with a palette knife so it flows down the sloping sides. Note: work quickly, as the icing will cool and set rapidly. Transfer the cake to a platter to serve.

Angel food cake

Angel food Cake

ANGEL FOOD CAKE IS A CURIOSITY, a frothy white cake which has captured popular fancy. It breaks many conventions. For instance, it is raised only with beaten egg whites to which a surprise spoonful of water is added as well as cream of tartar. Special cake flour with a low gluten content must be used. The tube cake pan is left unlined, the theory being that the cake climbs better up the untreated sides. Instead of being unmoulded while still warm, the pan is propped upside-down and left undisturbed. The result is a sweet, oddly chewy sponge with a deep golden crust from the high sugar content. Texture is so light that special comb-like cutters exist for cutting it, though I find that a serrated knife works fine. The cake is traditionally served without frosting. Vanilla and salt are the only flavourings, though a chocolate version exists – the devil's work, purists say.

There is some debate about the origins of this American confection, originally baked in a square tube pan. By the 1870s it was popular in Pennsylvania and New Jersey, a favourite among the thrifty Pennsylvania Dutch who still bake these cakes in order to use the egg whites left over from their traditional yolk-enriched noodles. Angel food cake is delicious served with Peppered Strawberry Coulis (page 136).

300 g/10 oz sugar
125 g/4 oz soft cake flour
10-11 egg whites, at room temperature
1 teaspoon cream of tartar

2 tablespoons cold water
1 teaspoon vanilla essence
½ teaspoon salt
25-cm/10-inch tube pan

Preheat the oven to 175°C/350°F/gas4 and set an oven rack in the bottom third of the oven. Note: do not grease the tube pan. Sift the sugar twice and set it aside. Sift together the flour and one-third of the sugar four times and set aside. Measure 375 ml/12 fl oz of egg white.

Beat the egg whites with a heavy-duty electric mixture on medium speed just until foamy, 1-2 minutes. Add the cream of tartar, water, vanilla essence and salt, and continue beating, increasing the speed to medium-high, until the egg whites are very stiff but not dry, 4-5 minutes. Beat in the remaining sugar, 2 tablespoons at a time, until the egg whites are glossy and form a long peak when the whisk is lifted. Fold in the sifted flour and sugar mixture, 2 heaping tablespoonfuls at a time.

Spoon the batter into the ungreased tube pan and bake in the preheated oven until a skewer inserted in centre comes out clean, 40-45 minutes. Invert the cake while still in the pan, resting the pan on a funnel, thin-necked bottle or tea cups to keep it above the work surface. Leave the cake until set and thoroughly cool, about 1 hour. Run a knife around the edge of cake and ease it away from the sides of the pan. Invert on a rack and remove the pan.

To serve, cut the cake into wedges with a serrated knife or divide it into wedges with a special comb.

PERFECTLY BAKED – batter nearly doubled in volume; cake springs back when lightly pressed, and just starts to shrink from pan; a skewer inserted in cake comes out clean.

PERFECT TEXTURE – when unmoulded, whole surface is an even golden brown; when cut, cake is even-textured and very spongy.

PROBLEMS

HEAVY AND SHRIVELLED
Why: under- or overbaked; egg whites poorly beaten; batter overfolded; cake cooled too rapidly or unmoulded too soon.
What to do: slice thinly and serve with fruit sorbet or coulis (see page 252 or 136).

STUCK TO PAN
Why: pan scrubbed with soap and water after previous baking. Note that angel food cake has a tendency to stick.
What to do: use a pan with a loose base; leave cake until cool, not cold, then run a thin flexible knife carefully around sides to loosen before unmoulding.

QUICK FIX

If angel food cake is heavy or sticks to the pan, cut the cake in large cubes and serve as a fondue with Salty Caramel Sauce (page 240) for dipping. For lightness, add some fresh strawberries.

Cakes, pastries and biscuits 281

Swiss rolls and logs

I WONDER WHO FIRST THOUGHT OF BAKING A THIN LAYER OF SPONGE, then rolling it while still warm so it would retain its curves to accommodate a contrasting filling, such as red jam for a pale vanilla sponge, whipped cream and cherries for a ginger cake, espresso buttercream for a chocolate sponge (overleaf), and so on. Any kind of sponge which remains moist when baked can be used. The batter is spread directly on buttered paper set on a baking sheet – pans are unnecessary as the batter is spread so thinly. Use quite a high temperature (for sponge) of 190°C/375°F/gas5, so the batter bakes quickly without drying, remaining pliable. It should brown around the edges, but only lightly elsewhere – overbaking is a common error.

To roll the cake, I find it simplest to flip it on to a dry cloth with the help of the paper, then to peel off the paper and quickly roll the cake inside the cloth. If your recipe suggests another method, try it as there are various approaches. It's important to work fast and roll the cake quite tightly while still warm. Leave it until cold, to retain moisture in the cake. Then unroll it, remove the cloth, trim dry edges and add the filling, being sure to re-roll it in a tightly shaped cylinder. Chill well so the roll is easy to slice, and add decorations at serving time, whether the piped coffee or chocolate 'bark' of a Christmas log, light-hearted rosettes of Chantilly cream or simply a sprinkling of icing sugar or cocoa. Trim the ends of the roll on the diagonal (trimmings are the cook's perks) and cut on the diagonal for a larger, more attractive spiral slice.

UNDERBAKED AND SOFT – batter puffed but still pale on top and underneath; very floppy when peeled from paper; cake is sticky to the touch; when cut, texture is soggy.
Why: cooking time too short; temperature too low.
What to do: continue baking, raising oven temperature if necessary; after baking, sprinkle with icing sugar.

PERFECT – batter puffed, lightly browned on top and underneath; cake is moist and still pliable when peeled from paper; when pressed with a fingertip, cake just holds mark, but is dry to the touch; when rolled, cake is firm but does not crack.

OVERBAKED AND CRACKED – batter dry and browned, particularly around edges; cake starting to shrink; cracks when peeled from paper.
Why: cooked too long; cooked too slowly, so batter dried out; cake not rolled while hot and pliable.
What to do: trim browned edges after cake is cool; moisten cake with sugar syrup and liqueur; once rolled with filling, cover cracks with whipped cream or buttercream, or sprinkle thickly with icing sugar or cocoa and add decorations such as meringue mushrooms (for Christmas log), herb sprigs and edible flowers; if very cracked, see Quick Fix.

OTHER PROBLEMS

SCORCHED EDGES
Why: heat too high; batter too near edges of baking sheet.
What to do: trim edges thoroughly before filling.

RISEN UNEVENLY
Why: batter unevenly spread; oven heat uneven.
What to do: during baking, rotate baking sheet; after baking, spread filling level on uneven surface so cake is even when rolled.

CAKE STICKS TO TOWEL WHEN ROLLED
Why: cake underbaked; cake batter very moist (common with chocolate); towel damp.
What to do: before rolling, if cake surface seems sticky, sprinkle towel with icing sugar; after rolling, coat cake with whipped cream or buttercream.

QUICK FIX

If cake for a Swiss roll cracks badly or sticks, make these triple-decker towers: cut 7.5-cm/3-inch rounds with a biscuit or pastry cutter, allowing 3 rounds per person. Reserve the best rounds for topping. Sandwich and top 2 remaining rounds with your filling, piping rosettes if possible for neat effect. Hide trimmings of cake inside the filling. Cut reserved rounds in half and perch them at an angle on the filling, like butterfly wings. Leave plain, or decorate with a 'body' of red berries or a single chocolate truffle.

Creamed cakes, including pound cake

I CAN JUST REMEMBER HOW OUR COOK, OLD EMILY, measured ingredients for pound cake. She put two eggs on one side of the scale and balanced them one by one with sugar, butter and flour. Perfect proportions every time. Some cooks add a teaspoon of baking powder to the flour, but not Emily. She relied on vigorous beating of butter and sugar until white and fluffy ('*blanchir*' is the graphic French expression, equivalent to our 'creaming'). This was followed by some equally hard beating as the eggs were added, a little at a time. It is at this stage that pound cake batter can curdle, making the cake heavy. Cold eggs are a likely cause, so Emily would beat directly with her hand for warmth. Watery eggs or inferior butter with a high water content can also cause curdling. If this happens to you, warm the bowl slightly and beat the batter until smooth again. If there are still eggs to be added, first beat in a tablespoon of the flour.

Pound cake is the queen of creamed cakes, and there are many others using different proportions, flours or ground nuts, and raising agents other than eggs. Typical are Australian pineapple and caramel cake with ground almonds, American devil's food cake, British Madeira cake and the Austrian hazelnut pound cake overleaf. These creamed cake batters are rich and much more varied than sponge cake, so they need less embellishment. Flavours like cinnamon, chocolate or cocoa, nutmeg or Cognac are sometimes added, but it's important not to blanket the taste of butter. A thin slice of candied citrus peel baked in the cake, or a transparent sugar glaze is often enough. Given its fat, a creamed cake keeps well – wrap it tightly and it will taste even better after a week.

bottom to top

PERFECTLY BAKED – batter nearly doubled in volume with deep golden crust; a skewer inserted in centre of cake comes out clean, though sometimes moist with fat; cake springs back when lightly pressed with a fingertip and starts to shrink from pan; flavour pleasantly buttery. Note: light cracking, particularly of loaf shapes, is normal.

UNDERBAKED AND SUNKEN CENTRE – sides of cake risen, but centre sunk; top often sugary; a skewer inserted in centre of cake is sticky when withdrawn.

OVERBAKED AND HEAVY – batter poorly risen, crust colour dark; cake very firm when pressed with a fingertip

PEAKED TOP – centre of cake rises higher than sides; crust often cracks to reveal paler crumb.

clockwise from bottom

PERFECT TEXTURE – when cut, cake is light, moist and even.
PEAKED TOP – texture uneven and slightly coarse; crust is rough.
OVERBAKED AND HEAVY – cake is dense and sometimes shows dry patches of flour and streaks of fat.
UNDERBAKED AND SUNKEN CENTRE – centre of cake is close-textured and soggy, often with soggy bottom layer.

QUICK FIX

If a creamed cake is heavy or underbaked, cut it in thick slices and brown in a toaster or under the grill. Top with jam or ice cream,

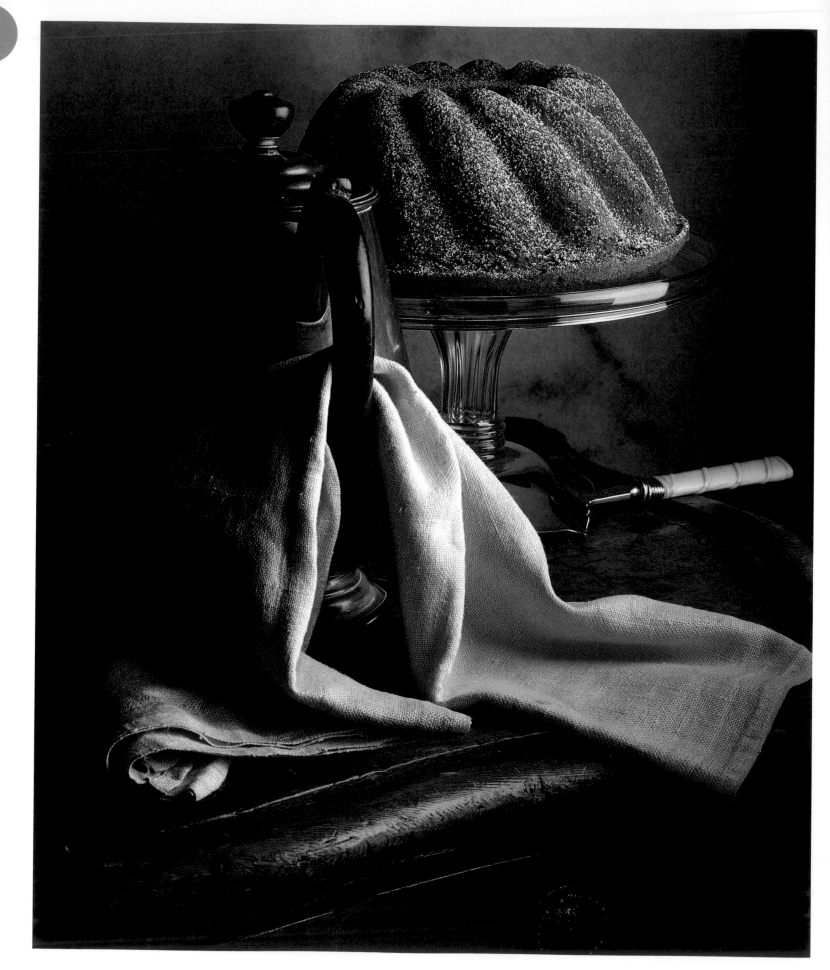

Hazelnut pound cake

Nusskuchen

SERVES 10-12

Toasted hazelnuts give this classic pound cake a rich flavour and crisp golden crust. For a warming winter combination, serve it with Chocolate and Stout Sauce (page 138). In summer try vanilla ice cream.

125 g/4 oz chopped hazelnuts	6 eggs
375 g/12 oz flour	2 tablespoons instant coffee dissolved in
1½ tablespoons baking powder	60 ml/2 fl oz milk
1 teaspoon salt	icing sugar, for sprinkling (optional)
375 g/12 oz butter, softened	
375 g/12 oz sugar	25-cm/10-inch tube cake pan

Preheat oven to 175°C/350°F/gas4. Spread the hazelnuts on a baking sheet and toast in the preheated oven until lightly brown, stirring once, 12-15 minutes. Let cool slightly, then grind the nuts in a food processor or using a rotary cheese grater. Note: do not overwork or they will be oily.

Brush the cake pan generously with butter and sprinkle with flour, discarding the excess. Sift the flour with the baking powder and salt.

Cream the butter with an electric mixer or wooden spoon. Gradually beat in the sugar and continue beating until the mixture is light and fluffy, 4-5 minutes.

Beat the eggs into the butter mixture one by one, beating thoroughly between additions. If the mixture starts to separate, beat in a tablespoon of flour. Stir in the ground hazelnuts and dissolved coffee. Finally, sift the flour over the batter in three batches, folding in each batch as lightly as possible.

Spoon the batter into the prepared cake pan and bake in the preheated oven until done, 50-60 minutes. Let cool for 5 minutes, then turn out on a wire rack to cool. Just before serving, sprinkle the cake with icing sugar.

Hazelnut pound cake

Chocolate roll with espresso buttercream

SERVES 8-10

As decoration, you may like to pipe a few rosettes of buttercream along this chocolate log, topping them with chocolate-coated coffee beans. When it comes to buttercream, I'm fussy about the butter – it must be the very best, unsalted.

45 g/1½ oz flour	75 ml/2½ fl oz water
30 g/1 oz cocoa powder	250 g/8 oz butter
½ teaspoon salt	4 teaspoons instant espresso coffee dissolved in 2 tablespoons hot water, or more coffee to taste
4 eggs	
125 g/4 oz granulated sugar	
½ teaspoon vanilla essence	
icing sugar for sprinkling	for the sugar syrup
	60 g/2 oz granulated sugar
for the espresso buttercream	45 ml/1½ fl oz water
4 egg yolks	2 tablespoons Cognac (optional)
100 g/3¼ oz granulated sugar	

Preheat the oven to 190°C/375°F/gas5. Butter a 25x40-cm/10x16-inch baking sheet, line it with greaseproof paper and butter the paper. Sift together the flour, cocoa and salt.

Put the eggs, sugar and vanilla in the bowl of a heavy-duty electric mixer and whisk until mixed. Turn the speed to high and continue whisking until the mixture is light and thick enough to leave a ribbon trail when the whisk is lifted, 8-10 minutes. Note: if whisking by hand, set the bowl over a pan of hot but not boiling water, whisk the mixture to the ribbon stage, then take the bowl from the heat and whisk until cool.

Sift the flour over the egg mixture in three batches, folding in each as lightly as possible. Spread the batter evenly in a rectangle on the prepared baking sheet just to the edges of the sheet. Bake in the preheated oven until done, 8-10 minutes.

Slide the cake off the baking sheet on to a rack by gently pulling the paper with the cake on top. Turn the cake over on to a tea towel. Peel off the paper and roll the warm cake inside the towel, starting with a long side. Leave the rolled cake to cool.

Meanwhile, make the buttercream filling: beat the egg yolks in a large bowl until mixed. Heat the sugar with the water until dissolved, bring to the boil and boil without stirring until the syrup reaches soft-ball stage (115°C/239°F on a sugar thermometer). Gradually pour the hot sugar syrup into the egg yolks, beating constantly, and continue beating until the mixture is cool and thick, about 5 minutes. Cream the butter and gradually beat it into the cooled egg mixture. Note: if the egg mixture is warm, it will melt the butter. Beat in dissolved espresso coffee, adding more to taste. Cover the buttercream and chill until just firm, 15-30 minutes.

Meanwhile, make the sugar syrup: gently heat the sugar and water, stirring occasionally until the sugar is dissolved. Boil until clear, about 1 minute. Remove from the heat and add the Cognac if you like.

Assemble the roll: unroll the cooled cake and trim edges. Brush the cake with sugar syrup. Spread the buttercream in a layer on the cake and roll it up. Chill until firm, 1-2 hours.

Just before serving, sprinkle the roll with icing sugar and trim the ends on the diagonal. Set the roll on a platter.

Fruit cakes

IT'S HIGH SUMMER NOW AND ALREADY WE'VE HAD THE CHRISTMAS CAKE ripening in a tin box for three months. Every so often I moisten the muslin in which it is wrapped with port or Cognac, so the fruit mellows and the crumb turns moist and dark; a cut apple in the tin helps too. When the children come home in December we'll add an icing of marzipan and candied fruits. On Christmas Eve, the first slice is cut by the oldest and youngest in the house, eyes closed with wishes for the New Year. For me, that's the start of the festivities. English Christmas cake is the richest of all fruit cakes, but equally traditional are combinations such as Irish porter cake with raisins, brown sugar and beer, or an Italian mix of toasted hazelnuts, almonds, figs and dark chocolate. One of my favourites is a blond pound cake dotted with whole red candied cherries. Fruit cake batter may be moistened with grated or puréed fruits such as apple or pineapple, and with Cognac or other spirits.

Dried fruits tend to fall to the bottom of the cake, especially if they are large. One trick is to toss them in flour so the batter adheres. And if dried fruits seem shrivelled, soak them for a few minutes in hot water, or better still in Cognac or whisky to plump them, being sure to dry them afterwards. Warm spices like ginger, cinnamon and cloves are common flavourings.

Fruit cakes may be made by the creamed method (page 283) or that for batter breads (page 288). They need plenty of eggs and raising agent for the heavy fruit. Plain fruit cakes are often baked in a loaf for slicing and spreading with butter, but richer ones are traditionally round. Oven temperatures also vary – the bigger the cake, the lower the heat – with slow cooking vital for dense cakes heavy with fruit. Testing a fruit cake can be tricky, as a skewer inserted in the centre may be moist with fat and crumbs even when the cake is cooked – to be safe, test it in several places. If a cake browns before it is done, cover it loosely with foil. All fruit cakes improve on keeping for a week or two, longer if rich.

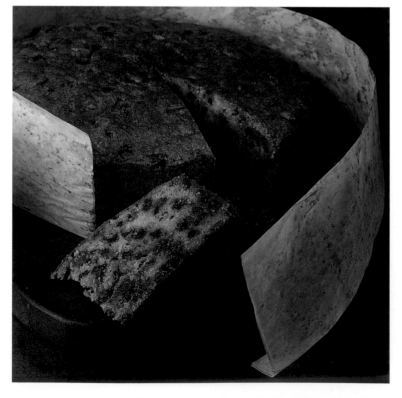

PERFECT TEXTURE – when cut, fruit is evenly distributed, crumb rich and moist; flavour mellow, especially if it has been stored in an airtight container.

PERFECTLY BAKED – batter risen half to two-thirds, depending on richness of recipe; crust an even deep golden brown, starting to shrink from pan; a skewer inserted in centre of cake comes out clean, though sometimes moist with a few crumbs; top of cake is level.

UNDERBAKED – upper crust of cake is shiny, with no fruit showing; often centre of cake is sunken and when cut, batter is separated, with fruit forming a dark lower layer in cake with lighter sticky layer above.

Why: baking time too short; oven heat too low; oven heat uneven or door opened causing draught during baking; batter not beaten enough; too much fruit; fruit not dry and not coated with flour; too little raising agent.

What to do: pretend cake is a pudding – cut it into fingers or chunks and top with whipped cream, custard or apple sauce.

PREPARING TO BAKE CAKES

Good organization is the key to successful cake baking. Remember to:

1 Preheat oven at least 20 minutes in advance.
2 While oven is still cold, arrange the shelves in a convenient position. In most cases, a shelf is best placed in the bottom third of the oven, but this does depend on the heat source, especially in a convection oven. In some ovens, cake pans are best placed on a shelf side by side, in others front and back. In any case, always turn cake pans during cooking so cakes bake evenly.
3 Be sure the pan is the size and shape indicated in the recipe – even a small variation can disrupt the baking of a delicate batter.
4 Prepare the cake pan according to recipe directions. To ensure a thin even coating of fat (usually butter), melt it and then brush the pan. For cakes which tend to stick, freeze the mould and brush again. After coating with fat, a sprinkling of sugar gives a crisp crust, but can caramelize and prevent even browning. Flour forms a light crust, helping delicate cakes detach from the pan. Sliced or slivered nuts will toast to be temptingly golden.

5 Most recipes will advise you to line the base of the pan with baking paper or greaseproof paper to protect the batter and prevent sticking. If so, be sure the paper is completely flat as any folds will mark the cake. For rich fruit cakes and gingerbreads, the sides of the pan should also be lined with paper, which is often left on the cake to keep it moist during storage.
6 In general, greaseproof paper is useful for lining cake pans which are baked in gentle heat. Baking paper is more robust, best for lining baking sheets and for tasks such as holding dried beans when blind-baking a pastry case. Sometimes, for very rich fruit cakes cooked for lengthy periods, the exterior of the cake pan is also wrapped in newspaper or brown paper to help prevent the surface of the cake from overcooking.
7 Before you start mixing, assemble all the equipment you need, weigh out ingredients and complete preparations such as softening butter, blanching nuts or tossing fruit in flour.

OTHER PROBLEMS

PEAKED TOP
Why: oven heat too high.
What to do: make peak an attraction, brushing cake with apricot glaze and adding decoration of candied fruits on peak. Brush them with glaze.

SUNKEN CENTRE
Why: underbaked; too little raising agent; too little flour; fruit separated from batter; oven temperature too low.
What to do: level the top by covering with icing; if deeply sunken, trim high edges and pack into centre hollow before adding icing.

OVERBAKED AND DRY
Why: baked too long; oven heat too high; too little fruit; too little fat; too much raising agent; cake overbaked; not stored in airtight container; not stored long enough.
What to do: poke holes in cake with a skewer, baste with orange or apple juice, sweet wine or Cognac, then wrap tightly and leave for 2-3 hours for cake to moisten; if cake is rich with fruit, leave to mellow for at least 2 weeks in airtight container.

LACKS TASTE
Why: too little or poor fruit; too little spice; not stored long enough for flavour to develop.
What to do: see Overbaked and dry.

Mrs Green's Christmas cake

SERVES 12-16

This recipe takes us back 100 years to Victorian England and Mrs Green, who was a cook in a great house with more than a dozen in the family. She would double or triple this recipe, using her hands to warm and dissolve the sugar, making mixing easy.

375 g/¾ lb flour	375 g/¾ lb sugar
½ teaspoon freshly grated nutmeg	6 eggs, at room temperature
½ teaspoon ground allspice	500 g/1 lb seedless raisins
½ teaspoon salt	125 g/4 oz flaked almonds
125 g/4 oz candied cherries	3 tablespoons Cognac
125 g/4 oz chopped candied orange peel	25-cm/10-inch springform pan
375 g/¾ lb butter, softened	

Preheat the oven to 150°C/300°F/gas2. Generously brush the springform pan with butter, line the base and sides with greaseproof paper and butter the paper. Sprinkle the pan with flour, discarding excess.

Sift the flour with the nutmeg, allspice and salt. Put the cherries in a small pan of cold water, bring to the boil and boil for 30 seconds to rinse away syrup or sugar. Drain the cherries on paper towels and coarsely chop them. In a small bowl, toss the cherries and candied orange peel in 2-3 tablespoons of the flour.

With your hand or using an electric mixer, cream the butter in a large bowl. Beat in the sugar until the mixture is soft and light, 8-10 minutes. Beat in the eggs one at a time, beating well between additions – if the mixture starts to separate, beat in a little flour between each egg. With your hand or a wooden spoon, stir in remaining flour in three batches. Finally, mix in the cherries, orange peel, raisins, flaked almonds and Cognac.

Transfer the batter to the prepared pan, leaving a shallow depression in the centre. Bake the cake in the preheated oven until done, 2-3 hours.

Leave the cake to cool in the pan. When cooled completely, unmould the cake and wrap it in muslin. Store in an airtight container for at least a month and up to a year, basting from time to time with rum, brandy or port.

Batter breads, including gingerbreads

BATTER BREADS (ALSO CALLED TEA BREADS) HAVE A MOIST, crumbly texture more like a cake than a bread. They are simple affairs, quickly mixed from ingredients which happen to be on hand – blackberries, blueberries, grated carrot or courgette may appear in summer, with apples, dried fruits, nuts and cranberries for autumn. Chemical leaveners are the main raising agents (see Bicarbonate of Soda and Baking Powder, page 271), though eggs may be included too. Spices are often a feature – allspice, nutmeg, cinnamon, cardamom, anise, and, of course, ginger in the multiplicity of ethnic recipes for gingerbread.

These breads, like pancakes, involve sifting flour, sugar, raising agents and spices, making a well in the centre, adding the moist ingredients, and then stirring the two together. A rough, almost lumpy batter is the aim – when overmixed, a batter bread is usually disappointingly heavy. Batter breads are also lighter when made with softer flours, ground from wheat that is relatively low in gluten.

Melted batter breads are also mixed like pancakes, except that the fat, sugar and liquid ingredients are melted until smooth, left to cool, then stirred into the flour. Melting is common for gingerbreads, helping develop flavour and mixing the spices evenly with ingredients such as honey and molasses. A medium-hot oven, around 190°C/375°F/gas5, helps the raising agent develop well. Often sweet batter breads are baked in a loaf pan and then sliced to serve plain or with butter or cream cheese. Most of these cakes keep well, mellowing and darkening to aromatic richness.

Sweet batter breads and melted batter breads are allowed imperfections which are forbidden in the perfect sponge or pound cake. A crack in the top is fine provided it is neither a high peak nor a gaping sunken crater. The crust of a melted cake is often moist, even sticky, so be sure to line the sides – as well as the base – of the pan with greaseproof paper before baking. When cut, a few bubbles in the crumb simply show a melted cake has risen well. A serious potential problem with all these cakes is dryness – this can be treated, but it's better still to avoid problems by careful mixing, and not allow the cake to bake too long.

QUICK FIX

If gingerbread or a spice bread is dry, use it to flavour ice cream: break it by hand or in a food processor to coarse crumbs. For every 250 g/8 oz crumbs, allow 1 litre/·1⅔ pints vanilla ice cream. Leave ice cream to thaw until slightly soft. Toast the crumbs in a 175°C/350°F/gas4 oven until dry and crisp, 10-15 minutes. Stir into ice cream and taste, adding more spice such as ground ginger or cinnamon if you like. Refreeze until firm.

PERFECTLY BAKED *above* – batter rises half to two-thirds; cake (here spice bread) is generous brown and starting to shrink from pan; a skewer inserted in centre of cake comes out clean, though sometimes moist with fat; top crust of cake is shiny and moist, often cracked. HEAVY, OFTEN UNDERBAKED *below* – cake poorly risen, centre is often sunken; crust dry, dark and shrinking from pan; a skewer inserted in centre is sticky when withdrawn.

PERFECT TEXTURE – when cut, consistency is open, firm and very moist; flavour is full-bodied, often with spice or fruit.

OVERBAKED AND DRY – when cut, crust of cake is dry, top often split; texture is firm, despite air bubbles; flavour is flat. *Why:* oven heat too high; baked too long; too much flour; too much raising agent. *What to do:* if there is time, pierce holes in cake with a skewer and baste with apple juice or a light honey syrup; wrap tightly and store for a week or more.

OTHER PROBLEMS

HEAVY, OFTEN UNDERBAKED
Why: batter overmixed; too little raising agent; too little flour; too much fat or liquid; if underbaked, cooking time too short, oven heat too low. *What to do:* if underbaked, continue cooking, raising oven temperature if necessary; serve with poached fruit, apple sauce or sour cream.
LACKS TASTE
Why: too little salt or flavouring used; spices past their best. *What to do:* spread with butter or cream cheese, or cube and serve with dip of Salty Caramel Sauce (see page 240).
PEAKED TOP
Why: too much raising agent; oven heat too high. *What to do:* serve in thick slices to disguise shape.

Muffins

THE PERFECT MUFFIN IS LIGHT IN YOUR HAND, risen to a shallow, cracked peak, moist and fluffy inside – nibble it with a slice or two of crisp bacon and, for me, you have the ideal breakfast. You can leave the muffin quite plain, or add the same fruits as in sweet batter breads, or use tasty cornmeal, oatmeal or bran. Muffins are so good I could not resist looking in detail at what can go wrong.

If heavy, muffins have almost always been overmixed – the batter should be stirred very lightly and remain almost rough. When the inside crumb is full of holes, overmixing may also be the culprit; alternatively it could be too much raising agent. How thoroughly should a muffin be baked? Well, a muffin should not be dry, but it is important to cook until the sugar in the batter toasts to a good brown crust. You need a hot oven, so the outside batter sets quickly, then rises in the centre for that pretty peak – typical temperature is 200°C/400°F/gas6. To avoid overflowing, don't fill muffin pans more than two-thirds full as the batter should rise one-third to half its volume.

PERFECT *front* – muffin is deep golden and starting to shrink from pan; centre rises to a shallow, cracked peak; a skewer inserted in centre comes out clean, but may be moist with fruit; inside texture is even and spongy, crumbling easily; taste is fragrant.

back, from left to right
FULL OF HOLES – muffin is tunnelled with holes, often with a high, broken peak.
UNDERBAKED – muffin is moist, wet in the centre; outside crust pale and batter not yet peaked and shrinking from pan; a skewer inserted in centre is sticky with batter flavour doughy.
HEAVY – batter scarcely rises and top of muffin is flat; crust is pale; texture is tight and dry.

Cranberry orange bread

MAKES 1 MEDIUM LOAF *pictured on page 277*

In summer, when fresh cranberries are out of season, I use blueberries or gooseberries.

250 g/8 oz flour	125 g/4 oz
150 g/5 oz sugar	cranberries
¾ teaspoon baking	grated zest of
powder	1 orange
½ teaspoon salt	
2 eggs	20x10x5-cm/
175 ml/6 fl oz milk	8x4x2-inch loaf pan
150 ml/5 fl oz	
vegetable oil	

Preheat oven to 175°C/350°F/gas4. Butter loaf pan and sprinkle with flour, discarding excess.

Sift flour, sugar, baking powder and salt into a large bowl and make a well in centre. In a small bowl, whisk together eggs, milk and oil. Add egg mixture to well and stir with a whisk until just mixed. Note: do not beat batter or bread will be heavy. Stir in cranberries and orange zest.

Spoon mixture into pan, filling it two-thirds full. Bake on lower rack of oven until done, 1-1¼ hours. Let cool slightly, then turn out on a rack to cool. Serve warm or at room temperature.

Summer strawberry mint muffins

Preheat oven to 200°C/400°F/gas6. Butter and flour 12 medium muffin cups. Prepare batter as for bread above, substituting hulled and chopped strawberries for cranberries and 3 tablespoons chopped fresh mint for orange zest. Pour into cups and bake until done, 20-25 minutes.

QUICK FIX

If muffins are heavy or stale, make rum balls: for every 175 g/6 oz of muffins, finely chop 125 g/4 oz walnut halves with the muffins in the food processor. Sift together 125 g/4 oz icing sugar and 2 tablespoons cocoa. Stir in 60 ml/2 fl oz rum and 1 tablespoon light corn syrup or honey. Stir in the crumb mixture – it should be moist enough to shape. Roll the mixture between the palms into walnut-sized balls. Set on a tray of icing sugar and roll with two forks until coated. Makes about 40 balls.

Tortes and flourless cakes

TORTE COMES FROM THE GERMAN FOR CAKE but we've come to think of it more specifically as a dense rich mixture, often containing ground nuts or breadcrumbs with little or no flour. Potato flour or cornflour may be used, but many tortes rely simply on eggs to hold them together. The almond torte here, taught to me by long-time friend, chef Fernand Chambrette, is a perfect example. Chocolate is another favourite flavouring as it also helps to bind the cake.

Don't expect torte batter to rise much when cooked – with very little or no raising agent other than eggs, it simply sets in a low oven to be firm and delectably moist. A springform pan is helpful, so the dense yet fragile cake can be slid easily on to a platter.

Tortes tend to be more of a dessert than a traditional cake, so plan on serving them that way, with a topping of ice cream, whipped cream or crème fraîche and an appropriate sauce. They'll make a grand end to dinner, and you can make them well ahead of time. Being so rich, they all keep well for at least a week, often improving in flavour all the while.

UNDERBAKED AND CENTRE SUNKEN – batter (here almond torte) rises poorly, often separated at base of pan; when unmoulded and sliced, texture is dense, even disintegrating.
Why: if underbaked, cooking time too short; oven heat too low; too few eggs or too little raising agent; not enough flour or nuts; batter overfolded.
What to do: if underbaked, continue cooking, raising temperature if necessary; serve with sauce, such as a fruit coulis or vanilla custard. See also Quick Fix.

PERFECT – when cut, texture is dense, often crumbling, very rich and moist; shape is even and shallow with a flat top; cake just starting to shrink from pan; for some but not all batters, a skewer inserted in centre comes out clean, but may be moist with fat; flavour is intense and mellows if stored in airtight container.

OTHER PROBLEMS

OVERBAKED
Why: cooking time too long; oven heat too high.
What to do: moisten with simple sauce of double cream, flavoured with powdered coffee or chocolate.

FLAVOUR FLAT
Why: too little sugar; too little flavouring, especially salt; overbaked.

What to do: if too little sugar, sprinkle with icing sugar; serve with caramel, chocolate or other intensely flavoured sauce.

STICKS TO PAN
Why: pan not lined properly; torte underbaked; oven heat too low, so batter melted rather than dried.
What to do: cut into wedges in the pan and serve on individual plates; cover cracks with Chantilly cream or crème fraîche.

Chef Chambrette's almond torte

SERVES 6-8

After 50 years in the restaurant business, Chef Chambrette is a master at making the most of what he has. From just three basic ingredients – almonds, egg whites and sugar – he makes this crunchy golden torte. If you like, decorate it with a trail of melted dark or white chocolate.

90 g/3 oz sliced almonds	granulated sugar
250 g/8 oz ground almonds	½ teaspoon vanilla essence
125 g/4 oz icing sugar, sifted	grated zest of 2 lemons
whites of 4 eggs	pinch of salt
2 tablespoons	23-cm/9-inch springform pan

Preheat the oven to 160°C/325°F/gas3. Butter the base and sides of the cake pan, line the base with greaseproof paper and butter the paper. Sprinkle the base and sides of pan with sliced almonds and chill until set, at least 15 minutes. Mix the ground almonds with icing sugar.

Meanwhile, make the batter: stiffly beat the egg whites, using a heavy-duty electric mixer or by hand, ideally in a copper bowl (see page 223). Add the granulated sugar and continue beating until the egg whites are glossy and form a long peak when the whisk is lifted, about 1 minute more. Stir in the vanilla, lemon zest and salt. Fold in the ground almond and icing sugar mixture in three batches.

Pour the batter into the prepared pan and tap on the counter to expel air bubbles. Bake in the preheated oven until done, 40-45 minutes. Remove the torte and let it cool completely before unmoulding.

Cheesecakes

THE FIRST POINT ABOUT CHEESECAKE is that every type is different – each calls for a specific fresh or cream cheese and woe betide the cook who makes substitutions. Fresh cheeses have differing fat and moisture contents and many now include stabilizers, so be sure to use the right kind – whether it be ricotta, mascarpone, cottage or cream cheese. Good flavourings, simple enough for the taste of the cheese to come through, include candied or dried fruit, vanilla, grated citrus zest and chocolate. Some cheesecakes are really very easy – mixtures of cheese and sugar set with egg in a pastry crust, which can vary from French pie or French sweet pie pastry (both usually blind baked, see page 295) to biscuit or cracker crust. Textures vary from firm to fluffy and light. It's the dense, rich cheesecakes like the one overleaf which are tricky, calling for gentle handling. As fresh cheese is moist, all cheesecakes tend to shrink a bit during baking.

PERFECT – top is pale cream colour; when cut, texture is even, creamy smooth or with curds depending on type of cheese; bottom crust is fully cooked; cake just starting to shrink from pan; batter is set around the outside, but trembles in centre when pan is tapped; flavour rich and fresh.

OVERBAKED – when cut, texture is uneven and centre of cake is dry and crumbling; cake shrunk from pan, often quite brown and tough.
Why: cooked too long; oven heat too high.
What to do: serve with a fruit coulis or sauce.

OTHER PROBLEMS

UNDERBAKED AND STICKY
Why: cooking time too short; oven heat too low.
What to do: if slightly underbaked and a bit softer than usual, served as planned, cutting with a knife dipped in boiling water; if very underbaked, see Quick Fix.

CAKE SEPARATED WITH SUNKEN CENTRE
Why: too many eggs; wrong type of cheese; eggs not whisked enough; baked too fast; under- or overbaked; removed from oven too soon, so cooled too quickly.
What to do: if firm and holding shape, top with berries, sliced poached peaches or pears and brush with glaze. If very underbaked, see Quick Fix.

QUICK FIX

When underbaked cheesecake sinks badly or collapses, refurbish it as a mousse to serve with gingersnap biscuits or fresh fruit. Scoop the cheesecake from pan, leaving as much crust as possible behind. For every 600 ml/1 pint underbaked batter, beat in 2 lightly whisked egg whites, using a mixer to obtain a stiff, smooth mixture. Taste and, if you like, add 1-2 tablespoons rum. Whip 125 ml/4 fl oz double cream and fold into the mixture. Pile the mousse in bowls and chill. Serves 4-6.

Classic American cheesecake

Serves 12-16

Snowy white and inches high, rich creamy cheesecake is an American dream. There are endless variations and all kinds of tricks, but the real secret is to use ordinary packaged cream cheese with nothing fancy added. Prepare at least a day ahead, to allow it to chill. If you like, serve with Berry Fruit Sauce (page 137), to cut the richness.

1 kg/2 lb cream cheese, at room
    temperature
200 g/6½ oz sugar
1 teaspoon vanilla essence
½ teaspoon salt
4 eggs
finely grated zest of 1 lemon

for the crust
75 g/2½ oz butter
200 g/6½ oz dry biscuit crumbs, such as
    gingersnap or cream cracker
45 g/1½ oz sugar

23-cm/9-inch springform pan

Preheat the oven to 150°C/300°F/gas2. Brush the cake pan generously with butter. Make crust: melt the butter, stir in the biscuit crumbs and sugar. Press the mixture into the bottom of the pan, spreading it evenly with the back of a spoon. Bake until lightly toasted, 13-15 minutes. Remove and leave to cool on a rack.

Make the cheesecake: in a heavy-duty electric mixer on low speed, beat the cream cheese until soft. Note: use the paddle attachment instead of the whisk, so air is not beaten into the mixture. Add the sugar, vanilla and salt and continue beating until light and creamy, 3-4 minutes. Add the eggs, one by one, beating until smooth. Stir in the lemon zest. Pour the batter into the cake pan and bake in the preheated oven until done, 1-1½ hours.

Turn the oven off, open the door slightly and leave the cake to cool for 1 hour. Transfer to the refrigerator and chill for at least 12 hours or overnight. To serve, warm the sides of the pan with your hands to melt the butter coating. Remove the ring from cake, loosening gently, if possible without using a knife. Set the cheesecake, with the pan base, on a plate.

Pie and sweet pie pastry cases

A CRISP PASTRY CASE, PALE GOLD OR DEEPER BRONZE FOR DESSERTS, is the foundation of a good pie or tart, sweet or savoury. Pastry doughs for pies (see page 311) are famous for demanding a light hand. Work them quickly and gently so the gluten in the flour is not developed (the opposite principle from bread and pasta, which need an elastic dough). Avoid adding too much water, or rolling with too much flour, as both make pastry tough. When shaping a pie case, take care not to stretch the pastry as it will shrink again in the oven. Some shrinkage is inevitable, so exaggerate the shape a bit, trimming to leave a generous overlap and pushing the sides high to make a deep container. Prick the base of the case to discourage puffing and shrinkage, and flute the edge if you like, a finish traditional for sweet pies and tarts. A sweet pie case, or one meant to hold a wet filling, is usually blind-baked (see opposite) so it crisps well and forms a delicious frame for open-faced tarts, particularly of fruit.

The importance of chilling pie pastry at every stage cannot be overemphasized – a freezer is useful for speed. After mixing the dough, chilling ensures that the butter or other fat sets, making the pastry easy to roll without sticking; at the same time, gluten in the flour relaxes so the baked pastry will not be tough. In a warm kitchen you need to work quickly. If you have trouble handling a soft pastry, try rolling it between two layers of greaseproof paper. After shaping, chill the pastry again to ensure that it sets immediately when hit by the oven's heat, rather than melting and losing shape.

Now, at last, we come to the filling, and I hardly know where to begin. Should we look at British steak and kidney, or French pear and almond, or Italian sour cherry and cinnamon? The filling may be arranged in spirals or flower shapes for decorative effect – fruit tarts are a good example. A custard or cream filling may brown to form its own decoration, as with a quiche. When adding a wet filling to a fully baked pie case, a coating of dry breadcrumbs or apricot jam glaze helps seal the pastry, so it won't turn soggy. Pastry cream is even more effective in insulating juicy fruits from their pastry case. Whatever your choice, with the perfect pastry case you're off to a good start.

PERFECT FULLY BLIND-BAKED – pastry an even light golden brown, with darker edge for pâte brisée (*left*) and rich golden brown for sweet and nut pastries (*right*); sides of case tall and shrinking from pan and border neatly finished; pastry thin, flaky and crisp for brisée, thicker and more crumbling for nut, pie and sweet pastry; for all pastries, case is without holes and firm enough to support the filling.

PERFECT PARTIALLY BLIND-BAKED – pastry (here sweet pie) set into firm shape, with no translucent moist patches; colour cream, with light golden edges; flavour still slightly mealy with uncooked flour. Note: a partially baked case is always filled and baked further.

SIDES COLLAPSED – sides of case shrunk unevenly down to base, so filling would leak; pastry may or may not be browned.
Why: pastry not chilled before baking; case not carefully lined, with paper and beans pressed firmly against side; oven heat too low; paper removed too soon.
What to do: if collapse has caused only small shrinkage, build up gap with trimmings of raw pastry and continue baking; if collapse widespread, see Quick Fix.

OTHER PROBLEMS

PUFFY BASE

Why: before baking, pastry not pricked to discourage rising; cases not carefully lined with paper and beans or with a second tartlet case; lining removed too soon.

What to do: during baking, prick puffy patches with a fork, press flat and continue baking; when baked, press puffed section flat, taking care not to poke hole in case.

HOLE IN CASE

Why: pastry rolled too thin; case shrunk and split during blind-baking.

What to do: before adding filling, seal with trimmings of raw pastry and bake 3-5 minutes; after filling added, bake at once, hoping heat will seal the leak. Note: if case has become thoroughly soaked with moist filling, it must be discarded.

UNDERBAKED AND PALE

Why: baking time too short; oven heat too low.

What to do: if not filled, continue baking, raising heat if necessary; if filled, place pie towards bottom of oven and continue until very thoroughly baked.

OVERBAKED AND DARK

Why: baked too long; oven too hot.

What to do: trim any scorched parts; if adding cooked filling, be sure to cover dark parts of pastry. Sprinkle scorched parts of a savoury pie with grated cheese, or add whipped cream to a sweet pie.

PASTRY ELASTIC, PASTRY TOUGH

Why: overworked during mixing or rolling; too much water in pastry.

What to do: before baking, chill as long as possible so pastry loses elasticity; after baking, nothing can be done.

LINING A TART PAN

Lining a tart pan correctly to form a deep case is important as it affects the amount of filling the tart can hold.

• Brush the tart pan with butter so the pastry does not stick. Roll out the pastry to a round about 5 cm/2 inches larger in diameter than the tart pan. Wrap the pastry around the rolling pin, lift it and unroll it gently over pan, taking care not to stretch it. Let the pastry hang over the edge of pan.

• Gently lift the edge of pastry with one hand and press it well into the bottom of the pan with the other hand. Roll the pin over the top of the pan, pressing down to cut off excess pastry.

• With forefinger and thumb, press the dough evenly up the sides of the pan from the bottom to increase the height of rim. Neaten the rim with your finger and thumb, fluting it for a sweet pie. Prick the base of the case with a fork to aerate the dough so it bakes more thoroughly. This also helps get rid of air bubbles which may puff up the base.

BLIND BAKING

Pastry cases for pies and tartlets are often partially or completely baked before a moist filling is added. This is called baking 'blind'. The shell is lined with baking paper and weighed down with dry beans or rice to prevent the sides collapsing and the base puffing.

• Preheat oven to 220°C/425°F/gas7. Heat a baking sheet in oven. Prick the base of the pastry with a fork so it does not puff. Line the case with baking paper, pushing it well into the bottom. Half-fill with dried beans or rice. Bake on the hot baking sheet until set and the rim starts to brown, 10-15 minutes.

• Remove paper and beans or rice (they can be reused) and reduce oven to 190°C/375°F/gas5. If filling is to be further baked, cook until base looks dry, about 5 minutes more. If completely baking case, continue until golden and crisp, 10-15 minutes. Cool on a rack.

Fill this festive fruit tart with at least three of the different types of fruit suggested, using what is fresh and in season. You can take an up-to-date approach, with the fruit resembling a bouquet of flowers or, if you prefer, overlap it in more traditional concentric circles. Coat lightly with apricot glaze for a touch of shine.

500 ml/16 fl oz plain yogurt
125 g/4 oz berries
 (strawberries, blackberries,
 blueberries, raspberries)
125 g/4 oz sliced fruit
 (start fruit, fig, kiwi)
few stone fruit
 (apricots, peaches, plums)
juice of ½ a lemon
125 g/4 oz seedless grapes
2 tablespoons icing sugar
4 tablespoons apricot jelly

2 tablespoons orange juice
small bunch of mint for garnish

for the French sweet pie pastry
200 g/6½ oz flour
½ teaspoon salt
100 g/3¼ oz sugar
3 egg yolks
1 teaspoon vanilla essence
100 g/3¼ oz butter, softened

25-cm/10-inch tart pan with
removable base

Put the yogurt in a sieve lined with cheesecloth and let drain until firm enough to cling to a spoon, 2-3 hours. Meanwhile, make the French sweet pie pastry. Sift the flour on to a work surface and make a well in centre. Combine the salt, sugar, egg yolks and vanilla in the well and mix the ingredients with your fingers. Pound the butter with a rolling pin to soften it slightly, add it to the well and quickly work it into the other ingredients. Using a pastry scraper, gradually draw in flour from the sides and continue working with the fingers of both hands until coarse crumbs are formed. Press the pastry into a ball.

Knead the pastry with heel of your hand, pushing it away and gathering it up until it is pliable and pulls away from work surface in one piece, 1-2 minutes. Shape into a ball, wrap it and chill until firm, at least 30 minutes.

Line the tart pan (see left above) and chill until firm, about 15 minutes. Blind-bake the pastry case completely (see left).

Prepare the fruit: hull the strawberries, rinsing them only if sandy. Halve them if large. Sort through the blackberries, blueberries or raspberries. Peel and slice the kiwis; slice the star fruits or figs. Halve the apricots, plums or peaches, discarding the stones. Cut large halves in crescents. Toss the peaches and apricots with lemon juice to prevent browning.

To finish: no more than 1 hour before serving, transfer the drained yogurt to a small bowl and stir in the icing sugar. Spread the yogurt in the baked case and arrange the fruits on top, adding generous quantities and covering the yogurt completely. Melt the apricot jelly with the orange juice, stirring until smooth. Lightly brush the fruit with this glaze and decorate the tart with mint sprigs. Chill until ready to serve.

Tartlets

A LIGHT LITTLE TARTLET, WINKING IMPUDENTLY AT YOU FROM THE PLATE, is the Cadillac of pies and tarts. Luxury fillings are invited, from lobster and smoked salmon to baby vegetables and seasonal fruits such as wild strawberries, giant blueberries or golden cape gooseberries set on a light pastry cream. Tartlets may also be baked together with a filling as an individual quiche or perhaps an almond cream tartlet (right). The case is so frail that tartlets do not keep well – they are by nature a gourmet item.

I like to line tartlet moulds with rounds of pastry cut with a fluted cutter 2.5-5 cm/1-2 inches larger than the mould itself. Boat moulds and miniature moulds, however, are more quickly lined by draping pastry loosely over them, then running the rolling pin on top to cut off the trimmings. In both instances, the pastry must be pushed well above the rim of the mould with your fingers. Be sure the pastry is even, so thinner patches do not scorch.

When the tartlet is to be blind baked, a neat trick is to line the case with a second tartlet mould – much easier than filling each with paper and beans. As when making a pie case, chill the pastry at every stage. Tartlet cases are baked in a hot oven, at 200°C/400°F/gas6 (sweet ones colour and scorch fast). They will be fragile, so let them cool a bit before unmoulding. If blind baked, leave tartlet cases in their moulds so they do not collapse when filled – even so, you are likely to lose one or two.

above

PERFECT – (here pear and almond cream tartlets) case deep, with high sides; pastry crisp and light, but robust enough to support a filling; colour delicately browned with darker edges; flavour of pastry is lightly toasted and filling is intense.

left

PERFECT *left* – case (here French pie pastry) deep with high sides; pastry crisp and light, but robust enough to support a filling; colour delicately browned with darker edges; flavour of pastry is lightly toasted and buttery.

PUFFY BASE *right* – base puffed, leaving less room for filling; case has shrunk, with sides fallen.

Pear and almond cream tartlets

Tartelettes aux poires normande

MAKES 8

Pear with almond is a classic combination in Norman tarts. Really ripe pears show at their best here, as the almond frangipane soaks up generous juice. Look for pears just shorter than the diameter of your moulds, or trim them to fit before slicing.

4 ripe pears
sugar for sprinkling
3-4 tablespoons apricot jelly
2 tablespoons water

for the French sweet pie pastry
275 g/9 oz flour
½ teaspoon salt
125 g/4 oz sugar
4 egg yolks
1 teaspoon vanilla essence
125 g/4 oz butter

for the almond cream
100 g/3¼ oz butter, softened
100 g/3¼ oz sugar
1 egg and 1 egg yolk, lightly beaten
100 g/3¼ oz ground almonds
pinch of salt

eight 10-cm/4-inch tartlet moulds
6-inch/15-cm round pastry cutter (optional)

Make the French sweet pie pastry: sift the flour on to a work surface and make a well in the centre. Combine the salt, sugar, egg yolks and vanilla in the well and mix the ingredients with your fingers. Pound the butter with a rolling pin to soften it slightly, add it to well and quickly work it into the other ingredients. Using a pastry scraper, gradually draw in flour from the sides and continue working with the fingers of both hands until coarse crumbs are formed. Press the pastry into a ball.

Knead the pastry with the heel of your hand, pushing it away and gathering it up until it is smooth, pliable and pulls away from the work surface in one piece, 1-2 minutes. Shape the pastry into a ball, wrap it and chill until firm, at least 30 minutes.

Meanwhile, make the almond cream: beat the butter with an electric mixer or wooden spoon until creamy. Gradually beat in the sugar and continue beating vigorously until the mixture is light and soft. Gradually add the eggs, beating well after each addition. Fold in the ground almonds and salt.

Preheat the oven to 200°C/400°F/gas6. Put a baking sheet in the lower third of the oven to heat. Brush the tartlet moulds with butter. Roll out the pastry to 6-mm/¼-inch thickness. Cut 8 rounds of pastry with the biscuit cutter or using a 15-cm/6-inch pan lid as a guide, rerolling the pastry if necessary. Line the tartlet moulds with the rounds, pressing them well into the bottoms and evenly up the sides to form neat cases. Chill until firm, about 15 minutes.

Meanwhile, peel the pears, halve them lengthwise and scoop out the cores. Cut the pear halves across in 6-mm/¼-inch slices and flatten the slices slightly. Spoon the almond cream into the tartlet cases, spreading it evenly. Using a palette knife, lay a pear half on top of the cream in each case. Sprinkle with a little sugar.

Bake the tartlets on the hot baking sheet until the pastry and almond cream are a rich golden brown, 15-20 minutes. Let cool slightly before unmoulding. Shortly before serving, make the apricot glaze: heat the apricot jelly and water in a small saucepan, stirring until melted. Brush the tartlets with the glaze and serve at room temperature.

PROBLEMS

STUCK TO MOULD
Why: filling overflowed or leaked; underbaked; mould scrubbed with soap and water after previous baking.
What to do: if underbaked, continue baking until pastry shrinks from mould; let cool before unmoulding; run knife around edge and scoop out; top with cream or ice cream.

COLLAPSED
Why: pastry too thin; underbaked; filling too moist.
What to do: see Quick Fix.

QUICK FIX

If a tartlet sticks or collapses, hide the damage with a frivolous decoration of herbs or edible flowers.

Filled pies and quiches

HERE I TAKE A LOOK AT PIES WHICH ARE BAKED WITH FILLING – quiche, pecan pie, almond frangipane, English treacle tart and the like. You can take two approaches: either add the filling at the start and bake both pie case and filling together, or partially blind-bake the case (see Blind Baking, page 295), then fill it and bake again. For quiches, custards and all moist fillings, blind-baking is advisable to avoid that unpleasantly doughy crust that we've all come across in poorly baked pies.

When you're adding a moist filling to a partially baked case, to keep the pastry crisp you might try sprinkling the base with a few dried breadcrumbs, or brush the pastry with lightly whisked egg white, drying it in the oven a few minutes before pouring in the filling. To ensure crisp pastry, it also helps to set a pie near the source of heat, usually low down in the oven, and to preheat a baking sheet so the pastry gets a jump start when the pan is placed on the hot sheet. In any case, a baking sheet is a sensible precaution to catch any filling that may leak.

Whenever possible, I'd advise quite a high temperature, around 200°C/400°F/gas6, for baking filled pies with a raw crust. Baking temperature for quiches, however, must be relatively moderate to avoid curdling the custard filling – yet another reason for prebaking the pastry case. Quiche and filled pies are at their best within an hour or two, as the pastry soon loses its crisp freshness despite all precautions. For fullest flavour, I'm a great believer in serving most of these pies, especially quiche, at room temperature or slightly warm. If hot, they taste of custard; if cold, their flavour is stifled.

OTHER PROBLEMS

CASE COLLAPSES WHEN UNMOULDED
Why: pastry rolled unevenly with cracks; underbaked; unmoulded when very hot; filling not set.
What to do: if possible, return to pan and, if warm, leave to cool and set; serve in pan; camouflage savoury pies with parsley and sweet pies with whipped cream.
FLAVOUR EGGY
Why: too much custard; filling ingredients tasteless or lack seasoning; underbaked.
What to do: sprinkle quiche with salty ingredients such as diced crisp bacon or Parmesan cheese, or simply with salt and pepper; top sweet custards with freshly grated nutmeg, cocoa or instant coffee.

UNDERBAKED, BASE SOGGY – filling (here bacon and cheese quiche) may be set and browned but, when cut, pastry base is soggy and filling runs; flavour flat.
Why: case not blind-baked; case underbaked before filling added; pie with filling underbaked; set too high in oven so top browned but underneath not cooked; kept too long before serving.
What to do: continue baking, setting pan on a heated baking sheet low down in oven; if already baked, cover pie loosely with foil and bake 10-15 minutes in a 200°C/400°F/gas6 oven to dry the crust.

PERFECT – filling set and, depending on type, also browned evenly on top; when cut, pastry base is crisp, not soggy, and holds a neat wedge; filling is even-textured, moist but not watery; flavour of all fillings is lively, for quiches and custards, pleasantly creamy.

OVERBAKED, FILLING CURDLED – top very brown; filling dry and shrunken; for quiche and custard (as here), filling is separated, with watery bubbles, and pastry base is soggy.
Why: baked too long; baked too fast.
What to do: add plenty of eye-catching garnishes such as radishes, lettuce leaves and cherry tomatoes for savoury pies, with strawberries, mint or basil sprigs, or chocolate sprinkles for sweet pies.

Double-crust and top-crust pies

WHETHER SWEET OR SAVOURY, DOUBLE- AND TOP-CRUST PIES each have their own quirks. The trick with a double-crust pie is to cook the under-crust thoroughly without the top getting too brown. Start by keeping the lower layer of pastry quite thin and bake the pie well down in the oven, on a preheated baking sheet so it heats rapidly. Moist fillings such as rich meats and juicy fruits are a hindrance to a well-baked bottom crust; one way of absorbing excess juice is to toss the meat or fruit in flour or cornflour. Another is to top the pie with a lattice rather than a flat crust, so moisture can evaporate – both expedients appear in the American apple pie overleaf. For their famous pork pies, the British use a hot lard pastry which is almost impermeable to moisture. When shaping a double-crust pie, take care to seal top and bottom crusts so they do not part company during baking.

With a top-crust pie you've only the upper crust to worry about, the problem here being that the pastry has no lower crust to cling to. If the pie dish has a flat edge, line it with a strip of pastry to support and reinforce the top crust. When covering the pie with pastry, drape it loosely to counteract shrinkage during baking. The crust on a deep-dish pie may collapse if the filling shrinks, as fruit is inclined to do. You can set a purpose-designed pie funnel in the centre of a dish or pan to hold up the crust; on occasion I've used an upturned demitasse cup. Note: it's helpful to bake double-crust pies in clear glass pie plates, allowing you to check the progress of the lower crust as it cooks.

A wet filling creates steam as it cooks, so be sure to slash a pattern of holes in a top crust for steam to escape. Glazes for the crust include beaten egg for a golden finish, whisked egg white sprinkled with sugar for crispness or a brushing of sugar syrup or milk for shine. And always chill the pie thoroughly before baking so the pastry holds its shape.

OTHER PROBLEMS

FILLING TASTELESS
Why: too little salt or sugar; not enough spice, vanilla or other flavouring.
What to do: for savoury pies, serve with ketchup, mustard, olives, pickles or other condiment; for sweet pies, sprinkle with icing sugar. See also Quick Fix.

top to bottom
PERFECT – top crust (here American apple pie) crisp and evenly browned, with a toasted edge; when cut, bottom crust is crisp, not soggy, and holds a neat wedge; filling is tender when pierced with a skewer; flavour of pastry is lightly toasted, buttery for brisée, rich for nut and sweet pastries, with a touch of salt to highlight sweetness.
UNDERBAKED, BASE SOGGY – top crust appears brown and filling may be tender but, when cut, inside pastry is soggy, particularly bottom crust.
Why: cooking time too short; pie placed too high in oven.
What to do: cover pie loosely with foil, set it on a hot baking sheet low down in oven and continue baking. If baked, let pie cool, remove top crust and cut into wedges; scoop filling on to individual plates, discarding bottom crust, and add wedges of top crust.

Fennel and Roquefort quiche

SERVES 6-8

Sharp Roquefort works well with this aromatic fennel custard filling, but other firm blue cheeses are fine.

750 g/1½ lb fennel bulbs,
    trimmed and sliced
30 g/1 oz butter
2 tablespoons chopped
    thyme
salt and pepper
175 g/6 oz Roquefort
    cheese, crumbled

for the French pie pastry
200 g/6½ oz flour
100 g/3¼ oz butter,
    softened

1 egg yolk
½ teaspoon salt
45 ml/1½ fl oz water,
    or more if needed

for the custard
1 egg
1 egg yolk
125 ml/4 fl oz milk
60 ml/2 fl oz double cream
pinch of grated nutmeg

25-cm/10-inch tart pan
with removable base

Make the French pie pastry: sift flour on to a work surface and make well in centre. Pound butter with a rolling pin to soften it. Put butter, egg yolk, salt and water into well. With the fingers, work moist ingredients until thoroughly mixed. Draw in flour and work in other ingredients with fingers of both hands until coarse crumbs form. If crumbs are very dry, add 1-2 tablespoons more water. Press pastry into a ball. Lightly flour work surface. Blend pastry by pushing it away from you with heel of your hand, then gathering it up until it is very smooth and peels away from work surface in one piece, 1-2 minutes. Shape into a ball, wrap and chill.

Line the tart pan (see page 295) and chill until firm, about 15 minutes. Partially blind-bake the pastry case (see page 295). Set the oven at 190°C/375°F/gas5.

Prepare fennel: heat butter in a frying pan and add fennel, thyme, salt and pepper – very little salt, as cheese will be salty. Press buttered foil on top, cover and sweat, stirring occasionally, until very soft but not brown, 20-30 minutes.

Meanwhile, make the custard: in a bowl, whisk the egg, egg yolk, milk, cream, nutmeg, salt and pepper just until mixed.

When the fennel is soft, add the Roquefort cheese and stir to melt the cheese. Spread the mixture evenly in the base of the pastry case and pour over the custard. Gently mix the fennel mixture and custard with a fork.

Bake until done, 30-35 minutes. Let cool slightly before unmoulding. Serve warm or at room temperature.

Fennel and roquefort quiche

Latticed American apple pie

In this American classic, spiced apples are tossed in flour to thicken lightly the juices which develop as the apples cook. Serve the pie still warm *à la mode*, with vanilla ice cream, or New England-style, with a slice of Cheddar.

1 kg/2 lb tart apples, preferably Granny Smith	for the American pie pastry
juice of 1 lemon	300 g/10 oz flour
100 g/3¼ oz sugar, more for sprinkling	2 tablespoons sugar
2 tablespoons flour	½ teaspoon salt
½ teaspoon ground cinnamon	150 g/5 oz vegetable fat
¼ teaspoon grated nutmeg	6-7 tablespoons cold water, more if needed
pinch of salt	
	23-cm/9-inch pie pan

Make the American pie pastry: sift the flour, sugar and salt into a large bowl. Add the vegetable fat and cut it into the flour mixture with 2 round-bladed knives or a pastry blender. Rub the fat into the flour with your fingers until it forms coarse crumbs. Sprinkle the water over the mixture, 1 tablespoon at a time, and mix with a fork until crumbs start sticking together. Press pastry into a ball – it should be quite rough. Wrap tightly and chill until firm, at least 30 minutes.

Brush the pie pan with butter and lightly flour the work surface. Roll out two-thirds of the pastry into a 28-cm/11-inch round. Lift on the rolling pin and drape over the pan, pressing well into the bottom and up the sides. Lift the pan and, using a knife, trim the pastry even with the outer edge. Add the trimmings to the remaining pastry. Chill the case and remaining pastry until firm, about 15 minutes.

Meanwhile, peel, halve and core the apples. Cut them into thick slices and toss with lemon juice. Stir to mix with the sugar, flour, spices and salt. Taste and add more sugar and spice, if necessary. Spread mixture in chilled pastry case and brush edge of the pastry with cold water. Roll out remaining pastry to a 25-cm/10-inch square, trim edges and cut into 1.25-cm/½-inch wide strips, preferably with a fluted pastry wheel. There should be 16 strips.

Set aside 2 strips. Lay half the remaining strips across the filling about 2-cm/¾-inch apart, letting the ends hang over the edge of the pan. Fold back alternate strips halfway. Set a strip across the centre of the unfolded strips, slightly on the diagonal. Unfold the strips to cover this one. Fold back alternate strips to cover the diagonal strip. Continue folding back and adding strips, about 2-cm/¾-inch apart, until half the surface is latticed. Turn the pan and repeat with the other half. Brush the ends of the strips with cold water and press to seal them to the pastry case, pinching off overhanging ends.

Brush the lattice with water. Set the reserved strips around the edge of the pie to cover the ends of the lattice. Brush them with water and sprinkle with 1-2 tablespoons sugar. Chill until firm, about 15 minutes.

Meanwhile, preheat the oven to 230°C/450°F/gas8. Put a baking sheet in the bottom third of the oven to heat. Bake the pie on the preheated baking sheet until the pastry is set but not brown, 10-15 minutes. Reduce the oven to 175°C/350°F/gas4 and continue baking until the pastry is done and the apples are tender when pierced with the point of a knife, 25-30 minutes. Cover the pie loosely with foil if the crust gets very brown before the apples are tender. Transfer the pie to a rack and let cool before serving.

Bouchées, feuilletés and puff pastry cases

AT THE HEIGHT OF THE NOUVELLE CUISINE PUSH towards purity and lightness, I was amused that puff pastry was the dough of choice. With its equal weights of butter and flour, what could be richer? Chapters could be written on how to make puff pastry dough, so let's assume you have in front of you a perfect batch of pastry, firm but not elastic, smooth but not sticky. Tucked beneath its pale surface are 729 layers of butter created when the pastry was rolled six times and folded each time in three. The pastry is very cold after chilling for at least half an hour. Shaping your puff pastry starts by rolling it evenly on a cold surface, preferably of marble. The edges of pastry are full of folds which must be trimmed if the layers are to rise evenly and form deep, straight-sided containers. Use a sharp, pointed knife or a metal pastry cutter for shaping, so the pastry is cleanly cut, not torn. All sorts of shapes are possible, large and small, round, rectangular or in a long band, the charm being that the pastry itself rises to form a retaining wall for the filling. Most difficult is undoubtedly the large vol-au-vent – at the Cordon Bleu School in Paris making one formed part of my graduation exam – with individual round bouchées a close second. Contemporary cooks incline more towards feuilletés, a loose term for any puff pastry case but more specifically 10-12-cm/4-5-inch diamonds, which are baked and then split horizontally to form a sandwich.

After cutting, pastry shapes should be set on a heavy, dampened baking sheet – steam gives them a boost. Press the shapes lightly to the sheet to discourage shrinkage. Fluting the sides with the back of a knife also helps rising. You'll have generous trimmings, which are valuable for making pie shells and little puff pastries which do not need to rise impeccably straight (see Sweet and Savoury Puff Pastries, page 306). Pile trimmings carefully so the butter layers are preserved as much as possible and wrap to store in the refrigerator or freezer.

Egg glaze adds that golden glow to puff pastry, but use a light hand so the glaze does not drip down the sides and glue the layers together. Then, with the point of the knife, slash your chosen design in the pastry, be it a lattice, a flower or the outline of a fish to indicate the filling. These are not just for decoration – they ensure that the pastry shrinks evenly in the heat rather than splitting in jagged cracks. Now chill again until the pastry is very firm, at least half an hour in the refrigerator, or 15 minutes in the freezer. Puff pastry keeps well for 2-3 days in an airtight container, thanks to all that butter. It freezes well too, baked or unbaked.

Puff pastry must be baked in a hot oven so that it creates its own steam within the pastry, thus raising and separating the layers. In an oven with bottom heat, set the shelf low down to give the pastry a boost. If heat is uneven, you may need to turn the tray during baking, but be sure the pastry is risen and set before you do so. Good pastry will rise in the oven by three or four times its original thickness. For full, nutty flavour, puff pastry should be baked to a deep toasted brown – probably much browner than you think. A few shapes are certain to fall sideways, as no cook ever has perfect puff pastry cases every time. Don't worry – I've never known puff pastry not to be consumed down to the last crumb. As the pastry case is such a decoration in itself, little more is needed, though a cross of chive stems or a small bouquet of sautéed mushrooms or baby onions can be welcome.

Fillings for puff pastry

When it comes to filling, the shape of a container to some extent dictates what can be put inside. A vol-au-vent is large enough for whole pieces of meat or shellfish, as in the *financière* garnish of sweetbreads, mushrooms, olives and truffles in Madeira sauce, or *fruits de mer* of shellfish with white wine and cream. Similar, usually creamy, mixtures of diced ingredients such as chicken *à la reine* are used for *bouchées* (which means literally a mouthful). Fillings for *feuilletés* often follow the modern taste for vegetables such as asparagus in butter sauce (see overleaf), wild mushrooms in warm vinaigrette, or ratatouille. Feuilletés of scampi, oysters and other shellfish are popular too, as are sweet versions with light pastry cream and fruit.

For serving, warm puff pastry cases in a low oven to crisp and freshen them, then add the filling as late as possible so it does not soak the pastry. (Trouble with a hole can be averted by blocking it with a lettuce leaf.) For full effect, the filling must be generous, spilling over the edge of a *feuilleté* or mounded in a vol-au-vent so its pastry hat can be perched elegantly to one side. This is why sauces need to be relatively thick, so the filling holds a shape.

PERFECT – pastry risen high and evenly, with generous room for filling (here, vol-au-vent is flanked by a *bouchée*); colour is deep golden brown; shell is crisp and all uncooked pastry has been scooped from centre.

UNDERBAKED – pastry case not deeply toasted, so inside soft and doughy; flavour undercooked and floury.
Why: cooking time too short.
What to do: continue baking, if necessary lowering temperature so pastry dries without browning further. Note: a little uncooked pastry in a large puff shell is normal. Simply scoop out and return case to oven to dry.

PERFECT – pastry risen high and flaky layers visible; layers risen to make an even shape; colour is deep golden brown; base very brown but not scorched; texture light and flaky; inside, soft underbaked dough is minimal; flavour is toasted, intensely buttery with hint of salt.

clockwise from left
PERFECT – case (here a *bouchée*) is well coloured, tall and with straight sides.
UNDERBAKED – though well-risen and apparently brown, pastry case remains uncooked in the centre.
RISEN UNEVENLY – pastry case rises high at one side but clings at other, so shape flops to one side; browning is uneven; inside, some uncooked dough remains.
NOT RISEN – case is flat, shape shallow with layers clinging; often baking sheet runs with butter leaked from pastry; colour deep golden brown, but inside much of pastry is soft and unbaked; flavour doughy and texture tough.

OTHER PROBLEMS

RISEN UNEVENLY
Why: layers within dough uneven; pastry not rolled flat; edges not trimmed to remove folds; pastry not chilled before baking; oven heat uneven; glaze dripped down side, gluing layers together.
What to do: split pastry case horizontally in half, reverse top so case appears level, then set on platter before adding filling as it may leak.

NOT RISEN
Why: pastry poorly made, so layers stuck together; not chilled before baking; oven heat too low; pastry deflated by draught when oven door opened too soon.
What to do: not much can be done. Scoop out uncooked dough and rebake case in low oven until dry. Note: even heavy puff pastry is delicious if cooked long enough.

PASTRY SHRINKS BADLY, LOSING NEAT SHAPE
Why: pastry is elastic as overworked, not left to rest, or not chilled before baking.
What to do: before baking, if pastry elastic when rolled, chill at least an hour before baking. After baking nothing can be done.

PASTRY TOUGH AND CHEWY
Why: pastry overworked; flour very high in gluten.
What to do: nothing can be done.

BASE OR TOP IS SCORCHED
Why: baking sheet too thin; oven heat too high. Note: some scorching often cannot be avoided if pastry is to rise well and be thoroughly cooked.
What to do: if base very brown during baking, set shelf higher in oven and put a cold baking sheet directly underneath hot one; if top very brown during baking, cover loosely with foil; when baked, scrape with serrated knife, as for burned toast.

LACKS TASTE
Why: too little salt.
What to do: before baking, add plenty of salt to glaze. Ensure filling is well seasoned.

QUICK FIX

If puff pastry looks a mess, add small bouquets of greens and edible flowers, draping them to hide the misery. If heavy, soggy or lacking flavour, add distracting flavourings such as chopped herbs, olives, red or green pepper, lemon juice and Cognac or Madeira to accent the filling

Asparagus in puff pastry

Feuilletés aux asperges

SERVES 6

This recipe is a classic French marriage of asparagus and puff pastry, ideal for spring when asparagus is in season. The sauce is made simply with softened butter, mounted with a little lemon juice and flavoured with tarragon – a natural partner for asparagus.

1 kg/2 lb green or white asparagus

for the tarragon butter sauce
juice of ½ lemon, or to taste
250 g/8 oz butter, cold and cut into pieces
3 tablespoons chopped tarragon
salt and white pepper

for the puff pastry
250 g/8 oz flour
1 teaspoon salt
250 g/8 oz butter
125 ml/4 fl oz cold water, or more if needed
1 egg mixed with ½ teaspoon salt for the glaze

Make the puff pastry. For the basic pastry dough (*détrempe*): sift the flour with the salt on to a marble slab or work surface and make a well in the centre. Add 30-45 g/1-1½ oz of the butter, cut into pieces, to the well with the water. Work together with your fingers until well mixed, then gradually draw in flour with your hand and a pastry scraper to make crumbs. Work just until the dough is mixed, adding more water if it is dry. Shape the pastry into a ball, cover and let rest in the refrigerator 15 minutes. Note: do not overwork the pastry, it should be quite rough at this stage.

Lightly flour the remaining butter, put it between two sheets of greaseproof paper and flatten it with a rolling pin. Fold it, wrap and continue pounding and folding until it is pliable but not sticky – the butter should be the same consistency as the *détrempe*. Shape the butter into a 15-cm/6-inch square and flour it lightly. Roll out the pastry to a 30-cm/12-inch square, slightly thicker in the centre than at the sides. Set the butter diagonally in the centre, and fold the pastry around it like an envelope, pinching the edges to seal the package.

Flatten the package of pastry slightly with the rolling pin and turn it over. Roll out the package to a 45x15-cm/18x6-inch rectangle. Fold over one of the short sides of pastry, then the other, so the rectangle is folded in three layers, like a business letter, and forms a square. Press the open ends lightly with the rolling pin to seal them.

Turn the package of pastry 90 degrees to bring the open edges towards you. Roll out again and fold in three. Keep a note of these 'turns' by marking the pastry lightly with the appropriate number of fingerprints. Wrap the pastry and let it rest in the refrigerator, until firm, 20-30 minutes. Give the pastry two more turns and let it rest again for 20-30 minutes. Shortly before using, give the pastry two more turns, wrap and chill for 30 minutes.

On a floured work surface, roll out the pastry to a 52x25-cm/21x10-inch rectangle and trim the edges. Cut the rectangle lengthwise to make two 50x11-cm/20x4½-inch strips. Cut each strip diagonally into 3 diamonds. Turn the diamonds over, put them on a baking sheet which has been sprinkled with water and press them down lightly. Brush with egg glaze and slash the diamonds in a lattice with the point of a knife. Chill until firm, 15-30 minutes. Preheat the oven to 240°C/475°F/gas9.

Bake the pastry until starting to brown, about 5 minutes. Lower the oven temperature to 200°C/400°F/gas6 and continue baking until done, 15-20 minutes longer. Split each in half horizontally and keep warm.

Prepare the asparagus: peel the asparagus spears with a vegetable peeler, working from the tips to the cut ends. Assemble and tie the spears in 6 bundles, lining up the tips evenly. Trim the ends level with a knife. Immerse the bundles in boiling salted water and simmer until just tender, 5-12 minutes depending on size and type of asparagus. Drain, refresh briefly with cold water, drain thoroughly again and keep warm.

Meanwhile, make the butter sauce: in a heavy-based saucepan, heat 30 g/1 oz of butter with the lemon juice, whisking constantly until the butter softens. Whisk the remaining butter into the sauce a few pieces at a time, working on and off heat so the butter softens and thickens the sauce without melting to oil. Whisk in the tarragon and season the sauce to taste with salt and white pepper.

Arrange the bottom halves of the *feuilletés* on warm individual plates. Discard the strings and lay the asparagus bundles on the pastry so the tips overlap at one end. Spoon over the sauce and cover with pastry lids, setting them askew. Serve at once.

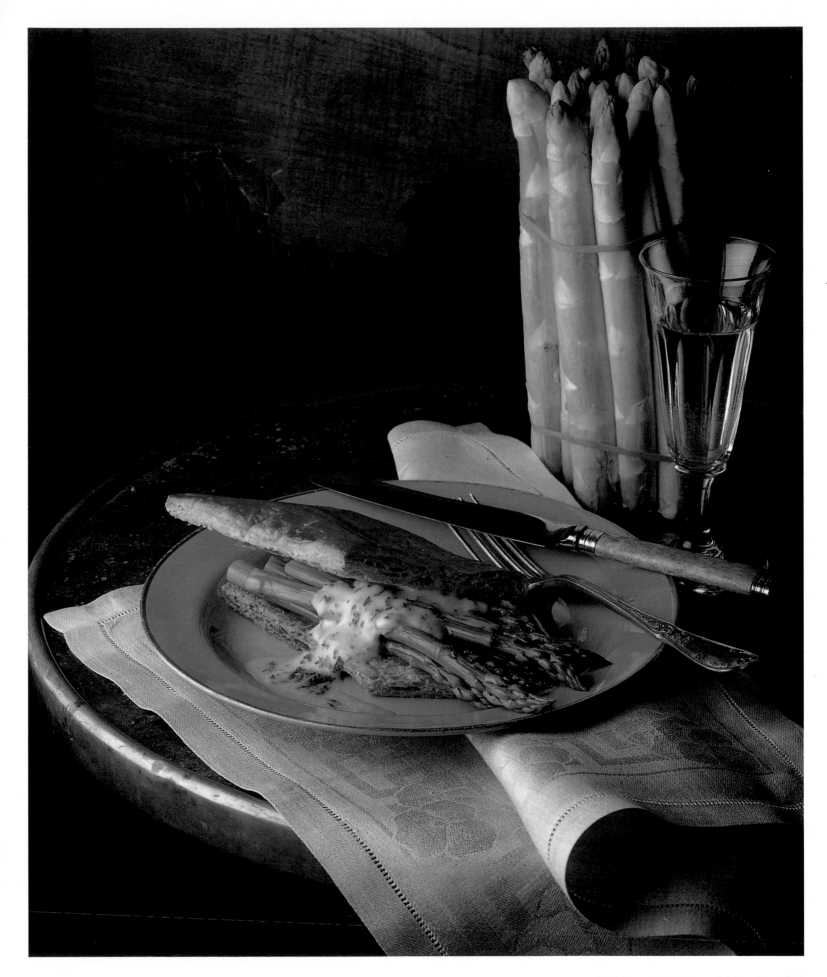

Sweet and savoury puff pastries

LET ME SAY AT ONCE that I would rather be offered a tray of golden crispy puff pastries, sweet with caramelized sugar or savoury with toasted cheese, than almost anything else I can imagine. I'm thinking of classics such as palm leaves, butterflies, bow ties and cheese straws. Many sweet puff pastries rely on caramel for that tangy bite, so you'll find them rolled or glazed with a surprising quantity of sugar. Be sure to bake them really thoroughly, so the sweetness is converted to pungent caramel. In savoury pastries, piquant, concentrated flavourings are needed to balance the butter – cheese, anchovy, anise, tomato paste, hot mustard, plus seeds such as celery, caraway and poppy.

Puff pastries are less demanding than containers such as vol-au-vents and *bouchées*, so they can be made with trimmings or from rough puff dough with fewer rollings than the classic six. Like all small cakes and pastries, you must shape them evenly so they cook at the same speed – a neat test of skill as the pastry puffs so much, exaggerating any imperfections.

Some cooks like to line the baking sheet for small pastries with baking paper so they brown evenly, but personally I think they cook more crisply directly on the sheet – much depends on your oven. Chilling is important, setting the pastry so it holds shape in the oven, and at the same time allowing the gluten in the pastry to relax, lessening shrinkage. Puff pastries keep well and they can be frozen baked or unbaked, making them a favourite with caterers and customers alike.

left to right
UNDERBAKED – though well-puffed, pastries (here *palmiers*) are scarcely crisp; centre of pastry is doughy; colour only light gold; flavours not yet developed.
PERFECT – pastries are well-puffed, crisp and light with shapes of even size; flavour is toasted, buttery and rich with caramelized sugar.
OVERBAKED AND SCORCHED – pastries shrunken and very dark, particularly with burnt sugar; flavour bitter.

PERFECT – pastries are from the top, palm leaves, cheese straws, cheese hats, caraway and poppy seed matchsticks. All are well risen and deep golden brown; with toasted, buttery flavour.

Giant palm leaves

Palmiers

OTHER PROBLEMS

UNDERBAKED

Why: baking time too short.

What to do: continue baking, lowering heat if necessary, so pastries dry and cook in centre without overbrowning on outside.

OVERBAKED AND SCORCHED

Why: baked too long; baked too slowly, so butter ran and then pastry shrivelled; pastries rolled and shaped unevenly, so some baked faster than others.

What to do: top savoury pastries with grated cheese and rebake until it melts, or sprinkle sweet pastries with icing sugar; if very scorched, discard burned parts and shred pastry to crumbs for topping salads or desserts.

NOT RISEN

Why: pastry poorly made, so layers stuck together; pastry not chilled before baking; pastries poorly shaped with little room to rise; oven heat too low.

What to do: nothing – pastries may be heavy but they will still taste good.

TASTELESS

Why: dough lacked salt; flavourings too few or too mild; pastries underbaked; sugar not thoroughly cooked to caramel (sweet pastries).

What to do: see Quick Fix.

Traditionally these heart-shaped *palmiers* are made from puff pastry trimmings and for this recipe you'll need 1.4 kg/3 lb of pastry trimmings. For sweet palm leaves, the pastry and work surface are sprinkled with sugar for the last two turns as instructed here. For savoury palm leaves, use grated Parmesan cheese.

400 g/13 oz sugar, more if needed	*for the puff pastry* *500 g/1 lb flour* *2 teaspoons salt*	*500 g/1 lb butter, softened* *250 ml/8 fl oz ice water, more if needed*

Make the puff pastry. For the basic pastry (*détrempe*): sift the flour with the salt on a marble slab or work surface and make a well in the centre. Add 2-3 tablespoons of the butter, cut into pieces, to the well with the water. Work together with your fingers until well mixed, then gradually draw in flour with your hand and a pastry scraper to make crumbs. Work just until the pastry is mixed, adding more water if it is dry. Shape the pastry into a ball, cover and let rest in the refrigerator 15 minutes. Note: do not overwork the pastry, it should be quite rough at this stage.

Lightly flour the remaining butter, put it between two sheets of greaseproof paper and flatten it with a rolling pin. Fold it, wrap and continue pounding and folding until it is pliable but not sticky – the butter should be the same consistency as the *détrempe*. Shape butter into a 15-cm/6-inch square and flour it lightly. Roll out pastry to a 30-cm/12-inch square, slightly thicker in the centre than at the sides. Set butter diagonally in the centre, and fold the pastry around it like an envelope, pinching the edges to seal the package.

Flatten the package of pastry slightly with the rolling pin and turn it over. Roll out the package to a 45x15-cm/18x6-inch rectangle. Fold over one of the short sides of pastry, then the other, so the rectangle is folded in three layers, like a business letter, and forms a square. Press the open ends lightly with the rolling pin to seal them.

Turn the package of pastry 90 degrees to bring the open edges towards you. Roll out again and fold in three. Keep a note of these 'turns' by marking the pastry lightly with the appropriate number of fingerprints. Wrap the pastry and let it rest in the refrigerator, until firm, 20-30 minutes. Give the pastry two more turns and let it rest again for 20-30 minutes. Just before using, give the pastry two more turns, wrap and chill for 30 minutes.

Roll out the pastry again to a 50x20-cm/20x8-inch rectangle on a work surface sprinkled generously with some of the sugar. Sprinkle the pastry with more sugar, fold in three to a square, then turn and roll again. Sprinkle again with sugar, fold and chill for 30 minutes. Note: thus the last two puff pastry turns have sugar instead of flour. Roll the pastry about 6 mm/¼ inch thick to a 55x36-cm/23x14-inch rectangle. Trim the sides and sprinkle the pastry with some sugar. Fold each short side to meet in the centre. Sprinkle with more sugar and fold the short sides to centre again. Bring one folded side of pastry on top of the other and press down lightly. Chill the folded pastry until firm, 15-30 minutes.

Cut the roll into 1.25-cm/½-inch slices – they'll be heart-shaped. Set on a baking sheet which has been sprinkled with water. Open the slices slightly so they are loosely folded, with a curve at the top of the heart to encourage rising. Chill for 15 minutes. Preheat the oven to 220°C/425°F/gas7. Bake the *palmiers* until done, turning them once or twice so they brown and caramelize thoroughly, 15-20 minutes. Transfer them to a rack to cool.

Baked choux puffs

AFTER YEARS OF TRIAL, I HAVE FINALLY MASTERED CHOUX PUFFS so they swell to the size of my fist, with the pastry crisp and golden on the outside, but warm and slightly soft in the centre. We flavour them with cheese for *gougères*, a pastry native to our part of Burgundy and the ideal partner for a glass of Beaujolais or chilled Chablis. I've even discovered you can freeze the shaped dough and bake it, still frozen, at the last minute. Choux is most familiar in cream puffs, profiteroles and éclairs, with a filling of pastry cream, whipped cream or ice cream. (The pastry remains crisp longer with pastry cream.) Savoury fillings such as a poached egg in red wine sauce are occasionally added. Choux pastry can also be deep-fried as fritters. Choux is based on a cooked paste (*panade*) of flour, butter and water, raised with whole eggs. The more eggs you add, the more the dough will puff. Stop when the dough just falls easily from the spoon but is still stiff enough to shape. Mound the dough on a buttered baking sheet – a piping bag helps with neat shapes – setting them well apart to allow steam to escape. This is important, as choux pastry bakes in two stages, first rising to form a hollow centre and then drying to a crisp, firm case.

Choux pastry is baked in a moderate oven, around 190°C/375°F/gas5. Do not be tempted to open the door wide until cooking is well advanced, as a draught will deflate the puffs for good. If you've a convection or gas oven, the flow of air will dry the puffs efficiently. However humidity can build up in an electric oven, so after 10 minutes open the door a crack – you'll be surprised by the rush of escaping steam. Repeat once or twice. Choux pastry can look ready – deceptively puffed and brown – long before it is done. To test, remove a puff – the cracks formed as it expanded should be brown, not pale. Let the puff cool and, if it remains crisp, it is done. Transfer puffs to a rack to cool – count on losing a few which have cooked unevenly or stuck to the sheet. Choux puffs are best used within an hour or two – they can be stored for a day if carefully wrapped.

QUICK FIX

When sweet puffs have fallen and cannot be filled, sandwich filling between two puffs, adding raspberries or other fruit if you like. Place the puffs on plates. Make a caramel: heat 200 g/6½ oz sugar with 125 ml/ 4 fl oz water until dissolved, stirring occasionally. Bring to the boil and boil without stirring to a deep golden caramel. Take the pan from the heat and plunge base in pan of warm water to stop cooking. At once trail warm caramel over the puffs in a lattice. Caramel will set to be crisp as it cools.

POORLY RISEN – flat and spread wide on sheet; base often hard and overbaked; little or no hollow interior.
Why: if small and dense, too little egg; if spread wide on baking sheet, too much egg.
What to do: add as much filling as possible, then pipe or spread rest on a platter or individual plates and set choux on top; if using a sweet filling, decorate with a lattice trail of raspberry coulis, chocolate, kiwi or other colourful sauce.

FALLEN – shape collapsed, so hollow interior lost; pastry often pale; inside of puff full of moist dough.
Why: underbaked; oven opened too soon during baking, so dough collapsed in a draft.
What to do: nothing can be done. Here's where you'd need to start again, or follow the Quick Fix.

PERFECT – pastry crisp and puffed high; colour a glossy, even golden brown; inside hollow, with little or no moist dough; flavour reminiscent of crackers.

Cheese choux puffs

Gougères

MAKES 9 LARGE GOUGÈRES

For parties, you can make little cheese puffs the size of an apricot, but I love them country-style, as big as your fist. Serve them warm and still slightly soft in the centre.

100 g/3¼ oz flour
175 ml/6 fl oz water
75 g/2½ oz butter
½ teaspoon salt
3-4 eggs
100 g/3¼ oz Gruyère cheese, coarsely grated

1 egg, beaten to mix with ½ teaspoon salt, for glazing

pastry bag fitted with 1.25-cm/½-inch plain tube

Preheat the oven to 190°C/375°F/gas5. Line a baking sheet with baking paper. For the choux pastry: sift the flour on to a piece of baking paper. In a saucepan, heat the water, butter and the salt until the butter is melted, then bring to the boil. At once take pan from heat, add the flour and beat vigorously with a wooden spoon until the mixture is smooth and pulls away from the sides of pan to form a ball, 30-60 seconds. Beat over low heat to dry the mixture, 30-60 seconds.

Whisk 1 of the eggs in a bowl until mixed and set aside. With a wooden spoon or using an electric mixer, beat the remaining eggs into the dough one by one, beating thoroughly after each addition. Beat enough of the reserved egg into the dough so it is shiny and just falls from the spoon. Note: all the reserved egg may not be needed. Beat in the grated cheese, reserving 2-3 tablespoons for sprinkling.

Put the dough into the pastry bag fitted with the plain tube and pipe nine 7-cm/2½-inch mounds on the prepared baking sheet. Brush with egg glaze and sprinkle with the reserved cheese. Bake in the preheated oven until done, 35-40 minutes. Let the puffs cool slightly, then transfer them to a rack.

from left to right
POORLY RISEN – puffs spread on baking sheet, so shape is flat with no clearly hollow centre.
PERFECT – puffs are light, hollow and crisp, an attractive golden brown.
FALLEN – shape has collapsed and doughy centre lacks a hollow.

OTHER PROBLEMS

UNDERBAKED AND SOFT, OFTEN PALE
Why: cooking time too short; oven heat too low; puffs wrapped before completely cold; puffs left in a humid kitchen.
What to do: if underbaked, rebake in a 190°C/375°F/gas5 oven until crisp, 5-7 minutes; if softened after baking, dry in a low oven.
OVERBAKED, HARD AND DRY
Why: cooked too long; oven heat too high; puffs stored in freezer and dried out; reheated for too long.
What to do: nothing – puffs will soften after filling is added but will lack fresh flavour.
BROKEN BASE, SO PUFF CANNOT BE FILLED
Why: oven temperature too high, especially bottom heat.
What to do: nothing can be done. Note: it is common to find one or two broken puffs, but a whole batch is very rare.

Layered pastries

LIGHT, FLAKY AND ADAPTABLE, LAYERED PASTRIES SUCH AS PHYLLO are enormous fun. Good commercial doughs are available so there's no need to attempt making them by hand and, indeed, I would not advise it. Rolling and pulling phyllo into paper-thin layers or leaves takes practice, and Moroccan brik dough is even more arcane. Only strudel is commonly made at home.

The key to handling these doughs is to work rapidly, keeping them pliable and moist, but not wet. Many packets come with protective plastic sheets to make handling easy. If not, lay the dough sheets on a tea towel and cover the pile with another, dampening the towels if the dough seems dry. Pull sheets from the pile as needed. Melted butter or oil (olive or walnut oil are delicious) is used to brush the leaves, which may then be layered in a baking dish, or rolled (in the case of strudel) or folded into a multitude of shapes (see opposite). Aim to coat the pastry lightly with fat, dabbing rather than brushing, so it is moistened without being soaked and heavy.

Fillings for layered savoury pastries must be pungent, given that the pastry takes much of the attention – consider salty ingredients such as feta cheese, goats' cheese, olives, ham and anchovy. A touch of green herb, particularly parsley and chives, or peppery greens like kale can be helpful; one unusual savoury pastry is filled with blanched cabbage. For sweet pastries, honey and nuts are by far the most popular filling, with cherries, apple and dried fruits for strudel. Spices add zest and national character – cinnamon in Austrian strudel, cloves and cinnamon in Greek *baklava* and saffron in Moroccan *bistelya*.

In the oven, a moderate, even heat is important so the pastry leaves bake through to the centre and brown on the outside without scorching. Too many layers or a filling which is very moist will make the pastry heavy. It's tempting to shape pretty, fluffy decorations from just a few layers of pastry, but take care as they scorch easily, baking faster than the main body of dough. Layered pastries keep well – warm them briefly in a low oven before serving.

OTHER PROBLEMS

SCORCHED EDGES
Why: dough shaped unevenly, with some single or loose layers; dough unevenly brushed with oil or butter; oven temperature too high.
What to do: break or lift off scorched portions; sprinkle pastry with grated cheese, chopped herb, or icing sugar for sweet pastries.

HEAVY
Why: too many layers; too much oil or butter; filling too moist; underbaked.
What to do: if underbaked, continue baking; when serving, sprinkle with chopped browned almonds, pine nuts or walnuts for contrast of texture.

BLAND
Why: lacks seasoning; ingredients too mild; too much pastry.
What to do: serve savoury pastries with black olive tapenade or Salsa of Tomato and Coriander (page 129); with sweet pastries serve a bowl of goats'-milk yogurt, or warm honey syrup.

UNDERBAKED AND UNEVENLY BROWNED – pastry is pale and pliable, lacking flaky texture; filling damp and heavy; flavour of pastry is doughy.
Why: baked too high or too low in oven; pastry layers arranged unevenly; brushed unevenly or too generously with butter or oil; filling too moist.
What to do: during baking, readjust oven shelves and rotate dish or baking sheet; after baking, rebake if parts very underdone.

PERFECT – pastry is crisp, lightly puffed and evenly browned; texture is flaky, not tough; flavour toasted with no trace of uncooked flour, and enhanced with butter or oil.

Small parcels of layered pastry

THINK OF A CONTAINER AND YOU CAN RECREATE IT IN LAYERED PASTRY. The picture below shows just a few of the dozen common shapes for layered pastry parcels, and you can make up many more. However you'll find that single leaves, detached from the main pastry in flyaway shapes, are a nuisance as the edges scorch easily. For example, a purse shape with its frilled crown is vulnerable and it bakes much better if the edge is neatly trimmed. Another limit to respect is the thickness of pastry – with too many layers the finished pastry will be heavy, with too few it may burst. Don't do as I often do and add too much filling as layered parcels are fragile and burst easily under pressure when the filling heats up. Mediterranean flavours are very much in order – small piquant spoonfuls of Poor Man's Caviar (Quick Fix, page 157), tapenade, chilli-spiced feta cheese and so on.

PERFECT – pastry crisp and golden brown; parcels are even in size, with fanciful shapes and no trace of burst filling; flavour is a nice balance of pastry and savoury or sweet filling.

PASTRIES FOR PIES AND PARCELS

Half a dozen different pastries can be used for making pies and parcels, each with different characteristics:

LAYERED PASTRIES such as phyllo and strudel are outstanding for crisp, flaky parcels both large and small. Fillings must be firm so they do not leak, with intense flavour as a high proportion of pastry to filling is usual. Layered pastry can also be shaped as a large round or rectangular pie (see overleaf).

FRENCH PIE PASTRY (*pâte brisée*) is made with butter, sometimes with an egg yolk or two, and is kneaded to become very pliable. It can be thinly rolled to form an unobtrusive background for fillings, best for quiche and tarts with a moist filling.

AMERICAN PIE PASTRY is more tender and crumbly, mixed quickly without kneading. Vegetable shortening (lard may be used in Britain) replaces part or all of the butter, also lightening texture. For stability, pie pastry should be rolled slightly thicker than French pie pastry, but its crispness is a plus. A few tablespoons of sugar may be added to sweeten either of these doughs, making them slightly more crumbling and easier to brown.

FRENCH SWEET PIE PASTRY (*pâte sucrée*) is even sweeter, in effect a biscuit dough, rich in butter, sugar and egg yolks. Be sure to chill it thoroughly to make it easier to handle. Ground nuts, often browned for flavour, may be added to the pastry and will make it even more crumbling. Both pastries collapse easily during baking unless thoroughly chilled and, if blind-baking, carefully lined with paper and beans (see Blind Baking page 295).

PUFF PASTRY, particularly trimmings, may be used for pies, especially those with with a top crust. The effect is deliciously crisp, flaky and rich. For a bottom crust, puff pastry should always be baked blind as the high butter content can make it soggy. Puff pastry is easy to handle if well chilled, but shells have a tendency to shrink during baking.

ROUGH PUFF, FLAKY AND QUICK PUFF PASTRIES are all versions of puff pastry with fewer layers and usually with less butter. They are an excellent compromise between plain pie pastry and the richness of puff pastry.

PROBLEMS

UNDERBAKED AND HEAVY
Why: cooking time too short; oven heat too low; too much oil or butter in pastry; too much rich filling; pastry too large.
What to do: continue baking, cutting pastry in half if large or fatty so it dries out.

SCORCHED EDGES
Why: pastry shaped unevenly, with loose sheets; temperature too high; shelf too high in oven.

What to do: trim scorched edges and mask savoury pastries with Savoury Cream Cheese Sauce (see Quick Fix), and sweet pastries with a Cooked Fruit Sauce (see page 137).

FILLING BURST
Why: oven too hot; too much filling; filling too moist; parcels poorly shaped.
What to do: trim overflow of filling and conceal opening with herb sprigs.

QUICK FIX

When savoury layered pastry parcels are scorched or heavy, add this sauce: in a food processor combine 125 g/4 oz soft cream cheese with 30 g/1 oz chopped tarragon or parsley, 1 tablespoon whole-grain mustard and enough sour or double cream to make a pourable sauce. Taste for seasoning. Serves 4.

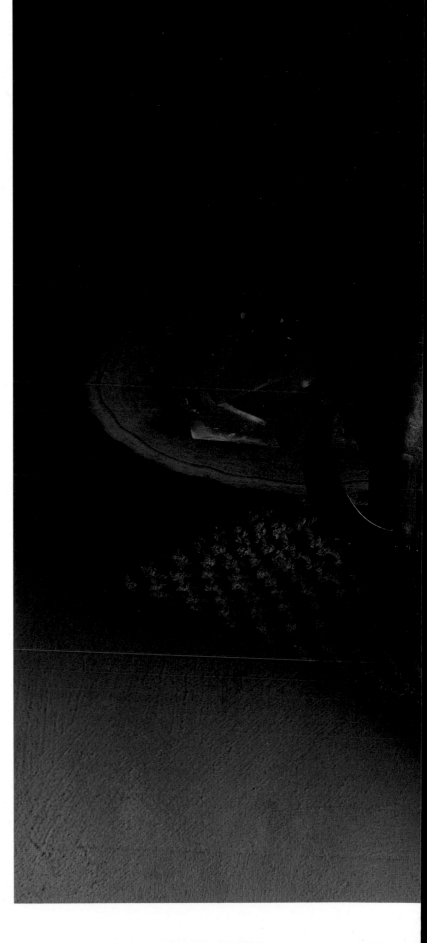

Greek spinach and cheese pie

Spanakopita

SERVES 6–8

You'll often see phyllo baked in individual parcels, but this large pie filled with spinach and feta cheese makes an eye-catching presentation.

500 g/1 lb phyllo	2 onions, finely chopped
60 g/2 oz butter, or more if needed	pinch of freshly grated nutmeg
60 ml/2 fl oz olive oil, or more if needed	salt and pepper
1 kg/2 lb spinach	250 g/½ lb feta cheese, crumbled
for the filling	small bunch of flat-leaved parsley, chopped
3 tablespoons olive oil	28-cm/11-inch tart pan with removable base

Make the filling: tear the stems from the spinach leaves. Wash the leaves well in plenty of cold water and drain off most of the water from the leaves. Pack the spinach in a large heavy-based saucepan, cover and cook just until wilted, stirring occasionally, 3–4 minutes. Let the spinach cool, squeeze it in your fists to extract water, and then coarsely chop it. Heat the olive oil in a large sauté pan. Add the onion and sauté, stirring, until soft but not brown, 3–4 minutes. Stir in the chopped spinach, nutmeg, and pepper. Cook, stirring, until very hot and any liquid has evaporated, about 2 minutes. Remove from the heat, stir in the feta cheese and chopped parsley. Taste, adjust seasoning and leave the filling to cool.

Preheat the oven to 175°C/350°F/gas4. Melt the butter with the olive oil. Brush the tart pan with some melted butter and oil. Lay a damp tea towel on the work surface. Unroll sheets of phyllo pastry on the towel. Using the tart pan as a guide, cut through all the sheets to make a round 7.5 cm/ 3 inches larger than the pan. Reserve the trimmings for decoration. Cover the sheets and trimmings with another damp towel.

Pull a phyllo round from under the damp towel and brush it lightly with melted butter and oil. Transfer the sheet to the tart pan, pushing it well into the bottom and sides. Repeat with half the sheets of phyllo, working quickly and brushing each layer with melted butter and oil. Keep the remaining sheets covered with a damp towel.

Spoon the spinach and feta mixture into the tart shell, spreading it evenly. Top with the remaining sheets of phyllo, brushing each layer, including the last, with oil and butter.

Fold the overhanging dough up around edge of tart pan, turning and pinching it to form a decorative edge. Cut the phyllo dough trimmings into 5-cm/2-inch wide strips. Crumple them lightly to make loose round flowers and arrange them on top of the pie so it is completely covered. Drizzle with the remaining melted butter and oil. Bake the pie in the preheated oven until done, 50–60 minutes. Let the pie cool slightly, remove from the tart pan and serve.

Rolled and moulded biscuits

THE VERY FIRST RECIPE ANY OF US EVER MADE was probably a rolled or moulded biscuit. In my case, the mixture was flavoured with golden syrup and ginger and the dough was rather better raw than cooked, so by no means all of it reached the oven. Those biscuits which survived were eaten every morning at 'elevenses', dipped into hot tea.

Looking back on it, they were the archetypal biscuit, bright with sugar and spice, plain enough to eat every day, and robust enough to keep a week or more without harm.

You'll find many rolled and moulded biscuits rely on spices such as ginger and cinnamon, on seeds like anise and caraway, and on the punch of chocolate, coffee and grated citrus zest. Sugar is often tasty and brown, or in the form of honey or syrup; butter is prime for flavour. Occasionally baking powder or bicarbonate of soda may be added to make the biscuit crumble. As with pastry, you'll find that hard or soft wheat flour makes quite a difference to the dough.

In fact, if you think of rolled and moulded biscuits as ultra-rich sweet pastries, you won't go far wrong. Like pastry dough, the mixture must be firm enough to roll. Dough for moulding may be somewhat softer, but it must be firm enough to hold a crisp shape in a mould, or be stiff enough to roll between your palms (for hand-shaped biscuits) or to slice (for refrigerator biscuits). Rolled biscuits can be large or small as you prefer — very large ones can be unwieldy, very small ones take more time to shape. Remember also that baking time will vary with the size of biscuit. Chilling is important both before and after shaping, so the dough is easy to handle and sets in the oven heat without spreading.

Always leave space between the biscuits to help them bake evenly.

Biscuits will bake differently on different baking sheets. A non-stick surface is good for doughs with a high sugar content. A heavy baking sheet browns the base of biscuits well, but very sweet doughs tend to scorch — you may want to line the baking sheet with baking paper, or use an insulated baking sheet. When done, rolled and moulded biscuits should be transferred to a rack to cool so steam escapes. As soon as they are cool pack them in an airtight container — any dough with a high sugar content softens quickly in the open air.

PERFECT – biscuits are golden brown and evenly coloured underneath and on top; texture meltingly crisp or quite hard, depending on fat and sugar content; flavour fragrant. Note: biscuits which seem soft when hot often crisp as they cool.

UNDERBAKED – biscuits scarcely browned, pale underneath; texture is soft and taste doughy.
Why: cooking time too short; oven temperature too low; biscuits low in sugar, so do not brown well.
What to do: continue cooking, raising oven temperature if necessary; if too pale after baking, add a white icing or chocolate frosting.

QUICK FIX

When biscuits are bland or need a pick-me-up, add this tart icing: beat 125 g/4 oz sifted icing sugar with the grated rind and juice of 1 orange until smooth. The icing should just fall easily from the spoon — if too thick, add more orange juice, if too thin, beat in more sifted icing sugar. Brush a teaspoonful or so of icing on each biscuit, leaving it to spread and set when cool. Makes 75 ml/2½ fl oz, enough for about 24 biscuits.

OTHER PROBLEMS

UNEVEN BAKING
Why: biscuits unevenly shaped; oven heat uneven; baking sheet too thin; oven shelf too low or too high.
What to do: during baking, adjust shelves up or down and rotate baking sheet. As soon as some biscuits are done, remove them and leave others to continue baking. After baking, divide biscuits into pale and dark batches, serving them separately; arrange biscuits overlapping on the plate, hiding overbrowned patches.

DOUGH SPREADS IN OVEN
Why: too much liquid, fat or sugar in dough; dough not chilled before baking; baking sheet warm when dough added.
What to do: when biscuits fully baked but still warm, trim to shape with a biscuit or pastry cutter.

BISCUITS CRUMBLE WHEN BAKED
Why: dough too dry; dough lacks flour or egg; biscuits too hot to move.
What to do: if biscuits pale, continue baking; let them cool to tepid before lifting.

STICK TO BAKING SHEET
Why: baking sheet not buttered adequately; biscuits underbaked; biscuits left to cool on sheet.
What to do: try to loosen biscuits from baking sheet with a sharp, flexible knife; if biscuits baked on paper, when baking sheet is still hot pour a little hot water under the paper — the steam will loosen the biscuits; if biscuits are still sticking, warm baking sheet in oven.

BLAND
Why: mixture lacks salt or sugar; ingredients bland.
What to do: before baking the next batch, brush with salt or sugar glaze; after baking, sprinkle with cinnamon sugar or top with tart icing, see Quick Fix.

Herb butter biscuits

Sablés aux herbes

MAKES 8-10 LARGE BISCUITS

When I first tasted herbs in sweet biscuits, I was surprised – but why? After all, herbs were a favourite flavouring for desserts and candies centuries ago and it is we who have forgotten their charms. Flavours which are good with sugar include lemon thyme, rose geranium, tansy, lemon verbena and, of course, mint. Any can be used in this recipe.

large bunch of chosen herb
100 g/3¾ oz butter, softened
200 g/6½ oz flour
4 egg yolks
100 g/3¾ oz icing sugar
½ teaspoon salt

1 egg beaten with ½ teaspoon salt for glazing
10-cm/4-inch biscuit cutter

Strip the leaves from the herb stems, reserving 10 large sprigs or leaves for decoration. Chop the remaining leaves, taking care not to bruise them. There should be about 4 tablespoons.

Sift the flour on to the work surface and make a well in the centre. Add the egg yolks, sugar, chopped herb and salt to the well and mix with your fingertips. Pound the butter with a rolling pin to soften it slightly, add it to the well and quickly work it into the other ingredients. Gradually draw in flour from the sides, working with a pastry scraper and rubbing the ingredients into the flour with your fingers to form crumbs. Press the dough into a ball.

Flour the work surface and knead the dough with the heel of your hand, pushing it away and gathering it up until it is smooth, pliable and peels from the work surface in one piece, 1-2 minutes. Shape into a ball, wrap and chill until firm, at least 30 minutes.

Butter 2 baking sheets. Roll out half the dough to a sheet 6 mm/¼ inch thick. Cut out rounds with a biscuit cutter and set them on the prepared sheets. Press the pastry trimmings into the remaining dough, roll and cut more rounds. Brush biscuits with the beaten egg glaze and press one reserved herb sprig flat on each round. Chill until firm, about 15 minutes.

Preheat the oven to 190°C/375°F/gas5.

Bake the biscuits in the preheated oven until done, 12-15 minutes. Let cool slightly, then transfer to a rack to cool completely.

Bar biscuits

Bar biscuits take rolled and moulded biscuits a step further, as the mixture is often so rich it must be pressed with your fist into the pan. Other mixtures are soft enough to pour as a batter – brownies are an example. With a square or rectangular pan, you can cut the biscuits into bars (hence the name) or you can substitute a round pan and cut them in wedges. Bar biscuits are normally left to cool in the pan. Slice them while still warm and moist, then let them cool and stiffen completely before unmoulding.

A good bar biscuit has lots of texture – it is chewy with oatmeal or coconut, melting with honey or chocolate, crunchy with nuts. Topping may be a lattice trail of thin icing or chocolate, or a melted frosting, but often bars are left completely plain. It can be difficult to bake them evenly, as the edges brown more than the centre of the pan. Rotating the pan during cooking can help. Beware of drying out the mixture too much in the oven – bar biscuits should be baked just long enough for the mixture to hold together when cool. If overbaked, they can lose their characteristic moist richness. Bar biscuits mature well if stored in an airtight container.

PERFECT (here oatmeal bars) – evenly coloured, firm, though soft enough to slice while still warm; a skewer inserted in the centre comes out clean; texture chewy but not tough; flavour full-bodied.

Drop biscuits

DROP BISCUITS ARE QUICKEST OF ALL, a matter of mixing the dough and dropping it in spoonfuls on the baking sheet ready to bake. But there's a catch — if the dough is not quite right or the oven temperature a bit off, the biscuits can huddle in dry little clumps — or even worse, spread all over the baking sheet. If you're trying a new recipe, or uncertain of your oven, I strongly recommend you bake a trial biscuit first.

Drop biscuits include some of the most famous — chocolate chip, macaroons, oatmeal and raisin, and peanut butter biscuits. Doughs are made all sorts of ways: always shape the mounds on the baking sheet neatly, leaving plenty of space for expansion. In terms of flavour, one or two ingredients often take the lead, whether it be coconut, dried fruit, chocolate or praline. Texture is important, with grains like oatmeal and cornmeal adding body. You'll see that many of my comments on rolled and moulded biscuits also apply.

PERFECT – biscuit spread to even thickness and lightly browned, darker at edges and underneath; slight depression left when pressed with your fingertip; shape an even round; texture crisp or chewy, depending on type; flavour generous. Note: crisp drop biscuits may be further cooked, so they are evenly browned on top.

PROBLEMS

TOO THIN
Why: not enough flour in dough; oven heat too low, so batter melted rather than baking at once; baking sheet warm when dough added.
What to do: before baking the next batch, add several tablespoons of flour, if biscuit edges jagged, trim with a round cutter. Note: the biscuits may be crisper than usual but will still be good.

UNEVEN BAKING
Why: oven heat uneven; baking sheet too thin; oven shelf too low or too high.
What to do: during baking, adjust shelves up or down and rotate baking sheet. As soon as some biscuits are done, remove them and leave others to continue baking. After baking, divide biscuits into pale and dark batches, serving them separately.

TOO THICK
Why: dough has too much flour or egg; oven too high.
Note: mounded shape with crisp outside and soft centre is correct for some biscuits.

What to do: before baking next batch, add a few tablespoons of melted butter or vegetable oil to dough; try lower temperature. After baking, if very dry, see Quick Fix.

STICK TO BAKING SHEET
Why: baking sheet not buttered adequately; biscuits underbaked; biscuits left to cool on sheet.
What to do: while biscuits are still warm, try to loosen them from baking sheet with a sharp flexible knife; if biscuits baked on paper, when baking sheet is still hot, pour a little water under the paper — the steam will loosen the biscuits; if biscuits still stick, try warming baking sheet in oven.

BLAND
Why: mixture lacks salt or sugar; ingredients bland.
What to do: before baking next batch, brush biscuits with a sugar glaze; after baking, sprinkle with sugar or top with tart icing, see Quick Fix on page 314.

Chocolate chunk macadamia cookies

MAKES 16 LARGE BISCUITS

Nothing tastes quite like these rich biscuits studded with chunks of dark chocolate and chopped macadamia nuts. Our adult children still wolf them down with a tall glass of milk.

175 g/6 oz dark chocolate
100 g/3¾ oz macadamia nuts
225 g/7½ oz flour
½ teaspoon bicarbonate of soda
pinch of salt
90 g/3 oz butter, softened
50 g/1¾ oz brown sugar
100 g/3¾ oz granulated sugar
1 egg
½ teaspoon vanilla essence

Preheat the oven to 190°C/375°F/gas5. Brush a baking sheet with butter. With a large knife, coarsely chop the chocolate into rough chunks. Coarsely chop the macadamia nuts. Sift together the flour, bicarbonate of soda and salt.

In a large bowl, beat the butter until soft. Gradually add the mixed sugars and continue beating until light and fluffy. Beat in the egg and vanilla. Add the flour mixture in two batches, stirring just until mixed. Stir in the chocolate chunks and chopped nuts.

Drop tablespoonfuls of batter on the baking sheet, leaving room in between as the biscuits will spread during baking. Bake in batches in the preheated oven until done, 12-15 minutes. Let the biscuits cool slightly, then transfer to a rack to cool completely.

QUICK FIX
When drop biscuits are dry or plain, let them cool and dip one edge in your choice of melted chocolate – dark, milk or white. Place them to cool and set on greaseproof paper.

Wafer biscuits and cigarettes

FRAGILE, EYE-CATCHING AND ELEGANT, wafer biscuits magnify the temptations, and the drawbacks, of their more robust relations. Even a very small variation in the batter can make the difference between success or failure, so I always play safe and bake a trial wafer before launching on a full sheet. Just a minute or two of baking time, more or less, affects a wafer's success. It should be baked in quite a hot oven only until brown around the edges, still pale in the centre. When cooked more evenly, a wafer is often too crisp to shape.

Your choice of baking surface has an influence, too. Wafer biscuits love to stick and a non-stick baking sheet makes handling much easier (a standard baking sheet must be thoroughly buttered). It does not help to line the sheet with baking paper as wafers must be baked directly on the hot surface, but the flexible silicone sheets used by professional bakers are invaluable. There's quite an art to removing wafers from the sheet. Work quickly as they harden and stick as they cool. Using a sharp, flexible knife, loosen all the biscuits, then lift one by one with a triangular metal spatula or palette knife. Tile biscuits can be draped over a rolling pin, or curved in baguette bread moulds; cigarettes are rolled around the handle of a wooden spoon. Be sure to cool flat wafers on a level surface. If the last biscuits on the sheet are too cool to shape, warm them briefly in the oven. With their high sugar content and delicate structure, wafer biscuits do not keep well – tiles soften within 2-3 hours, though I know a trick for reviving a limp one (see Quick Fix). If keeping, transfer wafers to an airtight container as soon as they are cool.

UNDERBAKED, PALE AND SOFT – wafer tears easily; hard to shape and not crisp when cool.
Why: cooking time too short; oven temperature too low; too much egg.
What to do: bake longer or raise temperature; if still hard to shape, add a tablespoon of sugar to batter.

PERFECT – wafer very thin, even and approximately round; colour beige or pale gold with darker edges; very pliable when hot, cools to be crisp and very fragile; flavour sugary, best with nuts, lemon or other tart flavouring.

OTHER PROBLEMS

CRACKS WHEN SHAPED
Why: oven heat too low, so wafer dried during baking; too much flour; waited too long to shape.
What to do: increase temperature; stir tablespoon melted butter into batter; shape sooner, while still warm.
TOO THIN – too fragile to shape, often with holes.
Why: too much sugar; not enough flour; spread too thin.
What to do: stir a tablespoon of flour into batter.
DOES NOT SPREAD
Why: oven heat too high; too much flour or egg.
What to do: lower oven temperature; add a tablespoon of melted butter to batter.

Almond tile biscuits
Tuiles aux amandes
MAKES ABOUT 12

These lacy wafer biscuits get their name from their curved shape, which echoes roof tiles in their home country of France.

125 g/4 oz sliced almonds	pinch of salt
125 g/4 oz sugar	1 egg
3 tablespoons flour	white of 1 more egg
60 g/2 oz butter	

Melt the butter over a low heat and let cool. In a medium bowl, combine the almonds, sugar, flour, salt and melted butter. Whisk the egg and the egg white until well blended and stir into the batter. Cover and leave to rest in the refrigerator for at least 1 hour.

Preheat oven to 200°C/400°F/gas6 and butter several baking sheets. Drop generous teaspoons of batter on the prepared baking sheets, leaving plenty of room for each biscuit to spread. With a fork dipped in cold water, flatten each spoonful of batter to a 10-cm/4-inch round.

Bake the biscuits in the preheated oven until done, 6-8 minutes. Let cool slightly, 30-60 seconds. Then, while still pliable, transfer with a metal spatula or thin sharp knife to a rolling pin and leave until crisp and cool, 3-5 minutes.

QUICK FIX

When tiles or wafer biscuits are soft, dry and crisp them in the oven, then reshape them: heat the biscuits on a baking sheet in a 175°C/350°F/gas4 oven for 4-5 minutes. They will collapse and become pliable. Reshape them while still hot and leave to cool.

Glossary

al dente Italian term (meaning 'to the tooth') used to indicate perfectly cooked pasta, i.e. tender but still gives a slight resistance to the bite. Now generally used of many foods, like vegetables, rice, etc.

bain-marie French term for the water bath, usually a shallow pan half-filled with hot water, in which items that require very delicate cooking at a low even temperature, like custards, are placed for cooking in the oven to protect them from its harsh direct heat.

baking blind When pastry cases are pre-cooked (either partially or totally) prior to filling, this is called baking blind.

blanch From the French for 'to whiten' this can mean putting food in cold unsalted water and bringing it to the boil to remove strong flavours (as with some offal) and/or excess saltiness (bacon and hams). Generally, however, it refers to brief cooking of vegetables in lots of rapidly boiling salted water, to fix their bright colour and soften them prior to further cooking. The process is usually followed by refreshing in cold water to arrest the cooking process.

bouquet garni A small bunch of herbs, usually including bay leaves, some parsley stems and a sprig of thyme, either tied together or wrapped in muslin or a paper sachet. Used to flavour stocks, soups and stews, it is removed before serving. The exact mix of herbs may vary from dish to dish.

braise This is a method of long slow gentle cooking in a little liquid (usually wine or stock) in a tightly closed pot. It is generally used on tougher cuts of meat, as it converts the abundant connective tissue into a meltingly tender result.

brunoise Small dice of vegetables, usually a mixture of carrots, celery, onion and sometimes leek, used to add flavour, texture and colour to soups and stews.

caramelize Cooking sugar or sugar syrup to the caramel stage (see pages 238-9). Also used when grilling a sugar topping on a dessert and when reducing meat or other cooking juices to a sticky glaze.

chantilly Crème chantilly is stiffly whipped cream that has been sweetened with icing sugar and flavoured with either vanilla or a liqueur. It is usually served with puréed fruit.

clarify Clearing a liquid, generally a stock or sauce, of impurities. Stocks are clarified by simmering them with added egg white (which traps impurities) followed by careful straining. Butter is clarified (so it cooks without burning) by melting it, skimming the surface and pouring off the liquid butter from the solids that separate out at the bottom.

concassé Meaning 'crushed', this term is most generally used of tomatoes that have been skinned, seeded and coarsely chopped for a garnish or a salad.

confit From the French for a preserve, this term was once limited to candied fruit, and meat and poultry simmered in its own fat and then preserved in it. It is also now used of onions cooked slowly to a 'jam' or 'marmalade' and, by extension, has come to be applied to similar condiments.

coulis A puréed sweet or savoury sauce with one predominant ingredient, such as tomatoes or raspberries. The purée may be smooth or coarse, but is usually thin enough to pour (couler is French for 'to run').

deglaze A pan in which something has been cooked is deglazed by adding some liquid (usually stock or wine) and then scraping vigorously with a wooden spoon as the liquid is brought to the boil to dissolve all the caramelized glaze on the bottom of the pan. The richly flavoured liquid that results is either used to make a gravy or added to a sauce.

devilled A dish or sauce that is highly spiced with a hot ingredient like chilli or mustard is said to be devilled.

emulsion A mixture of two liquids that are not capable of being blended, such as oil and water, drops of one becoming suspended in the other. For example, in mayonnaise globules of egg fat become suspended in the oil.

flambé Pouring a highly alcoholic liquid like brandy over food and then setting it alight is called flambéing or flaming. The process burns off the harsh alcohol taste and concentrates the flavours of the added spirit.

glaze Something brushed or sprinkled on food to give colour and shine is called a glaze, e.g. warmed apricot jam over a fruit tart. Some food, especially vegetables like carrots, may be cooked with butter and sugar to glaze them. The term is also used of a stock reduced to a thick liquid.

gluten Proteins in flour that develop when it is mixed with liquid and the resulting dough kneaded to make it elastic.

gratin A dish that is finished in the oven or under the grill to give it a crisp crust.

infuse When an aromatic element, usually herbs, is soaked in hot water to extract their flavour this is termed infusing and the resulting liquid an infusion.

macerate When food is soaked in a liquid to soften and flavour it this is termed maceration. It is most often used of fruit in syrup or alcohol.

marinate Immersing food in a cooked or uncooked seasoned acidulated liquid to tenderize it and add flavour prior to cooking is called marinating and the liquid a marinade. Apart from enhancing flavour, the process is usually employed on tougher foods and meats like game that have so little fat they may dry out when cooked. Dusting or brushing food with spices is called dry marinating.

panade This is a thick mixture, often a white sauce, used for binding mixtures like croquettes or stuffings, or as the basis of a soufflé.

poach Very gentle cooking in liquid held just below boiling point so that it is barely trembling is called poaching. It is normally used to cook very delicate foods like fish or eggs.

reducing Boiling liquids like stocks rapidly to concentrate the flavour is called reducing and the result a reduction.

refresh See blanching

roux This is a mixture of flour and fat (usually butter) used as the basis and thickening agent of many sauces.

sauté This method of cooking, usually employed on smaller pieces of food, involves browning over a highish heat with lots of turning (sauter means 'to jump') to ensure uniform browning. This may be followed by subsequent stewing in a little liquid, covered, to cook the food through.

sweat Preliminary very slow cooking in a little fat or oil until food (usually onions or other aromatic vegetables) just softens (without browning) and gives off its own moisture.

tapenade This highly flavoured Provençal preparation is a thick paste of anchovies, olives, garlic and capers. It is served as a condiment and used to dress vegetables and eggs, or spread on canapés, etc.

zest This is the coloured outer layer of the skin of citrus fruit containing all the aromatic oils. Be careful when paring it off not to include the bitter white layer beneath. Many citrus fruits, particularly lemons, are coated in a chemically impregnated wax to prevent them going mouldy. This must be washed off in hot soapy water before using the zest.

Index

040-877-1